BLITZ OVER BRITAIN

In the Spellmount/Nutshell Military list:

The Territorial Battalions – A pictorial history
The Yeomanry Regiments – A pictorial history
Over the Rhine – The Last Days of War in Europe
History of the Cambridge University OTC
Yeoman Service
The Fighting Troops of the Austro-Hungarian Army
Intelligence Officer in the Peninsula
The Scottish Regiments – A pictorial history
The Royal Marines – A pictorial history
The Royal Tank Regiment – A pictorial history
The Irish Regiments – A pictorial history
British Sieges of the Peninsular War
Victoria's Victories
Heaven and Hell – German paratroop war diary
Rorke's Drift
Came the Dawn – Fifty years an Army Officer
Marlborough – as Military Commander
The Art of Warfare in the Age of Marlborough
On the Word of Command – A pictorial history of the RSM
Scandinavian Misadventure
Epilogue in Burma 1945-48
Indian Army of the Empress 1861-1903
A Medal for Life – Capt Leefe Robinson VC
The Fall of France
Kitchener's Army – A pictorial history

In the Military Machine list:

Napoleon's Military Machine
Falklands Military Machine
Wellington's Military Machine

In the Nautical list:

Sea of Memories
Evolution of Engineering in the Royal Navy Vol I 1827-1939
In Perilous Seas

In the Aviation list:

Diary of a Bomb Aimer
Operation 'Bograt' – From France to Burma

First published in the UK in 1990 by
Spellmount Ltd, Publishers
12 Dene Way, Speldhurst
Tunbridge Wells, Kent TN3 0NX
ISBN 0-946771-89-8

British Library Cataloguing in Publication Data
Webb, Edwin 1943- and Duncan, John, 1926-
Blitz over Britain – (Pictorial history series)
1. England. Air raids by Germany. Luftwaffe
I. Title II. Webb, Edwin III. Series
940.54212

ISBN 0-946771-89-8

Design by Discourses Ltd, Tunbridge Wells, Kent
Typesetting by Vitaset, Paddock Wood, Kent
Printed and bound in Great Britain

Blitz over Britain

EDWIN WEBB
&
JOHN DUNCAN

with contributions from
Pat Barrett, Cahal Dallat
Sam Dodd and David Price

edited by
John Walton

maps by
András Bereznay

SPELLMOUNT LTD
Tunbridge Wells, Kent

Contents

Acknowledgements

The authors would like to thank Pat Barrett, Cahal Dallat, Sam Dodd and David Price for their valuable contributions to this book. We should also like to express our gratitude to our team of researchers – Alan Simmonds, David Kelly, Anne-Marie Dallat and Sandra Gaffney – for all the work they have undertaken on our behalf.

In the research and preparation of this book we have also been helped by a number of individuals and organisations. To the individuals named we are grateful for the assistance they so freely gave, often making the task of research that much swifter and more certain. And we would like to place on record, too, the access provided to us and our researchers at the various Reference Libraries we have used where, without exception, we were given most courteous attention:–

Peter J. Ainscough, Chief Officer, Leisure Services, Humberside Libraries and Arts Unit; P. G. Ashton, Librarian, *Southern Evening Echo*, Southampton; Patrick Baird, Local Studies Librarian, Central Library, Birmingham; Steven Brown, *East Anglian Daily Times*; Nick Carter, Editor, *South Wales Evening Post*; Central Library, Coventry; Jill Crowther, Local Studies Team Leader, Hull Central Library; Mr A. Cutting of Yarmouth; Howard Davies, *Liverpool Post & Echo*; Derby Local History Library; Robert Harrison, Local History Librarian, Reference Library, Bristol; J. A. Fisher, Local Studies Librarian, Mitchell Library, Glasgow; D. Hinds, Director of Leisure Services and J. P. Hall, Central Museum and Art Gallery, Sunderland; Catherine Hodgkinson, Local History Library, Manchester Central Library; R. E. Hollingsbee, *Folkestone Herald*; Imperial War Museum; Brian Jewell, Factfinder Research, Harrogate; Christine Kelso, Ipswich Central Library; Leeds Central Library; Central Library, Leicester; Sheila Livingstone, the Dalmuir Education Resource Centre, Clydebank; Pat Malcolm, Information Service Librarian, Central Library, Clydebank; F. Manders, Local Studies Librarian, Central Library, Newcastle-upon-Tyne; Mass Observation Archive, University of Sussex; J. M. Olive, Local Studies Department, Sheffield Central Library; Geoffrey Oxley, City Archivist at the Hull City Record Office; Corinne Phillips, Local Studies Section at the Nottingham Central Library; Plymouth Central Library; RAF Museum; Peter Seagraves; The Science Museum; David Reynolds, Photopress, Plymouth; Mrs P. Sheldon, Central Library, Newcastle-upon-Tyne; Southampton Public Library; Aubrey Stevenson, Local History Librarian, Reference Library, Leicester; David Taylor, Local History Librarian, Central Library, Manchester; Mrs Tranter, Local Studies Department, Central Library, Birmingham; Derek Walker, Managing Editor, *Sunderland Echo*; Sheila Welsh, *Exeter Express & Echo*; Derek Wills, *Leicester Mercury*; West Glamorgan County Library and Cardiff and Swansea Public Libraries; The Ulster Museum.

We should also like to acknowledge the help given by the librarians of Thames Polytechnic (Roehampton campus) for their unfailing willingness to trace and obtain texts required for this study.

EDWIN WEBB
JOHN DUNCAN

Illustrations

Belfast Telegraph pp 152-157
Birmingham City Library pp 76-81
Bristol United Press pp 83, 84, 86, 89
Clydebank Central Library pp 114, 116
Eastern Daily Press p 172
Exeter Express and Echo pp 167, 168
Glasgow Daily Record p 115
Glasgow Herald pp 111, 113, 118
Hulton-Deutsch pp 64, 65, 66, 68, 71, 73, 174
Imperial War Museum pp 10, 11, 12, 13, 14, 16, 17, 18, 25, 26, 29, 32, 33, 34, 36-47, 64, 67, 69, 74, 75, 94, 135, 138, 144, 149, 150, 168, 170, 183, 184, 186
Kent Messenger pp 176-181
Leicester Mercury pp 137, 139, 140, 141
Liverpool Daily Post pp 97, 99, 102, 103
Manchester Evening News pp 119-126
Newcastle Chronicle and Journal pp 160-165
Nottingham Evening Post pp 127, 129
Nottingham Central Library pp 130, 131
Photo Press Library pp 142-147
Portsmouth Publishing & Printing Ltd pp 33, 47-57, 158
RAF Museum pp 15, 30, 32
Science Museum pp 8, 10, 11
Sheffield Central Library pp 104, 109
South Wales Evening Post p 92
Southern Newspapers pp 59, 60, 62, 63

'I see the damage done by the enemy attacks;
but I also see, side by side with the devastation
and amid the ruins, quiet, confident, bright
and smiling eyes, beaming with a consciousness
of being associated with a cause
far higher and wider than any human or personal issue.
I see the spirit of an unconquerable people.'

WINSTON CHURCHILL

12 April 1941

First cross-Channel flight

The first aeronaut to cross the English Channel was a Frenchman, Jean-Pierre Blanchard, who made his historic flight on 7 January 1785. His hydrogen-filled balloon took no more than two hours to fly from Dover to Guisnes. Though few realised it, from that moment Britain was no longer an island. Blanchard was probably the first professional aviator, giving many exhibition flights and setting a long-distance record with a flight of 300 miles in a hydrogen-filled balloon.

A contemporary print showing Henry Giffard's steam-powered balloon in flight: 24 September 1852

Prelude

From the day in 1783 when a young French physicist, François de Rozier made a 25-minute, 5-mile flight in Joseph Montgolfier's hot-air balloon not only did ballooning become an exciting new pastime for the adventurous, it also introduced the possibility of war in the air. When two years later in January 1785 another Frenchman, Jean-Pierre Blanchard, made the first cross-Channel flight in a hydrogen-filled balloon, Britain's security as an island began to be questioned. But it took more than another hundred years for this new strategic reality to be fully recognised.

In the 19th century balloons were regularly used for military reconnaissance purposes: in the American Civil War (1861-65), the Franco-Prussian War (1870), and by the British in their colonial wars in Africa and the Boer War (1899-1901). The first attempt at aerial bombardment was made by the Austrians, in 1849. They launched a number of small hot-air balloons, each carrying a 30-lb bomb, to drift over Venice. There were no casualties, and the Venetians were undismayed.

The first successful powered aircraft that could carry a man was Henry Giffard's aerial steamer. This splendid-looking airship, which was steerable ('dirigible') but only in calm weather, was 144 feet long and propelled by an airscrew driven by a 3-hp steam engine. In September 1852 Giffard, wearing a top hat and frock coat, flew from Paris to Trappes, a distance of some 17 miles – man's first powered flight.

It was the arrival of the petrol-powered internal combustion engine that made powered aircraft a practical possibility, in the shape of airships and other heavier-than-air machines. In 1885, the German inventor Gottlieb Daimler designed an efficient petrol engine, and collaborated with a fellow German designer of airships, Dr Karl Wolfert, to produce a new airship much larger than its predecessors. Unfortunately, their first venture exploded in mid-air, killing Wolfert and his mechanic. Undeterred, an Austrian engineer, David Schwartz, built a rigid airship of aluminium on an aluminium frame, also powered by a Daimler engine (12-hp). This, too, crashed on its first flight, but Schwartz escaped unhurt.

The idea of a large rigid airship as a new weapon of war was now taken up by a patriotic German ex-cavalry officer, Count Ferdinand von Zeppelin, whose name became for the British a synonym for the dreaded German raiders in World War One. His first airship, produced in 1900, was 420 feet long and powered by two 16-hp Daimler engines. It was fabric-covered on a rigid aluminium frame. By 1908 the German Army had its first 'Zeppelin' – the LZ 1 – and the next few years saw the building of many new and improved Zeppelins. For the German people were more enthusiastic about the airship than the aeroplane. They were convinced that in the Zeppelin they had a new kind of war weapon – one that could win wars on its own.

At that time many people could see no future in flying. Then, on 17 December 1903, at Kitty Hawk, USA, two brothers, Wilbur and Orville Wright, took off in a heavier-than-air flying machine they had christened 'Flyer', and flew all of 40 yards. They made three more flights the same day. From then on they built 'Flyers' of ever increasing power and efficiency, making longer and longer flights. The aeroplane had arrived.

First men in the air

Joseph Montgolfier's hot-air balloon made the world's first man-carrying flight on 21 November 1783, over the Bois de Boulogne in Paris, in the presence of Louis XVI and members of his family. Passengers on previous flights had been a sheep, a duck and a cockerel, carried in a wicker cage, and then the King ordered that two condemned criminals should become the first men to fly – on the promise of a pardon if they survived. But the Marquis d'Arlandes persuaded him to allow him and Joseph de Rozier to make the first ascent. This Montgolfier balloon was 40 feet in diameter and was made of tough cloth lined with paper. In it the two first aviators flew about five miles, and were airborne for some 25 minutes.

Not all hot air . . .

Hot air had obvious disadvantages for cloth and paper balloons, and an ingenious French scientist, Jacques Charles, succeeded in inflating a balloon of silk coated with rubber with hydrogen (then a new discovery and known as the 'inflammable gas') produced by pouring sulphuric acid on iron filings. On 1 December 1783 Charles's balloon rapidly climbed to a height of 3000 feet over Paris and stayed airborne for 45 minutes, coming to earth 15 miles away.

The first real aeroplanes

Orville and Wilbur Wright were bicycle manufacturers in Dayton, Ohio, who were fascinated by the problems of flight by heavier-than-air, fixed-wing aircraft. They experimented for years with gliders, and built three powered biplanes, designing their own 12-hp engine. On 17 December 1903, the first *Flyer* took off at Kitty Hawk, and flew about 40 yards. It made three more flights that day before it was wrecked by a gust of wind. But the Wrights had proved for all time that men could fly in heavier-than-air machines.

Not until Wilbur Wright took *Flyer III* to Europe in 1908 did the world begin to sit up and take notice. When he made banking turns, circles and figures of eight (in a biplane without wheels – it was launched by pulleys and weights and landed on skids), all onlookers were astounded. 'Compared with Wright,' said one, 'we are as children.'

In one flight Wright performed the then amazing feat of flying nearly 80 miles and remaining airborne for 3 hours. (And this was less than 90 years ago!)

'A POWER WHICH WILL CONTROL THE FATE OF NATIONS'

Their success was greeted with some scepticism in Europe until in 1908 Wilbur Wright made a series of spectacular demonstration flights in France, circling, turning, banking and making figures of eight with apparent ease. 'Wilbur Wright,' remarked one observer, 'is in possession of a power which will control the fate of nations.'

By this time there was a bewildering variety of flying machines invading the skies of Europe and America – airships, monoplanes, biplanes, and even triplanes – all with their passionate advocates. Aircraft were flying ever longer distances at ever greater speeds. By 1909 maximum speeds of 40-50 miles an hour were possible, and some machines could fly a distance of 80-100 miles without great difficulty. Only two years later a French monoplane flew on the level at what seemed the incredible speed of 126.67 miles an hour. But undoubtedly the event that most impressed the world at large was the first cross-Channel flight by Louis Blériot in 1909. From then on it was clear to all that flying machines were much more than strange-looking and dangerous contraptions designed by crackpot inventors for the amusement of the adventurous and wealthy. Those daring young men in their flying machines meant business – and power.

The first army to take a serious interest in aeroplanes for military use was the American, and in 1909 the US Army took delivery of its first aircraft – a Wright biplane. Two years later the US Army achieved the dubious distinction of dropping the first high-explosive bombs – on a dummy target. But the first to drop hostile bombs on an enemy were the Italians. During the war with Turkey in 1911, Italian pilots dropped modified 4½lb grenades from airships on Turkish encampments in Tripolitania. They were immediately accused of bombing a hospital – an accusation which, on many occasions since, has been made by the victims of air bombardment.

Louis Blériot made the first powered flight across the English Channel on 25 July 1907, in a light monoplane powered by a 25hp Anzoni engine. The crossing, from Baraques in northern France to a point on the English coast near Dover, lasted 38 minutes

'FLYING CAN NEVER BE OF ANY USE TO THE ARMY'

'Tell Sykes he is wasting his time; flying can never be of any use to the Army', wrote the future Field-Marshal Haig (Commander-in Chief of the British Army in the First World War) in 1911, of the man who became commander of the military wing of the Royal Flying Corps. About the same time the Admiralty was telling the Wright brothers that their aircraft 'wouldn't be of any practical use to the Naval Service' – which was more interested in airships.

In spite of these negative views, the Royal Flying Corps was established in 1912 and the Royal Naval Air Services in 1913. These two new services were in fact as ready for war in 1914 as the more senior services. In October of that year British naval aircraft bombed the German Zeppelin sheds at Düsseldorf and later those at Lake Constance – making possibly the first ever strategic air strikes. Meanwhile, on the Western Front the Royal Flying Corps was engaged in attacks on railway junctions, advancing troops, supply dumps and other military targets.

The first serious strategic air attacks by one side on the other were initiated by the Germans using their rigid 'Zeppelin' airships. The objective was to attack military targets in England, including London, but with strict instructions from the Kaiser to avoid royal palaces and historic buildings. The first raid was on Norfolk in January 1915 when two people were killed and 13 wounded. London was bombed for the first time in May of that year, when a ton weight of

In the early days of powered flight German interest in airships resulted in the development of *Zeppelins*, used for bombing raids on England. They were an easy target, however, and once defensive tactics had been worked out, many were shot down in flames

Early in September 1917 a German plane dropped a 50kg bomb on the Thames Embankment in London. It landed near Cleopatra's Needle, breaking through the pavement and setting fire to a gas main in the subway below. In a passing tramcar, three passengers were killed and three others injured

bombs killed seven people and injured thirty-five. From then until nearly the end of 1916 Zeppelin raids increased in severity. The most destructive raid was in September 1915 when over £500,000 worth of damage was done in London alone, and the biggest bomb to date was dropped (660-lb).

But in all such raids the Zeppelins could fly only on dark nights and at such a height – to avoid being shot down by British interceptor planes or by AA guns – that it was extremely difficult to navigate or drop bombs with any degree of accuracy. Typical was the airship commander who thought he was about to land in Norfolk when he was, in fact, over Kent. In the biggest raid of the war fourteen Zeppelins crossed the coast but not one reached London. In all the Germans lost over 30 airships and some 1100 crew members, while the British lost 38 aircraft and six pilots. British civilians killed or injured in Zeppelin raids amounted to about 1700.

The defeat of the Zeppelin was due partly to the inherent difficulty of navigating and bombing with accuracy, and partly to the skill and courage of British pilots and the effectiveness of the British defences. Some of the credit for this goes to Winston Churchill, to whose responsibilities as First Lord of the Admiralty in 1913 was added the protection of Britain in the air. Churchill's arrangements for the deployment of Royal Naval aircraft, the siting of coastal airfields, AA guns and searchlights, as well as for instructions for the police and fire services, became the framework for air-raid defences in both world wars.

After the failure of the Zeppelin, the Germans turned to the heavy bomber. In November 1916 a single German aeroplane flew over London and dropped six bombs between the Brompton Road and Victoria Station, causing little real damage but a great deal of amazement and

Churchill and the Zeppelin

Winston Churchill was one of the few pre-1914 men in a position of power (he was First Lord of the Admiralty) who believed in the future of the aeroplane, but not of the airship. He learned to fly in 1911. In his book on World War One, *The World Crisis* he wrote, 'I rated the Zeppelin much lower as a weapon of war than almost anyone else. I believed that this enormous bladder of combustible and explosive gas would prove easily destructible. I was sure the fighting aeroplane, rising lightly laden from its own base, armed with incendiary bullets, would harry, rout and burn these gaseous monsters.'

The enemy below is about to get the message as this British airman takes aim from the side of his airship

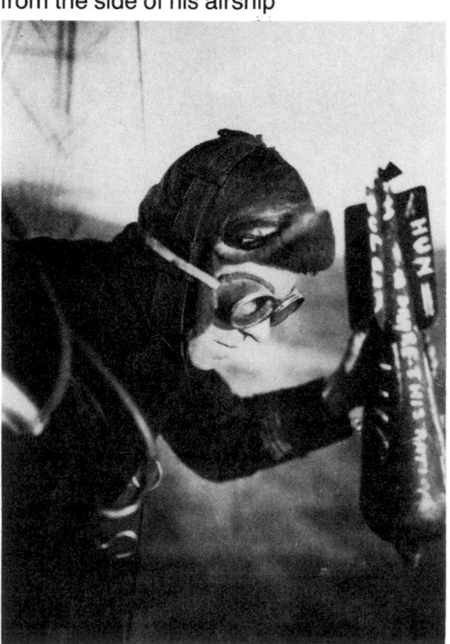

'Zepp Sunday'

Early on the morning of 2 September 1916, sixteen German airships were being got ready for the heaviest yet air attack on London, for the German High Command still believed that bombing could reduce the enemy to submission. Most of the 'Zepps' – to use the current British name for all German airships – crossed the coast around midnight, closely watched by the British, and bombs began to fall in and around London in the early hours of Sunday 3 September. Caught by searchlights and attacked by intense AA gunfire, the airships were unable to drop their 500lb bombs where intended, and the north-east suburbs of London – such as Ilford, Edmonton, Ponders End, Tottenham and Finsbury Park – suffered a good deal of damage. But the British had a new and secret weapon that was about to bring disaster to the Zeppelin – the explosive bullet. Aimed by a skilful and daring fighter such as the hero of 'Zepp Sunday' Lieut W. Leefe Robinson VC, the explosive bullet was deadly for a hydrogen-filled airship. So when the huge SL11 German airship was caught by searchlights over Finsbury Park and also spotted by Leefe Robinson in his BE2C fighter aircraft, there could only be one end. 'Robinson fearlessly gave chase' to the Zeppelin, and 'pressed home his attack . . . flying alongside at 11,500ft, raking the ship from end to end without any apparent effect. He turned the fighter to approach from the rear, some 500ft below, and pumped his last drum into the belly of the giant . . . Suddenly he saw a glow of red light appear on the airship which grew within seconds into a blazing inferno. He banked away quickly to avoid the intense heat . . .'* The stricken Zepp came down, a blazing wreck, into the little village of Cuffley, Herts – which immediately became a place of pilgrimage for thousands of sightseers. The crew of SL11 were buried in a mass grave near Potters Bar, with an RFC escort – but some of the crowd threw eggs at the coffins.

*from *A Medal for Life: Biography of Capt W. Leefe Robinson VC* by Leslie Wm Bills.

Famous planes from the First World War. The German *Gotha III* heavy bomber, the British *Sopwith Camel* and *Handley Page* heavy bombers

alarm. Speaking better than he knew, a *Times* leader writer commented:

> If I were asked what event of the year has been of most significance to the future of humanity, I should reply . . . the appearance of a single German aeroplane flying at high noon over London . . .

From then on for a whole year German heavy bombers, squadrons of the twin-engined Gotha and the bigger Riezenflufzieg, attacked Britain about once a fortnight. London was bombed on six out of eight nights in October 1917. In the last year of the war, some 200 tons of bombs were dropped on England, 857 people were killed and the cost of damage to property was estimated at £1,500,000.

'Like a manifestation in the Heavens'

Zeppelins seemed to have struck people of the time with wonder as well as fear. The novelist D. H. Lawrence described a Zeppelin attack on London in September 1915: 'One evening . . . across the Heath . . . there, in the sky, like some god vision, a Zeppelin, and the searchlights catching it, so that it gleamed like a manifestation in the heavens, then losing it, so that only a strange drumming came down out of the sky where the searchlights tangled their feelers. There it was again, high, high, high, tiny, pale . . . And the crashes of the guns, and the awful hoarseness of the shells bursting in the city. Then gradually, quiet. And from Parliament Hill, a great red glow below, near St Paul's. Something ablaze in the City . . .'

from *Kangaroo* by D. H. Lawrence, published in 1923.

These were modest enough figures by later standards, but undoubtedly the raids hardened British hearts, increased their hatred of the 'Huns' and influenced their attitude to 'the shadow of the bomber' during the next two decades. Partly in response to the demand for reprisals, Britain's air forces engaged in a sustained night bombing campaign on munitions factories in Germany, during which the civil population suffered much as the British had. Three huge Handley Page V/1500 bombers were waiting, with bombs loaded, to take off for a raid on Berlin on 11 November 1918 when the Armistice was announced.

BETWEEN THE WARS: THE SHADOW OF THE BOMBER

In the twenty years between the two world wars probably the national air force which gained the greatest experience of the use of air power was the Royal Air Force. The Spanish employed aircraft in their campaigns against the Riffs in Spanish Morocco, the French campaigned against the same guerrilla forces in French Morocco, and in Libya and East Africa the Italians used bombers to subdue rebellious tribes. Across the Atlantic, US Marines, helping the governments of Haiti, Dominica and Nicaragua put down rebels and jungle bandits, made effective use of air power, and became the first to employ dive-bombing tactics. But it was above all the RAF that systematically developed air power as an instrument of colonial policy – an economical method of policing territories with recalcitrant populations. Aircraft soon proved to be more mobile than conventional expeditionary forces, and dropping bombs on villages (after due warning) became an extremely effective punitive measure.

Viscount Trenchard was one of a powerful deputation, led by Winston Churchill, who in 1936 tried to persuade the British prime minister, Stanley Baldwin, to strengthen Britain's air defences to meet the growing threat from Nazi Germany

The first use of air power in a colonial war by the RAF was immediately after the end of the First World War, in the third Afghan War, on the North-West Frontier of India. Some six squadrons of aircraft were sent to the area, and the great Handley Page V1500 bomber, which had been produced too late to bomb Berlin, as intended, was used to bomb the Afghan capital, Kabul, instead. In the Arab revolt in Iraq in 1919-20, RAF squadrons were constantly in action, dropping some 100 tons of bombs on the rebellious population. By 1922 Iraq was in effect being governed by the local RAF commander, Air Vice-Marshal Sir John Salmond, as the British GOC in the area.

Air enthusiasts, notably Lord Trenchard, the Chief of Air Staff, held the view that the bomber would be the decisive factor in any future war. In this he followed the views of the Italian General Giulio Douhet, the apostle of air power, who claimed that wars could be won by destroying an enemy's cities and terrorising its population. This, in effect, was the strategy adopted by the Luftwaffe and by RAF Bomber Command in the Second World War. It was, in the words of a celebrated military historian, 'the most uncivilising means of warfare that the world has known since the Mongol invasions'. (Liddell Hart – *The Revolution in Warfare*, p. 93.)

The British people had few illusions about the realities of air power, and their rulers harboured serious doubts about the strength of civilian morale under heavy aerial bombardment. It was a British Prime Minister, Stanley Baldwin, who in 1932 made the chilling statement in the House of Commons that 'no power on earth can protect him (i.e. the man in the street) from bombing, whatever people may tell him. The bomber will always get through . . .' Newsreels of the effects of heavy bombing in three wars in the thirties merely darkened 'the shadow of the bomber'. In Abyssinia, Spain and China, aerial bombardment was seen to be totally destructive and decisive. Photographs of these events in the press and, more potently, on cinema screens up and down the country, helped to develop in the mind of the public the phobia about air attack which already existed, based as it was on vivid memories of the air raids on Britain from 1915 to 1918.

During the last days of Empire, Britain used her air power to patrol remote and potentially hostile borders in many parts of the world

In the Italian invasion of Abyssinia in 1935, well-armed infantry and tanks were supported by over 300 aircraft – bombers, fighters and troop carriers. This was the first time air power was used in conjunction with a mechanised army. Against a primitive, poorly-armed enemy the effect was devastating. Bombed, machine-gunned from the air, attacked with mustard-gas, Ethiopians stood little chance. The world protested – and noted the power of the bomber.

In August 1937 eighteen Japanese Mitsubishi medium bombers flew across the South China Sea and bombed Han-chow, despite the desperate resistance of Chinese fighter planes. In that 'undeclared war' the Japanese air forces, numbering some 1000 aircraft, made hundreds of ferocious raids on Chinese cities, as well as unceasing attacks on their air bases and troops. The vastly superior air power of the Japanese overwhelmed the Chinese, even though they were supported by strong squadrons of Russian bombers and fighters. The two years of war in China prior to the Second World War saw some of the fiercest air combats since 1918 in Europe, but Europe was too preoccupied with its own crises to take much note of events in far-away China and Manchuria.

GUERNICA – SYMBOL OF TERROR

Guernica is a small town in northern Spain, some 10km from Bilbao and 30km from the sea. On 26 April 1937 a single devastating raid by German Heinkel 111s and Junkers 52s wiped out the centre of the town and made the name of Guernica forever the symbol of the terror of the bomber.

'At half-past four in the afternoon,' wrote Hugh Thomas in *The Spanish Civil War*, 'a single peal of church bells announced an air raid . . . At twenty minutes to five Heinkel 111s began to appear, first bombing the town and then machine-gunning the streets. The Heinkels were followed by . . . Junkers 52. People began to run from the town. These also were machine-gunned. Incendiary bombs, weighing up to 1,000lbs, and also high explosives, were dropped by waves of aircraft arriving every twenty minutes until a quarter-to-eight. The centre of the town was then destroyed. 1654 people were killed and 889 wounded . . . This story was attested by all witnesses, including the Mayor of the town . . . by the Basque Government, and by all the political parties . . . It was vouched for by *The Times*, *Daily Telegraph*, *Reuter*, *Star*, *Ce Soir* and *Daily Express* correspondents, who visited the scene that night . . .'

Probably more than any other event before the Second World War, Guernica told the world what to expect from air bombardment, and in particular from the Luftwaffe. It was in Spain that the Nazis developed the tactics of terror bombing and the blitzkrieg that they later used to such powerful effect in Poland, the Low Countries and France.

BEHIND THE PROMISES – TERROR

As leader of the National Socialist party, Hitler used his remarkable gift of oratory to convince the German people that he would restore national honour after the humiliation of Versailles by tearing up the Treaty and cancelling all reparation payments. As well as making Germany strong again, he promised to put food on every table and guaranteed a job for each able-bodied man.

But these attractive electoral promises masked the darker side of the Nazi movement, with its ill-digested Nietzchean theories about an Aryan master race, its insistence on the need for more 'living space' for the German people and, above all, its implacable hatred of the Jews.

Behind the promises and the theories stood a highly-organised party machine, ruthlessly efficient in operation, with trained gangs of brown-shirted thugs ready to do its bidding. And as if all this were not enough, the whole sinister apparatus found a brilliant propagandist in Dr Josef Goebbels, who fully understood how the power of the press, the radio, the cinema and the organised rally could help to serve the interests of a one-party state.

Hitler made no attempt to conceal his contempt for the parliamentary process. Using it as a means to an end he set to work at once, as soon as he gained power through the popular vote, to destroy the system and to crush all political opposition. When the aged President Hindenburg died in 1934, Hitler felt sure enough of his position to assume the role of 'Führer and Chancellor', setting the seal on one of the most malign and oppressive regimes the world has known.

The first, and in many ways his greatest, gamble in pursuit of an expansionist foreign policy came in 1936, when he decided to re-occupy the Rhineland. Had the numerically vastly superior French army moved against him, Hitler would have been forced to retreat and face almost certain arrest by his own generals. But the French did nothing, and the German people acclaimed their Führer as a national hero. From now on, all members of the armed forces were obliged to swear an oath of personal loyalty to him.

Later that same year the Berlin Olympic Games provided the Nazis with propaganda opportunities to present their achievements to the world, and the outbreak of the Spanish Civil War gave German airmen a chance to test their new aircraft under actual battle conditions – training and experience they put to good use when the Second World War began.

In 1938 Hitler moved against Austria, and in a bloodless coup absorbed the land of his birth into the greater German Reich. Czechoslovakia was the next victim, and after intervention by the British prime minister, Neville Chamberlain, an agreement was signed in Munich which ceded 11,500 square miles of territory to Nazi Germany. A month later more land was transferred, this time to Poland and Hungary, and by March 1939 the rest of Czechoslovakia had disintegrated to fall under direct German occupation and control.

Versailles: the bitter legacy

The humiliation imposed upon Germany by the Treaty of Versailles in 1919 reflected the totality of her military defeat at the end of the First World War. The Allies wanted to ensure not only that Germany would never fight again, but also that she should make full reparation for the cost of the war. Her overseas colonies were shared out among the victorious powers, her fleet (later scuppered at Scapa Flow) was to be surrendered, Alsace-Lorraine was ceded to France, the Rhineland was occupied by the Allies and many German enclaves in the east were lost to resurgent Poland and the newly-created state of Czechoslovakia.

The German people regarded these terms with a hopelessness already fuelled by defeat and its consequences – recession, unemployment and, within a few years, uncontrolled inflation. This national mood provided a fertile breeding ground for the spread of new and radical nationalistic ideas put forward by Adolf Hitler. His first attempt to seize power landed him in gaol, but he put the time to good use by writing a political treatise, *Mein Kampf* in which he elaborated his anti-Communist and anti-Semitic theories and set out a detailed programme for national reconstruction. This included pushing back the eastern borders of the Fatherland to provide more living space (*lebensraum*) for the German people.

Secret re-armament

Early in 1935 the Heinkel He111 medium bomber had its first test flight, and the keel of the first *Scharnhorst* class battleship was laid. In June of that same year the first U1 submarine was commissioned, having been built in secret, and was later joined by eleven more of the same class.

All able-bodied young men had to do national service, and by the end of the year, conscription had brought the number of active servicemen in Germany to at least 350,000. The army had taken delivery of more than 350 tanks, and the fledgling Luftwaffe now boasted 48 squadrons with more than 500 front line aircraft.

The Allies expressed disapproval of so flagrant a breach of the Treaty of Versailles, but took no action. Some felt that the time had come for Germany to regain her rightful place in the world: there was even talk of restoring some of her former colonies. Others considered that Communism was a greater threat to the future stability of Europe than Fascism, and that compared with Stalin, Hitler was the lesser evil. Above all other considerations was the conviction in Britain and France that war must never be allowed to break out again, and that the use of military force no longer had any part to play in the conduct of international affairs.

To many people in Britain and France a major war now appeared to be inevitable, especially after guarantees were given to Poland. Hitler chose to disregard these warnings, either because he felt that the Allies would not honour their commitments, or because he was convinced that they could be bought off with a face-saving peace agreement once Poland had been conquered. In a brilliant diplomatic coup he made a non-aggression pact with the Soviet Union, and marched against Poland on 1 September 1939. Britain and France sent an ultimatum demanding the withdrawal of German troops, which was ignored, and two days later the Second World War began.

Peace For Our Time

Chamberlain was given a hero's welcome when he returned to London after signing the Munich Agreement with Hitler. Through his endeavours war had been

avoided, and Europe saved. Publicly he declared 'Peace For Our Time', but privately even he began to realise that neither Hitler nor Mussolini could be trusted to honour treaties or to keep good faith. Some say that he knew this all along, and simply bought time at Munich to allow Britain to rearm. Others claim that Chamberlain sincerely believed that he could deal with Hitler, and that it was not until Germany seized Bohemia and Moravia in March 1939 that he came at last to accept the inevitability of war.

Winston Churchill had no such doubts. Speaking in the House of Commons after the signing of the Munich Agreement, he said:

> We have sustained a total, unmitigated defeat. We are in the midst of a disaster of the first magnitude . . . All the countries of middle Europe and the Danube valley, one after another, will be drawn into the vast system of Nazi politics. And do not suppose that this is the end. It is only the beginning.

Churchill was shouted down by the appeasers as he uttered these words, but only a few months later more and more of his fellow-countrymen paid heed to his warnings and braced themselves for the coming conflict.

BLITZKRIEG!

The German onslaught on Poland in September 1939 remains, to this day, a textbook example of *blitzkrieg* tactics in action. Fast-moving armoured columns with dive-bombers in close support moved across the open countryside, encircling the Polish defenders in a double pincer movement. Five days after the attack, Poland's frontiers no longer existed. Within a week Warsaw was threatened on two fronts. A spirited counter-attack against overwhelming odds delayed the German advance west of the capital, but only by a few days.

On 17 September Russian troops started to occupy the eastern provinces in accordance with the Nazi-Soviet pact. After sustained and heavy bombing Warsaw capitulated ten days later, and by 6 October the last remnants of the Polish army surrendered to the invaders. Despite heroic resistance, Hitler achieved the subjugation of Poland in just under five weeks, with the loss of 13,000 German dead and 30,000 wounded. In grim contrast, over 200,000 Poles were killed or wounded and nearly 700,000 taken prisoner by the German army alone. Polish losses to the invading Russian forces are not known, but they include at least 15,000 officers later slaughtered by Stalin's secret police at Katyn. Responsibility for this atrocity was not admitted by the USSR until April 1990.

In France the British Expeditionary Force took up its positions. But other than a limited, token advance by nine divisions of the French army into the Saarland, no action was mounted against the Germans on their thinly-held western front. Allied paralysis on the ground extended to operations in the air, for apart from a number of ineffective leaflet raids no offensive strikes were mounted against the enemy. The RAF wanted to bomb targets in the Ruhr where, as Göring later admitted, in the absence of Luftwaffe defences, Germany's war industry could have been dealt a powerful blow. But the French feared retaliation against their own undefended cities, and the British reluctantly agreed to stay their hand. Even at sea, after an eventful first week in which 65,000 tons of Allied shipping were sunk by Admiral Dönitz's submarines, there came a lull on Hitler's express orders.

'Why didn't you attack?' asked the General

In giving evidence at his Nuremberg Trial, General Keitel declared that the German High Command could hardly believe their good fortune when France failed to attack the western front while they were so involved in the Polish campaign.

'Our astonishment was great,' he said, 'to find only minor skirmishes undertaken between the Siegfried and the Maginot lines. We did not understand why France did not seize this unique opportunity, and this confirmed us in the idea that the Western Powers did not desire war against us.'

With Poland at his mercy, and beyond reach of any practical Allied help, he made overtures to the Allies in an attempt to arrive at a face-saving formula that would bring the war to a speedy conclusion. After the fall of Warsaw, German propagandists stepped up the peace campaign. 'Why do Britain and France want to fight?' they asked: 'Germany wants nothing from the West.' The answer came early in October when Neville Chamberlain told the House of Commons that Hitler's offers were nothing more than talk, and that there had been no indication that Germany was prepared to put right the wrongs committed in Poland or in Czechoslovakia.

Hitler responded at once by stepping up his preparations for an attack on the western front 'at as early a date as possible'. Various plans were considered, but they had one thing in common: the great Maginot line was to be by-passed, and the main blow was to be delivered in the north through Holland, Belgium and Luxembourg. The objective was the destruction of the French army and those of its allies, and the occupation of the neutral Low Countries and of northern France to provide bases for a 'promising' air and sea war against England.

Once more Hitler found himself at odds with his generals. He knew better than his advisers that Germany could not afford a long and protracted war. But they put obstacle after obstacle in his path. It would take time to re-equip the army and move it to the western front; the supply bases in the west were not yet ready; the risks of a winter campaign were too great; insufficient account had been taken of the strength of the French army; a final choice had not yet been made of the actual plan of attack against the Allies.

To the Führer's mounting fury, the launch of *Fall Gelb* [Case Yellow – the code-name for the attack in the West] was repeatedly postponed for one reason or another. But in the end it was the weather, not his generals, that frustrated Hitler's plans. The whole of central Europe fell into the grip of one of the coldest winters in living memory, and even he had finally to concede that no major offensive in the west could be mounted before the spring of 1940.

The lull in military operations on land and in the air which followed the successful campaign against Poland, interrupted only by fighting on the Finnish front after a Russian invasion in November 1939, was later dubbed the 'Phoney War' – much to the fury of sailors and merchant seamen, for whom the war was anything but phoney. Admiral Dönitz, who had told Hitler, probably with good reason, that with 300 U-boats he could bring Britain to her knees in six months, launched a major attack against British shipping with the 50 submarines he actually had at his disposal. On 14 October 1939 one crept into Scapa Flow at night and

The screaming dive bomber

The Junkers 87 dive bomber, better known as the *Stuka*, was one of the most feared and most effective German weapons during the early part of the Second World War.

At 15,000 feet the aircraft dived at an angle of 80 degrees to 3,000 feet in order to release the bombload, by which time a maximum speed of 350 mph had been achieved.

As a precaution against black-out an automatic device brought the bomber out of its dive, enabling the pilot to resume normal control. *Stukas* were fitted with sirens that produced a high-pitched scream to destroy the morale of the enemy below.

sank the battleship HMS *Royal Oak* as she lay at anchor. Two days later German aircraft bombed a British flotilla in the Firth of Forth, damaging two cruisers and a destroyer, and followed up this attack with an air raid on Scapa Flow.

Meanwhile, magnetic mines continued to take an increasingly heavy toll of allied and neutral merchant shipping at the entrances to British harbours until, towards the end of November, two of these secret weapons fell on mud flats near the mouth of the Thames. They were recovered, carefully dismantled, and effective counter-measures taken against them.

The war at sea provided a few days of high drama in mid-December 1939 when in a running engagement in the South Atlantic three British cruisers damaged the German pocket battleship *Admiral Graf Spee*. She was forced to seek refuge in Montevideo harbour, where her commander scuttled her before committing suicide. This was an action that caught the imagination of the British public: it was in the true bulldog tradition and gave a boost to public morale that was disproportionate to the importance of the actual victory.

SCANDINAVIAN DISASTER

It was at this time that as First Sea Lord, Winston Churchill put forward a proposal to deny Germany access to essential supplies of Swedish iron ore by capturing Narvik and other Norwegian ports. The Germans, well aware of their vulnerability in this regard, already had a precisely opposite proposal to consider from Admiral Raeder. This was to occupy Norway in order, among other things, to safeguard vital supply lines. The British War Cabinet went as far as to authorise the mining of Norwegian waters. On the other hand, as soon as the Führer was convinced of the soundness of Raeder's ideas, he gave orders for the invasion of Norway and Denmark to go ahead, and to take precedence over the long-delayed attack on the western front.

And so, while Britain and France dithered, the Germans launched a brilliant combined operation against the two Scandinavian countries on 9 April 1940. Denmark capitulated at once, and Oslo fell to an airborne force. But the Norwegian army succeeded in holding up the German advance to the north, allowing enough time for British, French and some Polish reinforcements to land. The Royal Navy inflicted heavy losses on ships supporting the German land forces whose success, for a time, was by no means guaranteed. However, their superiority in numbers, equipment, quality of planning and boldness of execution eventually won the day, and Allied forces were steadily forced to withdraw from Norway amid scenes of great confusion and at considerable loss, taking with them King Haakon and his government in exile.

But this is to anticipate disasters of far greater consequence on the western front, where German forces crossed the boundaries of Holland and Belgium on 10 May 1940. Neville Chamberlain, his position undermined by the failure of the Norwegian campaign, was forced to resign in favour of Winston Churchill, who honourably acknowledged in full his own share of blame for the Scandinavian disaster. Nevertheless, he carried the confidence of the House and immediately formed a national government.

Within four days of the German onslaught Holland surrendered, after the Luftwaffe had carried out its threat to bomb Rotterdam. The Belgian army, bravely resisting the advancing *panzers* on the Meuse, was forced back towards the southern border, where the French 1st Army and the BEF had taken up their positions.

Meanwhile, in accordance with their master plan, the Germans had thrust through the thinly-defended Ardennes area, by-passing the Maginot Line to spill out into open countryside. Further attacks in the northern sector forced the Belgians to surrender, but now the main threat came from the south as the German *panzers* completed their bold encircling movement to reach Abbeville, on the mouth of the Somme, on 20 May. After ten days of *blitzkrieg*, Hitler's forces had succeeded in driving a wedge through the Allies defences, pinning three French armies, remnants of the Belgian army and the whole of the BEF against the sea.

British forces fell back to a perimeter around the northern port of Dunkirk, while units of the French army covered their retreat with a fiercely-fought defensive action near Lille. Meanwhile, a call went out in Britain for every available craft to make for the Dunkirk beaches to bring back the beleaguered BEF. During the evacuation the RAF flew over 2,700 sorties, although the length of time each aircraft could spend over the battle zone was limited by its fuel capacity, all flights now having to be made from mainland Britain. Despite intense enemy pressure, the operation was carried on from 27 May to 4 June, and nearly 340,000 men were rescued, two-thirds of them British.

As the full extent of the evacuation became known a feeling of relief swept across Britain, and many people came to regard Dunkirk as a kind of miracle, instead of the great military disaster it undoubtedly was. In his report to a tense and hushed House of Commons Winston Churchill observed that wars are not won by evacuations. By the time of the French surrender on 19 June 1940 a calmer, more determined and resolute mood had settled upon the country. The Battle for France had been lost: the Battle of Britain was about to begin.

Hell-Fire and Brandy

In his history of the Second World War, Churchill recalls that after Neville Chamberlain's famous broadcast telling the British people that they were at war with Germany, 'a strange, prolonged wailing noise, afterwards to become familiar, broke upon the ear . . . we made our way down to the shelter assigned to us, armed with a bottle of brandy and other appropriate medical comforts . . . my imagination drew pictures of ruin and carnage and vast explosions shaking the ground; of buildings clattering down in dust and rubble, of fire-brigades and ambulances scurrying through the smoke, beneath the drone of hostile aeroplanes. For had we not all been taught how terrible air raids would be?'

Tears of defeat

During the war Mrs Albinia Adams was a nurse at Pembury Hospital in Kent. She reported for duty one morning to find every bed in the ward occupied by young French survivors from Dunkirk, all of them in need of surgery.

'They could not speak English and we could not speak French, but we managed somehow,' she remembers. 'I had a portable battery radio and after a few days when the French boys were much better I lent it to them. They tuned it in to a French station, and next day I found them all in tears. I did not need a knowledge of French to guess what had happened. France had fallen.

The Many and the Few

The Battle of Britain lasted officially from 10 July to 31 October 1940 – 82 days – but unlike most land and sea battles of the past this was a conflict that had no easily recognised beginning and end. Long before the official starting date the Luftwaffe was attacking convoys, bombing ports and bases such as Portland, and making reconnaissance sorties over Britain. And as this book shows, the Germans' attempt to win the war by air power did not come to an end with their failure in the Battle of Britain.

At the time Germany and Britain were evidently reluctant to engage in a battle which was to prove decisive for them both. Having overwhelmed the great French army and made himself master of all the countries of north-west Europe, except Great Britain, with their coastlines and airfields from Narvik to Brest and beyond, Hitler paused. He had some reason to hope and expect that Britain might agree to a compromise peace in view of what he called 'her hopeless military position'. He also needed a breathing-space in which the Luftwaffe could regroup its forces and occupy airfields in France and the Low Countries, and in which to make 'preparations for and, if necessary, to carry out the invasion of England.'

Across the Channel Britain, too, needed this breathing-space. Apart from the Army's urgent need to re-equip the troops returned from Dunkirk and to train and equip fresh divisions against a likely invasion, the RAF needed time to recover from its efforts in the battle of France (in which at one time all but three of its fighter squadrons were engaged) and to rebuild its strength in aircraft and men. Above all, Fighter Command needed many more fighter planes and trained pilots. For Air Chief Marshal Dowding, Commander-in-Chief of Fighter Command, on whom fell the day-to-day control of the battle, every day's delay brought a welcome increase in the forces at his disposal. Indeed, it might almost be said that Dowding won the forthcoming battle by his strong and uncompromising insistence, in the face of the imminent defeat of France, that no more RAF fighter squadrons should be sent across the Channel 'no matter how desperate the situation may become.' The RAF had suffered significant losses over Dunkirk, and having just sent a further 10 squadrons to France, he reminded the Air Council on 26 May that '. . . the last estimate . . . made as to the force necessary to defend this country was 52 squadrons, and my strength has now been reduced to the equivalent of 36 squadrons.' Pressing his view to the point of offering his resignation, he was supported by Churchill, who told the War Cabinet on 8 June: '. . . if we cast away our defence the war would be lost, even if the front in France were stabilized, since Germany would be free to turn her air force against this country, and would have us at her mercy.'

HITLER'S INVASION PLAN

Early in July Hitler realised that Britain was not going to sue for peace, and he issued his Directive for the invasion of England (Operation *Sea Lion*): 'This operation is dictated by the necessity to eliminate Great Britain as a base from which the war against Germany can be fought. If necessary the island will be occupied . . .' The landing operation was to be a surprise crossing on a broad front from Ramsgate to a point west of the Isle of Wight, and the preparations to be made by the middle of August. '. . . to make a landing in England possible . . . the English Air Force must be eliminated to such an extent that it will be incapable of putting up any substantial opposition to invading troops . . .'

In preparation for Operation *Sea Lion* 13 divisions, each of some 13,000 men, were moved to the Channel coast as the vanguard of the 39 divisions of the total invasion force. In the first three days of the operation it was planned to land some 125,000 men in Kent and Sussex. To carry them across the Channel the Germans assembled a fleet of over 160 large transport vessels, 1,500 barges, and hundreds of small tugs, trawlers and motor boats. The German Navy could provide only four cruisers and eight destroyers to cover the proposed landings, and so it was clearly essential that the Luftwaffe should destroy the RAF in order to gain control of the Channel and prevent the Royal Navy from attacking the invasion fleet. Accordingly, the German High Command issued orders to the Luftwaffe for:

(1) The interdiction of the Channel to merchant shipping, to be carried out in conjunction with German naval forces by means of attacks on convoys, the destruction of harbour facilities, and the sowing of mines in harbour areas and the approchaes thereto . . .

(2) The destruction of the Royal Air Force.

Meanwhile, the breathing-space had enabled the RAF to increase its fighter strength from 36 to 54 squadrons in July and to 60 by September. Thanks largely to the immense vigour and drive of Lord Beaverbrook, then Minister of Aircraft Production, 'everything in the supply pipeline was drawn forward to the battle', wrote Churchill. 'New and repaired aeroplanes streamed to the delighted squadrons in numbers they had never known before.'

Reichsmarschall Hermann Göring, the German Air Minister and Commander-in-Chief of the Luftwaffe, assured the Führer that his requirement for the elimination of the RAF could certainly be fulfilled. He clearly overlooked the fact that the Luftwaffe's successes had hitherto been gained against air forces weaker than the RAF, and that even so it had suffered heavy losses in the spring campaigns, especially in combat with British fighter planes. However, he established numerous bases for his *Luftflotte* in the occupied territories of France, Holland and Belgium. *Luftflotte 2* operated north of a line from Le Havre to just north of Paris, and *Luftflotte 3* to the south of this line. *Luftflotte 5* was based in Norway, and its task was to mount attacks on the eastern flanks of England and Scotland. From these bases Göring confidently expected to send out his bombers and escorting fighters to smash the RAF within a month of launching a major assault. The proposed tactics were to use the bombers as a bait to lure the RAF fighters into the air, where they would be shot down by the escorting Luftwaffe fighters.

OPPOSING FORCES

In the first week of July Göring's force in France totalled 2,075 aircraft – 900 fighters, 875 bombers and 300 dive-bombers. A further 123 bombers and 34 twin-engined fighters were based in Norway. Against these odds, in that first week of July, the RAF had 48 operational squadrons (including two squadrons of Defiants, which were quickly transferred to exclusively night-fighting duties) and also four squadrons in the course of formation, as its total fighter strength for the protection of the whole of Britain.

In spite of the disparity in numbers there was perhaps little to choose in quality between the two air forces. The

The Battle at 'Hellfire Corner'

On 14 July 1940 a BBC recording van stood on the cliffs of Dover above the stretch of water nicknamed 'Hellfire Corner', and Charles Gardner, a well-known BBC reporter of the day, broadcast an eye-witness account of a Luftwaffe attack on a convoy steaming up the Channel. His running commentary on the battles between the Luftwaffe and RAF fighters was broadcast live that evening, and perhaps for the first time the listening British, sitting beside their 'wireless sets' realised that the war had come to their doorsteps. They could hear Charles Gardner's voice, rising and falling with emotion, as he described what was in effect an opening move in the Battle of Britain. 'There are one, two, three, four, five, six, seven German dive-bombers, Junkers 87s. There's one going down on its target now . . . he's missed the ship! . . . There are about ten ships in the convoy, but he hasn't hit a single one . . . the British fighters are coming up . . . here they come! Now . . . there's a terrific mix-up over the Channel! It's impossible to tell which are our machines and which are German . . . you can hear the rattle of machine guns . . .' As his breathless voice reported the dog-fights between Spitfires and Messerschmitts ('Go on, George, you've got him!'), he brought the air war right into the listeners' homes. Not everyone liked it, and there were protests that it was not a proper subject for broadcasting, but most rejoiced to hear first-hand how so many of the Luftwaffe had been shot down and the rest put to flight. It showed them that the Battle of Britain had begun – and they were going to be in it.

'Stuffy' Dowding

Air Chief Marshal Sir Hugh C. T. Dowding, GCVO, KCB, CMG, (1882-1970), later Lord Dowding and popularly known as 'Stuffy' Dowding, was Commander-in-Chief of RAF Fighter Command throughout the Battle of Britain, and was undoubtedly the architect of that victory. In 1940 he was 58 – a reserved, even austere, pipe-smoking man who could sometimes seem rather grumpy. Dowding had been a pilot and squadron commander in the Royal Flying Corps on the Western Front in the First World War. Between the wars he had been Director of Training at the Air Ministry, Air Officer Commander-in-Chief in Transjordan and Palestine, and Air Council Member for Research and Development (in which post he came to see the great potential of Radar) before taking over Fighter Command in 1936.

In the few years before the war, it was Dowding who persuaded th RAF to abandon the out-of-date wooden biplane fighters then in service in favour of high-speed all-metal monoplanes such as the Hurricanes and Spitfires with which the Battle of Britain was fought. It was Dowding, too, who was the moving spirit in establishing the detection and reporting system (through the radar chain and the Observer Corps) and the efficient communications network used to plot the moves of enemy aircraft and control the fighters sent to intercept them. And it was, above all, thanks to Dowding's insistence that Britain's remaining fighter squadrons were kept in England at the height of the Battle for France, thereby making it possible for the Battle of Britain to be fought and won.

'Stuffy' Dowding's pilots – 'Dowding's chicks' as Churchill called them – knew that in that melancholy-looking man they had a truly great Commander. There is little doubt that it was Dowding's leadership and almost uncanny strategical sense that saved the RAF and Britain from being overwhelmed in 1940. But he himself had no doubts as to whom the credit should go: 'They were a wonderful set of fellows, my pilots,' he said years later. 'I don't think there has ever been anything quite like (their) light-heartedness and spirit in the face of an issue that was anything but light-hearted . . . If those lads hadn't had this absolute refusal to be daunted, they would never have put up with the casualty rate they had to suffer.'

Luftwaffe's Messerschmitts were rather faster, with a better rate of climb, than the British Hurricanes and Spitfires, but the latter were better armed and more manoeuvrable. The German aircrews had the confidence born of their triumphs in Poland, Norway, the Netherlands and France, while RAF pilots were quite confident they could beat the Luftwaffe, even when outnumbered three or more to one. The Luftwaffe had the immense strategic advantage of widely-spread bases from which they could deploy their forces and concentrate their attacks, but as against this they had the disadvantage of having to fight above and across the Channel. When their aircraft were shot down, the crew were usually lost, either in the sea or in enemy territory, whereas British crews, being on home territory,

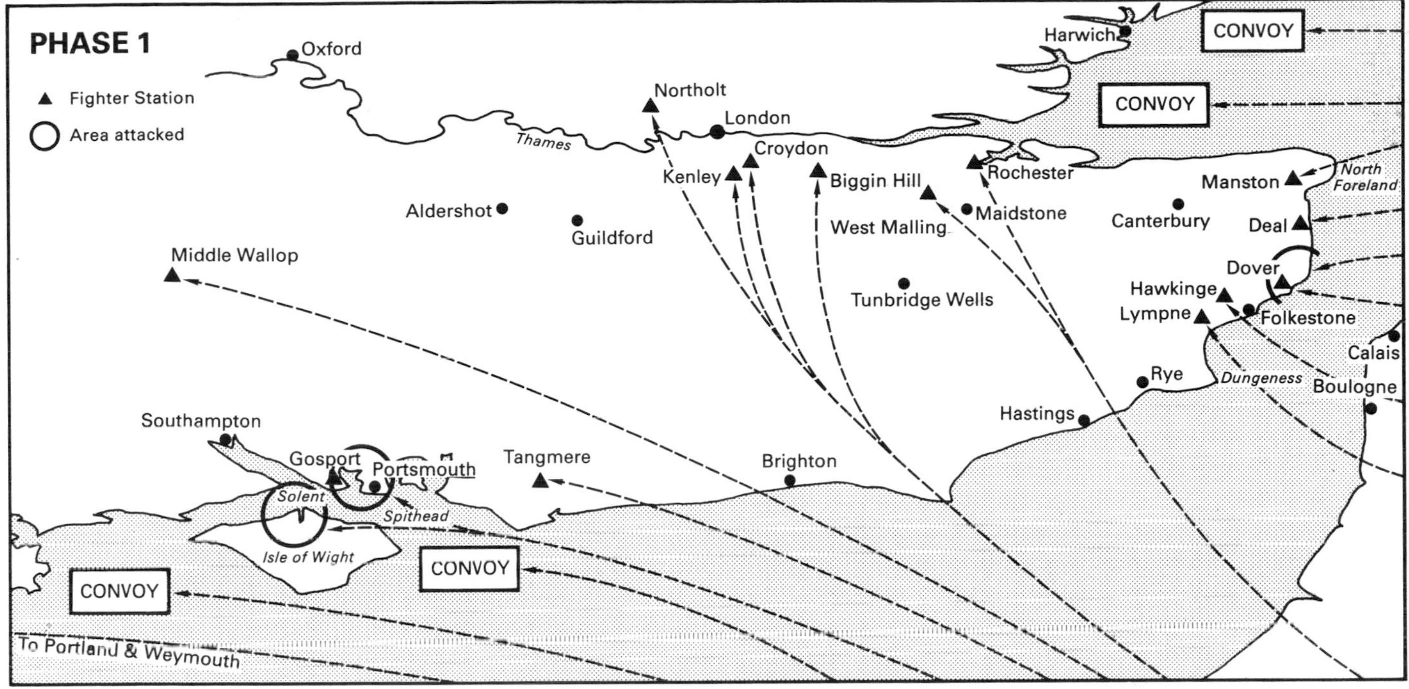

PHASE 1: Attacks on Convoys and Airfields

were usually saved. Unlike the RAF, the Luftwaffe rarely had the opportunity during the Battle of Britain of gleaning information from shot down aircraft and their crew.

It is possible to distinguish four successive and overlapping phases in the German attacks, in each of which the enemy pursued a different overall objective.

In the first phase (10 July to mid-August), the Luftwaffe's objective was to win superiority in the air over the Channel and Southern England. In the second phase (from mid-August to 7 September), the aim was to destroy the RAF as a fighting force by attacking its fighters, its airfields and its installations. In the third phase (7 September to 27 September) the Luftwaffe attacked London and attempted to force RAF fighters into the air in order to destroy them. In the fourth and final phase (27 September to 31 October) the Luftwaffe concentrated on night bombing of London and other major cities, which continued long after the official end of the Battle of Britain.

From airfields captured by the Germans in the course of their occupation of the Low Countries and Northern France, they were able to build up steadily their attack on shipping in the English Channel, and on the South Coast towns from Dover westwards, particularly those intended as landing places in Operation *Sea Lion*. In this phase of the Battle of Britain, the Luftwaffe probed and tested the strength of the RAF, intensified its attacks on convoys, and began fighter sweeps over south-east England.

On 10 July two heavy and significant onslaughts took place. In the Channel a British convoy rounding North Foreland was subjected to a series of attacks by 120 German bombers and fighters. By the end of the day's fighting nine German aircraft had been shot down, with the loss of one British fighter, which collided over the sea with a Heinkel 111. Only one ship was sunk.

In the west, on the same day, 70 bombers of *Luftflotte 3* raided Falmouth and Swansea, killing thirty people. Ships, railways, a power station, dockyards, and a munitions factory were hit. There were sporadic and widespread night raids in this period, and the Luftwaffe laid more mines around the coasts and in all the river estuaries.

Attacks on convoys continued throughout the month, and by the end of the third week the British were forced to suspend most Channel convoys until new defensive measures could be arranged, which included revised timing of convoys, stronger escorts, and ship-borne balloon barrages. Many Atlantic convoys were re-routed to western ports, but as the railways found it difficult to handle the increased freight traffic, Channel convoys had to be continued.

Attacking and defending them, however, proved to be expensive for both sides. Within a month the Luftwaffe had lost nearly 300 aircraft, most of them shot down by RAF fighters – at a cost of

Supermarine Spitfire

'The little Spitfire,' said the test pilot who first flew it, 'somehow captured the imagination of the British people at a time of near despair, becoming a symbol of defiance and victory in what seemed a desperate and almost hopeless situation.' The Supermarine Spitfire I in service with Fighter Command during the Battle of Britain was powered by a 1,030hp Rolls-Royce Merlin engine. Its normal range was around 400 miles and its maximum speed about 350mph. It carried eight Browning machine-guns, four in each wing, and each firing 300 rounds of ammunition. Pilots loved the Spitfire because it was easy to fly and 'had no vices.' It 'was the most beautiful machine ever invented,' enthused a wing commander who flew every Spitfire from Mk1 to Mk 24. 'I used to talk to mine all the time . . . and it almost talked back to me.' Although Hurricanes outnumbered them 3 to 2 in 1940, Spitfires were responsible for more than half the losses of Luftwaffe aircraft in the Battle. But Spitfire losses were very heavy – 237 lost to strength in August and 281 in September.

half that number of their own. But the RAF found these operations difficult to sustain, for often by the time the intercepting fighters were airborne, the raiders had already made their attack. In the course of these attacks between the North Foreland and Land's End 30,000 tons of merchant shipping and three destroyers were lost.

What was clear for all the world to see at this time was the fierce nature of the fighting between the RAF and the Luftwaffe over the south-east corner of England. It was obvious that the Luftwaffe was out for the kill, and the raids on RAF forward airfields, such as Manston in Kent, were so frequent and ferocious that the pilots christened the area 'Hellfire Corner'. The name stuck; here they learned combat lessons that were to be invaluable in the battle that was to come later in the summer. They found that attacking in twos and fours was much more effective than maintaining the formation-flight tactics learned in their pre-war training.

They learned, too, that the dreaded Junkers 87 (Stuka) dive-bomber, which had created so much terror in the *Blitzkrieg* tactics in Poland, the Low Countries and France, was in fact a highly vulnerable aircraft, especially if attacked when coming out of its dive. The Messerschmitt 110 heavy fighter was also an easy prey.

Perhaps most important of all, they discovered the value of the Fighter Command system of communication and control – which was very much Dowding's personal creation. The Dowding system linked radar and observer corps reports of incoming German raiders with Group controls, so that orders for squadrons to scramble could be given at precisely the right moment. There was some evidence that the Germans did not yet fully understand the RAF's operational procedures, and they lacked the ingenious and effective report and control system of RAF Fighter Command.

The severity of the battle for control of the air over southern England was about to be increased. On 1 August Hitler gave the order in person, in his Directive No. 17, that the Luftwaffe should use all its forces to 'destroy the British Air Force as quickly as possible.' 'An intensification of the air war' was to begin on, or some time after, 5 August, under the code-name *Adler Tag* – the Day of the Eagle. Some days later Göring issued his personal order to his Luftwaffe: 'within a short time you will wipe the British Air Force from the sky.' The immediate targets were RAF aircraft on the ground and in the air, 'their ground installations and their supply organisations'. Aircraft and anti-aircraft equipment factories were also to be attacked. The decision to invade (or not) hung on the outcome of these operations.

Between 8 and 12 August German attacks on convoys in the Channel and on east coast shipping were renewed and intensified. On 9 August, 300 German aircraft attacked radar installations along the south coast. Eighteen of them were shot down. The radar stations were attacked again the next day. While aerial towers and buildings were damaged, the radar system on which Fighter Command depended was not put out of action. On 11 August the Germans mounted a diversionary attack in the Dover area, while 150 bombers, escorted by Messerschmitt fighters, attacked Portland naval base and docks, as well as oil tanks, gas-works and army barracks in the area. Spitfire and Hurricane squadrons scrambled to engage them, and both sides suffered heavy losses: 38 German aircraft and 32 RAF fighters were shot down.

PORTSMOUTH BOMBED

On 12 August the Luftwaffe again tried to knock out radar stations on the south coast. In fact, they put the Ventnor station out of action although they were not aware of it. Portsmouth docks and town were heavily bombed, and extremely fierce attacks were made on airfields at Hawkinge, Lympne and Manston. At

PHASE 2: Concentrated Attacks on Radar Stations and Airfields

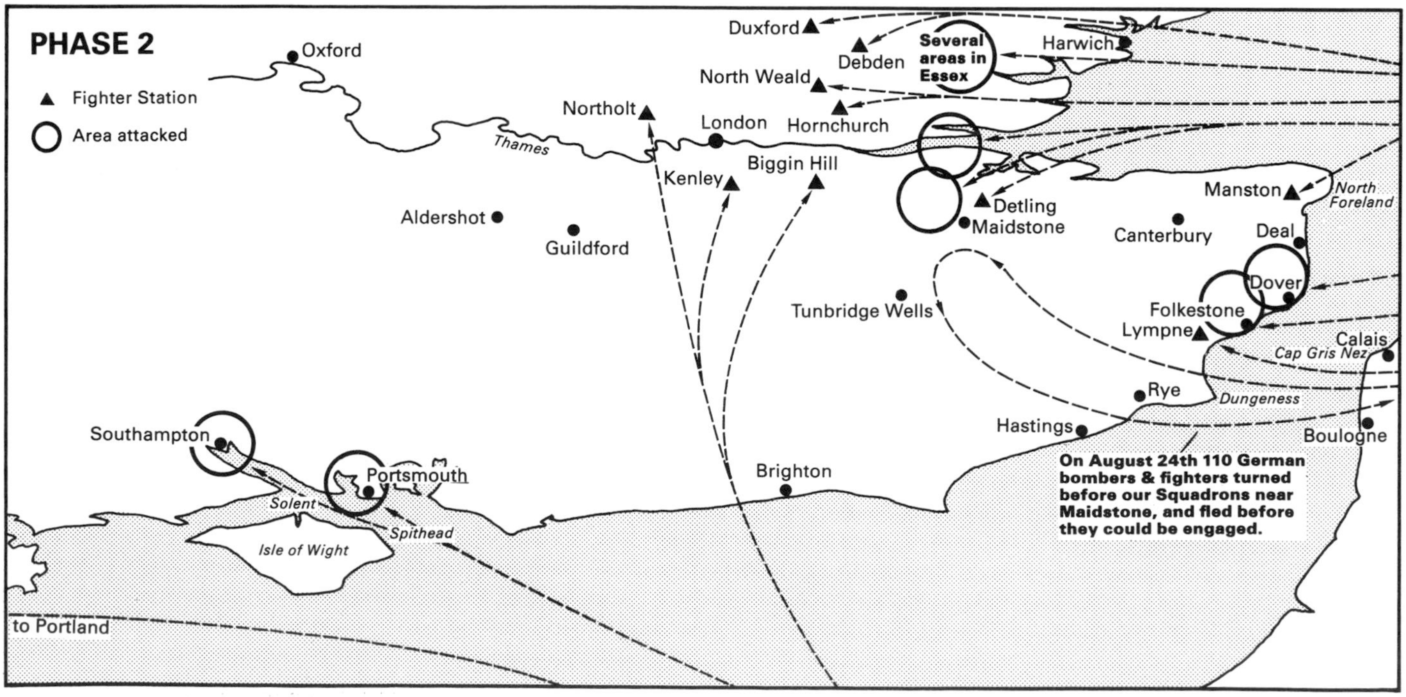

PHASE 2
Fighter Station
Area attacked
On August 24th 110 German bombers & fighters turned before our Squadrons near Maidstone, and fled before they could be engaged.

Radar stations along the south coast of England came under heavy attack

Manston most of a squadron of Spitfires managed to escape by taking off even as the bombs were falling. All these raids were intended as a prelude to *Adler Tag*, the date of which depended on a fine weather forecast. The forecast was set fair on 11 August, and Göring announced that 05.30 hours on 13 August would be zero hour for *Adler Tag*.

But the morning of 13 August was overcast, and the Reichsmarschall postponed zero hour until the afternoon. Eastchurch airfield, however, was bombed by Dorniers (the 55-strong formation not having received the postponement order) and five Blenheims were destroyed, hangars were damaged and runways cratered.

In the afternoon large successive waves of German bombers with fighter escorts crossed the Channel and attacked Portland and Southampton, as well as airfields in Kent and Hampshire. Spitfires and Hurricanes scrambled to intercept them. The Hurricanes were supposed to engage the bombers and the Spitfires the Messerschmitt 109s, but things did not always work out that way. By the end of the day the Luftwaffe had lost 45 aircraft and the RAF 13 fighters and three pilots. The *Adler Tag* attack was a failure.

The next day, 14 August, Luftwaffe activity was less intense, only about 500 aircraft being used throughout the day. The main targets continued to be RAF airfields, and Manston was bombed yet again. Middle Wallop and several other airfields, operationally less important, were also attacked.

On 15 August, however, came the heaviest German raids on any one day. All three *Luftflotten* took part in massive attacks along nearly 600 miles of the British coast, from Newcastle in the north-east to Weymouth in the south. Between 11.30am and 6.30pm the Luftwaffe flew 1,786 sorties, and the RAF hit back with 974. If the day's onslaught succeeded in carrying out Göring's order to smash the RAF, the planned invasion of England, the long-delayed Operation *Sea Lion*, might still go ahead. As Churchill said later, 'it was indeed a crucial day.'

RAF airfields were still the prime target for the Luftwaffe. Manston was raided once more, and two parked Spitfires were destroyed. Bases at Eastchurch, Middle Wallop, Worthy Down, and Odiham were all hit, and radar stations at Foreness, Rye, and Dover were attacked and damaged. Towards evening some 70 German aircraft heading for Kenley and Biggin Hill dropped their bombs on Croydon and West Malling in error.

In the north, *Luftflotte 5* took part in the air war for the first time. Operating from bases in Norway, it was directed to bomb targets in Newcastle-on-Tyne, the Tees and the Humber. The first two of these were to be raided by 65 Heinkels escorted by 34 heavy fighters, and a flight of unescorted Junker 88s made for the Humber. Radar detected both forces far out in the North Sea, and they were intercepted by British fighters. Sixteen German bombers and seven fighters were then shot down for the loss of one Hurricane. The Luftwaffe High Command had underestimated the number of RAF squadrons, and they assumed that when the squadrons in the south were fully engaged, their Group commanders would be compelled to call on reserves from the north. This would give the raiders from Norway a clear run. They were unaware that early in August Dowding had foreseen this possibility and had transferred seven fighter squadrons from the south to the north. His almost uncanny foresight undoubtedly contributed to the heavy defeat of *Luftflotte 5* that day, and in consequence it took no further significant part in air attacks on Britain. Later in August its bombers were transferred to *Luftflotte 2*.

The Luftwaffe's total losses on 15 August amounted to 75 aircraft. The RAF lost 34 fighters.

Despite this mauling, the Germans resumed their attacks the next day, 16 August. RAF airfields were again the principal targets, and once again Manston and West Malling were bombed, the latter being rendered unserviceable for four days. In the afternoon some 350 enemy aircraft made for three different target areas – the Thames Estuary, the Solent and Southampton, and Dover. The RAF fighter base at Tangmere was hit, as was the airfield at Brize Norton. The Germans again suffered significant losses – 45 aircraft shot down compared with the RAF's 22.

Junkers Ju 87 'Stuka'

The Junkers Ju 87 two-seater dive bomber was another German combat plane with a fearsome reputation before the Battle of Britain. The Germans used Ju 87 Stukas ('Stuka' is derived from the German word *Sturzkampfflugzeug*, the term for *all* dive bombers) in the Spanish Civil War to test precision bombing and ground strafing techniques, and there its characteristic screech as it hurtled towards the ground first struck terror in all who heard it. The Ju 87B Stukas used in the Battle of Britain carried one 500kg bomb and four 50kg bombs (with fin 'screechers') and three machine guns – two forward and one rear. In Poland, the Low Countries and France, the Ju 87 had a devastating effect – but against relatively weak opposition. RAF fighter pilots soon found that the Stuka was slow and vulnerable when coming out of its dive, and in August 1940 they shot down so many that, like the Me 110, it had to be withdrawn from the Battle.

RAF fighter pilots relax between sorties at the height of the battle

On 17 August Luftwaffe raids were reduced, perhaps in preparation for the heavy attacks mounted on the following day. Only reconnaissance flights were made during the hours of daylight, and at night there were small raids in Wales, the North and the Midlands.

Meanwhile, the Luftwaffe High Command made an updated assessment of RAF losses in the preceding six weeks, from 1 July to 15 August. They calculated that 553 Spitfires and Hurricanes (plus 21 Defiants and Curtisses) had been destroyed in the air or on the ground. Allowing for 196 aircraft destroyed 'in crash landing, landing damaged beyond repair, accidents etc.' and also allowing for the supply of new aircraft and a serviceability rate of 70%, their estimate concluded that 'there are now 300 combat-ready fighters'.

In fact, RAF fighter losses were far less than this crude estimate. Losses of Spitfires, Hurricanes, and Defiants (Curtisses were not operational!) amounted to 318 – less than half the German estimate. British aircraft factories were producing new fighters at twice the rate estimated by the Luftwaffe, and so by 15 August the RAF was numerically stronger than it was on 1 July. More than 1,000 Spitfires, Hurricanes, and Defiants were available to the RAF's squadrons – 80% of them serviceable. Additional fighters were held in storage, and 84 were in training units. On the date of the Luftwaffe's estimate, the true number of fighter aircraft available to the RAF was 1,438. Göring and his Luftwaffe were very far indeed from smashing the RAF as quickly as he had promised his Führer.

STERN TEST

On 18 August a stern test awaited RAF fighter pilots. Encouraged by its estimate of RAF Fighter Command's dwindling reserves, the Luftwaffe planned to make a final breakthrough. Concentrated assaults were to be made on four of the airfields where the bulk of the RAF's defences for the south-east of England were based: Biggin Hill, Kenley, North Weald, and Hornchurch. These attacks were to be conducted by *Luftflotte 2*, while *Luftflotte 3* was to launch itself at the Portsmouth area with waves of Stuka dive-bomber attacks. As all along, the tactics were to destroy fighters – on the ground by bombing, and in the air by Messerschmitt 109s.

At Kenley the attack was particularly severe. Low-level bombing destroyed four Hurricanes and several hangars. Even though one formation of high-level Dorniers was broken up by a Hurricane attack, 100 of its bombs fell from about 15,000 feet on or near the airfield, and some of the bombers released their loads on railway lines north of Kenley and others on Croydon aerodrome. Others turned for home with their bombs still on board. Twelve Junkers 88s, following up these attacks, found Kenley so thickly covered in smoke that their planned dive-bombing was impossible, and they re-routed to their alternative target at West Malling. No sooner had they done so than, with their fighter escort, they were pounced on over Biggin Hill by Spitfires and Hurricanes.

As the fighting over Kenley came to an end, at about 1.30pm, 60 Heinkel 111s escorted by 40 Messerschmitt 109s approached Biggin Hill. The Heinkels dropped their bombs from a great height, and most of them fell on the airstrip or in the woods to the west. In their retreat, the attackers of Kenley and Biggin Hill were chased across the south coast and out to sea by Spitfires and Hurricanes, who inflicted heavy losses on them.

Even as these raids were taking place, *Luftflotte 3* were assembling formations of aircraft for an offensive against the airfields at Gosport, Ford, and Thorney Island, which the Luftwaffe wrongly supposed to be Fighter Command bases. In fact, Ford was a naval air station, Thorney Island housed two RAF Coastal Command squadrons, and Gosport was the site of a torpedo development unit. The other target in this offensive was the radar station at Poling, near Littlehampton. For the attacks on these targets, the Luftwaffe committed 109 Junkers 87 'Stuka' dive-bombers: 28 for Thorney Island, 28 for Ford, 31 for Poling, and 22 for Gosport, and 157 Messerschmitt 109s were to escort this largest single formation of Stukas.

At 2pm the radar station at Poling logged the first indications of the approaching raiders. East of the Isle of Wight, the Germans divided, part heading for Gosport, a second part for Ford and Poling, and the remainder for Thorney Island. They began their attacks at about 2.30pm.

The Stukas, with their ability to pinpoint their bombing, inflicted considerable damage at two of their targets. At Ford 14 aircraft were destroyed, together with hangars and other buildings, and defenders on the ground were killed. At Gosport four aircraft were destroyed, buildings wrecked, and hangars damaged. At Poling, one of the high-receiver towers was partly knocked down, and the long-range early-warning system (the Chain Home) was put out of action, but its short-range radar detection was undamaged and remained in use. At Thorney Island the damage included three aircraft on the ground as well as damage to hangars and other buildings.

The attacking Stukas and their fighter escort were ferociously and repeatedly attacked by squadrons of Spitfires and Hurricanes. The Stukas proved very vulnerable: their lack of speed and manoeuvrability exposed them to fighter attack, particularly as they came out of their dive. Two of them were brought down by AA gunfire that day and others were damaged. Fifteen Stukas were destroyed and another damaged beyond repair in the four raids. As a consequence, the Luftwaffe no longer employed Stukas in raids against England, at least until late summer.

But the day's fighting was not yet finished, for later the Luftwaffe assembled formations to bomb the airfields at Hornchurch and North Weald. Fifty-eight Dornier 17s were despatched to Hornchurch, and 51 Heinkel 111s to North Weald. The whole force was protected by 140 Messerschmitt 109s and 110s. The raiders were detected by radar, and squadrons of Hurricanes and Spitfires scrambled to await them, attacking the North Weald force over the Essex coast, and the Hornchurch force over Kent, but they had to break off on running out of ammunition. The weather, in fact, prevented the Germans from reaching their objectives: low cloud at 3,500-5,000 feet made their targets invisible to aircrew flying at 12,000 feet. At this period of the war, instructions to German pilots forbade indiscriminate bombing, so both forces headed for home. At this point they were spotted by RAF fighter squadrons, who gave chase, and a furious action followed.

THE CRUCIAL DAY

This day – 18 August – proved to be particularly significant in the progress of the battle. The Luftwaffe had flown close on 1,000 sorties for the loss of 71 aircraft. The RAF lost 27 fighters in daytime operations, but when losses of aircraft on the ground are added, the RAF total is very close to the Luftwaffe's figure. However, the Germans lost 94 aircrew killed and a further 40 were taken prisoner. The RAF lost only ten pilots. The loss of trained aircrew was perhaps even more damaging to the Luftwaffe than the loss of aircraft. But what was possibly most significant about that day was the failure to defeat the RAF and the Führer's consequent decision to postpone Operation *Sea Lion*.

On the day following these concentrated raids there was no German air attack on Britain. 'A big mistake', commented Winston Churchill, who the next day – 20 August – made his famous speech in the House of Commons in which he praised the courage of the RAF fighter pilots, saying 'Never in the field of human conflict was so much owed by so many to so few.' He added – what is largely forgotten by the common memory – that the thanks of the nation should also go to the British bomber squadrons who night after night were conducting raids on German military installations and communications, air bases and storage depots.

Largely as a result of bad weather, the lull in German air attacks continued for several more days, and heavy fighting was not resumed until 24 August. Now came a change in Göring's strategy as the Luftwaffe was ordered to concentrate its attacks on RAF fighters and airfields. 'Our first priority,' he declared, 'is to destroy the enemy's fighters. If they do not take to the air, we shall attack them on the ground.' Earlier he had seemed to think it did not matter what were the Luftwaffe's targets so long as they lured the RAF fighters into the sky to be destroyed by his fighters. The new tactics drew RAF fighter squadrons, who needed to protect their bases, into ever-increasing conflict with Luftwaffe escorting fighters, and they came under very severe pressure. At this time Fighter Command enjoyed the support of Polish, Czech, and Canadian units, and numbers of American volunteers were also to be found in RAF fighter squadrons.

Airfields in the south-east came under renewed attack on 24 August, as did Portsmouth. That day the Luftwaffe flew 1,030 sorties compared with the RAF's 936. Breaking the RAF was now an urgent necessity if Operation *Sea Lion* were to be undertaken before the autumn – and before the deterioration in the weather made the invasion plan less and less feasible. But on the night of 24 August, as is described in the next chapter, there occurred one of those accidents of war whose consequences change the course of a battle, and even of history.

A group of Heinkel bombers missed their targets at Rochester and Thameshaven, and inadvertently, but against Hitler's express command, they released

Junkers Ju 88A

The Junkers Ju 88A was the Luftwaffe's newest bomber at the time of the Battle of Britain and played a prominent part in the Blitz. Between 1940 and 1943 some 2,000 were produced each year. Designed to meet the need for a high-speed, long-range bomber capable of carrying a substantial bomb-load, the Ju 88A was powered by two 1,340-hp engines. It carried a crew of four, and its maximum bomb load was approximately 6,000lb. For defence it had machine-guns mounted forward and aft of the cockpit, as well as in the ventral gondola, and as with most such warplanes the armament varied in different models. With its high diving speed and manoeuvrability the Ju 88A could evade RAF fighters on occasion, but although its tough construction enabled it to sustain substantial damage, the number of Junkers bombers lost during the Battle of Britain and the Blitz was very considerable.

Messerschmitt Bf 109E

When the Messerschmitt appeared in the Battle of Britain it had acquired a reputation, carefully promoted, for invincibility, having first proved itself a great combat aircraft in the Spanish Civil War. The Bf 109E was in fact a worthy opponent for the Spitfire, and there was little to choose between them in performance. The Messerschmitt tended to be difficult to handle at high speeds. It was armed with two machine-guns mounted on its fuselage and a pair of 20mm cannon mounted on the wings, but as with most other fighter aircraft the armament varied in different models. The Bf 109E (also often referred to as the Me 109) was therefore treated by RAF pilots with considerable respect, and indeed most of the RAF aircraft shot down during the Battle fell victim to its guns. If Göring had not insisted on confining the Me 109 to bomber escorting duties in the later phases of the Battle, there might have been a rather different result.

The *Messerschmitt Bf 110*, an elegant stablemate of the Bf 109 also had an awesome reputation, built up by intense publicity, and its intended role was to clear a way for bombers through opposing fighters. It was much favoured by Göring, but its designers never envisaged that it might have to face determined and highly-trained fighter opposition. In the Battle of Britain it was a failure, and had to be withdrawn.

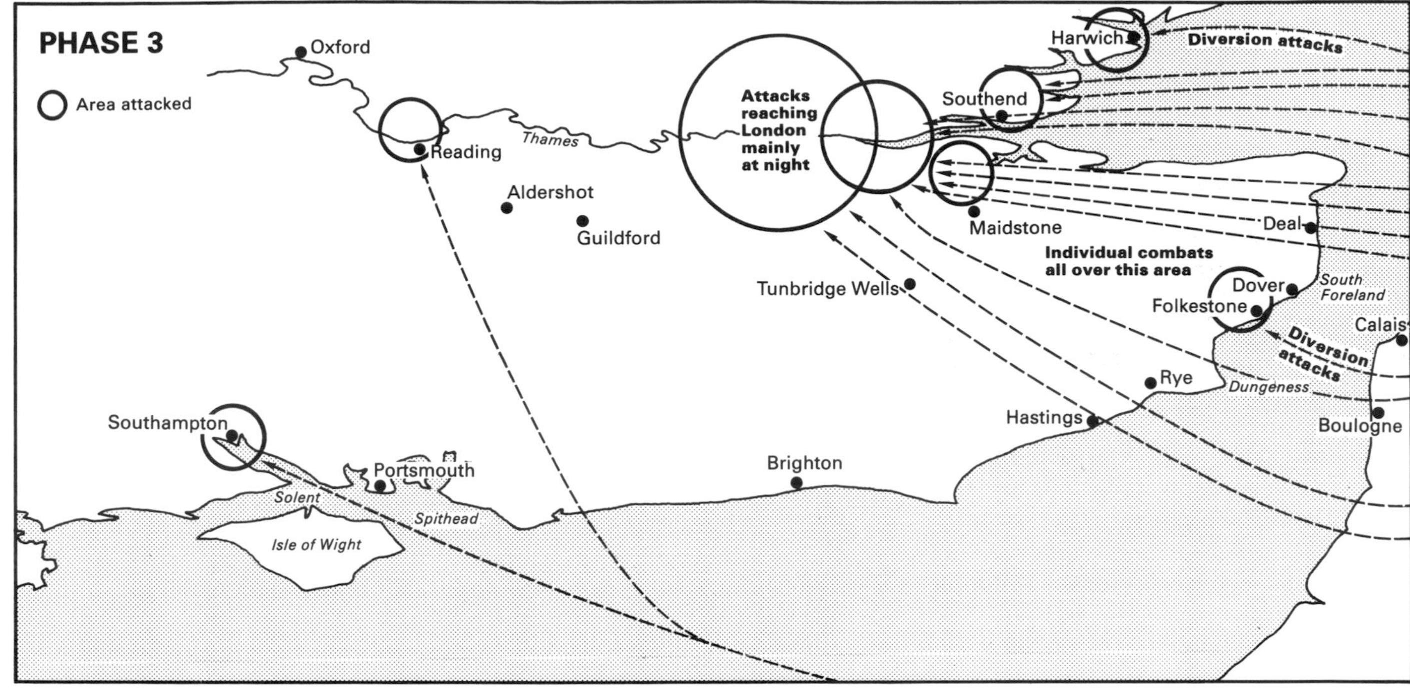

their bombs on the city of London. Churchill's response was immediate. The very next night RAF Bomber Command made a reprisal raid on Berlin, but the world noted – as Churchill had fully intended – that it was the Germans who were responsible for starting the attack on civilian targets. The British raid produced little real damage except to civilian morale in Germany, but Hitler's fury brought about yet another change in Luftwaffe strategy. London became a major target for its bombers, and German forces were consequently diverted from the prime objective of destroying the RAF.

Luftwaffe pressure continued relentlessly, however, in the last days of August and the first week of September, and the RAF had to endure while its airfields were constantly attacked. In that period virtually every airfield in the south-east was repeatedly bombed, and by the end of August RAF Fighter Command's losses were mounting alarmingly. On each of the last two days of the month RAF fighters flew 1,000 sorties against the Luftwaffe's massive formations. The RAF lost 77 aircraft, the Luftwaffe 64, and 1,075 civilians were killed in August as a result of German bombing raids.

LOSSES MOUNT UP

In the first week of September Fighter Command's losses increased markedly, and continued to exceed those of the Luftwaffe. In seven days the RAF lost 161 aircraft. Although production of new aircraft was just about keeping pace with the numbers destroyed, the strain on fighter pilots was growing, and they often had to make several sorties a day. Sometimes pilots in the front-line zone flew five or even six sorties in daylight hours, so persistent was the German assault. The pilots suffered from fatigue, and the losses among them were such that Dowding had to begin to feed into No. 11 Group – the Group which had all along taken the brunt of the German attacks – squadrons from Nos. 10, 12, and 13 Groups. From the end of August to 9 September fifteen squadrons were transferred, and before then there had been smaller infusions of pilots and aircraft. This clearly indicates the scale of the inroads the Luftwaffe was making into Fighter Command's resources.

The losses among the squadrons transferred from relatively quieter zones into the maelstrom of furious fighting in the south-east were proportionately greater than those of the earlier No. 11 Group squadrons, among whom it began to be a cause for alarm that so many experienced squadrons and flight leaders were being lost. The situation at the end of the first week of September looked grim indeed. Fighter Command was hanging on, but

Heinkel He 111

Like other German warplanes, the Heinkel 111 began its combat career with the German Kondor Legion in Spain in 1937. Its success (as with the Junkers 87 and 88A and the Dornier 117) led the Luftwaffe commanders to think their aircraft were invincible. Their triumphs in Poland and the Western Front tended to confirm this view, and it was not until the Battle of Britain and the Blitz that the Luftwaffe discovered how vulnerable they were. But the He 111 was a beautiful aircraft by any standard. Its main distinguishing feature was perhaps its glazed nose formed of transparent panelling to allow the crew all-round vision (but also giving a mirror effect when the sun was aft). It was powered by two 1,110hp engines and had a maximum range of about 750 miles. Its bomb-carrying capacity was approximately 4,500lb, and it was normally fitted with machine-guns for multi-directional firing. But against RAF fighters the He 111 was inadequately armed for daylight raids, even when strongly escorted, and it proved an easy prey; it was therefore confined to night bombing duties from September 1940. But when it was more heavily armed and provided with extra crew to man the guns, it became a lumbering machine and a sitting target for fighters. Even so, the He 111 was retained in service until the end of the war.

how much longer could it continue at the current rate of losses and against the increasing waves of Luftwaffe raiders?

What was not at all clear at the time, however, was that by hurling itself against the RAF in so frenzied a manner the Luftwaffe was on a path of self-destruction. In the cold light of retrospective wisdom, it can now be seen that for every RAF fighter pilot killed or grounded by wounds, five German aircrew were lost – killed or wounded in action, or taken prisoner. These figures were not fully known, nor was their significance grasped while the battle raged, which explains why at some levels there was a suppressed sense of a possible, impending defeat for the RAF. But although its ordeal was far from over and there were plenty of fresh trials to come, from 7 September 1940 – the date that marks the next phase in the Battle of Britain – pressure on RAF airfields started to ease, and Fighter Command began to recoup its strength.

PHASE 3: LONDON

While Hermann Göring publicly welcomed Hitler's decision to switch the attack to London (he could hardly do otherwise), it seems that he entertained private doubts about the wisdom of changing policy. The bombing of civilian targets with the aim of breaking morale and forcing the British government to surrender was to have a material and beneficial effect on Fighter Command, whose airfields and aircraft were no longer to be regarded as the Luftwaffe's prime targets.

To some extent this change caught the RAF on the hop when the devastating raid on London started in the late afternoon of 7 September. However, the scale of this attack marking the start of the blitz on London soon became apparent, and when RAF fighters appeared they attacked to good effect the marauding force of 300 Luftwaffe bombers escorted by a fighter screen of twice that number.

Losses on both sides were high: 28 RAF planes were shot down and 19 pilots killed. The Luftwaffe lost 41 aircraft, of which 22 were Messerschmitt 109s and 110s. On the ground, immense damage was caused by the raid in which 448 Londoners lost their lives.

Just after 8pm that evening (at 8.07 to be precise), during the bombing, the code-word 'Cromwell' was relayed to military units throughout Britain – the signal for the immenently expected invasion. Church bells rang throughout the land – another pre-arranged signal to carry the message to the general public.

But no signal had been issued by the German High Command, for the invasion of Britain depended on the success of the new policy of bombing the capital and on the outcome of air battles which it would force. To transport a large army across the Channel required total air superiority – a requirement the Germans had clearly not yet achieved.

The bombing of London continued relentlessly. From that first raid on 7 September, London was bombed almost every day and every night until 13 November. Well before the end of that period Hitler decided to postpone Operation *Sea Lion* until 1941, and the RAF had re-asserted itself and was again extracting unacceptable losses from the Luftwaffe.

'LONDON BURNED – BRITAIN WAS SAVED'

'It was the turning point,' writes one authority on the battle, who fought in it. 'London burned, but Britain was saved.' From that first week of the sustained attack on London the ratio of losses began to turn once again in favour of the RAF. Pilots drafted to squadrons in No 11 Group were becoming battle-wise, with a better understanding of combat

Hawker Hurricane

Like the Spitfire, the Hawker Hurricane was powered by a 1,030hp Rolls-Royce Merlin engine and carried eight Browning machine-guns in the wings. The Hurricane in service in the Battle of Britain had a normal range of 340 miles and a maximum speed of 312mph. Though slower and less nimble than the Spitfire, the Hurricane was well able to deal with bomber formations, and in fact bore the brunt of the fighting in the summer of 1940 – if only because there were more squadrons of Hurricanes than Spitfires. The German Messerschmitt 109 seems to have been able to climb faster, fly level faster and dive faster than the Hurricane, but it was less manoeuvrable and less powerfully built – which made the Hurricane its match at relatively low altitudes. Three hundred Hurricanes were lost in France, and a further 1,700 fought with Fighter Command in the Battle of Britain, of which 696 were lost permanently or temporarily. The Hurricane, less glamorous than the Spitfire, continued in service with the RAF (and the Navy) in many other roles and campaigns until the end of the war.

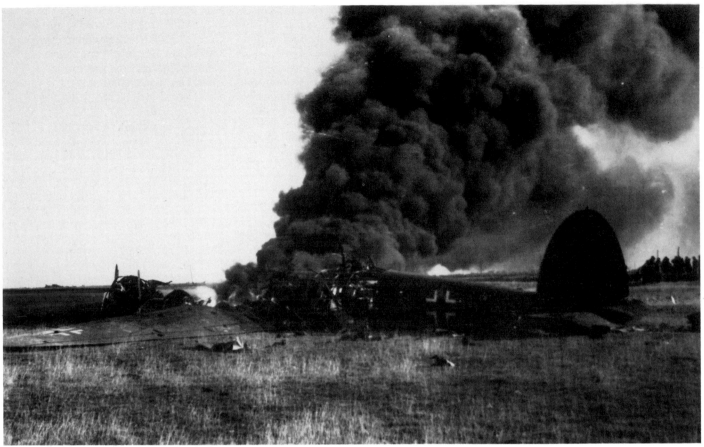

A Messerschmitt Me 110 burns after being shot down 'somewhere in Kent'

tactics, and the Group began to recover its formidable deterrent powers.

The Luftwaffe raids continued every day, although 8 and 11 September were, comparatively quiet, and reached a climax on 15 September – the day set aside after the war as the Anniversary of the Battle of Britain. It was during those days that Hitler, having postponed Operation *Sea Lion* from early September to 11 September, started to make plans for war in the east against the Soviet Union. But on 14 September he promised to give his commander his decision whether or not to go ahead with the invasion of England on 17 September, after which date the weather would start to deteriorate and with it the prospects of success. So, on Sunday 15 September, the Luftwaffe mounted massive attacks in a final effort to enable the invasion plan to go ahead.

Two massed formations of German bombers and fighters, in successive waves, swept in across south-east England. That day Luftwaffe fighters flew about 700 sorties and their bombers 230 sorties, and some of them flew a return sortie in the second attack. They were met over Kent, Sussex and Greater London by numbers of Hurricane and Spitfire squadrons, who 'waded into one huge enemy formation after another and dispersed it.' At one point every available fighter in No 11 Group had to be scrambled.

Winston Churchill witnessed this critical moment himself. Alerted by Ultra (top secret information obtained by breaking the German High Command's 'Enigma' code) that the day's actions would be decisive, he went to the headquarters of No 11 Group and sat in the Operations Room where the Group Commander, Air Vice-Marshal Keith

Dornier Do 17

At one time known as 'the flying pencil' for its slim outline, the Do 17 was a two-engine, three-seater medium bomber. It enjoyed great success in Spain in 1937, but the modifications made in the light of operational experience spoilt its pencil-slim figure. Its range was about 750 miles and its bomb-load about 2,200lb. Dornier 17s were used in the early stages of the Battle of Britain for attacking Channel convoys, and they were the bombers of the Group that attacked Eastchurch on *Adler Tag*, having failed to receive the postponement order. The Do 17 was highly manoeuvrable and could make low-level diving attacks to good effect, but its defensive armament was inadequate, and its crew were virtually unprotected. However, Do 17s were considered the most popular and reliable of German bombers during the early part of the Blitz.

Bullet? No, tea!

Typical of many stories of shot-down Nazi pilots in the summer of 1940 is the adventure of Mrs Betty Tylee and Miss Jean Smithson who were first to reach the young pilot of a Messerschmitt when it was shot down by an RAF fighter 'somewhere in England'.

He was lying some distance from his machine and he wore the Iron Cross. His first question, in very good English: 'Are you going to shoot me now?'

'No,' said Mrs Tylee, 'we don't do that in England. Would you like a cup of tea?'

'Yes, please,' he said eagerly.

So they made the Nazi airman a cup of tea. Then the ambulance called to take him to hospital.

The Battle of Britain – seen from below

For the general public in south-east England in the summer of 1940 the Battle of Britain meant the roar of fighter engines, the chatter of machine-guns, vapour trails in the sky, and the occasional glimpse of parachutes descending. A government information officer in Tunbridge Wells once saw 180 German planes in the sky from his office window, and on another occasion he watched five parachutes descending together. For all too many, of course, that summer brought bombs, death and loss of their homes. To the immense delight of many a schoolboy, however, it brought the new sport of spotting crashed Nazi planes, and if possible, collecting a souvenir from one of them. Headmasters and the police tended to spoil the fun by confiscating wreckage, and 'graveyards' of such debris could be as high as a house – confirming for many people the British claims of huge German losses.

Park, directed his fighter force. Watching the battle being played out and having heard Park ask Dowding for three squadrons from No 12 Group to be put at his disposal, the Prime Minister . . .

> . . . became conscious of the anxiety of the Commander, who now stood still behind his subordinate's chair. Hitherto I had watched in silence. I now asked: 'What other reserves have we?' 'There are none,' said Air-Vice Marshal Park.

But despite the nearness of the call, the day ended with a clear victory for the RAF, who shot down 56 Luftwaffe aircraft and lost 23 of their own. As if to emphasise the nature of this victory, the following day was relatively quiet. It was now becoming obvious to the German High Command – and to many Luftwaffe pilots seeing waves of RAF fighters homing in on them from the skies – that the RAF was very far from being a spent force. Its reserve strength had been badly underestimated by German Intelligence, but Göring still continued to believe that his Luftwaffe was within a few days of total victory in the air.

On 16 September, therefore, in conference with his commanders, the Reichsmarschall laid down his new strategy: the number of bombers in a formation would be reduced, but they would be supported by maximum fighter cover. The RAF fighters would be compelled to engage the bombers and when they did so the Luftwaffe fighter pilots would destroy them. Göring's strategy continued to be followed long after his Führer had announced his decision, taken on 17 September, to postpone the long-delayed Operation *Sea Lion*, 'until further notice.'

For the rest of September and into October, Göring's strategy continued to be followed. On some days there was comparatively slight air activity, especially when the Luftwaffe confined itself to fighter sweeps, or sent large formations of fighters escorting a few bombers as a bait: an obvious ruse which the defenders ignored more than once. On other days, the fighting could be as fierce as any from the start of the battle. On 27 September, for example, Messerschmitt 109s and 110s – which now carried bombs to compel attention – headed for the south coast in an attempt to exhaust the defenders' flying-time and ammunition, and so allow a force of raiding Junkers to get through. In the west a formation of Heinkel 111s and Messerschmitt 110s (fighter only and bomb-carrying mode) headed for Bristol. At the end of the day's fighting, the RAF had lost 28 more fighters, but had accounted for 55 enemy aircraft. At the time this day seemed to be as significant, and certainly as concentrated, as 15 September. On the following day, in attacks on London and on the Solent, the Luftwaffe scored a notable success, shooting down 16 RAF planes for the loss of only two of their own.

On the last day of September there was more intense activity, with German fighter sweeps in the south-east and two waves of attacks on London. Weymouth was bombed and the day ended with raiders heading for the Westland factory, but hitting Sherborne instead. Daylight raids continued into October, but from early in the month they began to give way to increasing raids at night. Such raiders generally operated in smaller concentrations, but the fighting with any one wave of attackers was as fierce as ever and demanded its victims on both sides.

Although these sporadic dogfights continued until the end of October, with hindsight it is now clear that the Battle of Britain – the Luftwaffe's attempt to destroy the RAF as a fighting force – was effectively over by the end of September, the critical turning-point being the 15th of that month. On that day the RAF won a decisive battle, after which the Luftwaffe contributed to its ultimate failure by allowing itself to lose sight of the original objective – control of the air.

The Battle of Britain lasted three-and-a-half months, and during that time both sides were severely mauled. The Luftwaffe's admitted losses were 1,733 aircraft and 3,089 aircrew, compared with those of the RAF which were 915 aircraft and 503 pilots. It was a battle that brought to an end the unbroken run of German victories, and it dealt the first blow to Hitler's military reputation. For the world at large could see that he had been defeated by the RAF and that he had been forced, as a result, to abandon his invasion plans.

This meant that the British army, humiliated earlier in France, no longer had to think in defensive terms as an anti-invasion force, but could start to plan and to train for a more aggressive role. And most important of all, the success of the RAF gave Britain's industries the freedom and the time to produce, in ever-increasing quantities, all those weapons needed to carry the war into the heart of enemy territory.

Few battles in recent military history show more clearly that avoiding defeat can sometimes be no less important than gaining victory. The men and machines of the Royal Air Force did not win the war for Britain, but they certainly ensured that she would not be defeated in the air by Göring and his Luftwaffe.

'The air was filled with Nazi aircraft . . .'

. . . reported one unnamed RAF fighter pilot on *Adler Tag*. 'There seemed to be thousands of Messerschmitts, Spitfires and Hurricanes all mixed up in a series of dog fights. The three hurricanes I was leading concentrated on six Messerschmitts. I saw one of the others shoot down his Messerschmitt. He broke away when only twenty-five yards from the German machine, which went streaming down towards the sea – but we did not see it crash into the water, so we have not claimed it as a victim . . .'

Keeping Track of Friend and Foe

Throughout the war RAF Fighter Command was able to keep track of every Luftwaffe raider from take-off and of every RAF squadron that scrambled – including all crashed aircraft and parachuted aircrew – both over land and off the coast. Immediate and accurate information came to Command plotting rooms from two networks of trained observers – the Observer Corps and the chain of RAF radar stations around the coast.

The Observer Corps (which became 'Royal' in 1941) was manned by volunteers and in 1940 'numbered upwards of fifty thousand men, women and youths . . . (who), devoted and tireless, were hourly at their posts' (Churchill). Equipped with field glasses and instruments for gauging the course, speed and altitude of aircraft, every post was connected to Fighter Command by landline. There were some 1,400 such posts throughout Britain charged with the enormous responsibility of detecting and reporting every aircraft movement over land. It was an Observer Corps post that spotted the first Flying Bomb in June 1944.

Radar for air defence was pioneered by the RAF, and by the beginning of the war there was a network of Chain Home (CH) radar stations with their 350ft steel towers all around the coast from the Isle of Wight to the Shetlands. CH stations could detect aircraft flying at a height of 15,000ft and at a distance of at least 40 miles – sometimes further – and some stations could even watch Luftwaffe squadrons forming up in Belgium and France. For detecting planes at lower level there was a second row of radar stations called Chain Home Low (CHL), with 185ft towers alongside the CH towers. CHL radar could see a fighter aircraft approaching at high speed, at sea level, and at a distance of 30 miles. But at this time CH and CHL looked out to sea and were virtually unable to see inland – this responsibility fell to the Observer Corps.

Advice to plane-spotters: 1940

Engines three, or engines four,
There's a Nazi at the door!
If the fly's head comes in view
Maybe paratroopers too.
If the wings as swallow's lie
'Still a Nazi' is the cry.
And among the other things,
Nazis like the square-clipped wings.
Britain's planes have underpart
Black as any Nazi's heart!

from the *Sunday Dispatch*

Regular air patrols were good for civilian morale and made excellent propaganda shots, but played only a minor part in keeping watch over Britain's skies. In the early days sound location equipment was used, without success, to track potential targets. Radar, when it was first introduced, could only scan sea approaches. So it fell to the Royal Observer Corps to keep a constant look-out for enemy aircraft.

Reichsmarschall Hermann Göring looks to London for a much-needed victory

Hermann Göring played such a key role in the early days of the Nazi movement and in the establishment of the Third Reich that it came as a surprise to no one, least of all to himself, when he was nominated Hitler's successor on the outbreak of war in 1939. This move merely confirmed in practice what nearly everybody understood in theory, namely that the Commander-in-Chief of the Luftwaffe, Minister for Air, Plenipotentiary for the Four-Year Plan, Chairman of the Council of Ministers for the Defence of the Reich, Minister President of Prussia, President of the Reichstag, was the second most powerful man in the land.

Yet less than a year later, in July 1940, when he added the rank of *Reichsmarschall* to his resounding list of titles and appointments, that power had already passed its peak. Not many of his friends in Germany knew about this significant shift in the power structure, and even fewer of his enemies. Those at the helm in beleaguered Britain had far too much on their hands to concern themselves unduly with stresses and strains inside the upper echelons of the Nazi hierarchy.

But for all his bombast and conceit Göring was not an unintelligent man, and during those momentous months of early summer 1940 his keen political nose would have told him that however much he still enjoyed the trappings, the reality of power was slowly slipping through his fingers.

In fact it was his conceit which was largely his undoing. He had watched with barely-concealed envy the battle honours being won by Guderian and other Panzer commanders during the campaign in France, and the adulation being showered upon the heroes of the Wehrmacht. Determined to secure some of the glory for himself and his beloved Luftwaffe, he persuaded Hitler to leave the destruction of the encircled BEF to his airmen. He gave an assurance that 'it would not be possible for the British to evacuate their forces from Dunkirk'. The Führer, ever-distrustful of his generals, readily acquiesced, and in doing so made his first serious blunder of the war.

Worse was to follow. When it became clear that the British would not capitulate after the fall of France, Hitler reluctantly agreed to the cross-Channel invasion plan, 'Operation Sea Lion', and told Göring that he must first secure complete air superiority. In reply, the *Reichsmarschall* boasted that in four days the air defences of southern England would be smashed, and in four weeks the RAF 'will be wiped from the skies'.

Failure to keep these promises was by no means lost on the Führer, and Göring knew that his credibility as a war leader now rested upon a successful outcome of a sustained air attack against the enemy. The BEF had eluded his grasp at Dunkirk. The RAF was still very much in evidence over the skies of southern England (Göring completely failed to realize just how close he had come to success at the end of the first crucial stage in the Battle of Britain). Now it was the turn of the ordinary men and women, children and old folk, in the mean and huddled streets of London, the glittering prize to be added to Warsaw and Rotterdam.

By bombing civilians into submission Göring and his Luftwaffe could still win the war for Germany single-handed, and so restore a somewhat tarnished image in the Führer's eyes. Such is the way in which tyranny works, and such was the lesson the Allies were not slow to learn and turn to their own terrible advantage in the years ahead.

London in the Front Line

The night the Luftwaffe set fire to London was the night Hermann Göring lost the Battle of Britain and, quite possibly, the war itself. That seems clear to us now, though at the time such a thought would have been far from the minds of those involved. But, fifty years on, the crucial question remains: *why did he do it?*

'The bombing of London on 7 September and for the four weeks following,' stated the British *Official Story of the Civil Defence of Britain*, 'can be understood only if it is seen as something different from the subsequent attacks on the capital and the onslaughts on other cities. Until the beginning of October the enemy sought to vanquish London by a knockout blow, as part of the same total operation that included attacks on the RAF and its aerodromes. He was plunging for a quick finish . . .' But that was not his only motive.

During the second week of the Battle of Britain there occurred one of those trivial-seeming incidents which can change the course of a battle or even a war. To wear down the defence as quickly as possible, Göring had ordered day and night bombing attacks, but – to avoid the risk of retaliation – London was not to be attacked. This was a direct order from Hitler, who, in his Directive of 1 August to the Reichsmarschall, had emphasised that only he, the Führer, had the power to authorise 'terror raids' on London.

On 24 August, however, a flight of Heinkel 111s which had been ordered to attack aircraft factories at Kingston-on-Thames, among other targets in the London area, lost its way and inadvertently dropped its bombs on the City of London, killing nine people. From that time until May 1941 London was rarely free from raids for long, even quite heavy raids. Here it is only possible to refer to the biggest of them.

The August raids gave Churchill the opportunity he was waiting for. Committed to the policy of attacking only military targets, he wanted Nazi Germany to receive the opprobrium for starting 'terror bombing', rather than Britain, for this would retain American approval and goodwill. But now he was free to order retaliatory raids on German cities, and on the night of 25 August 80 RAF bombers took off for Berlin. Only half of them succeeded in penetrating the dense cloud and reaching the target. Very little damage was done by this raid (or, indeed by subsequent attacks) except to German morale and the prestige of the Nazi Party. Unlike London, Berlin had come through the First World War unscathed by bombers, and Hitler had given assurances to the German people – no doubt underwritten by Göring – that enemy aircraft would never reach the capital. More recently, he had told them that the Luftwaffe had destroyed the RAF. 'Then how is it possible', hard-headed Berliners asked, 'that the RAF is now dropping bombs on us?'

A Foolish Mistake

In the second volume of his *History of the Second World War*, entitled 'Their Finest Hour', Winston Churchill recalled the sense of relief experienced by Fighter Command when, on 7 September, it became clear that the enemy had switched his main attack to London.

Only a few days earlier, on visits to RAF stations at Manston and Biggin Hill, he had seen for himself how 'they were getting terribly knocked about, and their runways . . . ruined by craters'.

Our ability to defend British air space entirely depended upon these and other similar airfields in the south of England, and Britain's wartime leader was quite clear that Göring should have carried on with his original plan of attack.

'By departing from the classical principles of war,' Churchill observes, 'as well as from hitherto accepted dictates of humanity, he made a foolish mistake.'

Elsewhere in the same book Winston Churchill describes the Luftwaffe's campaign against Britain as 'a tale of divided counsels, conflicting purposes, and never fully accomplished plans. Three or four times . . . the enemy abandoned a method of attack which was causing us severe stress, and turned to something new. All these stages overlapped one another, and cannot be readily distinguished by precise dates.'

Carriers of Death

The prototype of the elegant, twin-engined Heinkel He 111 made its first flight in 1935, and later underwent extensive secret trials as a medium-range bomber – medium-range, that is, by the standards of the day. It was introduced to the world at large as a civil airliner, although even in Deutsch Lufthansa livery the Germans could not resist using the aircraft for photo-reconnaissance missions over Britain, France and the USSR.

With a maximum speed of 258 mph, and a range, fully-laden, of about 745 miles (1,200 km) the He 111 was faster than most single-seat fighters of the late 1930s. For this reason the defensive armament was restricted to three machine guns mounted in the port beam, the dorsal position and in the nose-cone. The internal bomb load varied from version to version, but the maximum stood at 2,000 kg/4,400 lbs. The bombs were carried nose-up in vertical cells in the main fuselage.

The He 111 B-1, with two 880 hp Daimler-Benz DB 600C engines, was taken into service by the Luftwaffe early in 1937, and immediately saw action in Spain with the Kondor Legion. A B-2 version with improved flight performance from more powerful engines, each generating 950 hp, quickly followed. It was the success of these early, elliptically-winged versions during the Spanish Civil War that convinced Göring and his senior Luftwaffe officers that there was no defence against Heinkels.

By 1940 their familiar silhouettes against the sky still struck terror in the hearts of civilians on the ground below, but their vulnerability to attack by faster aircraft, such as the Hawker Hurricane and Super-marine Spitfire, had already become apparent. As a counter, more defensive guns were added and the crew numbers increased to five or six, with a consequent reduction in the payload. In this way the pride of the Luftwaffe became increasingly a liability, but no real attempt was made to replace it with a more up-to-date weapon. Putting their faith in rocket technology, the Germans were content to carry on building the aircraft, in many modified forms, right up until the end of the war.

Heinkel production in Germany and Rumania amounted to at least 6,000 – possibly even 7,000 – throughout the Second World War. Powered by Rolls-Royce Merlin engines, the plane, in a version designated as C.2111, continued to be built in Spain until as late as 1956.

'... A STROKE RIGHT INTO THE ENEMY'S HEART'

The day Göring described as 'the historic hour when our air force for the first time delivered its stroke right into the enemy's heart' was a fine Saturday afternoon. Suddenly, about 5pm, 'a great black rash,' in the words of one Fire Officer, was seen against the clear, sunlit sky. What he saw was a V-formation of Heinkels and Dorniers sweeping up the Thames estuary from the east. Then came the crump of bombs dropping, the dull roar of distant explosions, and columns of black smoke spiralling over the docks area. Soon a strange orange glow, which had nothing to do with the evening sun, was to be seen over the whole of London's East End.

Offices and warehouses were ablaze in the docks at Limehouse, Millwall, Rotherhithe and by Tower Bridge, as well as in Surrey Docks. Woolwich Arsenal, West Ham Power Station and Beckton Gasworks were all hit, and countless little terraced houses and shops were reduced to rubble. As the waves of raiders moved westward on this, London's biggest daytime attack, they dropped their bombs over a wide area, causing destruction in the City, Westminster and Kensington. By 6pm they had gone – all 375 of them.

The Cenotaph in dramatic silhouette against a background of burning incendiary bombs in Whitehall

'Send all the pumps you've got – the whole bloody world's on fire'

This *cri de coeur* went up from a desperate fire officer at the height of the raid on London's dockland. As installations and warehouses blazed all around them, exhausted fire crews struggled to prevent their pumps from becoming clogged with mud from the river. After a hot, dry summer the Thames water level was dangerously low. The heat from the fires was so intense that telegraph poles burst into flames, and barges burned at their moorings along the canals and river bank. There had been early warning of the raid with the result that every one of London's 2,000 regular, and 23,000 auxiliary, firemen had been mobilised. They were joined by other brigades from places as far away as Rugby and Portsmouth, responding to the call for help. Somo of the men, and their pumps, worked without pause for 40 hours or more.

How London prepared for bombing

In the years before the war everyone expected that bombs would rain down the moment war was declared – which was why nobody was surprised to hear the sirens almost the moment Chamberlain finished broadcasting the declaration. What did surprise many people was that no bombs fell.

Received opinion was that 'the bomber will always get through', and the official and unpublicised estimate of casualties – based on First World War experience and possibly on accounts of Guernica – was many thousands more than actually occurred in the worst raids of the Blitz. For this reason thousands of cardboard coffins were held in readiness, and London hospitals were ordered to empty their wards to receive huge numbers of casualties.

It was also the official view that air raids would cause great panic, and thousands, possibly millions, would attempt to flee from the capital. There was little official confidence in the people's morale, and no support for building deep underground shelters, which were thought of as bolt-holes. The only people encouraged to leave were children with or without their mothers. As to shelters, millions of Anderson shelters were provided, and many fewer communal or street shelters built.

Gas attacks were also generally and officially expected, and gas masks issued for the whole population, including babies in arms.

Air Raid Precautions were organised from 1937, air raid wardens recruited, warning systems constructed and much information issued to the public, but no real enthusiasm was displayed until the Fall of France showed that the air raid threat was real and aimed at this country.

AIR RAID WARDENS

VOLUNTEERS ARE WANTED as Air Raid Wardens. In urban areas there will be a wardens' post of five or six wardens to every 400 to 500 inhabitants. Wardens will be responsible for keeping in touch with the inhabitants of their sector and giving them advice, and must know the location of gas mains, electric cables, telephones, shelters and trenches.

QUALIFICATIONS. Men who are over the age of 30 are needed, and men between 25 and 30 may also apply if not available for more active service. Some women over the age of 25 are also needed.

CONDITIONS OF SERVICE AND TRAINING. Training is necessary, but will take place out of working hours and need not ordinarily interfere with a warden's occupation or employment.
In war time most of the wardens would give part-time service when they were able. There are also vacancies for a number of senior wardens who would, in war time, give whole-time service for which payment would be made at the rate of 60*s.* a week for men and 40*s.* a week for women.

HOW TO JOIN. Fill in the form overleaf and post it to your Local Council now.

NATIONAL SERVICE

In 1938 a national call went out for volunteers to act as Air Raid Wardens 'responsible for keeping in touch with inhabitants of their sector and giving them advice'. They wore white helmets and gas mask carriers to make them more visible in the blackout.
(left) Anderson shelters being delivered to householders in the Muswell Hill area of London in February 1938

Hitler was livid, and he ordered a sustained air attack to be made on London as soon as possible. 'If they attack our cities,' he shouted, 'we will simply erase theirs.' The order delighted senior Luftwaffe commanders, who did not agree with Göring's strategy of attacking the RAF's airfields and Fighter Command. In particular, Kesselring, whose *Luftflötte 2* had suffered the most losses at the hands of RAF fighters, was strongly in favour of bombing London and other cities; he believed they would prove a much easier target, and that many fewer men and machines would be lost in such raids.

There was another compelling motive for switching the attack to London: it would force RAF fighters, or what was left of them, back into the skies to defend the capital. Fighter Command had recently chosen to rest pilots and fitters rather than be lured into attacking 'bait' in the shape of heavily protected German bombers, and this seemed to Göring to be depriving the Luftwaffe of an easy victory. Time was running out, and if 'Operation *Sea Lion*' was to be launched by mid-September, it was vital to seize command of the air. Göring now aimed to knock out the RAF and London in one great blow. So, on 7 September, the Blitz came to London.

As it happened, Churchill and the senior RAF commanders welcomed the new situation. They knew, as Göring evidently did not, that the RAF was very close to being overwhelmed by the Luftwaffe. The sudden end to the raids on Fighter Command's airfields and bases gave hard-pressed ground crews and other staff an opportunity to repair, reorganise and regroup their resources – not to mention a chance for exhausted pilots to get some much-needed rest. It also became clear to the RAF commanders that with the Luftwaffe's main target no longer in doubt, British fighter strength could be concentrated on the Germans' mass formations to make them pay dearly for the death and destruction they aimed to inflict on London.

Follow my Leader

One of the many remarkable features of the Heinkel He 111 bomber was the degree of all-round forward visibility enjoyed by the pilot. Good in a normal flying position, it was made even better in some later versions by giving the pilot the choice of a raised seating position and a separate, retractable windscreen through which he could keep constant watch. Ready to hand was a 7.92mm Rheinmetall MG 15 machine gun on a manual mounting. During an approach run the bomb-aimer took up his position on a 'prone pad' in the forward part of the nose-cone. At other times during the flight he occupied a collapsible seat to the pilot's right. Above the pilot was a sliding roof hatch, and behind him was the main bulkhead separating the flight deck from the bomb bays.

The other component of the Luftwaffe's strike against London on 7 September 1940 was the Dornier Do 17, the so-called 'flying pencil'. Unlike the Heinkel, this aircraft, first flown in 1934, was actually designed for civilian use. But Deutsch Lufthansa decided that the narrow fuselage made cabin conditions too cramped for the six passengers, and it was left to the Air Ministry, under Hermann Göring, to decide whether or not the aircraft was worth developing as a medium-range bomber. In its military guise the Dornier, like the Heinkel, was originally armed with three machine guns, but the payload was considerably less (1,000 kg/2,200 lbs) and the airspeed about 30 mph slower.

A German bomber over the Thames

But two hours later the Luftwaffe's night-raiders arrived. The still-blazing fires by the river guided some 250 bombers to their target. Until 4.30am next morning they fed the fires with high explosive bombs. Three of London's main line stations were put out of action, many small factories were hit, and thousands of homes were destroyed by bomb or fire. In the docks and Thames basin some 60 vessels were sunk and many more fire-damaged. The human cost was heavy: 430 people were killed and 1600 seriously injured.

Dawn on Sunday revealed a spectacle of smoking devastation. Wrecked and gutted buildings, many still burning, others just a shell or a pile of rubble, were all that remained of many streets. Roads were blocked by enormous craters and piles of debris, gas and water mains were severed, electric cables torn up, and under many a ruined building there were bodies, some still living, to be dug out. Broken glass, bricks, roof tiles, splintered wood, wrecked cars and vans were everywhere. Clouds of evil-smelling smoke drifted over the whole area. Aware that the Luftwaffe might return to the attack at any moment, London's firemen, ARP wardens, police and other rescue services worked non-stop to get fires under control, release people trapped in fallen buildings, clear blocked streets and prepare themselves and their equipment for the next attack.

That night the bombers came back. For nine and a half hours from 7.30pm some 200 aircraft showered high explosive and incendiary bombs on the East End, as earlier, but this time on the City too. Once again, enormous fires were started and many factories and houses were destroyed. The casualties were: 412 killed, 747 seriously injured.

And so began for London 10 weeks of continuous bombing. Every night from 7 September until the end of November the capital was attacked by waves of 50 to 300 aircraft. During those three months some 36,000 bombs fell on London, killing 12,696 people and seriously injuring about 20,000 others. In September and October the enemy appeared to be going for the kill by destroying the life and morale of London, the nation's capital. That having proved unsuccessful, in November the onslaught was extended to include provincial cities and ports, and Coventry, Birmingham, Bristol, Southampton and Liverpool were all heavily attacked that month. In December Sheffield and Manchester were added to the Luftwaffe's visiting list – and of course many centres other than London were being frequently attacked on a lesser scale.

On the third night of the London blitz – 9 September – the Luftwaffe widened the range of its attack, and some 200 bombers 'visited' most parts of the town between 8pm and 4.30 next morning. Among other famous buildings, the Law Courts and Somerset House suffered damage. That night 370 people were killed and 1,400 injured. The following night Londoners' spirits were cheered by the sound of the anti-aircraft barrage

Bombs on the Palace

On 13 September 1940 a single German raider flew boldly down the Mall in broad daylight and dropped six bombs on Buckingham Palace. "We all wondered why we weren't dead," said the King, who was watching as two of the bombs made large craters in the quadrangle. Earlier the King and Queen had been booed when visiting the bombed East End of London – now they were received with warm cheers of fellow-feeling: their home too had been bombed. As the King noted, "we have found a new bond with the people." The Central Office of Information wanted to censor the story as bad for morale. "Dolts! . . . Fools!" roared Churchill. "Spread it at once! . . . Let the people know that the King and Queen are sharing their perils!" Like the King, he understood that people needed to feel that the Royal Family was facing the same dangers as everybody else.

Winston Churchill (*extreme left*), King George VI (*with his back to the camera*) and Queen Elizabeth examine bomb damage at Buckingham Palace

in action for the first time – a sound, as someone said, like 'gigantic doors being slammed in the sky'. At that stage few German aircraft were shot down, but AA gunfire hardly made their task easier and it certainly made their potential victims feel that something was being done to protect them.

'. . . A WONDERFUL MOMENT FOR US WHO ARE HERE IN LONDON'

And so it went on, night after night of terror and destruction, but somehow there was no break in morale or loss of will to resist which the Germans (and not only them) had anticipated. Londoners remained almost absurdly resilient and cheerful, and even insisted on going to work amid all the debris, as if everything was normal. Their homes could be reduced to rubble overnight, their office, factory or shop be burned to a shell, but still they expected everything to be 'business as usual'. People grumbled, of course, as they always do. They grumbled, in particular, about the lack of shelters – *deep* shelters – and they grumbled about the condition of the shelters

A burning City, seen through the dome of St Paul's Cathedral

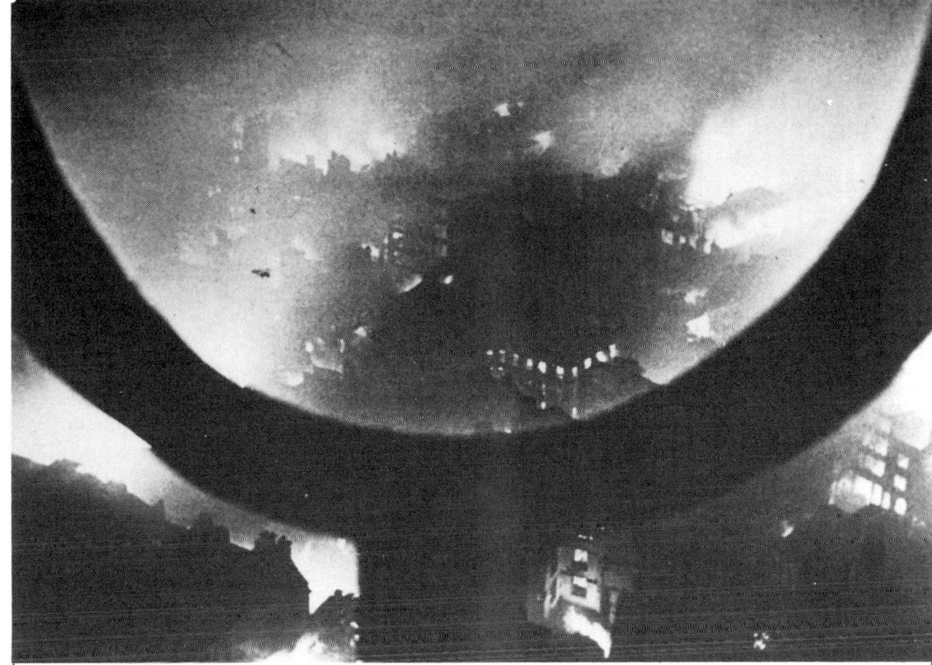

The 'Great Fire' again

'The Thames, with its riverside fires, created a spectacle probably unmatched since the Great Fire of 1666,' writes Neil Wallington in *Firemen at War: the work of London's Firemen in the Second World War*. 'Parts of the southern warehouse frontage below Tower Bridge were alight for over 1000 yards – a continuous wall of fire. Many moored vessels were ablaze from end to end, and numerous burning 100-ton barges, whose moorings had burned through, drifted down river with the ebbing tide like funeral pyres.' The huge stocks of such commodities as timber, rum and paint in the warehouses caused spectacular blazes, and liquid fire poured across the surface of some dock basins. 'At one inferno in Bermondsey the air was heavy with pepper and firemen found breathing an unpleasant and difficult task . . . There were paint fires, sugar fires, and tea fires. At a dockside building full of grain, rats poured out in a steady stream to escape the fire and smoke inside.' *(Ibid.)*

Farringdon Street and Shoe Lane, seen from Ludgate Circus, on the morning of 10 May 1941

that were available. They grumbled when there was no AA gunfire and then grumbled about the noise made when the guns did go into action.

Everyone seemed to want to carry on normally, and yet everybody seemed to relish the drama of the Blitz. People were much readier to talk to strangers on the train or in the street – often to exchange bomb stories – for almost everyone could tell of a wonderful escape. Many enjoyed the sense of danger and the sheer pleasure of waking up alive after a night of bombing. 'This is a wonderful moment for us who are here in London,' said the writer J.B. Priestley, 'in the roaring centre of the battlefield. We are not civilians who have happened to stray into a kind of hell on earth, but soliders who have been flung into battle . . .'

The full moon became known as the 'bombers' moon', and London's heaviest raid in October came on the 15th – the full moon. Over 400 bombers reached the city that night and dropped more than 1,000 tons of bombs. Again the casualties were severe: 430 dead and 900 injured. This time the Germans also dropped some 70,000 incendiaries, and it became obvious that new people and new methods were urgently needed to cope with the menace of fires on such a scale. A body of 'fire-watchers' and fire services covering the whole of London (and soon the provinces too) was quickly set up. The fire-watcher's job was to stay on a roof (protected only by a 'tin hat'), look out for incendiary bombs, report

'WE NEVER HAD ENOUGH WATER'

their position, and if possible extinguish them at once. At first fire-watchers were volunteers, usually from among residents or employees in a building, but so many were needed that it was soon felt that everyone should take their turn, and fire-watching was made compulsory. Training schemes were organised, and all fire-watchers learned how to deal with the different kinds of incendiary bombs. As a result thousands of incendiaries were extinguished as soon as they fell, and many buildings saved from the flames.

November saw the same procession of nightly raids, every night of the month except three (in September it was every night, and in October every night except one). Once again the heaviest attack was on the 15th. However, from that time the raids, though regular, became rather less severe as the efforts of the Luftwaffe were diverted to targets in the provinces. Instead of aiming a knock-out blow at the capital, the Luftwaffe seemed to be bent on a war of attrition by bombing industrial centres and ports. But London still had to suffer many terrible onslaughts.

Eight more major raids were to come before the Luftwaffe's attention was turned eastwards for the attack on the Soviet Union. On 8 December 250 people were killed and 600 injured when between 300 and 400 bombers showered 3,000 'baskets' of incendiaries over a wide area. That night the House of Commons was hit for the first time, but after this rehearsal of its attempt to destroy London by fire, the Luftwaffe took a three-week pause until after Christmas. Then, on the night of Sunday 29 December, came the Second Great Fire of London. That night, as the Germans well knew, there was an exceptionally low tide on the Thames, and as yet there was no network of emergency water tanks. Most office buildings were empty and locked when a

In a freak blast this double-decker bus – 'empty of passengers', the official caption assures us – ended up against the wall of a shattered terrace of houses in the 7 September raid on London

St Paul's Cathedral stood alone in a sea of destruction after the worst of the London bombing

hundred bombers flew over and dropped thousands of incendiaries directly on the City itself.

'We came as close as London ever came to a fire storm that night,' said one observer. 'We never had enough water.' At the start of the raid the water mains had been broken by parachute mines. Very soon the narrow streets between St Paul's and the Tower of London were a mass of flames and generating enormous heat. From the Guildhall to St Pauls, from Moorgate to Aldersgate Street, and from Old Street to Cannon Street, the great blaze burned out nearly every building. Some 1500 fires had to be fought, and many had to be left to burn themselves out. The damage was indescribable. The City's ancient Guildhall was 'smitten by fire and blast', as were eight Wren churches, including St Bride's Fleet Street and part of the Temple Church. The Old Bailey suffered great damage, and the whole of Paternoster Row, then the home of many publishing houses, was burned down, with the loss of many thousands of books. Amid all the fires stood St Paul's, the biggest and most vulnerable target of all. 'It floated but at times it was engulfed,' observed the writer H.M. Tomlinson, 'and we thought it had gone; then the fiery tide lowered and the Cathedral was above the capital as ever, except that it was red-hot.' Thanks to the heroic efforts of the St Paul's Watch and the restoration of the water supply, the Cathedral survived that terrible night almost unscathed.

Some hard lessons were learnt that night, and as a result fire-watching was made compulsory at all business premises, and an extensive system of emergency water tanks was set up so that firefighters need no longer be dependent on vulnerable mains supplies. These measures were tested when the Luftwaffe returned on the nights of 11 and 12 January, with formations similar to that of 29 December. In spite of the hail of incendiaries, few fires became really serious – thanks to the efforts of the new fire-watchers. The damage was comparatively small, and by morning the fires were out.

Two months later, there were heavy raids on 8 and 9 March – with 150 bombers on each occasion. Over 200 people lost their lives, and the damage to buildings was heavy. The heaviest raid since 15 October, even including the night of the Great Fire (when few lives were lost) came ten nights later. Three hundred bombers caused exceptionally heavy

'UXBs'

Early in the Blitz the Luftwaffe used a new and damaging form of attack – the delayed-action or time bomb – large numbers of which were dropped in most big raids. By the end of October there were 3000 of these unexploded bombs or 'UXBs' waiting to be dealt with in London. While most were potentially dangerous (10% of bombs dropped on London were duds), their sheer nuisance value was enormous. Streets had to be closed and houses evacuated for 600 yards around a UXB, which had to be dug out, rendered harmless or removed and exploded. The presence of a UXB could block a railway line, a main road or an approach to a vital factory for many hours. 'The rapid disposal of unexploded bombs,' wrote Churchill, 'is of the highest importance. Any failure to grapple with this problem may have serious results on the production of aircraft and other vital war material.' Had the Germans fully realised the effectiveness of these bombs they would surely have dropped more of them.

The most famous of all UXBs dropped very close to St Paul's Cathedral on 15 September and penetrated deep into the ground beside the foundations. It was eight feet long and weighed a ton. For three days a Royal Engineers bomb disposal unit struggled, with cool courage, to extricate it. Meanwhile the cathedral was closed and traffic in the area slowed down to reduce vibration. When the UXB was at last brought to the surface it was driven on a lorry at top speed through empty streets, all houses on the route having been evacuated, to Hackney Marshes where it was exploded, leaving a crater measuring 100 feet across.

damage, and 751 people were killed and 1,170 injured. There followed, in April, the two raids known, for obvious reasons, as 'the Wednesday' and 'the Saturday'. On 16 April 450 bombers and on 19 April 350 bombers released a large tonnage of very big bombs over the Centre and south of London. Each night they killed about 1,000 people and injured 2,000. Many hospitals, churches, telephone exchanges and other public buildings were severely damaged, among them the Houses of Parliament, the Law Courts and St Paul's Cathedral once again.

THE LUFTWAFFE'S FINAL FLING

The Luftwaffe's last attack before leaving for the eastern front was on 10 May, and it could be said that it was a fitting farewell, for it was one of the heaviest and certainly the most costly in lives of all the raids on London – indeed, on the country as a whole. The toll was 1,436 killed and 1,792 injured. Among the many public buildings hit were the House of Commons (where the Chamber was blown to pieces: 'it was lucky,' said

One of the most dramatic photographs taken during the London blitz is this famous shot of the frontage of the Salvation Army headquarters in Queen Victoria Street, Blackfriars. The building collapsed on 11 May 1941, the day after the heaviest of all the German air raids on London

Churchill, 'it was by night and not by day, when empty and not when full'), Westminster Abbey, the British Museum, the War Office, the Tower, the Mansion House and the Law Courts (again). Many well-known churches were damaged and five City Company Halls destroyed. But this time the Germans did not escape unscathed, for the RAF and AA between them shot down some 33 bombers.

In the next two months raids on London were comparatively light, and the last of all (except for V1s and V2s) was on 27 July 1941. It has been estimated that in the eleven months between September 1940 and July 1941, the Luftwaffe dropped up to 50,000 bombs on London, together with uncountable incendiaries.

NO MORE GLORY

What was the effect on Britain's war effort and what did it achieve for the Nazi cause? Apart from the incalculable human cost and the damage to property and irreplaceable buildings, the effect on Britain seems to have been remarkably little. It is doubtful if the nation's war effort was impeded in any significant way, and the blind violence of the bombing attacks seems to have stiffened morale, rather than the reverse. As for the Luftwaffe, the Blitz must surely be counted a failure. The attempt to provide a bridgehead for *Sea Lion* failed, the attempt to knock out London failed, as did the attacks on the cities, industrial centres and ports. After 1940/41 there was no more glory for Göring's Luftwaffe.

Not so much a miracle – more a stirrup pump

'All we can do now is pray,' said a verger of St Paul's when showers of incendiaries were hitting the cathedral roofs. One was actually lodged in the dome and melting the lead. 'Then pray standing up with your stirrup pump handy', said the Dean. The bomb fell from the dome and was put out, and once again the great Cathedral escaped disaster. But it was preparation and care, rather than miracles and prayer, that kept St Paul's safe. Before the war, 300 volunteers from all walks of life got together to form St Paul's Watch. They learned to find their way around all the passages and stairs leading to the roofs, they installed tanks, baths and buckets of water at strategic points, they equipped themselves with plenty of stirrup pumps, and above all they kept watch every night. So when the incendiary bombs showered down on that fearful night of 29 December 1940, they extinguished each bomb and fought each fire – and saved St Paul's.

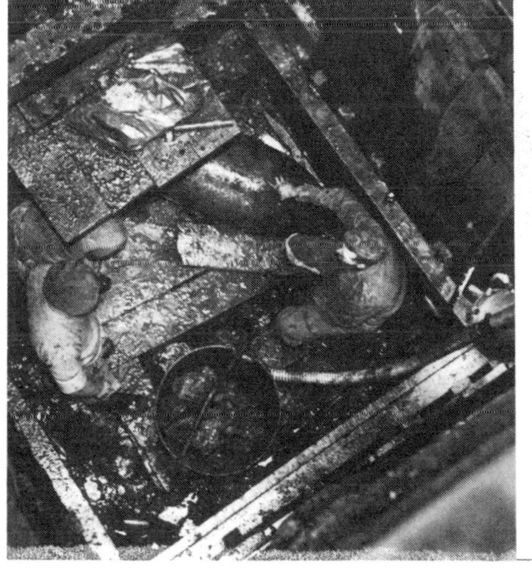

Somehow their faces seemed different

UXBs produced a new brand of heroes – the bomb disposal squads. In all towns and cities special teams were formed for 'the deadly game' of defusing unexploded bombs. All were volunteers, and few survived for long. 'Somehow or other their faces seemed different from those of ordinary men,' reported Churchill, who met them wherever he went, 'They were gaunt, they were haggard, their faces had a bluish look, with bright gleaming eyes and exceptional compression of the lips.'

One squad he remembered as symbolic of many others. It consisted of three people – the Earl of Suffolk, his lady secretary and his elderly chauffeur, and they called themselves 'The Holy Trinity'. They tackled 34 unexploded bombs with smiling efficiency, but 'the thirty-fifth claimed its forfeit. Up went the Earl of Suffolk in his Holy Trinity. But we may be sure that . . . "all the trumpets sounded for them on the other side".'

The task of clearing unexploded bombs continued for many years after the war. One of the trickiest operations, as the photograph shows, was removing a UXB from the bed of the lake in St James's Park, in the heart of London.

Balloons over Britain

Barrage balloons were a regular feature of the wartime skies around Britain's cities, ports and other sites vulnerable to air attack. Many people saw a strange beauty in these silvery shapes floating above them, and found them comforting, especially when raids were threatened.

Balloon barrages were a form of passive defence which forced enemy raiders to fly higher, making their aim less accurate. Planes at 10,000 feet or more, unlike low-flying, high-speed aircraft, were easier to hit with AA fire. So balloons were an effective deterrent to the dreaded dive bomber. Hitting a cable meant almost certain destruction – but for the RAF, unfortunately, as well as for the Luftwaffe.

Balloon barrage in 1917

As a defence against night raids on London by the Germans' giant Gotha bombers in 1917, about 20 'balloon aprons' were suspended in an arc to the north, east and south of the city, from Tottenham to Lewisham. Each apron consisted of a line of balloons whose cables were linked by wires from which other wires were suspended, effectively forming a curtain. The idea was to make low-flying attacks unattractive to bomber crews, and force them to fly at greater heights. Balloon aprons seem to have been successful enough to warrant the revival of the scheme in 1936 when German bombing attacks on London again seemed likely.

The first balloons over London, some 40 of them, were seen in 1938 – evidence of the approach of war and of the city's vulnerability to attack. Eventually the RAF had 55 squadrons in Balloon Command operating thousands of balloons, each about 60 feet in length and 30 feet in diameter at their widest point. They were filled with some 20,000 cu ft of hydrogen gas and could be set at various heights. Crews hoisted the balloons up and down either from winch-equipped lorries (for greater mobility) or from permanent sites in parks, squares and other open spaces.

Weather was an enemy, and at one period losses due to unexpected changes were such that squadrons were forced to keep two-thirds of their balloons, deflated, on the ground. Buried railway sleepers or sandbags were often used as anchors.

Handling balloons was a strenuous and sometimes dangerous job. At the start of the war it was considered too tough for women, but with the manpower shortage crews of 16 WAAFs* took over from 10-men RAF crews, releasing the men for more active duty. By 1942 most barrages were operated by women who, rank for rank, were the highest paid of all WAAFs.

The obvious method of siting barrage balloons was to station them around the perimeter of the area to be protected. But it was found that if they were set at equidistant points over the whole area a much better barrage was formed. Known as 'field-siting' this method provided a better defence against dive bombers, and the 'staggered' formation meant that the balloons did not have to be so close to each other, which could be dangerous.

Balloons made good targets for enemy fighter pilots, of course, especially in fine weather – when fighter planes and AA guns could be used to best effect – and they were safest from enemy attack at night or in poor visibility, which was just when they were most needed.

How many German aircraft were brought down by barrage balloons is

difficult to estimate, but the official figure given in Parliament in October 1945 was as low as 24 piloted and 278 non-piloted. But these figures do not, of course, begin to represent the true value of the balloon barrage as a means of defence.

Enemy losses caused by striking cables were difficult to record. Many barrages were on the coast, and a crash was only credited if on land. Confirmed Luftwaffe losses include Heinkels brought down at Newport (Mon.), at South Shields, and in the River Mersey, as well as seven other aircraft early in 1941. But RAF losses of men and machines caused by barrage cables were most carefully recorded, and rose to alarming levels. The official total by the end of the war was 91 collisions with cables and 38 actual crashes, but the true figure may have been much higher.

Balloons came into their own when the V1 offensive started. When Intelligence learned early in 1944 that an attack was planned with these 'pilotless aircraft', urgent defence measures included a Curtain Balloon Barrage south of London. At first this was to consist of a belt of 500 balloons sited on high ground and flying at 4-5,000 feet between Gravesend and Sevenoaks. By June 1944 most of these were in position. That month the Curtain Barrage brought

*Women's Auxiliary Air Force, founded 28 June 1939, later renamed the Women's Royal Air Force (WRAF).

(*left*) Photo-montage shows balloons above Buckingham Palace
(*right: top*) A well-known painting by Dame Laura Knight RA of a balloon crew in operation
(*right: below*) At home in suburbia 'somewhere in southern England' at the height of the V1 offensive

down 46 flying bombs, and as a result it was extended and thickened.

In July, 1,750 new sites were built, and by August the number was increased to more than 2,000. By this time over 100 V1s had been brought down. As far as possible, the sites were kept away from populated districts, and often access roads had to be very hurriedly laid across fields and through woods to remote anchorages. Even so, some villages in Kent and Sussex were badly damaged when V1s hit nearby balloon cables. As the bomb tended to slide down the cable it struck, crews were at risk and several were killed. Many balloons were also destroyed when hit by lightning. But by the time the V1 sites in Europe had been captured by Allied armies, RAF Balloon Command could proudly claim that they had brought down 278 (later confirmed as 233) V1s.

In practical terms, what was the real value of the balloon barrage to the war effort? The number of enemy aircraft brought down seems so small (even if V1 successes are added to the account) and the number of Allied planes destroyed so high, that the question has to be asked – was the cost worth it? And the answer has to be that the benefit of the balloon barrage lay not in the cold figures, but in the unquantifiable deterrent effect on Luftwaffe pilots. Another important factor that cannot be measured is the sense of security given, in those bomb-scarred days and nights, to the millions who lived under the protection of those 'strangely serene and beautiful shapes.'

Balloons and the ferry pilot

New aircraft were usually delivered to airfields by special ferry pilots (often women). In her book *The Forgotten Pilots* Lettice Curtis shows how balloon barrages added to the dangers and difficulties of ferrying. Sometimes ferry pilots had to be briefed by the RAF on the location of balloons and recommended safety lanes. All of which indicates how difficult barrage balloons must have made life for German pilots.

Pompey's Pride

When a couple of dozen Luftwaffe bombers flew over Portsmouth on the evening of 11 July 1940 and dropped sticks of high-explosive bombs, the attack could hardly have come as much of a surprise to most of the inhabitants. They were all well aware that their town must be one of Göring's top targets. Portsmouth, with Gosport, was a principal home base and port for the Royal Navy, and with its docks, arsenals and associated industries it was a prime and legitimate military objective.

Later, as the raids became indiscriminate, areas around Portsmouth and its suburbs – places such as Fareham and Havant – also received a full measure of the falling bombs.

Affectionately known to many generations of sailors as 'Pompey', the town had always taken great pride in its centuries-old association with the Royal Navy. It was after all the port from which Nelson had embarked on board HMS *Victory* for Trafalgar and his death. At the time of that first Luftwaffe raid a German invasion was expected almost hourly, and it seemed very likely that Portsmouth would be one of the main invasion points.

'THE APPEARANCE OF AN EARTHQUAKE'

This first raid on Portsmouth was in fact the first serious air raid of the war on any British city – though it seems doubtful if the censors would have been happy for this to be known to the world, or even to the townspeople themselves, eighteen of whom were killed that evening. Scores of others were seriously injured. One bomb scored a direct hit on a first-aid post in Drayton Road, and fifteen others destroyed or badly damaged houses, offices, pubs and a couple of hotels. The *Portsmouth Evening News* reported that 'the principal thoroughfare of the neighbourhood presented the appearance of an earthquake having taken place.' Reporters had not yet run out of epithets for describing bomb damage, and they were not to know that this raid was no more than a modest curtain-raiser for much greater devastation to come.

It was only a foretaste of what was to follow, and it generated a false optimism about the effectiveness of Anderson shelters which, it was claimed, came through the attack unscathed. Later, there were harrowing incidents in which the shelters failed to protect their occupants.

A month later, on the morning of 12 August, the Luftwaffe returned in force. At this time many points along the south coast were being attacked in preparation for Hitler's planned invasion. Portsmouth was chosen as the major target on this occasion, while a section of

A group of sailors helping to clear rubble near the Theatre Royal after the raid on 24 August 1940, pose rather unconvincingly for a local news photographer. Such shots were commonplace during the war and were intended to keep up civilian morale

Eight people died when a bomb pierced the roof of the Princes Theatre in the raid on 24 August 1940. Much of the building was destroyed, but there were many lucky escapes for the audience, most of whom were children (*right*) In Shearer Road, Buckland, survivors pick their way through 'an anonymous pile of rubble', to quote a local reporter at the time

the raiding force split off to attack a radar base on the Isle of Wight. In the teeth of 'terrific anti-aircraft fire', 80 Junkers 88 bombers headed for the city through a gap in the balloon barrage at the mouth of the harbour, while a few others overflew the city and then turned around to bomb it from the north. Short as it was, the dive-bombers' attack was ferocious and its consequences severe. Though aimed at the docks and surrounding military targets, including Lee Airfield, nearly half the bombs dropped that day fell on residential areas in Portsea and Old Portsmouth. Many houses were wrecked, 29 people were killed and 126 injured.

The damage done that morning included the destruction of Portsmouth Harbour Station by one of the early incendiary devices used by the Luftwaffe. This consisted of a large metal drum filled with oil and detonated by a TNT charge. Such devices were apt to be unreliable, but this one exploded with spectacular effect, demolishing the station and three trains standing in it. Similar incendiaries caused fires in Old Portsmouth and Portsea which blazed through most of the afternoon. And the raiders succeeded in hitting their main target – the docks, where

Wait For It: 1

During the night of Saturday, 2 September 1939 a violent thunderstorm broke over Portsmouth. Four barrage balloons were struck by lightning and set on fire, and rumours quickly spread through the city that the war had already started.

NEARLY 700 PEOPLE MADE HOMELESS

their bombs tore up railway lines and dislocated services.

This raid heralded much worse to come. Within a fortnight the Luftwaffe was back and unleashed what proved to be by far the worst raid of the summer – indeed, the worst suffered by any British city, except London, during the period of the Battle of Britain. In the late afternoon of Saturday 24 August – at a time when the city's streets were crowded with shoppers – and when the Alert gave all too short a warning of the imminent bombardment, waves of Junkers 88s (about 50 in all), escorted by Messerschmitt 110s, roared over the city, releasing more than 60 high-explosive bombs. The effects were appalling – 117 people killed instantly and 143 badly injured.

The southern half of the city suffered very badly. Extensive damage was done to property, and nearly 700 people were made homeless. Close to the Commercial Road shopping centre a large high-explosive bomb crashed through the ceiling of the Princes Theatre in Lake Road. Many children were among the large audience at a matinée performance, and when the bomb wrecked the inside of the theatre it was feared that many lives were lost. Luckily, most of the audience had reached the rear exit before the explosion, but eight people lost their lives and 17 others were badly injured.

Only nine bombs fell within the docks area. The torpedo base of HMS *Vernon* was hit, but the damage done to the docks and services was slight. But many dock workers were killed and many more injured when a bomb cut through into an underground vault which they were using as a shelter.

People's confidence in shelters was badly shaken by this raid. In a number of explosions Anderson shelters were simply blown apart – destroying at a blow the

Wait For It: 2

In an attempt to drum up business during a slack period of the Phoney War an ingenious newsvendor in Portsmouth displayed a placard reading 'GERMANY ATTACKS HOLLAND', well before the actual event took place. He explained that not being much good at grammar he had mistakenly left out the word 'IF'. This defence seems not to have cut very much ice with the magistrate, who sentenced him to two months in jail for spreading false information in time of war.

The end of the line. The scene at Portsmouth Harbour Station after the Luftwaffe attack

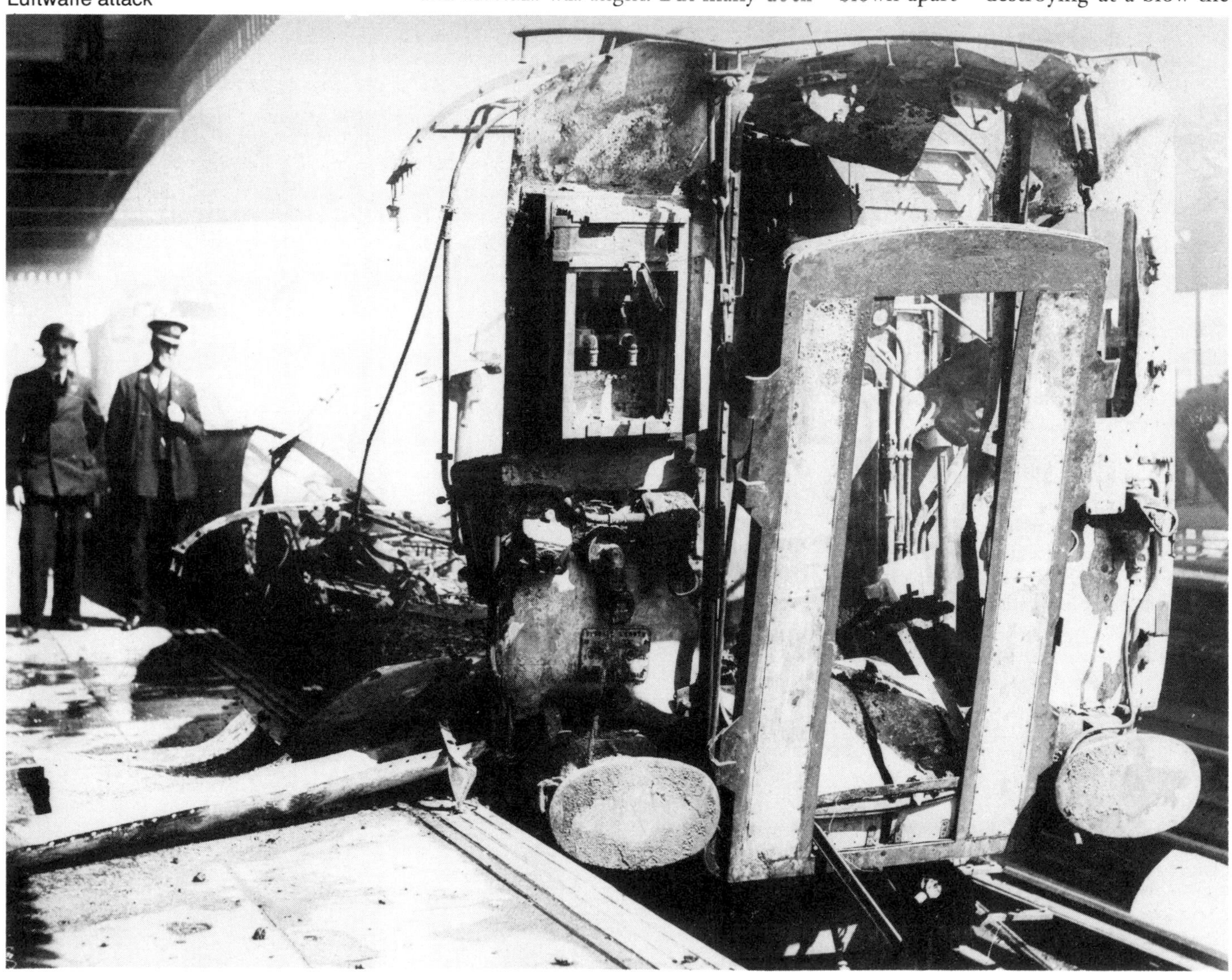

Green Road, Southsea

complacency induced by reports of their effectiveness in the city's first raid. Public shelters were also shown to be less safe than expected, and the number of casualties in all types of shelter was significant and worrrying.

Two more raids occurred before the end of August. In the first, on 26 August, the attacking force was the same as in the raid two days earlier – Junkers 88s escorted by Messerschmitt 110s. Most of their bombs fell into Langstone Harbour, but hits were made on Hilsea gasworks and on the Royal Marine Barracks at Fort Cumberland, where there were several casualties.

The next raid, on 28 August, was the first night attack on the city, and the first of many nights that the people of 'Pompey' were to spend in their shelters listening to the drone of bombers and the screech and crump of the bombs. This time a modest force of bombers released a shower of magnesium incendiaries, together with conventional high-explosive bombs. Small fires were started, but little damage was done.

Portsmouth enjoyed something of a lull in September 1940 – when, of course, the Luftwaffe was busy elsewhere. Most of its attention was switched away from the Channel ports in favour of heavy attacks on the RAF's airfields and its supply factories. London was also heavily attacked in order to draw British fighters away from coastal areas – and also by way of retaliation for the raid on Berlin. But Alerts continued to be heard in the Portsmouth area for the rest of the year, and there were many minor raids – 25 in the last four months of the year. Many of them were undertaken by just a few aircraft – or sometimes only one. Some caused substantial local damage. On 6 September, for example, a lone raider

Run, Rabbit, Run!

An unexpected bonus from the bombs that fell in rural areas that summer was seen in the *Portsmouth Evening News*. 'There was a remarkable mortality of rabbits on the downs. They have been the curse of this particular district for years, and farmers are well pleased by this aspect of the raid. Small boys were to be seen later in the day joyfully bearing back big "bags" for supper.'

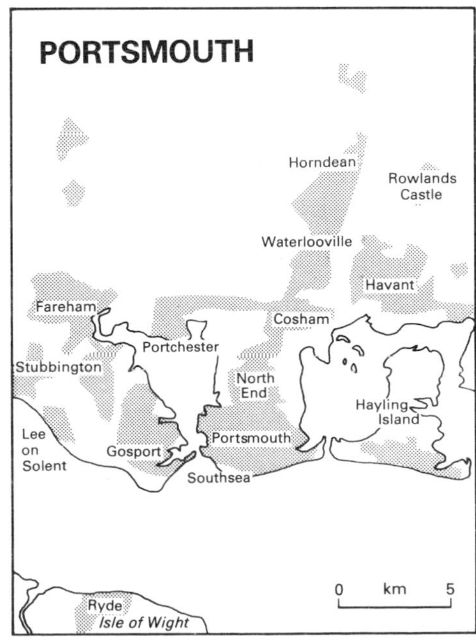

'Lit up like Fairyland'

The manager's vivid memories of the night the Carlton Cinema was bombed were reported many years later in *The Hampshire Telegraph*:

The film we were showing was 'Elizabeth and Essex' starring Bette Davis, and the bomb struck just as Essex was about to be beheaded. Two projectionists and a member of the audience were killed and 60 people were injured . . . I had cleared everybody out of the Circle, and they were all standing downstairs, but the man who was killed declined to move out and said he would be all right upstairs.

The manager also recalled standing at the entrance to the cinema that night and seeing Portsdown Hill 'lit up like fairyland by incendiary bombs'.

scored a direct hit on a house whose inhabitants, having heard the 'All Clear', had just left their shelter and gone back to bed. Another solitary hit-and-run raider, detached from the main force, destroyed St Alban's Church at Copnor. That aircraft was shot down and its pilot killed.

In October there were only four raids – the heaviest on 29 October, when a dozen Junkers 88s caused extensive damage in the Fratton area. The 'visitors' were now calling mainly at night, and they kept up their harassing attacks throughout the following month, causing much damage in such places as Cosham, Copnor, North End, Farlington, and Fratton, as well as in other parts of the city. Then, on the evening of 5 December, Portsmouth was once again subjected to heavy and intense bombing.

The raid started at about 8pm. Large numbers of high-explosive and incendiary bombs were scattered across the city. This time the Luftwaffe succeeded in doing a vast amount of damage to the dockyard. Big fires were started here as well as elsewhere in the city. Casualties were severe: 44 killed and 140 injured. Three of those killed were in the Carlton (later the Essoldo) Cinema in Cosham High Street, Copnor. About 600 people were in the cinema when it was hit just before 8.30pm, the standard closing time for all cinemas at this period of the war.

POMPEY 'COVENTRATED'

Portsmouth's decoys were not yet in place when the city suffered its worst raid of the war. At close to 7pm on 10 January 1941 the sirens wailed their warning, and soon afterwards the first waves of bombers droned overhead. For two hours they dropped their loads of high-explosives as well as thousands of incendiaries. After a lull the fury started again just before midnight, and continued for a further two hours. The glare of fires lit up the whole city and could be seen for miles around. Three hundred German aircraft took part in those four hours of destruction. Hundreds of bombs struck all parts of the city, and an estimated 25,000 incendiaries added their special threat to the terror and devastation.

The very first bomb scored a direct hit on the electricity generating station,

The ruins of Madden's Hotel seen from the platform of Portsmouth & Southsea railway station. It was estimated that 28 people lost their lives when the hotel was hit in the last major raid on Portsmouth, which took place on 27 April 1941

and the whole of Portsmouth was plunged into darkness. Buildings were blasted apart or burst into flames, countless craters appeared, streets were deep in debris, and a thick pall of dust and smoke hung in the air.

The shopping centres at King's Road, Commercial Road and Palmerston Road were all reduced to rubble. Many shops were ablaze, including C & A Modes, Timothy Whites and Woolworths. Cinemas and hotels, among them the historic George Hotel in Old Portsmouth, were totally demolished. Clarence Pier was ablaze, and three large factories were gutted by fire. To prevent fires from spreading some buildings had to be dynamited. Six churches were destroyed, and the Eye and Ear Hospital and a part of the Royal Portsmouth Hospital were blown up. In Southsea alone more than 2,000 buildings were destroyed.

One of the major fires started that night was at the Guildhall. Incendiaries fell on its wooden roof, and the Council's own firemen attempted to deal with the situation by dropping sandbags on them. Then firewatchers on the roof of the Post Office reported the fire at the Guildhall. Ken Hampton, then a boy fireman in the combined police force brigade, was sent to investigate. How he dealt with the situation is told in the panel but the Guildhall became an inferno which raged all night. The last flames, at the top of the clock tower, did not die out until noon the next day. It was many days before the gutted interior was cool enough to be entered.

Boy Fireman finds 'A Ball of Fire'

In Nigel Peake's *City at War* the story is told of boy fireman Ken Hampton, who discovered the fire in the Guildhall after a couple of incendiaries fell through the roof ventilators. With the aid of a policeman, some soldiers and other helpers, he attempted to douse the 'ball of fire' by throwing bags of sand down the ventilators – but without effect. 'It was hopeless,' he recalled later. 'We came down floor by floor, with the fire coming down after us. When we got onto the floor of the Great Hall, we could see the whole roof burning furiously . . . Burning debris was coming down, and we even tried smashing the basins in the washrooms and lavatories so that we could get the buckets under the taps and form a bucket chain, but it didn't get us anywhere. The frustrating thing was that by the time we were on the ground floor, the water was back on, and when we were in the basement, we were paddling up to our ankles.'

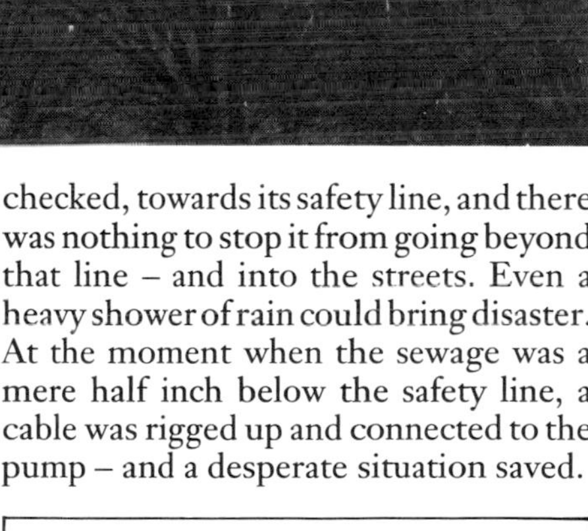

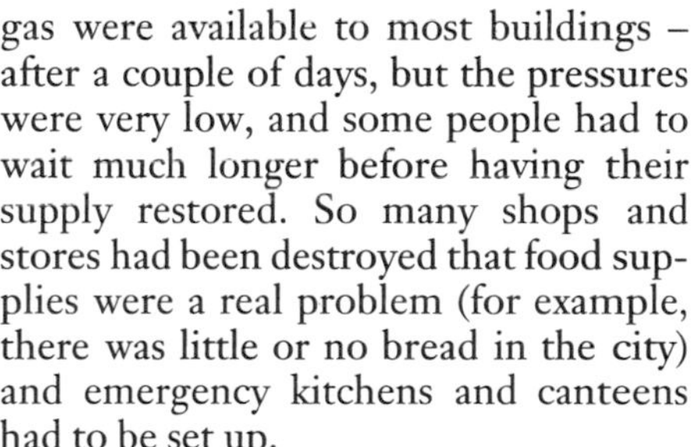

SCENES OF UTTER DEVASTATION

When dawn broke next morning so terrible were the scenes of death and devastation that many photographs taken at the time had to be censored. The dead totalled 171 and hundreds more were seriously injured – though of course such figures could only be guessed at that day. More than 3,000 people lost their homes and hundreds their jobs. Hundreds, again, decided to get out of the stricken city, and many of them – as in Southampton – became 'trekkers' travelling daily to and from Portsmouth.

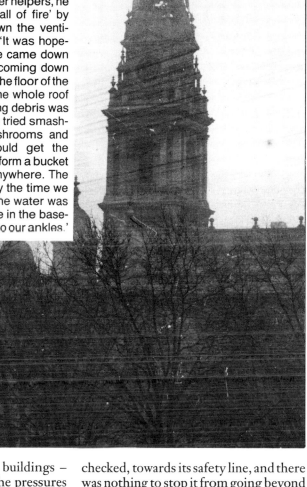

For those who remained there were great hardships. For two days there was no electricity in the city, and some people had to wait as long as three weeks before being re-connected. Water and gas were available to most buildings – after a couple of days, but the pressures were very low, and some people had to wait much longer before having their supply restored. So many shops and stores had been destroyed that food supplies were a real problem (for example, there was little or no bread in the city) and emergency kitchens and canteens had to be set up.

But that day Portsmouth was threatened by a fearful danger which was known only to its authorities – and, not surprisingly, they were keeping their mouths shut about it. The danger was – sewage overflow, which would mean that the city would have to be evacuated completely. When that first German bomb knocked out the city electricity supply, it had also put the sewage pumps out of action. This meant that sewage continued to rise, unchecked, towards its safety line, and there was nothing to stop it from going beyond that line – and into the streets. Even a heavy shower of rain could bring disaster. At the moment when the sewage was a mere half inch below the safety line, a cable was rigged up and connected to the pump – and a desperate situation saved.

Out of a Hot Spot – or Freed in the Nick of Time

The fire in the Guildhall was rushing down floor by floor and was about to engulf the whole building when someone remembered that there were prisoners in the police cells on the ground floor. So relieved were those petty offenders at being let out that not one of them seized a unique opportunity to escape hotfoot.

No Connection

Local fire brigades in Britain jealously guarded their independence before the war, with the result that their equipment was not fully standardised. A disastrous consequence of this was that when appeals went out for help from burning cities like Plymouth and Portsmouth, some units travelled great distances from other parts of the country only to find on arrival that they were unable to connect their apparatus to the local hydrants.

Portsmouth had been bombed close to complete destruction, but soon its life returned, and the essential work at the docks started up again. But many of its citizens had a clear sense that Pompey had not seen the last of its tormentors, and so it proved. On 28 January they were back and dropped bombs into the harbour. No damage was done, and the raiders were chased off by RAF fighters. Lee and Gosport were next attacked, and early in March the Luftwaffe again dropped bombs in the harbour area, doing only limited damage. However, these sporadic raids gave the city, as a local newspaper put it some years later, a sense that it 'was living on the edge of a precipice'. The lull in raids on the city itself lasted only two months. But as Luftwaffe bombers often flew over Portsmouth on their way to attack other targets, there were many Alerts in that period, and the town's inhabitants had many a sleepless night.

When the Luftwaffe returned in earnest they attacked on three successive nights – 9, 10 and 11 March. On the first date (a Sunday evening) they bombed harbour installations for four hours, but it was buildings in the neighbourhood that suffered most damage, including offices and shops, a maternity and nursing home, and the Rialto cinema.

The Germans returned in greater force the following night. Three capital ships in the harbour were obviously among their major targets. After dropping flares, relays of bombers attacked the harbour for seven hours, but they also dropped bombs all over Portsea Island. This time they had to face the heaviest anti-aircraft barrage yet mounted in the Portsmouth area, but among the casualties were eleven gun crew members at Southsea (see panel). As in earlier raids, heavy showers of incendiaries were scattered over a wide area, and the firefighters had to cope with about 30 serious fires, some of which were not fully under control until after midnight.

Stanley Road, Southsea

The imposing Central Hotel building on Commercial Road, Portsmouth, was so badly burned out in the 1941 blitz that it had to be pulled down a year later. Here, two demolition men can be seen working at the top of the parapet on the left

Queen Street suffered badly, the Royal Sailors' Club Home was demolished, and a hotel and a synagogue were hit. Many shops and offices were destroyed, and among the 150 'incidents' reported from across the city was the destruction of ten buses at the Corporation Bus Station at Eastney.

Casualties were very high that night – 93 killed and more than 200 injured. The next night (11 March) a further 21 people were killed, six of whom were taking refuge in a garden shelter.

'A TOMB OF DARKNESS'

The Luftwaffe's repeated attacks were producing a feeling of helplessness in many of the citizens of Portsmouth. As a major military target, the town had suffered badly, and it was clear that more raids could be expected. Many people had left the town or become trekkers, and many others said that they would leave if they could afford to do so. Everywhere there were huge areas of bomb damage, and as one visitor said at the time, Portsmouth was 'a tomb of darkness'.

The Germans came back the following month – on the nights of 8, 11, 17 and 27 April. These raids again inflicted a great deal of damage across the city. But on 17 April the brunt of the attack was borne by Hayling Island, a decoy target zone which successfully diverted bombers from the city.

The heaviest raid of the month was on 27 April, which turned out to be the last intensive raid Pompey had to endure. During this assault a number of parachute landmines came floating down to create their special form of widespread destruction. Once again incendiaries caused many fires, and shops, offices and other public buildings were gutted, including the City Museum in the High Street. A block of the Infectious Diseases Hospital was set on fire, but fortunately it was unoccupied at the time. One of the worst incidents was at Madden's Hotel, close to the railway station, where a direct hit killed 28 people.

Site Unseen: The use of Decoys

Following the fire blitz on Coventry (see p 64) much thought was given to devising an effective means of protecting urban areas likely to be 'Coventrated'. It was obvious that the combined efforts of RAF fighters, AA guns, barrage balloons, and all that the ARP services could do would not save target cities from the total devastation threatened by concentrated night bombing. Already a technique was being used for deflecting the radio beams relied on for their guidance by Luftwaffe navigators and so diverting them from their course (see p 00), and now somebody (who?) came up with the idea of providing dummy target areas to draw the attention of the raiders – 'decoys'. Such decoys were skilfuly planned structures erected in areas some distance from likely target towns and designed to suggest the presence of a built-up area at night. Some of the structures would let out a certain amount of light – as from poorly blacked-out buildings. There would also be fires and flares, many of them oil-fuelled, to simulate the glare that a night-bomber's crew might expect to see on approaching a target city under attack.

Although Portsmouth was for the time being spared the full attention of the Luftwaffe, it was obviously still a major target. In order to divert raiders from the docks and city, decoy sites were prepared at Langstone Harbour, Sinah Common and Hayling Island. It is to be supposed that the local residents were not wholly in favour of this idea – Portsmouth's loss being, as it were, their none-too-welcome gain. But the decoys did a good job, particularly in one raid in 1941, when Hayling attracted most of the bombs intended for the city. What the people of Hayling felt about it must be another story . . .

The Royal Portsmouth Hospital, with its wards all occupied, was hit three times during this raid. The first was a direct hit on the Casualty Department, killing nine people. Another bomb started a fire in the administration block. As might be expected, the nursing staff worked heroically throughout the raid, moving their patients to the cellars for greater safety. There were no casualties among the patients and nurses. But once again the city's casualty toll was very high: more than 100 dead and 150 injured.

More raids on Portsmouth were to come, but the days and nights of concentrated bombardment were over. The resources and attention of the Luftwaffe were being diverted from Britain to support Hitler's invasion of Russia. After the raid of 27 April 1941 the next heavy raid came more than a year later. On 15 August 1942, about 25 Luftwaffe bombers with fighter escorts attacked Portsmouth, and again casualties were recorded and fires started. After this raid there was another lull until April and May of 1944, when Allied forces were being assembled for the invasion of Normandy. This time the Luftwaffe came up against such formidable anti-aircraft defences that only a few of them got through to their target, and most released their bombs in the sea or on the open countryside.

As something of a postscript to Portsmouth's trials came two flying bombs (V1s). One fell in June and another in July 1944, the first on Locksway Road and the second, which killed 14 people, on Newcomen Road. Many were injured by the blast from both bombs.

Ack-Ack Toll

In his account* of Britain's defence against air attack during the Second World War, the General Officer Commanding-in-Chief Anti-Aircraft Command 1939-1945, General Sir Frederick Pile GCB, DSO, MC, describes a typical action during the raids on Portsmouth:

On the night of March 8-9 (1941) the first of three concentrated and consecutive attacks on Portsmouth began. On the last and heaviest of these three nights the attack lasted for six hours. It was a clear night with brilliant moonlight and searchlights, which had been grouped around the city in pairs to dazzle the bomb-aimers, were badly hampered by the smoke from the rapidly-spreading fires.

Two heavy bombs fell on one of our gun sites. An officer and ten other ranks were killed. All the instruments and one of the guns were put out of action. But two guns were kept going with the remaining men, and by the end of the night four of the raiders had been destroyed by the guns, making our total bag for twenty-four hours 9 bombers and 1 fighter.

**Ack-Ack*, by General Sir Frederick Pile, published by Harrap & Co Ltd, London: 1949.

POMPEY'S PRIDE

From the beginning of the Battle of Britain in the summer of 1940 until the Invasion of France some four years later Portsmouth was constantly in the front line, enduring as much as any city in Britain.

As a great naval port and base, the town was a prime target and it suffered 67 raids and lost 930 of its citizens. A further 1216 were seriously injured. About 7,000 properties were destroyed, including 6,000 homes. It was a heavy price to pay, but that was Pompey's Pride.

Counting the Cost . . .

No. of raids	67
Bombs dropped:	
High-explosive	1,320
Incendiary	38,000
Parachute mines	38
V1s	2
Properties destroyed	7,000
including homes	6,000
Properties badly damaged	6,000
slightly damaged	42,000
Area devastated (acres) est	160
Persons killed	930
seriously injured	1,216

Portsmouth wardens make themselves at home in their local ARP post

Southampton's Worst Weekend

'We'll have to abandon the whole damn place and build it afresh,' remarked a typical resident after the Luftwaffe had devastated Southampton at the end of November 1940. 'There's nothing left for them to hit now, is there?' observed another. In one never-to-be-forgotten weekend (30 November/1 December) successive waves of Luftwaffe bombers had 'Coventrated' the city, reducing its heart to rubble and causing death and injuries on a scale not yet seen even by much-bombed Southampton.

'Everyone who can is leaving,' noted the Bishop of Winchester (Dr Cyril Garbett) on the Monday after that worst of all Southampton's 57 air raids. 'Everywhere I saw men and women carrying suitcases or bundles, the children clutching some precious doll or toy, struggling to get anywhere out of Southampton.'

No Medal for Ron

When Ron was 15 he joined the ARP in Southampton as a messenger boy, but he lied about his age: ARP recruits had to be at least 16. His job involved taking messages when the phones were out of order, and sometimes he ran through the streets with windows shattering and bombs dropping all around him. Once he arrived at a post and was told by its warden that it was too dangerous for him to go back, and he had to stay where he was until it was safe – several hours later. Ron felt he was quite a hero and thought he ought to get a medal for bravery. Instead, his father – who had been beside himself with worry – gave Ron the biggest tanning of his life.

Many of these 'trekkers' moved into the New Forest or even as far away as Winchester, but most of them came back to work each day. As one observer commented, 'they were not dumb or shattered or groaning.'

For Southampton, the 'Gateway to Britain', was an obvious target for Göring's bombers. A major entry port for much-needed supplies, with extensive docks, shipyards, railway lines and factories (including the Vickers Supermarine (Spitfire) Works at Woolston and Itchen), all vital to Britain's war effort, it was clearly marked for special attention by the Luftwaffe – and it got it.

'WE SAW THE PLANES HEADING UP THE RIVER'

At first the raids were light – sometimes there was only one aircraft – and the target was the Old Docks at the south end of the town, where there were closely congested houses and shops. In the first of the raids in August, a bomb made a crater 25 feet across in the back garden of a large house. The back of the house was wrecked, but the three people in it at the time escaped unhurt. In another suburb a bomb fell only five yards from an occupied Anderson shelter, demolished the rear of a nearby house and made a huge crater, but the people in the shelter emerged unharmed. In the days of bombardment to come there would be many more such escape stories. Throughout August and the first half of September these occasional raids continued, and the Spitfire Works at Woolston were given special attention.

It was on 15 September 1940 (now commemorated as Battle of Britain Day) that Southampton's days of light and occasional raids came to an end, and the Luftwaffe made its first concentrated attack on the Vickers works at Woolston. Late in the afternoon of that day about thirty Messerschmitt 110s, adapted to carry bombs, dropped 12 tons of high-explosive bombs in the area. A fierce anti-aircraft barrage was put up, but many small houses and shops were destroyed or damaged beyond repair, twelve people were killed, and Woolston railway station was wrecked. The only damage to the Spitfire works was broken windows.

Later that month the raid was repeated – with a smaller number of aircraft – and again the Vickers factory was the target. On the afternoon of 24 September there were two raids, and this time there were many casualties – 42 killed and 65 seriously injured. Many years later, a fuselage builder (who was also a Home Guard gunner) recalled his experiences for *The Southampton Echo*.

> We saw the planes heading up the river, so we had plenty of time to man the guns. It seemed a long time to wait. The sky was full of aircraft . . . The planes came so low we could plainly see the rear-gunner's turrets bringing his guns to bear on us.

The defenders returned the fire with the air-cooled Browning – the same gun that was mounted in the Spitfire. Then the bombs struck:

Belvedere Terrace, 24 September 1940

The ground appeared to be shaking up and down violently as each bomb was dropped . . . I thought the end of the world had come as day was turned into night in a few seconds.

Two days later the raiders returned, this time with devastating force in two massed waves of about 60 and 100 aircraft – by far the heaviest raid on Southampton up to that date, both in the number of aircraft and the tonnage of bombs dropped. The targets were the gasworks and the Spitfire factory once more. Thirty-five tons of high-explosive bombs killed 55 people and seriously injured nearly as many. The Luftwaffe's strategy in this phase of the Battle of Britain was to attack RAF airfields and aircraft factories, and on this occasion it was a complete success. The Vickers Supermarine works were reduced to rubble.

These severe raids were no more than a prelude to the indiscriminate bombing in store for Southampton. The next few weeks were relatively quiet, with occasional light attacks, until on 17 November in a daylight raid the Germans dropped the first of their parachute mines. This was followed the same night by the longest Alert: it was thirteen hours before the All Clear came soon after 7.30am. In seven attacks during that day and night, 55 people lost their lives and as many were seriously injured. But worse was to follow.

Just a week later, on 23 November, virtually the whole of Southampton was shattered by massed bombing. For several hours that evening 80 German aircraft released some 50 tons of bombs on the town. To start with, flares lit up the sky, then came sticks of incendiaries and high-explosive bombs. In all parts of the town, houses, shops, banks, offices, hotels and public buildings were hit, including two cinemas with fairly large audiences. People were trapped in damaged buildings, some having to wait hours to be released. The Fire Services managed to contain the worst fires, but this raid produced the heaviest casualties so far – 77 people (including Firemen and Home Guards) lost their lives, and a further 134 were seriously injured. Thousands were made homeless.

But even this was no more than a rehearsal for what was to come the following weekend – Southampton's worst weekend. As at Coventry on 14 November, the aim of the Luftwaffe was to demolish the city completely and to destroy its inhabitants' will to resist. Such a raid was intended to be an act of terror – what Nazi propaganda already called the 'Coventrieren' principle. The method of attack was to begin by releasing showers of incendiary devices to act as flare-paths for the bomb-aimers and to set fire to buildings on the ground. The succeeding high-explosive bombs would then cause the maximum devastation and spread further the fires already started.

Ordeal by Fire

Fire bombs caused more damage, killed or maimed more people, and probably created greater terror than high-explosives. The Luftwaffe had adopted the tactics – later to be followed by the RAF over Germany – of sending 'pathfinder' aircraft ahead of the main bomber force. The pathfinders dropped showers of incendiaries on the target, and the resulting glare from burning buildings showed the following waves of bombers more or less exactly where to release their high-explosives bombs. On Southampton's worst weekend of the war (30 November/1 December 1941) many fires started on the Saturday night were still burning when the raiders returned on Sunday night. The city's own Fire Service was reinforced by 2,000 firemen and 160 appliances that weekend, but by the Sunday evening, the situation began to look uncontrollable. In particular, leaks caused by fractured mains and damaged hoses – impossible to repair or even trace amid all the chaos – made the water pressure totally inadequate for fire-fighting.

THE 'COVENTRIEREN' OF SOUTHAMPTON

For six hours wave after wave of Luftwaffe bombers droned in over Southampton from Saturday evening (30 November) until early Sunday morning. In all, about 120 aircraft dropped their sticks of incendiaries and high-explosive bombs on the centre of the town in their attempt to reduce it to rubble, but bombs hit all parts of the town. On Sunday evening the same number of aircraft returned to carry out a follow-up raid of equal ferocity. This also lasted several hours – into Monday morning. An estimated total of 800 bombs was dropped, equivalent to 105 tons. The devastation was widespread, and the casualties were on a scale not previously seen in Southampton. Those killed that weekend numbered 137 (96 in direct hits on air-raid shelters), and 242 people were seriously injured.

More than 1,100 buildings were destroyed or damaged beyond repair, and once again many houses, shops, offices, public houses, churches, cinemas and public buildings were hit. A district police station received a direct hit, but there were no casualties, all the officers stationed there being on duty in the streets at the time. Five churches (of different denominations) were destroyed or damaged, including St Luke's, All Saints' and St James's. The Congregational Church in Above Bar, Portland Street Baptist Church and St Mary's were also hit. St Mary's lost its roof completely, but when the rubble had been cleared, it was used for open-air services.

Above Bar, as it was before the war, and after the Luftwaffe attack

Among the many commercial and industrial buildings that suffered were Edwin Jones (the well-known department store), Pirelli's cable factory, the Ordnance Survey offices, Ranks Flour Mill, the General Motors factory in Western Docks, and a timber yard. Fires caused more damage than the blast of high-explosive bombs. Some fires that were started on Saturday were still burning when the Luftwaffe came back on Sunday evening. To help Southampton's Fire Service, more than 2,000 fire-fighters came from 75 other districts – even from as far away as Nottingham. But in some areas, particularly in the lower part of the town, water pressure was not adequate for their needs, the mains having been damaged by bombing.

All this death and destruction caused many to 'trek' out of the city each night, as we have seen. For those who remained there were great hardships. Gas and electricity were cut off in most parts of the town, and so cooking was impossible or very difficult. To deal with this situation mobile canteens were brought into the town from outside, and for a few days bread also had to be brought in. The water supply could not be restored quickly to all areas, and for some time all water had to be boiled before it could be drunk. Candles, matches and lamp oil all ran out and were unobtainable for days. Telephones were generally out of service, and for obvious reasons many bus services had to be re-routed, causing more disruption.

People in Southampton naturally compared their experience with that of Coventry a fortnight earlier. At first, an observer noted, they said it was 'as bad as Coventry', but a little later they claimed that it was 'worse than Coventry', and they were annoyed that the press had not made so much fuss over Southampton's raids as they had over Coventry. Indeed, as in other heavily-bombed areas, there was 'a suppressed feeling of pride' in having endured, but little demand for retaliatory bombing of Germany. Such 'tit-for-tat' feelings were observed to be more common in unscathed villages and rural areas close to bombed towns. In Southampton people were generally in good spirits, and the level of mutual help and co-operation was high – but there was a good deal of criticism of the

Nazi Airmen's Funeral

Despite all that Southampton had suffered from the Luftwaffe and the oft-quoted desire to hit back, this *Southern Daily Echo* report of the funeral of two German airmen tells another story . . .

Military Honours in South Coast Town

Ober Leutenant Gunther von Seidlitz and Feldwebel Franz Hummer, of the Luftwaffe, whose bodies were found in a scrap metal merchant's yard after their machine had been shot down by an R.A.F. fighter during a raid on a South Coast town, were buried with military honours yesterday afternoon.

Twenty-five R.A.F. men formed an escort, and, doing a slow march, preceded the coffins, which were covered with German flags, from the cemetery chapel to the grave.

Behind the escort marched a Royal Air Force officer and the Baptist minister who conducted the service.

Each coffin was borne by six R.A.F. men, and behind them marched a sergeant carrying a wreath of pink carnations and tulips from the squadron according the military honours.

When the coffins had been lowered, one on top of the other, into the grave, and the committal sentences beginning "In the midst of life we are in death . . ." had been recited, the officer stepped forward and saluted the dead airmen.

The sergeant placed the wreath on the edge of the grave, saluted, and the parade was dismissed.

Several women who were tending graves in the cemetery filed silently past the open grave as the R.A.F. men marched away.

The two men were buried beside five other Nazi airmen who were killed when their bomber was shot down on the edge of the same town recently.

From the *Southern Daily Echo*, 19 April 1941

"SILVER THING" IN A BATH

Fire Bomb That Did Not Explode

RAIDER ON OUTSKIRTS OF S.C. TOWN

FIRE bombs were sent down towards a block of flats on the outskirts of a South Coast town by a Nazi raider last night

Most of them fell in gardens and were quickly put out by residents. One hit the only skylight in the flats, fell through the only trap door in the ceiling into a bathroom, and into the bath. It failed to ignite.

This morning Mrs. James went to the bathroom with her daughter, Sheila, aged 12, who said: "Look, mummy, there's a silver thing in the bath."

Mrs. James called her neighbour, Mrs. Cole, an A.R.P. warden, who at once put the fire bomb into a bucket of water and took it in the garden. Mr. James, who then came home from night duty, took the unexploded incendiary to the police station.

From the *Southern Daily Echo*, 17 May 1941

authorities for inefficiency in coping with the emergencies. When this charge was made public many years later, it was strongly and convincingly denied.

Among those who remained in Southampton, there was a strong view that the Luftwaffe would leave them alone – at least for some weeks – because 'there's nothing left to bomb now'. As one resident put it . . . 'there's nothing to come for now – their bombs would just fall on places that had already been bombed flat . . . If you think about it . . . they sent over 250 planes, didn't they, and dropped 600 tons of bombs. Well, they're not going to waste that again.' (In fact, the estimated tonnage of bombs dropped in the whole of 1940 was 260). Others tended to take a less optimistic view and expected that the Luftwaffe would come back sooner or later. However, when the Alert was sounded, 'scarcely anyone took any notice, and carried on just the same'. Even when an aircraft was heard overhead and the AA guns boomed, people simply grouped together in the streets or stood at the entrances to shelters. When more gunfire was heard, some went down the steep steps into the shelter, but one woman refused, explaining to the ARP warden:

> No, I'm not going down. But after having my husband blown out of bed . . . when I hear the sirens now I'm all like this . . . (hands shaking). But we've got to keep ourselves in hand, haven't we? . . . But it makes you nervous, after you've been bombed once and blown out of bed.

So most people expected their city would be left alone and not troubled by the Luftwaffe for some time to come. In fact, one solitary raider did attack the town just before the end of the year, apparently aiming for the Thorneycroft works. During the first six months of 1941 there were a number of sporadic attacks, and apart from a minor raid in January, most of them took place in March. On 11/12 March, sixteen aircraft dropped bombs on all parts of the town, and the resulting casualties were 22 dead and 24 seriously injured. Similar raids, but with no more than six aircraft, were repeated on another six nights of the month. The Luftwaffe returned with another six-plane raid on the night of 10/11 April. This time they dropped one-ton parachute mines. These did not dig themselves into the ground on impact and so were liable to do a lot more damage than the ordinary high-explosive bomb. The massive destruction caused by the twelve mines dropped on this occasion included severe damage to the South Hampshire Hospital and a school.

Plummers, one of the large department stores destroyed in the Southampton blitz

Why They Trekked

During and after the war there were stories that people in Southampton lost confidence in the city authorities and 'cracked'. An entry in the ARP log at the time – quoted in *The Southern Evening Echo* in 1984 – attempts to put this rumour in perspective. 'A very large amount of evacuation was necessary, and in addition a large number of others whose homes were not damaged would not sleep in the town after November 30 . . . Bearing in mind that the town was without gas – largely without water – without telephones – and, in some cases, without electricity – as well as the possibility of further bombing (which possibility materialised on December 1), this wish to get away from an obvious danger spot is not surprising, however regrettable it may be.'

More devastated shops and offices along Above Bar

'All Clear' for Courting

The Luftwaffe sometimes gave courting couples a helping hand. For many a girl the sound of the air-raid siren spoke more loudly than an angry father . . . as one former Southampton resident later recalled: 'We were not allowed out of the cinema' (when the sirens sounded) 'until the "all clear" at about 2am . . . Not being allowed out meant that at least I had a good excuse for being late home.'

But the pattern of small raids by lone aircraft tended to continue until in June the Luftwaffe stepped up its raids, and on 22 June twenty aircraft released eighteen one-ton parachute mines over the town, together with incendiaries and high-explosive bombs. At the end of the first week of July, they mounted their biggest single attack of the year when 50 aircraft rained 150 high-explosive bombs, together with incendiaries, on the town. In these two raids 50 people were killed and 65 seriously injured. Blocks of flats, shops, houses, a garage and a school were all badly damaged. The blast from one bomb produced a freak effect on some of the windows of a nursing home: the outside shutters were blown off, but the glass remained intact. The only other raid before the end of 1941 was carried out by two aircraft about 10 weeks after the big attack in July.

For Southampton the worst was over. There were minor raids in April and May 1942, and the last heavy attack came in the early hours of 22 June 1942. Very substantial damage was done to the central and eastern parts of the town, and the casualty figures were high: 36 killed and 44 seriously injured. Later in the war there were a couple of high-explosive bombs and a couple of V1s, but the bombardment of Southampton was effectively over soon after midnight on the longest day of 1942.

From April 1941 onwards raids on Southampton and other places, though intended to damage Britain's war effort, were also a cover for a change in Hitler's conduct of the war. Their object was to direct attention away from his preparations to attack Russia. Relocation of most of the Luftwaffe's resources to the eastern campaign inevitably reduced the frequency of raids that could be mounted on Britain. But there were still leaflet raids, and in addition to more damaging missiles Southampton had to endure showers of Nazi propaganda leaflets proclaiming that Britain had lost the Battle of the Atlantic and therefore was about to lose the war . . .

Counting the Cost . . .

No. of raids	57
Duration of Alerts	1551 hrs
Bombs dropped (includes 36 parachute mines)	est 2,605
Incendiary devices	32,000
Tons of explosives	530
Residential properties destroyed	4,000
Residential properties damaged but repairable	over 36,000
Other properties destroyed	2,500
Lives lost	633
Seriously injured	922

Note: Undoubtedly much damage was avoided and many lives saved because many bombs aimed at the town fell into the Itchen, the Test or Southampton Water.

Coventry – 'Our Guernica'

On 8 November 1940 – the 17th anniversary of Hitler's attempt to seize power in Bavaria – British bombers attacked Munich. A highlight of the celebrations in the city was a Party address to be given by the Führer himself, but the impending arrival of the RAF made it necessary to bring forward this key event by one hour. The German High Command smarted at the humiliation, while Hitler was incandescent with anger. He and Göring immediately decided to exact a terrible price for this 'attack on the capital of the Nazi movement'.

Something special was needed. Coventry, a compact city with a population of about 220,000, with its aircraft factories and the many engineering works that served them, all in a limited area, fitted the bill admirably. A full moon, due in a few days' time on 14 November, provided the perfect occasion for the retaliatory attack, which would also strike a savage blow at one of the major centres of Britain's industrial war effort.

The people of Coventry, of course, had no idea that they had been selected by the German High Command for this signal honour. They knew all about the sufferings of Londoners, as reported in the newspapers during the past weeks, and felt for them in their plight. But London was an obvious target not only because it was the capital, but also because it was close to German bases in France and the Low Countries. Coventry, on the other hand, located in the Midlands some distance from the coast and protected by anti-aircraft batteries and the RAF, seemed somewhat safer. And so the citizens of Coventry felt relatively secure or, at least, they thought that the scale of destruction visited upon London would not fall upon their own city.

It was not that precautions against air bombardment had been, or were being, neglected. Every night hundreds of the city's population practised their drills for dealing with air raids, confident that they would be ready if 'Jerry' came.

Coventry had already had some experience of being bombed before the war. During the summer of 1939 the IRA had chosen the city as a target, and in one of their outrages five people had died in Broadgate, a central shopping area. With

On the morning after the raid the people of Coventry pick their way through the city's shattered streets

Coventry Cathedral

The Cathedral Church of St Michael at Coventry probably originated in a small Norman-style chapel built in the twelfth century, but it did not become a cathedral until 1918. The old chapel was extended in the thirteenth century when a nave, north and south aisles, south porch (still existing) and Lady Chapel were built. The tower and spire, which rise to nearly 300 feet above the ground, were begun in 1373, and the nave and chancel were rebuilt early in the fifteenth century – all in the classic Perpendicular style. The building is extremely wide (130 ft) and owing to successive rebuildings and additions (prior to the disaster of 1940), its proportions became distinctly assymetric and irregular, giving St Michael's a charm all its own. The post-war rebuilding, controversial at the time, can certainly be said to have added to the assymetry and the interest of Coventry Cathedral.

Churchill's Fury

Exactly a week before the raid on Coventry, a plane from the Luftwaffe's special KG 100 squadron, with the latest *Knickebein* navigational equipment on board, came down just off the Dorset coast near Bridport.

The Army claimed that it was up to them, and not the Royal Navy, to salvage the wreck. They refused access to the naval authorities, but made no attempt to secure the aircraft themselves, with the result that together with its equipment it was totally lost.

In a curt memorandum to General Lord Ismay, head of the Military Wing of the War Cabinet Secretariat, Churchill 'prayed' that proposals be made 'to ensure that in future immediate steps are taken to secure all possible information and equipment from German aircraft which come down in this country or near our coasts, and that these rare opportunities are not squandered through departmental differences'.

this experience behind them, Coventry people felt they had been 'bloodied' in some way. However, nothing could have prepared them for the devastation about to be visited upon them. Coventry would be remembered in the future not only for Lady Godiva and Peeping Tom, but also for a new word: 'conventration'. The German equivalent, coined by the Nazi prpaganda machine, was *Conventrieren*. The languages are different but the meaning is the same – to raze to the ground; to destroy completely.

While Coventry went about its business as usual, the Luftwaffe prepared for the raid. The code name 'Moonlight Sonata' was given to the operation as a whole, while that chosen for Coventry itself was 'Korn'. As yet, 'Ultra' – the highest classified information derived from Enigma decrypts – had no identification for 'Korn', so no advance warning could be given.

TARGETS MARKED WITH RED CIRCLES

All that was known was that a major air attack was in preparation, and it was assumed that London would be the target yet again. Indeed, so strong were the indications that Churchill decided to turn back from his journey into the country in order to be with Londoners during a raid which was expected to be one of the heaviest yet.

It was on the night of November 14–15 that the Germans introduced a new tactic in night-time bombing, which was later used by the RAF to devastating effect. This involved sending a highly-trained and specially-equipped advance group, later known as 'pathfinders', to lead the raid. On arrival it was their job to release parachute flares to mark the targets, and to start fires with incendiary bombs to guide the main force of bombers following on behind.

The briefing given to this Luftwaffe pathfinder group included detailed street maps of Coventry on which the targets, all industrial, were marked with red circles. The officer carrying out the briefing outlined to the pilots and the crews the aims of the raid: these were to avenge Munich and, in the light of Coventry's industrial importance, to strike a paralysing blow at Churchill's war effort. He also made it clear that civilian housing was *not* a target.

As darkness fell, flights of Heinkel 111s took off from a base near St Nazaire on the west coast of France. Their flight would take them 200 miles, crossing the Dorset coast, and flying down the *X-Gerät* (X-apparatus) radio beam transmitted from Cherbourg. This main approach beam, code-named 'Weser', would be intersected at various points by other radio beams from Calais and Boulogne. These also carried code names of German rivers and were, in order, 'Rhine', 'Oder' and 'Elbe'. The last intersection was crucial, for less than a minute after each aircraft reached the point where the 'Weser' and 'Elbe' beams crossed, its bombs were automatically released to fall upon Coventry below.

Bombs carried by the pathfinders were incendiaries many of which were, for the first time, of an exploding type. Their purpose was, as we have seen, to light up targets for Junkers 88 bombers carrying the high explosives that were to rip out the heart of one of the most beautiful medieval cities in England. For eleven hours, from shortly after 7pm until the approach of dawn the following morning, the bombers pounded Coventry to rubble.

Winston Churchill inspects the ruins of Coventry Cathedral

'Conventration' in practice. Gutted buildings and piles of rubble stand in what was once a busy shopping centre

NO NEED TO COME IN LOW

Coventry's vulnerability to air attack was much greater than might have appeared to many of its inhabitants. At this stage of the war there was very little defence against night bombing. For low-flying attacks the Bofors gun was the standard defence weapon. But the Coventry raid was carried out from a high altitude: on such an exceptionally clear night, and with as 'bombers' moon', there was no need to come in low.

Anti-aircraft guns protecting the city, of which there were only 40, were not very effective, largely because it took so long to plot the enemy's position. By the time the calculation was complete and the gun made ready for action the aircraft could be as much as six miles away, in any direction, from the position in which it was first sighted. The guns were deployed on a 'sixteen-gun density' principle, but the theory on which this was based seemed entirely to overlook the mismatch between the speed and accuracy of the guns and the speed of attacking aircraft.

General Sir Frederick Pile, C-in-C, Anti-Aircraft Command, once told Churchill that he doubted if one enemy bomber was brought down for every 15,000 shells fired. Certainly the Coventry experience showed that even this high figure was a generous over-estimate of the effective strike-rate.

The other strand of defence against air attack were the searchlight units, whose beams picked up aircraft and held them for the gunners. Unfortunately the beams also served as excellent navigational markers for the bomber pilots. On one occasion, at Birmingham, General Pile ordered all searchlights to be switched off, with the result that the city enjoyed one of its most peaceful nights for a long time. Without the guiding beams, the navigation of enemy bombers became very uncertain and unreliable. Even under the most favourable conditions aerial bombardment was remarkably inaccurate. Coventry presented a compact target, well-lit by blazing fires, but even so bombs fell anywhere within a seven-mile radius from city centre.

It was generally believed that radar provided the best defence, but at this point in the war the device was still at an early stage of development. The direction of an aircraft could be determined,

'If the King was there everything was all right . . .'

As soon as the King heard of the destruction of Coventry, he decided to visit the stricken city. He arrived next day – so informally that he was stopped on the way into the town and asked for his Identity Card. 'Poor Coventry!' he noted in his diary. 'I was horrified at the sight of the centre of the town . . . The water, electricity, and gas services had ceased to function . . . The people in the streets wondered where they were . . . nothing could be recognised. I talked to many of them. I think they liked my coming.'

He was right. As one survivor put it: 'We suddenly felt that if the King was there everything was all right, and the rest of England was behind us.'

but not its height. Radar therefore was unable to give any indication to crews of the angle of elevation required to hit their targets, with the result that their guns could not be used to maximum effect.

By 12 November RAF Intelligence knew that a major operation was being planned by the Germans to take advantage of the full moon, but the actual target remained a mystery. Rumours that circulated much later to the effect that the target was known some three days in advance, but that it was deliberately decided to let Coventry burn so that the Germans would not know that their codes had been broken, have no basis whatsoever in fact.

The number of front-line aircraft thought to be assembled for the raid was greatly over-estimated. In the event, 440 Heinkel 111s and Junkers 88s were involved: of these only one bomber was lost, and that crashed for unknown reasons. British Intelligence was on firmer ground when it identified no less a person than Kesselring as the operational commander. Clearly this was to be a raid very close to the heart of the German High Command.

Armed with this knowledge the British authorities mounted 'Operation Coldwater', which consisted of a number of strategies aimed at disrupting the attack. The first of these was to strike at the source of the radio beams, whose importance had already been correctly assessed. Accordingly, the base of *Kampfgruppe 100*, the pathfinder group, became the target for specially-assigned bombers. Beam transmitters, as well as those airfields most likely to be chosen by the Luftwaffe for mounting the attack, were also bombed by the RAF in an attempt to put them out of action. In addition, German radio traffic was continuously monitored, and attempts made to interfere with their navigational beacons. The RAF sent up their own planes to listen to the enemy's signals, details of which were then reported to the boffins back at base.

Other less effective measures were also adopted. Maximum night-fighter and anti-aircraft cover was ordered, but the night-fighters were largely ineffective because they had not yet been fitted with radar interception devices. Every available plane was pressed into service that night – Hurricanes, Blenheims, Beaufighters, even ancient Gloster Gladiator biplanes – and 135 sorties were flown by Fighter Command. And yet there were only seven sightings of the enemy. No wonder the question was asked: 'Where is our Air Force?' Sir Charles Portal, Chief of Air Staff, could report only one engagement during the whole night.

The anti-aircraft batteries, on the other hand, expended a prodigious amount of ammunition during the raid. The official Ack-Ack figure shows that 6,700 rounds were fired, an average of ten rounds a minute for the eleven hours. General Pile later reported that the German raiders:

> . . . came over at intervals of ten to fifteen minutes and in batches of about 20.
>
> The early attack was met with an intense barrage, and the barrage system remained in operation throughout the night, though as communications broke down, such barrages naturally became less effective and considerable independent firing was used.

Just what is meant by 'effective' in this context is difficult to say, since not one enemy aircraft was destroyed by anti-aircraft fire during the whole of the raid. Indeed, it is difficult to escape the conclusion that much of the firing was simply a discharge of ammunition to keep up civilian morale. At least Coventry's defenders could be heard to be doing something.

The evening of Thursday 14 November 1940 fulfilled all the expectations of the German High Command. A clear, sunny, autumn evening with a fresh breeze saw the first of the Heinkel 111s crossing the Dorset coast near Christchurch just before 6.20pm and flying down the beam heading straight for Coventry, despite the attempt made by British Radio Counter-Measures to interfere with the guidance system.

Thursday was early closing day in Coventry. At 1pm shopworkers and shoppers hurried home. Soon after 4pm

As paths were cleared through the rubble, dazed survivors gathered in the streets to stare in disbelief at the scale of the destruction of their city

housewives began the daily routine of putting up the blackouts, putting mattresses under tables, or under stairs, preparing thermos flasks of hot drinks. Suitcases, outdoor clothes, hats, gloves, outdoor boots, were all placed near the door ready for a quick getaway should the warning siren sound. In addition, torches, candles, bottles of water, maybe baby food, had all to be placed close to hand in preparation for a night in the shelter. Many of the better organised would have stoves, hot water bottles and anything else that would make life bearable, should the night be disturbed by the air raid sirens.

Blackout time that evening was 5.46pm. Ten minutes after seven o'clock the sirens sounded. The Germans were early. People were caught, their preparations incomplete. The major job at the hospital of making patients safe under the beds was still under way. Activity became frantic as the first bombs fell in large numbers. The barrage balloon control office ordered the raising of the barrage at Baginton at about 7.25pm. Without warning Coventry's ordeal as the target of the biggest air raid in history till then had begun. Morning would see the fruits of this 'revenge' strike, and would also show how pitifully inadequate against sustained attack were the defences and defence strategies.

The nightmare of Coventry began when ten Luftwaffe pathfinders dropped 1,000 incendiaries over the city centre, the clear intention being to start the maximum number of fires which in turn would illuminate the target for the main bomber force to follow. Some of the incendiaries were no more than flares that provided light and started fires if they landed in the vicinity of combustible material. Citizens had experience of dealing with these. The standard practice was to put them out as quickly as possible, thus preventing both fire and illumination of targets. The fire hazard was great because the number of incendiaries dropped was so enormous and many fell in places not imediately accessible to the fire-watchers. In addition, Coventry, being a medieval city, contained many buildings built of highly combustible materials. That night there was a new

Terror by night

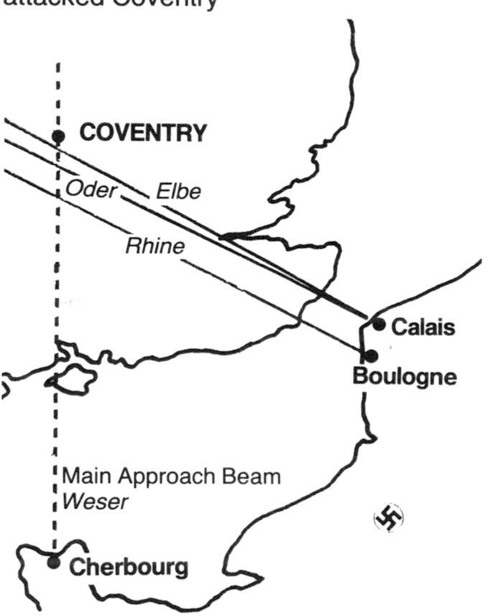

How radio beams guided the bombers

Early in 1940 the Germans started using a radio-guidance system (code-named *Knickerbein*, or 'crooked leg') for directing night-bombers to their targets in Britain. Two slightly overlapping radio beams were aimed at the target from giant transmitters on the Continent. Pilots knew they were keeping to the correct course if they heard in their earphones a continuous dot-dash signal. But if they strayed to either side of the overlap and heard only dots or only dashes, they knew they would have to adjust course accordingly. A second beam, from a station in another part of the Continent, cut across the main beam telling the pilot when to drop his bombs to fall on the target.

Bending the beam

The *Knickerbein* system was detected by Dr R. V. Jones of Air Intelligence, who devised an effective counter-measure known popularly as 'bending the beam'. Detector planes were sent up to detect the German beams (called 'Headaches'). False beams ('Aspirins') were then transmitted by the British to strengthen the *Knickerbein* Morse dashes. This confused many Luftwaffe pilots, who lost touch with the overlap in their guidance system and so missed their target completely.

X-Gerät

The Germans then adopted the *X-Gerät*, or X apparatus, a new device that was much more accurate than *Knickerbein*. At 200 miles the width of its beam was only 60ft, compared with *Knickerbein* which was one mile wide at 180 miles.

X-Gerät was an automatic system in which three radio beams, linked to instruments for calculating speed and distance, crossed a main approach beam ('Weser') at different points. The first cross-beam ('Rhine') warned the pilot to keep his aircraft in the centre of the main beam. The second ('Oder') was the signal for the bomb-aimer to activate a small on-board mechanical computer that calculated the precise moment for bomb-release, and at the third ('Elbe') the bombs were dropped. The main approach beam was transmitted from Cherbourg, in the case of the Coventry raid, and the cross-beam from Boulogne and Calais (see sketch map).

Coventry was the first British city to be bombed using this new system. The Luftwaffe also employed for the first time their new, elite path-finding force (*Kampfgruppe 100*) to fire the target with incendiaries for the follow-up bombers to home in on.

As with *Knickerbein*, the 'back-room boffins' in Britain soon found a way to jam *X-Gerät* by transmitting false signals on the same frequency to mislead Luftwaffe pilots and cause them to drop their bombs, if possible, on open countryside.

Unfortunately, on the night of the Coventry raid things went disastrously wrong for British counter-measures. Owing to a mistake in measurement, the false beams were not sent out on the *X-Gerät* frequency. German pilots were not misled, and the city of Coventry was duly 'Coventrated'.

hazard: exploding incendiaries. A number of citizens approached what were thought to be the familiar type of incendiary, to be dealt with in the usual way, only to lose their lives to this more deadly type.

The incendiary onslaught seemed to go on forever. Many reported that Coventry seemed to be alight from end to end. The city was gripped in a fire storm. The deliberate creation of uncontrollable fire would terrify the citizens of many cities on both sides, many more times, before this war came to an end.

The arrival of the Junkers 88s brought the high explosive bombs. The biggest of these were the so-called landmines. These floated down on parachutes, exploding on impact. Some were fitted with delayed-action fuses, creating an additional terror. Landmines had enormous explosive power. The parachute bomb had the additional terror, on a bright night, that it could be seen coming slowly to earth with the consequent psychological effect. Later in the war the whistling doodlebug was to create something of the same kind of effect.

Some of the more densely inhabited areas, such as the Butts, suffered badly. The narrow streets, alleys and courtyards of this area were like traps, from which screaming people ran blindly. Ambulances and fire engines were helpless to go to their aid. The hospital wards and the casualty stations filled up rapidly. The two hospitals were very vulnerable. Within an hour or so of the start of the raid, a string of incendiaries landed on the roof of the Mens' ward, the Womens' ward, and the Eye ward of the Coventry and Warwickshire Hospital. Staff had to transfer their patients, as best they could, to other parts of the hospital. No sooner was this completed, than high-explosive bombs fell on the wards marked by the incendiaries. The operating theatres were completely swamped with casualties. Many of the bomb-blast lacerations required surgery, because this type of injury often concealed much more damage under an apparently superficial surface wound. Sub-surface tissue and organs were often damaged by the compression of the blast while the surface remained relatively intact. Limb injuries such as fractures and amputations were also common. Surgeons worked nonstop to deal with the continuous flood of patients in theatres constantly shaken by the blast of exploding bombs. Electricity failed about midnight and the hospital was reduced to functioning on its own generator. Frequently during operations, doctors and nurses had to throw themselves under the operating tables as the bombs crashed down nearby. When a patient died, the corpse was just removed and another victim put on the table. Thousands passed through the hospital during that terrible, long night.

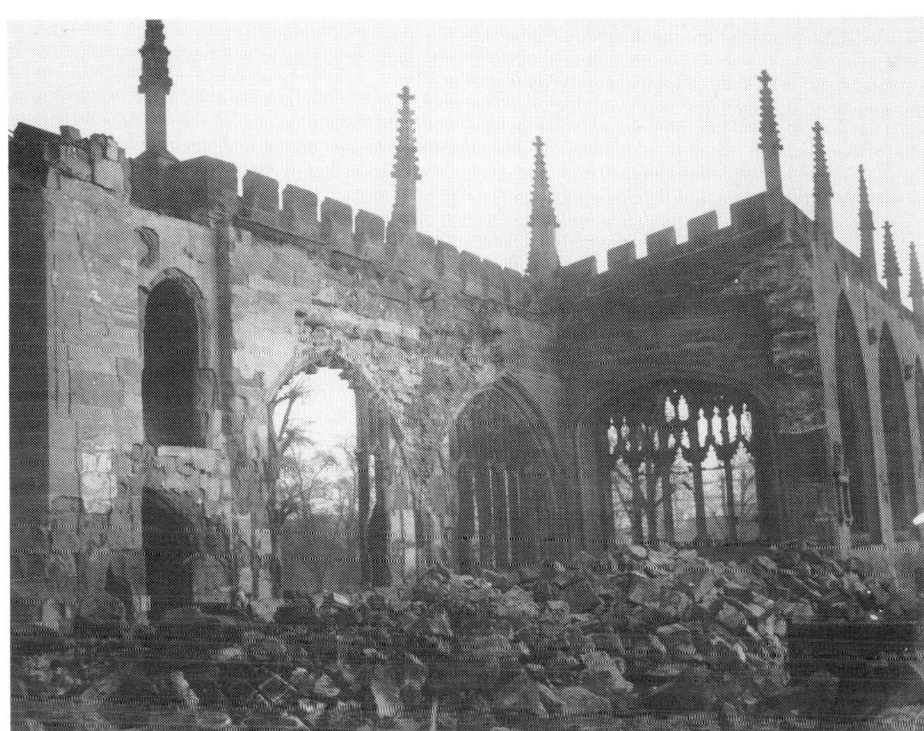

Waves of incendiary bombs destroyed the 13th-century Cathedral, but some of its treasures were saved

One of the most unsettling ordeals for the people of Coventry was having to move from one shelter to another, when fire and smoke made it impossible for them to stay put. Some people had to move several times in the course of the night. Terrified and near panic-stricken, they followed the ARP wardens whose job it was to guide them. The journey from one shelter to another was a fearful experience amidst explosions, wreckage, and fire on all sides. A quarter of a mile seemed an endless trek. As more and more shelters were put out of commission, those remaining became more and more crowded. In many, there was not even enough room for everyone to sit down at the same time. People took it in turns. Where there were bunks they were shared. To add to the fear and and discomfort, the electricity supply to the shelters failed, leaving their inmates in darkness. Observers commenting on the state of the shelters the next day, highlighted their inadequacy, their dampness, the foetid water on the floors, the lack of sanitation, and the overpowering, all-pervasive stench.

Coventry Control Centre was beneath the Council House, close to the Cathedral. The function of the Control Centre was to co-ordinate all the services during an air raid. This meant plotting all the incidents on the map, and communicating the needs by telephone to the appropriate services. By 8pm 240 fires had been reported to the Central Fire Station. Within minutes of 8pm all outgoing telephones failed. A short-lived attempt was made to use a messenger service, but this had to be abandoned because of the ferocity of the bombing. It became impossible to co-ordinate services. ARP wardens were left to their own devices to help as best they could, wherever they were. Doctors in the casualty stations even tried to tend the injured in the streets, wherever they found them. Doors blown off hinges were used as makeshift stretchers, any cloth material was pressed into service as splint supports, slings, and covers. People just managed as best they could. The bright moonlight that was such a help to the bombers now impartially helped the bombed to see their way when the electricity failed.

The fire-fighting service was quickly overwhelmed by the sheer number of fires. Crews and appliances were rushed in from the surrounding district, but to no avail. Streets became impassable with rubble, masonry, collapsed buildings and bomb craters, and the failure of the communications system cut fire services off from Control. Even when they got to the fires, such as at the Cathedral, the water supply quickly dried up because the mains were broken. Coventry was indeed burning.

Officers and staff at the Central Police Station which was close to the Cathedral and the Council House, tried to fill the gap left by the breakdown of communication with the Central Control. Unfortunately, this attempt failed when the station itself hit, lost its telephones, and the messenger service broke down.

The Cathedral, which had stood for six hundred years in the heart of the city was symbolic of the burning of Coventry. The first report of fire in the Cathedral came just after 8pm. The police relayed the message to the Central fire station. By then all fire appliances were out and the communication system was already breaking down.

The provost and three helpers were on fire watch that night. Their vantage point was the roof. Soon after 8pm the first incendiaries landed on the roof of the chancel and nave. The fire watchers tackled these with their buckets of sand and water. The oak beams were very difficult to deal with because the lead had to be stripped back and the sand poured through the holes. No sooner had the little group got on top of these fires than the next wave of incendiaries arrived. This wave penetrated the roofs of the Cappers Chapel and the Smiths Chapel. These fires were also dealt with by the fire watchers, whose supply of sand and water was rapidly running out. When the third wave of incendiaries arrived the Girdlers Chapel and the Children's Chapel were hit. By now the Cathedral was well and truly alight. Smoke and flames were billowing through the holes in the roof.

About 9.30pm the first appliance arrived. The first jet of water was played on the flames and then stopped as quickly as it had started. More hoses were attached to other hydrants – but all in vain.

NUMBED AND DAZED

Other appliances arrived but without water they were helpless. The provost and his helpers rescued as many of the Cathedral treasures as they could and took them to the safety of the police station. There was nothing left to do now but watch the Cathedral and Coventry burn.

Morning found Coventry blitzed and Coventry folk numbed and dazed. The scale of the onslaught was so great as to take them beyond the limits of human endurance. People wandered about in a daze of incomprehension. There was a real sense of terror as well as of helplessness. People just did not know what to do.

In the narrow streets of the ancient city 568 people lost their lives, of whom more than 400 were so badly burned that they could not be identified. They were buried in a communal grave. More than one square mile of the city's centre was reduced to rubble, and no less than 80% of its buildings were destroyed or badly damaged. The destruction of so many shops, offices and hotels hampered the recovery of the city and made life very difficult for those who had stayed on, as well as for those who had fled in terror and had later returned.

The long-term consequences for the stricken city were very grim. About three-quarters of the total housing stock had been either destroyed or badly damaged. The main commercial area around Broadgate had been almost completely gutted. On Monday, 19 November, the report from Whitehall was brief, but telling:

> By dawn most of the water supply of the city had been cut off . . . Almost the whole of the city was without light or power . . . The city was entirely without gas . . . There was considerable damage to sewers.

The effect of the Coventry raid on vital war industries was also immediately apparent. 27 major factories were hit, including 12 directly connected with the crucial aircraft industry. Among those damaged were factories and engineering works belonging to GEC, Humber Hillman, Triumph Engineering, Sir Alfred Herbert Ltd, Daimler, Alvis, Rover, Armstrong Siddely and many others. Bearing in mind the extent of the destruction it is surprising that production in some of these got under way again at all, although it was noted at the time that machines often fared better than the buildings in which they were housed. At all events, some factories were able to resume production quite quickly. Others remained out of action for weeks while essential repairs and rebuilding works were carried out. The damage done to the people of Coventry and to their living conditions took longer to repair.

Drinking water was a major problem. Failure to deal with this could have resulted in an outbreak of typhoid. How far fractured sewers contaminated what little mains water there remained was not known. Chlorination was immediately put into effect at the pumping stations, while notices were posted around the city to 'boil all drinking water'. In addition a crash programme of immunisation was instituted. In the first few days following the raid about 30,000 injections were given, most of them at people's workplaces, where workers lined up in batches of 100 for the injections. Water tankers were brought in from around the Midlands to reduce the risks from contaminated water in the Coventry system.

Recovery was seriously hampered by the large number of unexploded bombs in the city. Royal Engineers bomb disposal teams worked solidly, in the most appalling and dangerous conditions, to deal with the bombs that littered Coventry. Among them there were upwards of twenty landmines, and a far greater number of 500lb bombs. Once the detonator types were established the work progressed quickly.

The number of extra troops drafted into Coventry for the rescue work created an accommodation problem in a city that already had an accommodation crisis. Officers fared quite well being billeted in the homes of the well-to-do. Other ranks were not so fortunate. They found themselves in such places as under the stand at Warwick race course, sleeping on the concrete floors with hardly a blanket to cover them, and with no food supply. When food did arrive for breakfast there was nothing to eat from or with. The ensuing row got the men individual billets.

Getting Coventry moving again was a task of mammoth proportions. The people had been traumatised by the experience. There was a terrible fear that the Germans would be back again the next

Cleared bomb sites reveal the ferocity of the attack

night. People were desperate to get out of the city. It was estimated that between 50,000 and 100,000 people left Coventry after the raid. As was noted at the time:

> 'the small size of the place makes people feel that the only thing they can do is *get out of it altogether* . . .'

They left in any way they could, and were representative of all classes. Many of these refugees were not homeless, they were just fleeing. They flooded the rest centres that were set up for the bombed-out. When those were full they occupied schools and churches.

The Ministry of Information bulletins spoke of the 'heroic calm' of the people. This was far from the truth. Herbert Morrison, the Home Secretary, had a rough ride when he met the Civic Authorities. He was blamed for the fact that the German bombers had been allowed to roam the skies at will for hour after hour systematically destroying the city, with neither the RAF nor the Anti-Aircraft able to do anything about it. Morrison, faced with what he saw as 'defeatism', threatened to place the city under martial law. In the end it was decided to leave the task of getting Coventry moving in the hands of the civilian Emergency Committee.

The 'Coventrieren' of Coventry aroused horror in the whole non-Nazi world. The *New York Herald Tribune* saw in the bombing 'the voiceless symbol of the insane . . . barbarity which has been released on Western civilisation' – a comment which, in those pre-Hamburg, pre-Dresden and pre-Hiroshima days, was reflected in many different ways by much of the press in most civilised countries. But perhaps the most succinct and telling comment of all appeared, two days after the attack, as a headline in the *Birmingham Gazette*, published in Coventry's neighbouring city. It simply read:

COVENTRY – OUR GUERNICA

The Luftwaffe returns

It goes without saying that Coventry's ordeal, terrible as it was, would have been even worse if the Luftwaffe had bombed the city the next night as well – a practice they adopted later in the Blitz. It is possible that Göring and his commanders believed that the city had been completely wiped out, beyond hope of recovery, and that no further action was necessary.

It was not until the night of 8/9 April 1941 that the Luftwaffe returned in force. More than 280 bombers were assembled for this second full-scale raid, of which over 230 found the target area and released their bombs. There was some cloud that night, but conditions were good enough for many of the crews to bomb visually. From 9.30pm onwards successive waves of bombers dropped more than 23,000 incendiary bombs and 300 tons of high explosive bombs. As in the first 'conventration', the intention was to fire-raze to the ground aircraft and motor assembly plants together with ancillary factories and workshops.

Fires were started in many parts of the city but the fire-fighting teams were more than ready for them, with the result that only two developed to major proportions. However, commercial, industrial and residential properties were demolished or burned out, and three major factories were badly damaged. Compared with the November 1940 raid this second concentrated attack lasted a much shorter time, three hours all told. Nevertheless, grievous casualties were caused, including 281 dead.

Two nights later the bombers returned, although there is now evidence to suggest that the Luftwaffe had not marked Coventry as its victim that night (10/11 April 1941). Birmingham was intended as the major target, but as a result of navigational errors many of the German air crews found themselves over Coventry, and bombs rained down on the city once again. Damage was widespread and several buildings, including the main Post Office, were destroyed by fire in this 'accidental' raid, which cost a further 126 lives.

Ack-Ack guns – the first to fire

• When war broke out, AA Command had less than a third of the heavy guns provided for in their establishment, and most of those were obsolete. It was much the same story with light AA guns and searchlights. Although strenuous efforts were made to equip all units fully as war production got under way, there remained many deficiencies when the German attack on British targets started.
• Women of the ATS took over from men on many AA gun-sites during 1941 to perform such duties as driving, plotting, radar operation, etc. – almost everything except actually firing the guns. In 1942, the Home Guard took over the full operation of many gun-sites and 'Z' rocket batteries.
• Searchlights were re-distributed in 1941 in order to give greater aid to night fighters, by creating boxes of light in the sky. Within the box a fighter circled a stationary vertical beam. When an enemy entered the box, other searchlights indicated its position to the fighter on patrol, who then went in to the attack.
• The first hostile aircraft to be brought down on British soil by AA fire was a Junkers Ju88, which was hit during the raid on Scapa Flow on 17 October 1940 and exploded over the island of Hoy.
• At the height of the Blitz one London borough asked an AA unit to move elsewhere because, they said, the thunder from their guns was cracking all the lavatory pans in a local council housing estate.

(*top*) General Sir Frederick Pile, KCB, DSO, MC, GOC-in-C AA Command
(*bottom*) Even while this photograph was being taken at Barry, near Cardiff, the unit shot down an enemy aircraft and probably 'accounted for another'

Anti-Aircraft gunfire (popularly known as Ack-Ack) was both welcomed and abused by the public throughout the war. It was cheered when it put up an ear-splitting 'barrage' – what the press invariably called 'a ring of steel' – against Luftwaffe bombers, but at the same time abused when the roar of guns robbed honest citizens of their sleep. But when the guns were silent during a raid the howl of criticism was also ear-splitting. 'I think the anti-aircraft defence of London the biggest scandal since Nero,' wrote one outraged citizen during the Blitz. Whatever it did AA Command couldn't win.

This was perhaps inevitable because, AA gunners – like the balloon barrage, but unlike airmen, sailors and even the infantry – could hardly be seen as potential war-winners. But their role in blunting enemy attacks at the height of the Blitz and later in the days of Flying Bombs was undoubtedly crucial. 'By the end of the Blitz,' wrote General Sir Frederick Pile, who was the redoubtable GOC-in-C of AA Command throughout the war, 'we had destroyed 170 night raiders, probably destroyed another 58, and damaged, in varying degrees, 118 more.' Churchill, an unswerving admirer of General Pile, noted that 'in the daylight attacks of the Battle of Britain the guns accounted for 296 enemy aircraft, and probably destroyed or damaged 74 more.' These are not insignificant figures – particularly for German pilots. The AA barrage over cities and airfields forced them to fly at a greater height than planned or to miss their targets, and undoubtedly contributed a great deal to the defeat of the Luftwaffe. Good AA shooting broke more than one massed raid on a fighter aerodrome, notably Hornchurch where (according to captured German aircrew) the AA gunfire was the most accurate they had ever met.

AA Command covered the whole of Britain, and was under the operational control of RAF Fighter Command. The two C-in-Cs (Pile and Dowding) worked together very effectively to defend vital aerodromes with a system of anti-aircraft guns and balloon barrages. Largely thanks to the ingenuity of General Pile huge batteries of guns and rocket projectors could be concentrated in a threatened area at short notice. The heavy AA guns (for example, the 3.7in and 4.5in) could hit Luftwaffe aircraft of the time even when flying at their ceiling. To attack fast-moving aircraft at lower levels, AA used the Swedish Bofors gun to good effect. But with high-flying planes, accuracy of aiming was all but impossible, and consequently the quantity of ammunition spent per 'kill' was extremely high. To hit an unseen bomber flying at 250mph and at a height of up to 35,000ft, above cloud or at night, even wth the aid of searchlights and sound locators, was very much a matter of luck – until the arrival of target-tracking radar in October 1940. With the aid of radar over 70 German planes were shot down by AA gunfire during the raids on London in May 1941 – more than in the first four months of the Blitz.

Much of the value of AA was as a boost to civilian morale. At the beginning of the London Blitz in September 1940, for example, Londoners endured nights of unrelenting bombardment to which there seemed to be no counter-attack. Then on 10 September, in Churchill's words, 'the whole barrage opened, accompanied by a blaze of searchlights. This roaring cannonade did not do too much harm to the enemy, but gave enormous satisfaction to the population. Everyone was cheered by the feeling that we were hitting back . . .' Such barrages, of course, were only possible when there were no night fighters, but at this stage of the war night fighter planes were not very effective. However, guns and searchlights enabled raiders to pick out their targets on the darkest nights. When the Blitz came to Midlands' cities (targets easier for the Luftwaffe to miss than sprawling London), Pile at one point ordered all searchlights to be switched off and all guns to be silent – with the result that several cities enjoyed bomb-free nights in the total darkness.

As the war went on, AA defences became ever more effective. Not only were there more powerful and varied guns, but such technical devices as radar control, mathematically-accurate predictors and the proximity fuse enormously improved the accuracy of shooting. As a result, AA hit 20% of all tip-and-run and Baedeker raiders and destroyed 10% of them – a disaster for the Luftwaffe. And when they again attacked London in January 1943, only 30 out of 75 aircraft managed to penetrate the city's defences.

But perhaps the greatest of AA triumphs was in the defeat of the Flying Bombs in 1944-45. This involved moving the entire anti-aircraft line of defences down to the coast so that the guns should get an uninterrupted view of the incoming V1s. There was thus a gun-belt from Beachy Head to Dover, 5,000 yards deep and firing 10,000 yards out to sea. In addition, there was a 'box' of AA guns north and south of the Thames to deal with V1s as they came up the estuary. These defences together accounted for 1,972 flying bombs.

'We had been the first troops in the country to go into action,' wrote General Pile after the war, 'and never since the beginning of the war had we ceased to be on the alert. The great battles in which we fought were famous . . . The Battle of Britain, the Battle of London . . . the "Baedeker" towns . . . the Flying Bombs; there had been long-drawn-out months of boredom and squalor and moments of high drama in which the skill and courage and endurance of the men and women of AA Command had done much to save Great Britain . . . The troops of AA Command had destroyed 822 enemy aircraft, had probably destroyed a further 237 enemy aircraft, and had damaged, in varying degree, 422 enemy aircraft.'

75th (Heavy) AA Battery, at Mount Kemel, near Dover, saw constant action throughout the blitz on Britain

All at sea . . .

Rather like modern oil rigs, offshore anti-aircraft forts were floated into position at various points in the estuaries of the Thames and Mersey to guard the approaches to London and Liverpool. They also proved to be a useful deterrent against mine-laying activity, and the crew of one of the forts even claimed to have sunk a German E-boat.

Birmingham: the obvious target

Before the war began there had been a survey of the country to establish those areas which would be at high risk of attack from the air. The degree of risk was calculated partly on the basis of geography and partly by the strategic industries in the area. Birmingham's position in the Midlands was felt to make it a difficult target to hit by bombers based in Germany as it was considered to be the farthest point of their range. However, its wide variety of engineering production made it an obvious place for the enemy to attack. These two opposing views led to a mixed reaction in the city. Plans were prepared to disperse factories so that the destruction of a production centre would not cause all manufacture of an item to cease. On the other hand, there was a certain complacency about the development of civil defence measures.

As it was, the enemy tested the defences of Birmingham relatively early in the war, although this first attack was conducted by a lone aircraft which probably attacked the city by mistake.

The great 'Gas Scare'

It was in 1941, according to Birmingham's *Evening Mail Special* that the 'gas scare' – the fear of gas attacks – really began to alarm the civilian population. The horror of incendiary and high explosive bombs had been experienced, but gas remained a terrible unknown.

In the spring of that year the newspapers were full of references which indicated how seriously the authorities viewed the possibility of a gas attack.

On 9 April 1941, for instance, the day of the city's last massive blitz, the Birmingham Coroner adjourned a hearing at midday so that 'the Court could comply with the Lord Mayor's appeal for gas masks to be worn periodically.'

On the same day, a reader's letter in the *Evening Dispatch* told animal lovers how to apply to 'Our Dumb Friends' League' for a leaflet about the care of pets in a gas attack.

Ten days later a most bizarre picture appeared in the *Birmingham Gazette* – no doubt intended to be cheering – of dancers at the Grand Casino in Birmingham doing the jitterbug wearing gas masks. The event was a Gas Mask Ball, during which an ARP official 'gave an instructive talk on the care of gas masks.'

FIRST RAID

This first raid occurred on 9 August 1940. The first bomb fell in Eversley Dale, a cul de sac off Bromford Lane. Several others fell in the same area. In Montague Road, Erdington, a family of five was sound asleep when a bomb hit the building. Neighbours and local ARP members rushed to the scene and began work to release those trapped in the rubble. The first brought out was the mother and then the father. Still trapped were two sisters and their brother who was at home on leave from the army. The two girls were brought out fairly rapidly, with only minor injuries. Then began the more difficult task of rescuing the son. They battled for two hours and eventually made a hole in the roof, through which he was carried. Since all the ambulances had been withdrawn by this time, he was taken to the General Hospital in a demolition vehicle. He died on the way to hospital and became the first casualty of the war in Birmingham.

A couple of months before this event a local paper carried an article drawing attention to the poor response from the citizens to calls for volunteers for ARP duties. It also criticised those who had joined because so many respirators were being lost or damaged. Now Birmingham could no longer afford to be complacent. If one bomber could create such damage, it was clear that a major attack could create havoc. As the Germans advanced westward it also became clear that decisions based on the range of their aircraft were now irrelevant.

It was not long before this truth was demonstrated more dramatically. A larger raid took place on the night of 13 August and Castle Bromwich Aero factory was hit and quite seriously damaged. Seven people died that night, five of them workers at the factory. The next night the raiders were back and areas of Erdington, Stechford, Yardley and Bordesley Green were hit. Two families in Bordesley Green East, using the same Anderson shelter, were all killed when it received a direct hit. Seven people died in this incident.

In all these early raids there were complaints that the warning sirens were not operated until after the attack had commenced. In several cases the Alert was sounded an hour after the bombs had started to fall. Naturally, the population of Birmingham was angry at this failure. To be fair, the original information had to come from a source outside Birmingham, but no one seems at that time to have decided that having

The Market Hall after the night raid on 25 August 1941

bombers overhead justified taking the initiative. This led to ARP wardens using their whistles as unofficial warnings to people in their locality. Another ruling at this stage of the war was that the public shelters would not be unlocked until the air raid warning had sounded! The authorities' attitude was that if they were open at other times they would be misused! The ARP Chairman stated:

> We cannot, as long as a certain, anti-social, filthy, Fifth Column element exists in the city allow the public shelters unrestrictedly open. Those who hold the keys should not wait for the sirens, but if they hear enemy planes or gunfire should open them at once.

These early teething troubles were overcome when it became obvious that lives were being lost because of such bureaucratic nonsense.

On the night of 25 August, Birmingham received its first concentrated raid of the war. In that raid the Market Hall in the centre of the city was burnt out and 25 people lost their lives.

For over a century the Market Hall had been the traditional shopping centre of the city. It was usually packed with stall holders selling a wide range of goods – though the war had limited the selection and rationing had meant that the usual good-natured bargaining had been replaced by careful allocations of food. One high explosive bomb scored a direct hit and started Birmingham's first major fire of the war. Showers of incendiaries fell on Corporation Street and the shops and businesses in the Bull Ring area. This destruction in the centre of the city and in an area frequently visited by the population brought home to them that the raids had begun in earnest. Luckily the raid took place on Sunday night and so there were no occupants of the basement of the Market Hall which was used as a public shelter, or the loss of life would have been heavy.

The next morning there were many reports of unexploded bombs. Some of these bombs proved to be defective, but others had been fitted with delayed action fuses. Police Sergeant Joe Flavell and Constable Bill Price were called to a huge bomb which had fallen through the roof of the Methodist Chapel in Hatchett Street, near Newtown Row. It was about six feet long and about two feet in diameter. In these circumstances it was a rule that the police had to make a note of the number on the bomb so that it could be identified for the bomb disposal squad who would know what equipment to bring.

The bomb was covered with dirt and plaster. Gingerly they rubbed the dirt away until they found the number and carefully noted it in their records. Once that had been done they evacuated the

area as rapidly as possible. They had only got about one hundred yards down the road when there was a tremendous explosion and the chapel was blown to smithereens. On that occasion the number of the bomb proved to be irrelevant!

For a while the enemy switched to daylight raids and on the afternoon of 27 September Fort Dunlop was attacked. Later, on 13 November, the Austin aero factory was raided and six workers were killed and 25 injured. But these raids were dangerous and expensive for the enemy to mount because the RAF was able to detect the bombers at a distance from their target. To mount further raids upon the city and its environs, it became clear to the Luftwaffe chiefs that their bombers would require a heavier fighter escort. The fighters usually had a shorter range and so targets like Birmingham, although very attractive to the Germans, were not very suitable for daylight raids.

Despite the difficulties of pursuing day raids, night raids could still be launched; and on 15 October 59 died in a heavy raid. Then on 19 November the city was attacked by a force of 350 bombers in a raid which led to the deaths of over 400 people; the greatest loss of life in any raid on Birmingham. Huge numbers of serious fires were started. The BSA Small Heath factory was hit by high explosive bombs and the New Building was burnt out. Sadly 50 workers who had been sheltering behind a blast wall on the ground floor were killed in this raid.

An ARP warden recalled that night:

> The sirens went off at just before 7pm that night and the all clear came at 4.30am. I walked back into town down Bradford Street. The devastation was unbelievable. I stood at the end of New Street, which was ablaze and watched the firemen fighting the flames which were shooting out of the top of the Marshal and Snelgrove building. They were on ladders high over the roof tops and by the time the water came down through the building to the street it was boiling.

The first firewoman to be recruited on Division C in 1939 told a tale of life at that critical time, a story which illustrates the amazing calm with which people could get on with their duties under severe duress:

> When I arrived I was asked to take messages for the control room on the switchboard, as the control in the basement was still

(*left*)(*top*) Gooch Street (*below*) One of many industrial targets hit was Dockers factory, part of the BSA group (*right*)(*top*) Miller Street tram depot (*below*) Devastation along New Street in the city centre

jammed with calls for assistance. The disc of the Fire Force HQ dropped and I plugged in to hear a calm voice say: 'I have a repeat message for you from 23.00 hours last night. We have to report that an unexploded landmine has fallen at the rear of your building. Please take necessary action immediately.' I promptly put on the klaxon for an emergency.

It was by now daylight so the fire officers searched the building and canal which ran behind it while everyone else left for the secondary control room. They found the landmine hanging about 40ft up in the air by its parachute, tangled up in a mass of telephone wires running between the buildings above the canal. It had swung against the building as it descended and had caved it in like a matchbox. It was a huge ball of metal with knobs sticking out all over it. I was requested to stay behind and ring other stations to tell them of our evacuation. The switchboard room was on the ground floor and only had an Anderson shelter built over it to protect against blast. One of the stations joked, 'Don't worry Jackie, you'll get a medal and a Union Jack over your coffin!' After about half an hour of phoning I was able to make my way to safety.

IF YOUR HOUSE IS BOMBED WHAT YOU SHOULD DO

The Lord Mayor desires us to make the following announcement —

In the event of citizens being bombed out of their houses they should first endeavour to find accommodation with neighbours or friends.

Where they cannot do so they should go to the nearest reception station — police or wardens will inform them where this is.

Public officials will then endeavour to provide for all their needs, including alternative accommodation.

To assist the public officials, the clergy, Salvation Army officers, school teachers (if not engaged on evacuation duties) and others are appealed to to attend at their nearest reception station to volunteer their services whenever the emergency arises in their locality and to act upon the instructions of the official in charge.

The bombers were back again on 22 November. This time there was a force of approximately 200 raiders and over 600 fires were started. Municipal buildings, the law courts and two gasworks were affected. Fisher and Ludlow suffered extensive fire damage and Klaxon Ltd was hit by high explosive bombs. Other factories hit were Joseph Lucas, Singer Motors, Bakelite, and Wright, Bindley and Gell.

In this raid it became obvious that Birmingham was particularly vulnerable to attack by incendiaries because its water supply for fire-fighting came in huge mains from the Elan Valley in Wales. Damage to these mains left many areas of the city without the necessary water supply to contain the fires. There was a danger that these could spread, producing the ideal conditions for a firestorm – such as that which completely destroyed Dresden later in the war.

Two 42-inch mains feeding the city from Frankley Reservoir were each fractured in two places near the Woodlands

One-and-six (7½p) for 8 hours

As in other centres, most of Birmingham's 22,000 air raid wardens gave their services completely free. They did their normal office and factory jobs in the daytime and then reported to the local wardens' post every night.

If there were no raids, they could enjoy a pleasant, sociable evening together, playing cards or chatting over mugs of cocoa or tea. But as soon as the sirens sounded, they had to put on their steel helmets, check their first-aid packs and other equipment, and go out into the streets ready to deal with any emergency.

They were allowed some expenses – sixpence for a sandwich, and 1/6d for a meal. But the Home Office decided that this was a little extravagant, and laid down that no man or woman was entitled to a meal allowance unless they had been on duty for not less than eight hours

Hospital. As a result the remaining pipes were filled with mud. Before the new pipe could be fitted it was essential to remove this mud. This meant that men had to dig inside a 42-inch diameter pipe, sometimes at steep angles. An hour at the face was totally exhausting. They rigged up a little trolley which was filled by the man digging and his mates then dragged it back to the surface.

There were additional anxieties: the fear of infection spreading because of contamination of the water supply, and the fear of sewerage infiltrating the system. Those with gardens were advised to dig holes for use as lavatories. Public trench latrines were made in the parks and recreation fields. Many mortuaries were without water. Soldiers were drafted into the area to act as grave-diggers.

This secret signal was sent to the Ministry of Home Security on the morning of 23 November:

> Water for fire-fighting does not exist in four fifths of the city. In case Birmingham is attacked tonight it is hoped to muster the Home Guard at full strength to be dispersed over the city to undertake incendiary bomb fighting. Work on the restoration of the water supply will start immediately, but large mains have been damaged in several places and this will take many days.
>
> Arrangements are being made for men to work during the blackout. A regional call is being made for all available water carts to be placed at the disposal of Birmingham Water Department. It is hoped to make use of railway water tank waggons to bring water to strategic points where it can be collected.

A partial mains water supply was re-established on 27 November, five days after the raid – and luckily there was a lull in serious raids until 3 December, by which time the necessary repairs had been effected and the peril averted.

But the Luftwaffe had not finished its visits to Birmingham in 1940, and on the night of 1 December 200 bombers carried out what was to prove to be the longest raid of the war on the city. This led to the deaths of 263 persons and serious injury to 245, and lasted over thirteen hours.

Then Birmingham had a respite. In the early months of 1941 the Luftwaffe expended most of its efforts on the ports, and between 2 January and 8 April there were only three raids on Birmingham and none of these was serious. It began to look to the more optimistic that the Germans had forgotten the city. In Easter week, however, all that changed.

Pioneering spirit

Men of the Pioneer Corps had long been regarded as the navvies of the British Army, but they earned a new respect during the Second World War for the magnificent way they responded to calls for help from Birmingham and other cities attacked by the Luftwaffe. In a Churchillian spirit of 'blood, sweat, tears and toil' they worked around the clock, and for days on end, clearing debris, blasting away unsafe buildings and re-opening highways.

Although the Prince of Wales Theatre was only performing matinees it had good audiences for the Anglo-Polish Ballet company. The cinemas also played to packed houses. Birmingham was getting back into a feeling of 'business as usual' after the heavy raids of 1940. The events of Easter week were to demonstrate that the enemy was far from defeated in the air over Britain.

On the night of 9 April the red warning was given at 9.32 and within minutes the first bombs were crashing down on Bordesley Green. Soon after other bombs fell in the east of the city, destroying homes in Stechford, Kings Heath, Small Heath and Aston. Incendiaries started fires in Washwood Heath and Nechells. The police station at Digbeth received a direct hit and one officer died and three others were injured.

At about midnight the attack was concentrated on the city centre. Soon serious fires were raging in an area within Moor Street, Masshouse Lane, High Street, Dale End, New Street, Bull Ring and Edgbaston Street. The worst fire centred on the Midland Arcade which was burning from end to end. Already the fire fighters were hampered in their efforts by low water pressure and preparations were made to blow up buildings to provide a fire break. Some firemen stood helplessly holding empty hoses and watching the flames spread. One reported afterwards how he felt at the top of a hundred-foot ladder gazing down at the blazing Midland Arcade.

Men of the Pioneer Corps helped to clear away tons of rubble in John Bright Street

A view of Temple Row, from the roof of Lewis's stores, after the raid on 10 April 1941

It was a frightening experience up there, by myself, hearing bombs exploding and having no protection, thinking the next one could be mine. Was I scared! Somehow we struggled on until towards dawn the raiders dispersed, reinforcements arrived and water was relayed to the site.

Flames leapt all around the Bull Ring. The Swan Hotel, the oldest in Birmingham, was destroyed. It was to be the last performance at the Prince of Wales Theatre. One high explosive bomb fell through the roof and exploded in the pink, white and gold decorated auditorium ripping it to pieces. Amazingly the ballet company were able to recover their costumes undamaged.

And that night probationary constable Ronald Jackson went on duty along the Coventry Road. A plane flew over and dropped flares which were the target for high explosive bombs which dropped on houses in a nearby street. 'The dust and debris rose in a gigantic spout,' he later reported, 'yet the shock-waves from the explosion were absorbed by the density of the surrounding houses. There were no other noises. No screams. No shouts. Just nothing.'

He went from house to house. 'At some of them dust covered corpses, one of them sitting on cellar steps in a quiet attitude of resignation, and others, with little more than a trickle of blood escaping from the mouth to indicate that their lungs had been burst by the blast, were grave testimony to the death and destruction falling from the skies on to an innocent population.'

Later he was sent to a block of flats in Garrison Lane, Small Heath, where a woman was trapped after a direct hit. Several attempts to rescue her had already failed. Jackson burrowed beneath the wall under which she lay. He discovered that some reinforcing rods were exposed and by working for an hour with just a hacksaw blade he managed to cut through one and relieve the pressure on her legs. He continued working until others were able to pull her free. At any moment the wall could have subsided and he would have been entombed. In June he learned that he had been awarded the George Cross for his gallantry that night.

About 650 high explosive bombs and numerous sticks of incendiaries rained down from an estimated 250 raiders during the raid. On this night was created what became known to many as the Big Top Site which was used by a circus for some time prior to its redevelopment.

The enemy returned the next night. During the two nights it was estimated that 110 tons of high explosives were dropped on the city.

BURNING RUBBER

The following night the roof of Fort Dunlop was set alight, and volunteers among the workforce climbed up to deal with the fire as the works fire brigade was on duty elsewhere. By the time the blaze was put out they were soaked and blackened by the burning rubber. They returned to their normal work still wet through. To compensate them for their ruined clothes they received about seven and sixpence each (37p).

This week marked the end of heavy raids on the city. It has been estimated that throughout the war Birmingham received 1,800 tons of high explosives. Only Liverpool/Birkenhead and London were more heavily bombed.

Occasional raids continued, and as late as 27 July 1942 the city was attacked by 70 bombers which inflicted heavy losses. The last actual raid of the war was on 23 April 1943, a 'hit and run' raid such as the one which started the attacks nearly three years before.

During the war Birmingham was subjected to 62 raids; over 2,000 people lost their lives and more than 3,000 were seriously injured.

Horrible as these figures are, it is obvious that Birmingham escaped what could well have been disasters of a huge magnitude. For on several occasions its defences were so weakened that if the Luftwaffe had continued heavy bombing without a break, the whole of the city could have been wiped out in a massive fire storm.

Rats gave the alarm

Birmingham's Caroline Street was rat-ridden, according to a former fire-watcher writing in the *Evening Mail Special*, who had caught over 60 of them with a wire rat-trap. But they proved useful during the blitz. 'By some mysterious sixth sense, they came scampering out of the buildings' (where he was on duty) 'long before the warning that the bombers were on the way. It was a heavy raid and we waited in an entry for cover when a bomb dropped not far away. We were bowled over.' The bombing continued for some time, but then stopped quite suddenly. We are not told if the rats returned after the 'All Clear'.

Bristol – the 'Neutral' City

Bristol was designated a 'neutral' area in the event of war, according to plans laid down by the Government in 1938. Its neutral status meant that the town could not send out, or receive, any evacuees. A city of medium size – its population was then 415,000 – Bristol was not considered to be one of the urban areas likely to attract concentrated attention from the Luftwaffe. Heavy bombing was not expected. Not until February 1941 – by which time the city had suffered a number of bombing attacks, several of them being major raids – were the first of Bristol's schoolchildren evacuated. Twenty-thousand boys and girls were eventually moved out of the city and its surrounding districts.

The bus driver's return . . .

Among the casualties of the single bomb which fell at Broad Weir on 28 August 1942 was a Bristol bus driver. He had just come off duty and was walking towards a bus on his journey home to Fishponds when the bomb fell.

Bomb splinters had blown a hole in his chest and his case seemed hopeless. At the hospital he was placed on a trolley ready to be wheeled into the hospital mortuary. His wife was notified that he was dead.

As he was being wheeled away down a hospital corridor, his next door neighbour who was serving in the ambulance corps, hurried past. The fact that the 'dead' man was in bus driver's uniform caught his eye.

'That chap is my next door neighbour', he told the hospital attendant. Then as he looked down he suddenly noticed a slight movement of the 'dead' man's eyelids.

The bus driver was taken back to the operating theatre for an emergency operation. Twelve weeks later the man who came back from the dead was back behind the wheel of his bus again.

from *The Bristol Evening Post*

objective. At the outbreak of war, therefore, in the words of C. M. MacInnes's history of *Bristol at War*, 'The unreadiness of Bristol was lamentable.' But even when German raiders began to be seen over Bristol and Avonmouth they seemed to show only minor interest in the area.

LEAFLETS AND 'DRIP-BOMBING'

In the event, Bristol was heavily and repeatedly bombed by the Germns, and the raids had clear strategic objectives. First, the docks at nearby Avonmouth made it an important distribution point at the end of the supply line across the Atlantic. Secondly, the area contained a production centre vital to the war effort – namely, the works of the Bristol Aeroplane Company at Filton. Luftwaffe reconnaissance photographs taken in the early summer of 1940 clearly identified a range of targets – the docks, the Filton factories, the railways, power stations and gasworks.

Although Bristol's ARP Committee was set up in 1935, and its organisation was fully established by 1938, its preparations did not offer an adequate level of defence against full-scale attack. Only 1521 trained wardens had been allocated to their sectors by the end of 1938, in spite of the Committee's appeals for volunteers. In the last three months of that year crisis only 52 men volunteered as fire-fighting reserves. This poor response largely reflected the feeling that if Bristol was not one of the 12 cities required to make evacuation plans, then it surely must have a low status as a Luftwaffe objective.

The first Luftwaffe attack in the Bristol area was recorded just a few minutes into 25 June 1940 – a small raid, probably by two aircraft, which released bombs near Temple Meads railway station. Comparatively minor damage was done to railway sidings, a steel works, a soap factory, and a brewery, but five people were killed. This raid set the pattern for repeated small and harassing raids by day and night. Some saw the morning raid of 4 July on the Bristol Aeroplane Company's works at Filton as the precursor of bigger attacks to come. So tension was reduced when a single German plane, flying high on 2 August, dropped propaganda leaflets instead of bombs. Even on 15 August, when there were five major raids on other parts of the country, the raid in the Bristol Channel area was slight and took place after midnight. That was the day when hundreds of Luftwaffe bombers and their fighter escorts attacked London, Southampton, Cardiff, Liverpool and the south coast in one of the Germans' last concerted attempts to destroy the RAF's fighter reserves.

By the end of August 1940 the Bristol area was rather the worse for frequent and usually small raids, which in them-

selves created no premonition of the heavy bombardment to come. The Luftwaffe's targets were the railways, oil tanks, Avonmouth docks and the aircraft factories, and the evidence of bombing was local and scattered.

TERROR BOMBING

Bristol and Avonmouth were frequently put on alert for these raids, and 'drip-bombing' continued. Then the Luftwaffe's policy was switched to one of smashing the RAF's aircraft-production resources, and the Bristol Aeroplane's

Morning after a fire-blitz on Broadmead

Broadmead, one of Bristol's many fine, historic streets, suffered enormous destruction during the Blitz – as this picture of a dawn scene after a fire-blitz shows. Historic buildings such as John Wesley's Chapel and the old Greyhound Hotel were not seriously damaged, but many commercial and industrial premises were completely destroyed.

Fire-fighters toiled unceasingly to control the effects of fire-bombs, as our picture shows. Their efforts were constantly hampered by shortage of water – usually because water mains had been hit – and shortage of men, appliances and hoses. In Bristol's biggest blitz no fewer than 77 other brigades sent help, and 20,000 feet of fire-hose were sent from Cardiff, Newport, Birmingham and Plymouth – but unfortunately too late to save the city. To make things worse, the phones were often completely out of action, and there was always a severe shortage of petrol. And then in the midst of a huge fire-bomb attack, firemen would be called upon to put down their hoses to carry out other rescue work – such as, on that terrible night, leading horses out of burning stables and rescuing 35 elderly women . . .

works at Filton received a savage pounding. Shortly before noon on 25 September, 27 Heinkel 111s with a large fighter escort crossed the coast at Weymouth heading – it was first thought – for Yeovil. But at 11,000 feet their course took them directly over the Filton works. In a single pass they released 100 tons of bombs simultaneously. Severe damage was done to the Rodney Works: eight aircraft under construction were damaged beyond repair, and a further two dozen required damage-repairs. Moreover, the potential terror of aerial bombardment was now fully realised, for 60 workers were killed while taking cover in six shelters in the engine works. Other bombs falling in the Filton area caused further deaths.

Two days after this harrowing event, the worst in the area to date, the Germans returned to Bristol. Though it was commonly thought that their target was once again the Filton works, in fact this time their objective was the Parnall Aircraft Works (making gun-turrets) at Yate. At about 11am 25 bomb-carrying Messerschmitts, with a fighter escort of twice that number, crossed the south coast and headed for Bristol. But this time they were met by five squadrons of RAF fighters and chased back across the coast. In the ensuing dog-fights, one Messerschmitt 110, both engines on fire, exploded over the Stapleton Institution at Fishponds. The crew were buried in Bristol's Greenbank Cemetery.

Throughout the rest of September, the whole of October and most of November, raids continued in and around the Bristol area. Bomb-drops appeared to be even more haphazard and scattered. Outlying districts and villages reported small numbers of bombs, and railways and docks were also attacked. But there was no marked increase in the frequency or severity of raids to give warning of the change of bombing strategy which was about to inflict so much suffering on Bristol.

For by November 1940 the Luftwaffe's policy had switched once more to the general bombing of urban areas, beginning with the devastation of Coventry on the 14th of that month. Bristol's first 'coventration' was scheduled for the night of 24 November – the third of the large-scale raids on provincial towns.

The riddle of Bristol's 'Dutch House'

Until it was reduced to a blackened ruin by Luftwaffe incendiaries on 20 November 1940 a fabulous, half-timbered building – known to all as 'the Old Dutch House' – had stood for centuries at the corner of Wine Street and High Street in Bristol. It carried the date 1676, and its black and white, four-storey façade overhung a shop. On the first-floor balcony a wooden soldier with rifle and pack stood sentry. According to a story in Bristol's 'Evening Post', 'An air of mystery had always hung over the old Dutch House. Some said it was shipped over from Holland, while others maintained that it was a fair imitation of a Dutch house built as a whim by a wealthy Bristol merchant.' But the story added that the riddle is 'for ever safe', because the German fire-bombs damaged the Dutch House so badly that it had to be pulled down – 'but at least some relics of it have been preserved.'

The illustrations show the old Dutch House after the raid of 20 November 1940, before it was completely pulled down, and as it looked in the 1880s.

SAMUEL
S & G

The bomb that wasn't . . .

One of the eccentricities of the Blitz was shown in the Bristol raid of 16 March 1941. Civil defence workers had been called to investigate a reported unexploded bomb in a house. Instead of a bomb they found a paving slab. The bomb blast had flung it 70 yards through the air to land on the roof of the house. Its force had taken it through the roof and ceilings, and it had buried itself in the front room floor.

from *The Bristol Evening Post*

A total of 148 long-range bombers of Luftflotte 3 was ordered to attack Bristol as their target objective – 134 of which claimed to have reached and bombed the city (12 aborting, 2 lost, and one attacking an alternative target); though it must be said that local observers in Bristol on that night put their estimates of attacking planes at half that number. That the German planes did not attack singly might help to account for the discrepancy.

Shortly after nightfall the sirens sounded. The first drone of approaching aircraft reverberated through the Sunday evening, at a time when many Bristolians were at services in their various churches. At 6.30pm the attack opened with the dropping of flares from the leading planes. They were recalled many years later by a correspondent to the Bristol *Evening Post*:

> The night sky seemed a dark backcloth for the hanging baskets of fire; rather pretty and like a Guy Fawkes celebration we thought . . .

The prelude to the bombing was also observed by a young boy, Ted Hill, who in middle-age recorded his first vivid impression of that night. His mother, who had gone into the garden, called him out: 'Quick! come and see this light.'

> It was a clear, starry night, but immediately I felt it was too light. The reason was a bright light in the sky, which seemed to be moving slowly to the earth. We watched it quietly as it cast flickering shadows about the garden and over the opposite houses . . . A high pitched note started in the pit of my stomach and rose to a shriek in my ear. The house shook with the explosion . . .

The first incendiaries and high-explosives were directed at the city centre docks. Soon these were followed by further drops, the German planes flying over the city in waves of two or three. Within a short space of time, as a local reporter described his experience: '. . . it was obvious that this was not the mild and innocuous air raid to which we had become accustomed in recent months.' Later, he records: 'We opened the church doors and half of Bristol seemed on fire!'

The incendiaries had by now started numerous fires across large areas of Bristol and its districts. Within the first hour of the commencement of the raid no fewer than 70 fires had been started – some of them developing into major proportions. Before the end of the raid more than 200 fires were burning simultaneously, of which ten were classified as major and 15 as serious. 'There were fires and bombs everywhere,' as a Bristol woman simply put it, 'for the city was enveloped in flame and clouds of smoke everywhere.'

During the raid the Luftwaffe dropped something over 12,000 incendiaries, including several hundred of the exploding variety, together with 160 tons of high-explosive. The destruction caused was severe. Whole streets were alight, blazing like torches – the fire-fighters supplemented by forces from other districts, their task made impossible in some places because of damage to the water supply mains.

Many parts of the city testified to the severity of the raid, though it was the heart of the city which bore the brunt of the destruction – the most concentrated effects shown from Broad Quay to Old Market. Here some streets were totally or very largely destroyed: Castle Street, Bridge Street, High Street, Union Street, Broad Street, and Mary-le-Port Street. Much of Wine Street, one of the oldest of the city streets and a busy shopping centre, had also been flattened, the remaining structures opened up with missing roofs and walls, the street littered with rubble and debris. Park Street was smashed. Churches were destroyed, as were warehouses, shops, and dwellings. Among the buildings of historic interest which were destroyed was Temple Church, a medieval church of more than 800 years' standing – though its leaning tower, for which it was famous, survived. A fine Tudor mansion (St Peter's Hospital) was destroyed, and the unique Dutch House in the High Street was damaged so badly that three days after the raid it had to be pulled down.

'What part of France is this?' asked the Nazi Pilot

One misty morning in July 1941 the first aircraft to land at the new airfield at Lulsgate Bottom was – a brand new German bomber. Men working on one of the runways watched, puzzled because the machine looked unfamiliar and because it was landing contrary to regulations on an airfield not yet open. It didn't seem to be in trouble, and it made a good landing and taxied towards them.

The pilot got out, followed by his crew, and walked across to the workmen. 'What part of France is this?' he asked the foreman in French. The foreman laughed. 'This isn't France,' he said. 'You're in England.' The pilot whipped out a revolver to cover the retreat of himself and his crew back to their aircraft, but at that moment soldiers protecting the airfield arrived with tommy-guns. The three Nazi airmen were marched off to the guardhouse.

The intelligence officer who questioned them was delighted: he discovered that their aircraft was a brand-new Junkers 88, a new type with new ideas, and it had come into British hands intact. At the time the censors would only allow the newspapers to report that a Junkers 88 had 'crashed in Somerset' and its crew captured: the Germans must not be allowed to know that we were in possession of a perfect sample of their latest Ju 88. In fact, the bomber was in good order and had plenty of petrol. So why had it landed at Lulsgate? At the time some people thought that perhaps the crew were fed up with the war and landed deliberately in order to get away from it all. But the truth was that they were on their way back from a raid on Merseyside, keeping over the sea. Unfortunately for them, they mistook the Bristol Channel for the English Channel and thought they were flying over northern France when they were over Somerset.

The uncensored story of the Junkers that landed at Lulsgate was told by 'Simon' in the *Bristol Evening World* for Monday 26 August 1945.

> **When even the hose froze . . .**
>
> Sub-zero temperatures during the raids on Bristol in the early part of 1941 made the already difficult task of fire-fighting almost impossible. Water turned to ice in the main pipes and even in the firemen's hoses. Appliances such as this water tower became clogged with ice and seized up, and the suffering firemen had to use reservoirs, tanks and swimming pools, but these were very soon exhausted. In the face of all these difficulties and the constant danger, firemen in Bristol performed countless miracles of damage limitation and rescue work.

AMONG THE SURVIVORS, A STUFFED GIRAFFE . . .

The museum was ruined – though it was recalled that one of the exhibits, a stuffed giraffe, was still standing the following morning, unharmed among the ruins. Parts of the University buildings also suffered, the most serious damage occurring to the Great Hall, which was reduced to a shell, and its fine hammer-beam roof destroyed.

Thousands of houses were damaged. In comparison with other urban areas hit by the Luftwaffe, Bristol was a sprawling city where targets were less densely packed, but all the same the loss of life was very high – generally much greater than the first official figures released at the time. The final death toll for this first fire-blitz on Bristol was 207, and 187 people were seriously injured.

The immediate clearing up and search for survivors took several days. In almost all parts of the city electricity was reconnected within four days of the disruption of supply. More than 300 unexploded, or suspected, bombs remained to be investigated and dealt with.

Some remains were still hot to the touch for a day or more after the raid. One man recalled how he returned several days later to what had been his offices, and the safes were hauled out of the ruins and opened. The books inside were 'in perfect order, but the impact of the fresh air turned the contents to ashes immediately.' And in the aftermath of Bristol's first blitz there were still flashes of grim humour; the notice on a collapsing wall: 'Stick no bills' and the chalked sign outside a baker's shop: 'Hitler has paid us a visit – why don't you?'

The German press announced: 'As a distribution centre and important railway junction Bristol has been wiped out.' Although this was very far from the truth, Bristol had been subjected to a great ordeal. But the Germans' own photographic evidence, following the raid, confirmed that, despite the considerable damage done, the city was far from being made non-operational. Bristol, the centre that the enemy had claimed to be 'wiped out', was revisited twice within a fortnight with the express intention of substantiating the Germans' claim.

The next attack, on the evening of 2 December, was much more scattered in character than the first major assault. On this occasion bombs fell in many districts of the city. The attack by 121 aircraft began shortly after 6pm, and adopted the now established procedure of dropping flares and incendiaries followed by high-explosive bombs. Visibility was bad, and two thick layers of cloud were reported over the area that night – factors which may well have accounted for the widespread bombing that followed. Residential property again suffered severely, and there was again much damage and destruction to churches and business premises. Within an hour of the beginning of the raid more than fifty fires had been started – a figure which increased to 167 by the end of this five-hour onslaught. More than 22,000 incendiaries were dropped together with 120 tons of high-explosive bombs. Gas, water and electricity were again disrupted, and Temple Meads station was hit once again, blocking some suburban lines.

When the Luftwaffe returned four nights later, on 6 December, Temple Meads was selected yet again for attention, and lines were again blocked. There were two direct hits on trains – the train for Salisbury and three coaches standing at No. 2 platform. This raid, the largest night-time Luftwaffe activity on this date, involved about 60 aircraft in an attack which began around 6.30pm and ended more than four hours later. Though the bomb-loads were on this occasion smaller – 76 tons of high-explosives and 5,000+ incendiaries – the damage was severe in some areas, causing considerable interruption to war production when two power stations were put out of action. Several factories were demolished or badly damaged, including British Oxygen's works and Parnall's aircraft works at Barton Hill. Residential property took the heaviest pounding, especially in the Knowle and St George divisions. In these two December attacks more than 200 people were killed and several hundred injured.

A brief respite came to Bristol for, apart from a minor raid on 11 December, the rest of the year passed out without further incident. For many Bristolians in that exceptionally cold winter, the greatest hardship of those weeks was the shortage of coal. The new year, 1941, was only just entered when the Luftwaffe came back in force on the evening of 3 January – one of the coldest nights of the winter. In a dusk-to-dawn raid two waves of Luftwaffe bombers attacked. The first wave, from about 6.30pm until gone half-past midnight, showered incendiaries mainly along a line running westwards from Temple Meads. Platforms 9 and 12 were set ablaze, as were buildings around. A second large wave attacked an hour later, an attack which lasted until almost 6am. In addition to the damage at Temple Meads and its vicinity, the raid as a whole inflicted severe damage to the City Docks, Bridge Street, High Street, and many other streets. One of the oldest churches in the city, St Augustine's, was burnt out, as was the Guildhall. Commercial and residential properties were destroyed. 2,500 houses in all were damaged that night.

Fighting the blazes in this, Bristol's longest raid to date, had to be conducted under extreme conditions. Water froze; huge icicles hung on buildings, and sheets of ice formed on the roads. So intense was the cold that spray froze on the fireman's helmets and clothing, and the men themselves suffered from frostbite. Yet they fought on, succeeding in staunching fire after fire, despite hosepipes turning into solid tubes when, as happened frequently that night, the water pressure dropped.

The final casualty figures for this raid show that 149 people were killed, and 133 were seriously injured. From this raid until the middle of March 1941 Bristol itself had something of a respite, though Luftwaffe bombers still paid some attention to the area, but mainly to the docks at Avonmouth. The next major attack upon Bristol was scheduled for the night of 16 March. It was to prove Bristol's worst raid of all – 'a night of horror and murder', as one account expressed the consequences of this raid in which 257 were killed and 391 injured.

'A NIGHT OF HORROR AND MURDER . . .'

Targets for this raid were marked by the Luftwaffe as being the west central and south-west portions of the city, together with the docks and installations at Avonmouth. In the event, bombs hit every part of Bristol, and residential and shopping areas were badly affected. Though fires were started in the docks, no major damage was inflicted.

Over 100 bombers attacked Bristol itself, another 50+ concentrated upon Avonmouth. Railways and roads were mauled, factories were damaged, as was Bristol General Hospital. Two public shelters received direct hits, in one of which 25 people were killed. Three hundred people sheltering in the crypt of

The non-stop press

'It can now be revealed that *The Western Daily Press* and *Bristol Mirror* office, Baldwin Street, was blasted by bombs that fell in a recent raid', according to a report in *The Western Daily Press* on 15 April 1941.

The bombing took place on 11 April, and the WDP gave a vivid description. 'Luckily our night staff were in the ground floor shelter at the time and were unhurt, but even so they had a very unpleasant time as the "swish-crump" of explosives mingled with crashes as the windows and doors were smashed in and the heavy plaster of the ceilings collapsed. The entire building quivered and shook.

Still, although many of our machines were covered with debris . . . the paper came out as usual as a single sheet. But work could not start until dawn, because of the damage to the roof and blackout . . .

Nearly every room was piled high with broken plaster, shattered window frames and black-out material, overturned tables, chairs and bookcases. Our valuable, irreplaceable books, files and collections of cuttings were buried under the wreckage. Wooden partition walls had suffered, and electric light fittings torn out – although most of the lights were still working.

Members of the entire staff . . . took off their coats and got to work cleaning up . . . They succeeded very well, although for several nights it was impossible to print the paper here . . .'

St Michael's escaped although the church itself was set on fire. In the crypt of St Barnabas's church 25 people perished. Damage from more than 100 tons of high-explosive – between 600 and 700 individual bombs – was widespread, the centre of the city suffering the greatest destruction. Water mains and electricity cables were cut and about 100 gas mains hit. About 6,000 houses were damaged in this raid, the most disastrous to date.

At the end of the month the raiders returned to Avonmouth when, in a sharp attack lasting under two hours, oil tanks were set ablaze, burning furiously. In a return raid upon Avonmouth early in April, 'The whole of Bristol was illuminated by a large number of "chandelier" flares, 15 of which were counted in the air at one time.' The reinforced A.A. defences, however, succeeded this time in driving away most of the raiders. But they could not prevent the attacking raiders from penetrating Bristol on the night of 11 April, which was Good Friday.

Again, the Germans mounted a two-phase attack in which altogether 150 Luftwaffe crews reported having located and bombed Bristol. The first phase, starting shortly after 10pm, concentrated bomb-drops along a line from the city centre (Bristol Bridge) out towards Horfield. The second phase, beginning shortly after midnight and ending almost four hours later, produced a more erratic pattern of hits. Mainly concentrated on the southern districts of the city, this phase was by far the more serious of the two in the widespread destruction it produced. Among the many fires which blazed that night was one in Cheltenham Road which burned out the Public Library there and a girls' school opposite. One famous Bristol building also burned out was the Coliseum, the one-time variety theatre in Park Row.

The number who died as a result of the Good Friday bombing was 180, with 146 seriously wounded.

Satan – the Superbomb

Satan, twice as tall as a man and weighing 4,000lb, plummeted from the bomb rack of a Nazi raider over Knowle during a dusk-to-dawn attack on Bristol in January 1941.

Satan, as the monster bomb was later christened, did not explode. In the end it was to serve a far different purpose from that planned by the Germans.

It narrowly missed the houses in Beckington Road and dug itself deep beneath the pavement. Its weight took it nearly 30ft down where it completely vanished from view.

Here 4,000lb of explosives that could have blown most of Beckington Road and its residents sky high, stayed hidden for three years.

A small amount of debris from a damaged garden wall was cleared away from what had been reported as a small exploded bomb. People walked up and down the street about their daily business little realising that Satan was just beneath their feet.

It was a chance remark at a meeting of special constables being instructed on how to report blitz incidents that led to Satan being discovered. Chief Inspector Walter Hill explained that the presence of a metal ring at the scene might well be the detached part of an unexploded bomb.

His remark rang a bell with one Special in his audience. The man jumped to his feet and said he had found a ring at the scene of a bomb incident in Beckington Road three years previously and still had it at his home.

The surprised folk of Beckington Road were asked to leave their houses and the Army bomb disposal men got busy. The paving slabs were lifted to reveal a gaping hole from which Satan was hauled up on chains rigged from steel legs.

Satan was taken by an Army lorry to a site beyond South Liberty Lane and harmlessly detonated after the occupants of all the houses on the route taken were evacuated.

Later Satan, with his teeth drawn, rode through London in the big Victory parade as a prize exhibit.

CHURCHILL TOURS THE CITY

That night the Prime Minister was travelling by special train to Bristol from London, in the company of John Winant, the American Ambassasdor, and Robert Menzies, the Australian Prime Minister. Churchill, as Chancellor of the University of Bristol, was due to confer upon them honorary degrees on the following day. His train stayed overnight in a siding on the outskirts of the city, in open country, from where he and his fellow-passengers could see and hear the raid as it proceeded. The train pulled into Bristol early next morning, just hours after the raid had ended, and Churchill toured the stricken parts of the city, some of them still smouldering, while the ARP Services were still at work and people were still being dug out of the ruined buildings. Later, prior to the award ceremony at the University, he took sherry with his guests and other dignitaries in a University room which adjoined the burned-out Coliseum.

Obviously much moved by the devastation he had witnessed, and by meeting people whose homes had just been destroyed, Churchill's speech at the ceremony gave encouragement to many:

> Here we gather in academic robes and go through ceremonials and repeat formulas – here in battered Bristol, with the scars of new attacks upon it. Many of those here today have been all night at their posts and all have been under the fire of the enemy, under heavy and protracted bombardment. That you should gather in this way is a mark of fortitude and phlegm, of a courage and detachment from material affairs worthy of all that we have learned to believe of ancient Rome . . .

'Good Old Winnie!'

After receiving his Honorary Degree from Winston Churchill at Bristol University the American Ambassador, John Winant, wrote to President Roosevelt about what he had seen that day: 'the Prime Minister arrives . . . unannounced, is taken to the most seriously bombed area, leaves his car and starts walking through the streets without guards. Before long, crowds of people flock about him and people call "Good old Winnie!", "You'll never let us down!"' Nobody in Bristol had got any sleep that night, and people were still shaken by the bombing, but within two hours of Churchill's arrival, 'the whole town was back on its feet again and cheering.' One of his aides noted that he got back into his train with tears in his eyes and hid behind his newspaper.

The terror at Broadmead, where the last German bomb to fall on Bristol in 1942 was dropped without warning on 28 August, killing 45 people

In the weeks succeeding the Good Friday raid, there followed minor skirmishes over the Bristol area, the most serious of which – classified officially as a 'medium' raid – occurred on 8 May. Several scores of fires were started, the worst being at Ashton Gate where a timber yard and buildings belonging to the Bristol Motor Company were set ablaze.

Counting the cost . . .

Air Raid Alerts	548
Raids	77
including major raids	6
High explosive bombs (tons)	919
Persons killed	1299
seriously injured	1303
rescued alive from debris	697
Bodies recovered from debris	833
Buildings damaged	89,080
including houses destroyed	81,830
or later demolished	3000+

Both the Bristol Royal Infirmary and the Bristol Eye Hospital were damaged, as were some 1,000 houses, where died most of the 20 killed in the raid. Other small raids followed, for example, on 12 June when parachute mines fell upon the city for the first time. Seventy houses around Victoria Park were completely wrecked, and there were 16 fatal casualties. From this point onwards, the summer of 1941 proved to be quiet. The skies above Bristol were very seldom invaded by Luftwaffe raiders – a welcome state of affairs which persisted well in 1942. In general, bombing was becoming far more infrequent, and the casualties fewer. Then happened one of those single events which shocked people at the time perhaps even more than the concentrated Blitz to which the entire population had been subjected – more shocking, perhaps, because of its isolation carried with it the sense of the randomness of fate.

At 9.20am on 28 August 1942 a single German fighter-bomber passed over the city at a height of 20,000 feet and released a single 500lb high-explosive bomb. It struck Broad Weir, close to the junction of Philadelphia Street. Within the impact area were three buses loaded with passengers, including many women and children on holiday. The buses were set on fire instantaneously. 'In a second,' as one report recorded the year after the war's end, 'they were like blazing torches, and so fierce were the flames that rescue work was well-nigh impossible.' The toll of dead from this incident was 45, twenty of whom were among those trapped inside the buses.

The sense of local outrage aroused, as MacInnes expresses it, 'a storm of bitter and almost hysterical protest.' The bomb which caused this anguish was the last to fall on Bristol in 1942.

Despite claims to the contrary made by the German propaganda machine, there were no raids on Bristol throughout 1943. In 1944 there was a single raiding incident at a time when Bristol and Avonmouth were important assembly-points for troops, landing-craft, and support material in preparation for the D-Day invasion of Normandy. A single casualty, a serviceman at a searchlight post, resulted from Bristol's last raid on 15 May.

South Wales faces the enemy

After the collapse of France in June 1940 it was only a matter of time before the industrial areas of South Wales would be attacked. From France it was an easy flight to reach these targets. Other parts of the Principality suffered in the Blitz, but space has limited this report to the bombings of Swansea, Cardiff and one major raid on Pembroke Docks.

In the early stages of the air attack on Britain no place was visited more frequently than Wales, which had over 50 alerts in a month after the first which occurred at 11.55pm on 19 June 1940. Yet no prolonged attack was mounted until September 1940.

SWANSEA – COMMUNITY OF COURAGE

Then, on 1 September, Swansea was bombed by waves of aircraft dropping thousands of incendiaries followed by high explosives, and Wales heard and felt the effects of a concentrated attack on a city. This was to reach a crescendo in the raids on three successive nights of 19, 20, and 21 February 1941.

Snow had fallen during 19 February, and this gave a softness to the scene which was to be shattered by the events of the night. Shortly after seven in the evening the first aircraft to arrive dropped flares which floodlit the city. These were followed almost immediately by incendiaries. These fell not only on the city but on the surrounding hills. An eyewitness reports bringing his family from the safety of the shelter to see the beautiful effect of the incendiaries scattered in the snow on Kilvey Hill, making it look like a giant birthday cake with candles ablaze. But in the city there was not time for such romantic visions as the civil defence services battled to save lives and property. On this first night Swansea was bombed for five hours and it was after midnight before the last raiders left. The attack was unusual because there were alternate waves of incendiaries and high explosive bombs. The normal attack method was to begin with incendiaries to start large fires and then for other bombers to home in on these fires and drop their high explosive loads on these targets. This meant that, for a period, the defenders could tackle the fires in some degree of safety. By mixing incendiaries and high explosive bombing the danger to, and destruction of, vital services were both increased.

In the centre of town a large, unexploded bomb lay in a huge hole it had made opposite the old Bovega Inn and this meant that Castle Street, Temple Street and Castle Bailey were closed off. It was not until the 21st that a bomb disposal squad could begin the task of removing it. They had raised it to the road level when it exploded and killed all six of the team.

The following night the raiders were back and further damage was inflicted on the town. But the worst night of destruction was Friday night, 21 February. The previous two nights had created so much damage that the defence services were struggling under an immense burden. Many water mains had been damaged and some routes through the city were impassable because of debris or the danger of unexploded bombs. Gas escaping from mains or damaged properties presented a further hazard with the likelihood of explosions. As a result, desperated decisions had to be made about where scarce resources should be deployed. Some parts of town were treated as evacuated areas and all except a few firewatchers were withdrawn. In some residential areas the defenders had to leave local citizens to fend for themselves, and there were many reports of householders striving manfully to deal both with incendiaries which had fallen in their area and with the resulting fires. At daylight Swansea's roads were covered in thousands of little piles of sand which marked the spot under which another incendiary lay. Everyone had their own raid stories. One group of citizens, attempting to tackle an incendiary blaze in a house, were assailed by the delicious aroma of stew. The heat had cooked a pan of vegetables prepared for a meal.

Even the rats left town

Mrs Rosalind Young of Swansea vividly recalls hiding in her garden as rats in their thousands made their way out of the blitzed town centre to parkland on the outskirts.

'There was one huge, black mass stretched right across the road,' she told a local reporter.* 'The noise of the squeaking was deafening. I was absolutely petrified – but I stayed behind the garden wall until they had all gone.'

'They had nothing in town because it was all flattened. It was just like the Pied Piper of Hamlyn,' she added.

**South Wales Evening Post*

The large covered market in Swansea, completely rebuilt between the two World Wars, was wrecked during the Blitz. Temporary arrangements were made for the duration, but now a fine modern building stands on this site

Another group decided to make some tea as there was a lull in the raid. The raid started up again and they took to the shelter in the cellar. They were horrified to hear the whistle of a bomb directly above them and threw themselves down to minimise the blast effect, only to realise that it was the sound of the whistling kettle.

At one time it seemed as if the whole town were ablaze, and further high explosive bombs were crashing into the flames, scattering red hot debris in all directions. The glow from the fires was visible from the Devon coast. The fire in the town centre spread rapidly until it became one huge blaze over an area of about a mile square. Castle Street to Lower Oxford Street was one long, continuous line of fire and it was impossible for the fire-fighters to approach the heart of the conflagration. All the big stores in Temple Street were alight and the fine old market became a roaring furnace. Fire-fighters endeavoured to surround the fire, and from slender ladders and roofs attempted to contain the fire within their boundary. Sometimes fires started behind them, either caused by further incendiaries or flaming materials carried high into the air which dropped on other buildings. These had to be dealt with as a matter of urgency lest the firemen become engulfed in the spreading inferno.

Temporary hoses run out from the North and South Docks were continually being ripped by high explosive splinters and so firemen would suddenly find the water supply failing at crucial moments, placing other buildings and sometimes their own lives in danger. So much water was drawn from the North Dock that the level in the dock fell by 11 feet. Near the New Cut Bridge, linking the docks to the town a bomb had wrecked an oil and grease store, and a trail of burning oil covering the road made it a river of flame. Damage to property was extensive. The town's shopping centre was completely wiped out, including the market. From Castle Street to the Union Street corner of Oxford Street was laid waste. No fewer than 282 houses were demolished and over eleven thousand severely damaged. Schools that were destroyed or severely damaged were: Brynhyfdryd, Brynmill, Cwm, Danygraig, Dyfatty, Hafod, Plasmarl, St Thomas, St Joseph's Nursery School, The Grammar School for Boys, Dynevor Secondary School for Boys, Delabeche Secondary School for Girls, Glanmor Secondary School for Boys and the Technical College. This catalogue in itself shows how widespread was the attack on the city. Among the churches lost was St Mary's, regarded as the city's mother church. It dated back to 1631. It had been substantially rebuilt in 1895, but all the ancient monuments had been carefully preserved. Everything was destroyed. Other religious establishments which were damaged or destroyed included Holy Trinity, Trinity (Welsh C.M) Chapel, Capel Gomer, the Wesley Chapel, Ebenezer Chapel and the Jewish Synagogue. One department of the General and Eye Hospital was put out of action. The Picture House Cinema was gutted. The Food Control Headquarters in Rutland Street and the BBC Studios in Alexandra Road were struck. No aspect of city life escaped during those nights.

Even the rats left Swansea. A huge, black mass of them stretching across the Sketty Road, ran towards Singleton Park one night. An eye-witness described how she hid behind a garden wall as thousands of rats scampered along. The noise of their squeaking was terrifying.

On Saturday morning a grim picture was revealed. Most of the main traffic routes were blocked by huge, gaping craters; some big enough to take a double decker bus. Fallen debris presented a hazard in all quarters – in others there was the threat of an unexploded bomb. No fewer than 57 public water mains had been damaged. Yet within a fortnight 44 of these had been repaired. Many of the townspeople had not been to bed for three nights. Civilians wandered the streets, searching for their homes, relatives, or even family pets abandoned in the rush to public shelters. Many carried pathetic bundles of belongings salvaged from the wreckage of their homes.

Blackened firemen and the Civil Defence services personnel remained on duty. A pall of smoke hung over the city. The three nights of raiding, the climax of the enemy's bombing of the city, had claimed a total of 230 lives with more than that number of persons reported seriously injured.

The dislocation of the city was severe. Telephones were cut off. Over 6,500 people were homeless and 171 food shops (among a total of 396) had been destroyed, not including the many stalls lost in the market. There was an acute problem in making arrangements to feed people. Gas and water had been cut off in many of the homes which still stood.

The Town Clerk and ARP Controller later reported to the Town Council on the situation that emerged that Saturday morning. Part of his report states:

> Dangerous buildings required immediate attention; the blitzed area had to be cordoned; rescues still had to go on; the dead had to be identified and buried; thousands of enquiries had to be answered.
>
> That was the position at the Civic Centre at nine o'clock on the Saturday morning. It just wanted a match to cause panic and consternation, and to put everything in hopeless muddle and disorder.
>
> During the raids, although the town outside was burning, everything in the Control Room was kept on a level keel. There was good order and perfect coolness. Yet on those three nights no fewer than 8,000 messages were dealt with, and 561 incidents reported – all without a single complaint.
>
> We foresaw there was a probability of trouble arising in the food supply. In the early hours of the morning, my ARP Officer telephoned through to the War Room at Cardiff for mobile canteens. The result was that soon after nine o'clock on Saturday morning 16 mobile canteens were in operation in the town.
>
> Then there were the homeless. Rest centres had to be opened. We also needed reinforcements for rescue work and the Military had to be called in.
>
> On top of this the electric light in the building failed; the telephones failed, but fortunately we had our alternative plans for both emergencies.

A conference was held at 11am. The report continues:

> The feeding of the population was vital. An official (Mr Gealer) of the Ministry of Food, was in the Control Room as early as 2.30 in the morning, and as the Food Office and all the records had gone we decided to establish an office in the Civic Centre. Many of the food traders and catering establishments had lost their premises. The dislocation of the water and gas services prevented the public from cooking. Bakers could not operate, or could only do so in a very small way by hand. So with the assistance of the Area Bread Officer 10,000 loaves were rushed into the town on Saturday morning.
>
> Two special cafes were opened which provided nearly two thousand meals a day. The mobile canteens were also out in the streets. We experienced difficulty in getting boiling water, but a butcher placed his boilers at the disposal of those loading the vans. Volunteers from the Food Office stoked the boilers in the Guildhall to ensure a constant supply of hot water for the canteens which were sent to districts where they were most needed. In addition we were able to obtain ten tons of cigarettes which were distributed to the various Services which were still valiantly doing their duty.
>
> From the 'blood, sweat and toil' of the triple bombardment, almost fantastic in its ferocity and effect, one feature emerged – clearly and proudly – the devotion and heroism of a people who seemed to be brought closely together by a common peril. Swansea was a community of courage. All were neighbours; there were no strangers within its battered gates. Swansea was scarred and stricken, but its spirit shone throughout with a glorious light, challenging the fury of the flames which destroyed the town centre. Buildings tottered, as if some strange visitation or earthquake had descended the slopes of Abertawe, but the people, although dazed, stood magnificently firm and steadfast.

This eloquent record of bravery, combined with details of the organisational problems that had to be overcome, shows clearly how the Blitz affected the whole community.

'Have you seen my two little sisters?'

February 1941

Swansea had three nights of hell. Today was Sunday. Wisps of smoke drifted up to the sky – as from an altar – and an eerie silence hung over an uninhabitable place. The 'Blitz' of three weeks ago seemed like only a feeble rehearsal. Today Swansea stands as a monument to the beastliness of war . . .

But the most pitiful sight of all was the little children, red eyed, walking from the ruins of their homes towards the sanctuaries in the town centre. Sanctuaries? Graveyards – poor pitiful little wretches. There's no one to take care of them. No one ever mentioned evacuating them to safety in their own country. They will have to suffer and to die . . .

In a school in town [a child] sat in the corridor watching the other children coming in. As they did so the child – a 10-year-old girl – greeted them thus, 'Have you seen them?' She kept on like this all morning. No one could comfort her because they all knew her two sisters were dead. 'Have you seen my two little sisters?' . . .

From: Aneurin ap Talfan-Davies, *Dyddiau'r Ceiigo Rhedyn* [The Locust Years], 1941 translated by Alan Rees.

There were many acts of gallantry, but one sustained effort over the whole three night period, gained King's Scout, Jack Evans, aged 19, the Bronze Cross which is known as the Scout's VC. On 19 February, the first of the three nights of bombing, he reported at a wardens' post where, despite a near miss by a high explosive bomb which severely damaged the building, he took charge of the telephone. The next night he tackled numerous incendiaries and assisted in dangerous rescue work, beside rendering first aid to the wounded. He found one small street with small fires everywhere. He climbed onto burning roofs and put out many fires with sand and water from the water tanks of the houses – despite the constant danger of further bombs. A report said: 'He had the strength of ten men, and encouraged the people all the time, acting as an inspiration to all. The Boy Scout movement is to be thanked for the training that turns out such citizens.'

There is still some dispute about the reason why the anti-aircraft guns ceased firing for a period on the Friday evening. Some reports suggest that it was to allow night fighter patrols to get among the bombers. Others claim that it was due to the fact that the control centre was temporarily put out of action by the bombing. Whichever it was, it meant the enemy planes were given the freedom to select their targets with ease. Some claim that the massive damage to the centre of town would not have occurred had the guns kept firing. Certainly, with the good visibility available that night, the city, without the defence of its guns, must have seemed a plum ripe for the picking to the enemy airmen.

PEMBROKE – 'A RING OF FIRE'

Early in the war, on 19 August 1940, an enemy aircraft carried out a successful daylight raid on the oil tanks at Pennar on the edge of Pembroke Docks. It dropped several bombs, one of which hit a tank and immediately set it on fire. This was the start of the biggest fire in Britain caused by raiders up till that point in the war. Over 600 firemen were involved in fighting the fire which burned for almost three weeks. Five Cardiff fire-fighters were killed when huge tongues of flames engulfed them and they were burnt alive as they fought to contain the conflagration.

The tanks were clustered on the top of a hill and were visible for miles. Eight of the sixteen tanks, each with a capacity of 12,000 tons, were destroyed. Thick clouds of smoke rose thousands of feet into the air day after day.

Initially it seemed that nothing could save the whole complex from being engulfed. Pembroke lived in a perpetual twilight as the dark, acrid smoke lay over it like a smelly blanket. Everything was spattered with oil droplets and as far afield as twenty miles crops were ruined by this thick, gluey rain. Luckily the wind directed the thickest smoke away from the town itself or those without protection might have suffocated.

Looking surprisingly cheerful, this bombed-out Swansea family rescue a few treasured possessions from the wreckage of their home

A deep moat surrounded the tanks. This became filled with oil which then ignited, forming a ring of fire which had to be crossed to get at the tanks themselves. Lengths of hose were run down to the sea and trailer pumps used to lift the sea water to attack the fire. This was very effective while the tide was high, but when it went out it was impossible for the pumps to be moved onto the mudflats and the frustrated firemen were left to watch for four hours at a time as the fire regained its hold on areas that they had won back earlier at such cost.

Foam was used, but without success. A tank was deliberately blown up in the hope of smothering the flames; still the fire raged. The enemy pilots were trying to create more havoc by machine-gunning the firemen and bombing more tanks. Luckily only one fireman was wounded in these raids. Forty Bristol firemen, brought in to assist local brigades, had a fantastic escape when their billet, the Temperance Hall, received a direct hit which wrecked part of it. But not one of them was injured.

Among gallantry awards made as a result of the bravery shown in fighting this fire there were no fewer than *thirteen* George Medals.

CARDIFF'S 'NEW YEAR GIFT'

It was not until the tenth raid on Cardiff, on 9 July 1940, that the first fatalities occurred when a lone bomber scored a direct hit on the SS *San Fillipe* in the docks. Men were killed in the hold, where the bomb exploded, and on the decks.

There followed six months of 'hit and run' bombing before the night of the huge attack which became known as 'The Luftwaffe's New Year Gift' on 2 January 1941. This raid began at 6.37 in the evening and the 'raiders passed' message was not received until 4.50 the next morning. There was a full moon and freezing temperatures. As usual, the raid began with showers of incendiary bombs and fires began blazing throughout the city. On that night there were 170 fire calls.,

Among the first buildings to be hit were a warehouse, a school, a rubber works and a paint works. Soon these were joined by Peacock's Bazaar in Queen Street and the Corporation Transport Offices in Paradise Place; both were completely destroyed.

Shortly after 7pm the Grangetown area was hit by high explosive bombs. A private shelter received a direct hit and many were killed inside. Such was the destruction that the exact number has never been established. At the Western end of the city, Wembley Road, Ninian Park Road and Neville Road were hit by high explosive bombs. The next morning in Neville Road part of a motor car could be seen hanging from a lamp standard. Seven people died in this street alone. In Blackstone Street a group of people who had been attending a funeral were sheltering in a house which was hit and almost all of them were killed.

At about 8pm Llandaff Cathedral was badly damaged when a parachute mine exploded in the churchyard. But on some allotments off Caerphilly Road a group of civilians had an extremely lucky escape. They thought they had located part of an enemy bomber and were pulling it from its crater when somoene realised that they were dealing with an unexploded parachute mine! The group dispersed at some speed . . .

Another parachute mine caused extensive damage at Cardiff Arms Park. It made a crater fifty feet in diameter and nearly fourteen feet deep. The Lyne grandstand lost its roof and most of the seating was destroyed.

In that raid 95 houses were totally destroyed and another 233 damaged so badly they had to be demolished. A total of 165 people died and 168 were seriously injured.

This was by far the worst single raid on Cardiff, but the city continued to receive regular attention from the Luftwaffe. On 4 March there was a raid which was centred on the docks. The north side of Roath Dock and the Mountstuart dry dock were both struck, as was the Spillers grain silo. On 30 April, six parachute mines caused extensive damage in the Riverside, Wyverne Road and Cathays areas. Thirty-three people were killed. In one house in Wyverne Road two parents and their eight children all lost their lives as a parachute mine landed within yards of their Anderson shelter. This was probably the worst raid on the city as far as residential destruction was concerned.

As late in the war as 18 May 1943, Cardiff was still under attack. In a short raid lasting no more than 41 minutes, about 60 high-explosive bombs and parachute mines were unleashed on the city. Severe damage was caused in the docks area and it probably produced more industrial damage than most of the previous raids put together. It seemed that at last the Germans were able to target their bombs with more accuracy in order to affect the war effort. But in fact, it was the last raid the city was to receive.

Wales suffered severely in the Blitz, as did other parts of Britain. And like other areas, the damage was caused mainly to people and properties not immediately involved in the war effort. However, if the intention was to terrorise the civilian population into submission, the result among the close communities of South Wales, as one reads the reports and records of the time, was in fact to bolster resistance and firm resolve.

Drinks all round

Lucky people in Swansea had drinks on the house when a bomb shattered the off-licence building under which they had taken shelter. When liquid started to flood into the cellar they at first thought it was water. Then someone tasted it and discovered that it was a mixture of wine and spirits.

Everyone grabbed a container of some kind. 'We were all quite tipsy when they came out to get us out,' said one survivor.

Counting the cost . . .

	Killed	Seriously Injured
Swansea	387	412
Cardiff	355	502
Newport	51	63
Glamorgan	82	120
Pembrokeshire	45	42
Monmouthshire	25	36
Denbighshire	18	10
Carmarthenshire	14	13
Caernarvonshire	5	14
Flintshire	3	6
Anglesey	–	3
Totals	985	1,221

Merseyside: the port they nearly destroyed

Early raids on Merseyside

Sunday 28 July 1940: first bombs in the Merseyside region fell on a searchlight post at Altaar and on Thurstaston, Lely and Neston on the Wirral. The craters in the fields attracted crowds of the curious.

Thursday 8 August 1940: six bombs fell at Preston, Birkenhead: one of them killed Joanna Mandale, a domestic servant. She was the first of the 3,875 people killed by air attacks on Merseyside.

Friday 9 August 1940: the Wirral was once again under attack. Seven bombs fell on Wallasey, damaging houses and a railway embankment with 32 casualties, including four killed and four seriously injured.

Saturday 17 August 1940: the first bombs to fall on Liverpool, landing on the Dock Road and damaging the Overhead Railway and a corn silo.

Monday 19 August 1940: the first of the thousands of incendiaries fell at Eaton Road, West Derby and Norris Green. Most fell in open spaces but some slightly damaged the Robert Davies Nursing Home.

Wednesday 28 August 1940: the first of four successive nights of bombing. These have been described officially as 'the first major night attack on the United Kingdom'. London had been bombed mainly by daylight, but this was a change of tactics. In the first of these attacks incendiaries fell on Fulwood Park and Grossendale with high explosives falling on West Derby, Mersey Road and Mossley Hill. The following night at Bootle incendiaries fell on Hawthorne Road Gas Works. On the 30th there was a small raid, with incendiaries, on the Docks and Mill Road Hospital, and high explosive on Grafton Street, Brodie Avenue, and Wallasey High School for Girls.

Saturday 31 August 1940: the first of a large number of serious raids. Liverpool had 100 fires, 23 people died, and 86 were injured. Cleveland Square was badly damaged and the Custom House set on fire. Other fires at the Dingle oil jetty, and houses damaged in Edge Lane. Bootle bombed and Wallasey Town Hall and its valuable organ destroyed.

September 1940: Merseyside not affected directly by day but 20 night raids, often short and sharp. Some were reconnaissance, others minelaying in Liverpool Bay. A raid on 18 September hit Walton Gaol; 21 bodies were recovered. The Governor insisted that there should be 22 prisoners. One was thought to have escaped. He hadn't. His body was found under rubble in 1951 – eleven years later.

October 1940: a month of 15 relatively light raids.

November 1940 will be remembered as the date of Merseyside's first blitz, although there was a series of smaller raids earlier in the month.

On seven successive nights in May 1941 the Luftwaffe heavily attacked Merseyside, and came close to putting its docks out of action. An eighth attack might well have succeeded, but – inexplicably – it never came. Though severely damaged, with many of its berths blocked and thousands of tons of shipping sunk, Britain's major port of the day continued to handle the cargoes the nation needed.

Merseyside had to endure 68 Luftwaffe attacks between its first on 28 July 1940 and its last on 9 August 1942. Eight of these were 'major' attacks by the German definition of one in which more than 100 tons of high explosive were released on a single target area. Of other British centres, only Birmingham and Plymouth were also subjected to eight major attacks, while Bristol suffered six and Glasgow five. Although London had 71 major raids, and was hit by 18,800 tons of high explosives, the 1,957 tons dropped on the much smaller area of Merseyside caused destruction that was, by comparison, more extensive and damaging to the war effort. A few hundred more tons of high explosive could have crippled the port – or some thousands more incendiaries, since it was these fire-raising devices that accounted for so much of the damage.

Merseyside's eight 'major' attacks occurred on the nights of Thursday 28 November 1940 – Friday 20 December and Saturday 21 December 1940 – Wednesday 12 March – Saturday 26 April –

A Merseyside family gazes on the wreckage of what was their home

Friday 2 May – Saturday 3 May – and Wednesday 7 May 1941.

In the first major attack, on 28 November 1940, 324 aircraft of *Luftflotten 2 & 3* dropped 356 tons of high explosive bombs and 30,960 incendiaries. The raid would have been even heavier, but 48 aircraft attacked alternative targets and 18 aborted. The sirens sounded (for the 58th time) at 7.23pm. The attack started with flares and did not end until 3.15am. The main raid lasted from 7.30pm to 10pm. The casualties were: 264 people killed and 62 seriously injured.

This raid was often referred to as the Night of the Land Mines, because the high explosives included 30 'land-mines' (which were actually adapted sea mines). These were designed to descend by parachute at 40mph and explode on impact, causing considerable damage from blast. On explosion they produced a characteristic earth-shaking thump, unlike the sound of a bomb. People in shelters soon learned to tell the difference.

One peculiar feature of this raid was the lack of 'incidents' occurring in the centre of the city. This may have been due to the variable cloud cover, which made it difficult for aircrews to find their target and to see it when located. Many crews bombed by dead reckoning, without seeing the ground; others aimed at fires or targets glimpsed through gaps in the clouds. Although they later claimed much damage, the docks were little affected. Several serious fires were caused, as well as great damage to houses, water and gas mains, electric cables, telephones, tram wires, and sewers. Only two instances of critical damage to industrial buildings were reported.

The suburbs sustained most damage, especially at the south end: Allerton, Childwall, Wavertree, Woolton, Edge Hill, Mossley Hill and Garston. Dogs escaped when Stanley Greyhound Track was hit, but only one of the dogs was killed.

The casualties were high. Just before 2am there occurred what Churchill later described as 'the worst single incident of the war'. Three hundred people were sheltering in the basement of the Junior Technical College in Durning Road. Apart from the regulars, there were others from nearby shelters already damaged, and passengers from two passing trams. The 3-storey building was hit by a parachute mine which crashed down into the basement, where the boilers exploded and fire broke out. The basement started to flood from a burst water main. A middle-aged warden behaved heroically in preventing panic and helping people from the wreckage. The final casualty list included 164 dead and 96 injured. Only a couple of dozen were uninjured out of 290. This was an incident talked about for years afterwards and is still remembered locally five decades later.

THE CHRISTMAS BLITZES

In September, October, and November, Merseyside had 44 raids, averaging one almost every other night, but none as severe as the series known as 'The Christmas Blitzes'. December 1940 had opened quietly enough with a single aircraft over Liverpool on Sunday 1 December, probably to check the damage caused the previous Thursday; and on Wednesday 11 December there had been a minor attack with incidents at Widnes. Merseyside was looking forward to its second wartime Christmas.

On Friday 20 December the sirens sounded at 6.30pm and the all clear was not sounded until 4.am next morning. A total of 205 aircraft from the Channel Islands, Fécamp, and Dieppe flew in eight main waves over the region, releasing 205 tons of high-explosive and over 27,000 incendiaries. After only one hour a very large fire developed in the city centre, surrounded by a half dozen or so large fires, with another 50 to 60 in other districts. Birkenhead had three large and half a dozen medium-size fires. By midnight further bombing caused a dense cloud of smoke to cover the area, rising to 13,000 feet. As many as 30 fires could be seen from 60 miles away.

The docks were hit, warehouses and timber yards set ablaze. At the Pier Head the Landing Stage was on fire as were the Cunard and Dock Board Buildings. In the centre the Town Hall, Municipal Buildings and Central Police Offices were all hit by incendiaries. The Adelphi Hotel was blasted by a mine which landed in nearby Copperos Hill, but as the guests were dining on the opposite side of the building most of them escaped unhurt.

There was another shelter tragedy when five railway arches in Bentinck Street collapsed after being hit. Masonry blocks, which were too heavy to lift and too tough to break, hampered rescue which took two days.

Worse was to come on the following night, Saturday 21 December, when nearly 300 aircraft bombed the target zone from 5.45pm for close on 11 hours, in which period 280 tons of high-explosives were dropped (including 80 bombs weighing over a ton), and over 33,000 incendiaries. These caused extensive fire damage, especially to the northern docks. By 11.pm an 'entire district' of Liverpool was reported to be ablaze. A pharmaceutical factory in Hanover Street went up like a rocket. In addition to the docks, city warehouses were on fire as was St John's Fishmarket, stocked with poultry for Christmas. The smell of roast turkey, chicken and goose, lingered in the streets. St George's Hall was hit by incendiaries but Civil Defence and the Fire Service saved its famous organ and a wooden covering saved the magnificent tiled floor. The Assizes were undamaged, but the Sheriff's and Chancery Courts, and the Law Library were burnt out. There was a dramatic incident when a bomb fell in Roe Street, producing a large crater between the Royal Court Theatre and the Victoria Hotel, both of which were only slightly damaged – but a fire engine drove into the crater and its crew of seven were killed.

The church of Our Lady and St Nicholas near the Pier Head was almost destroyed by fire, with only the walls remaining and the tower, which was saved from the flames by an oak door. Two charred beams in the form of a cross were found, and incorporated in the porch when the church was rebuilt.

Hospitals damaged included the Royal Infirmary and Mill Road. Mines blasted houses on Queen's Drive and Wyncote Road near Penny Lane. The Anfield district was badly hit, with yet another shelter tragedy in which 74 were killed. The other districts of Merseyside were all hit but none as badly as Liverpool, especially its centre.

On the following night, Sunday 22 December, when the major Luftwaffe effort was directed against Manchester, the fires still burning on Merseyside guided the raiders to their target.

THE 'FORGOTTEN' RAIDS

The year 1941 opened 'quietly' on Merseyside with four days of minelaying and minor attacks on 10-13 January, followed by more raids and minelaying operations, leading to a 'major' attack, on Wednesday 12 March – the Merseyside raid least talked about in years afterwards. The November, Christmas and May blitzes all seem to have left deeper impressions on people, yet in March great damage was done in Birkenhead and Wallasey, with a share of the damage inflicted upon Liverpool too. A total of 316 aircraft was sent to attack the docks, shipyards and factories of Birkenhead and Bromborough. Wallasey was heavily attacked and lost its water supply early in the raid, when a main pipe was fractured. Birkenhead, whose churches suffered badly, was hit by no fewer than 180 heavy bombs and 40 mines.

In Liverpool the Cotton Exchange, General Post Office, Municipal Annexe and White Star Building were all damaged by fire. A land mine landed in the quadrangle of the University. Railways were badly disrupted. There were many unexploded bombs, whose presence caused severe accommodation problems. The military gave considerable help in fire-fighting, first-aid and rescue operations.

The death toll was high: 264 died in Birkenhead, 198 in Wallasey, and 49 in Liverpool.

Liverpool comedian Stan Boardman has often claimed that the Germans 'bombed our chip shop during the war'. It could not have been the one in the Scotland Road area, which was one of the few buildings left intact. Soldiers and

Street scene in Liverpool the morning after a major attack

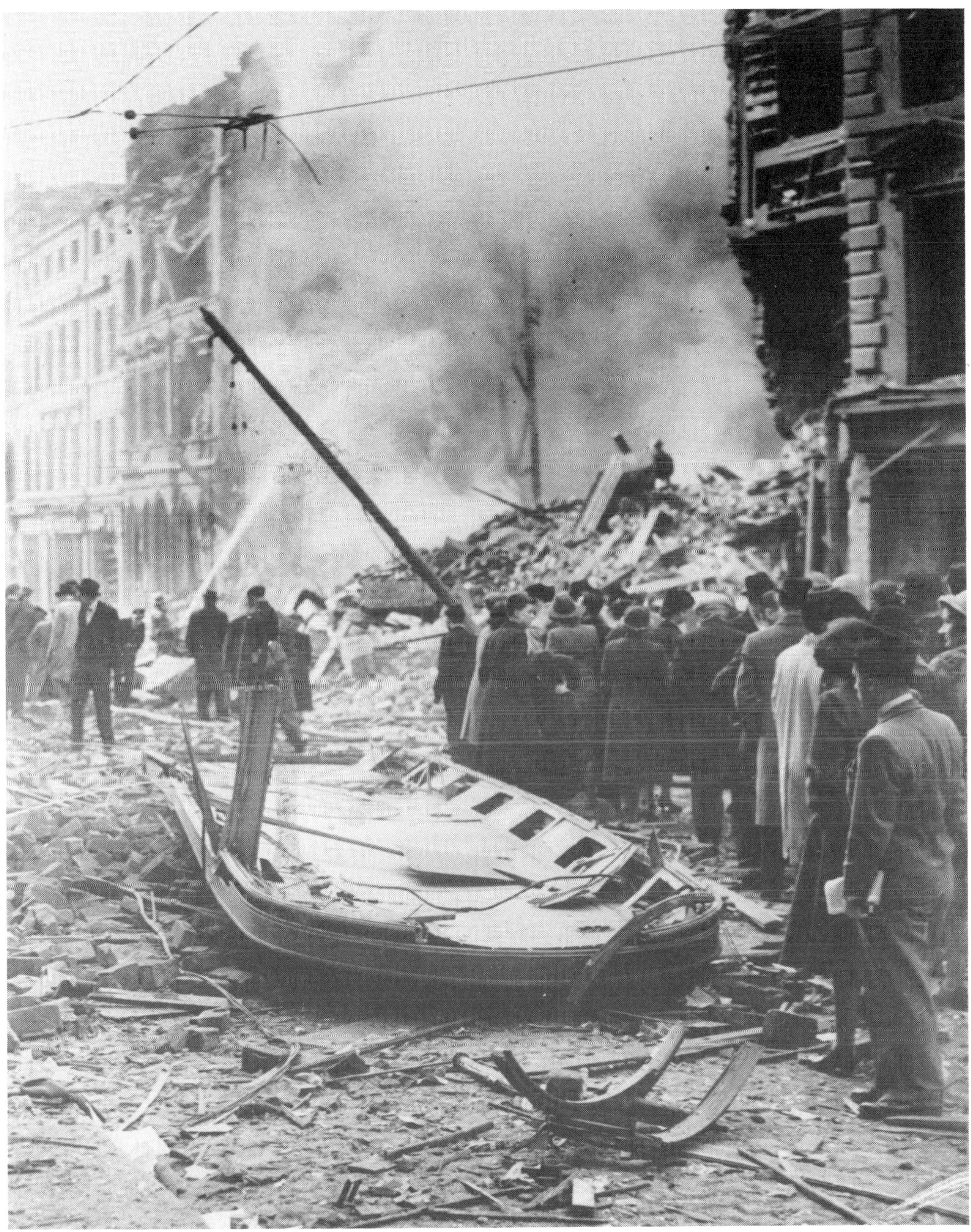

The Mystery Bomber

Thursday 3 October 1940: a mysterious incident received much local coverage and was also covered by the BBC. In daylight a *three-engined* German bomber allegedly swooped on a bus taking women factory workers home, and started to machine gun it. The driver claimed to have heard the rattle of the guns. He accelerated and swerved across the road. The chase was described by a 17-year-old girl passenger: 'We heard the plane first' she said 'and then we could see it clearly diving towards us. We heard a pinging noise and guessed it must be bullets spattering off the roof. The driver of the bus went at great speed and he did marvellously. He had us at a shelter in a very short time. The German plane was still machine-gunning as we raced for the shelter. There was an auxiliary fireman near and we saw his hat knocked off, presumably by a bullet. We saw the funny side of that later'.

On November 12, the BBC came to Liverpool to broadcast and the bus driver told his story.

It all sounds plausible, but the mystery is that the Luftwaffe had only one type of three-engined bomber, the Junkers 52/3m which had not seen service as a bomber since the Spanish Civil War in 1937. It was used as a transport plane for equipment and dropping paratroopers, but not over Britain. In addition no Luftwaffe activity seems to have been recorded outside the London and Midlands areas at the time of the alleged 'incident'.

Royal Marines from Seaforth Barracks, who had been helping with rescue work for hours, were tired and hungry. The grateful owner of the chip shop re-opened his premises in the early hours of the morning and fed them with fish and chips.

In Lancaster Avenue, Wallasey, three rescue workers heard what they thought was the mewing of a kitten from a wrecked house. They dug into the rubble and found a baby girl, a few months old, who had been buried for 3½ days. After first-aid treatment she made a complete recovery.

A record number of 261 RAF night fighters were on patrol during the night of this raid. One Heinkel 111 bound for Liverpool was shot down over Surrey by a Defiant from Tangmere. A second Heinkel, having bombed Birkenhead, was attacked by a Hurricane. It struck a balloon cable and crashed at Widnes. A third was attacked by a Defiant over Birkenhead. Later it crashed into the sea off Hastings. The strangest victim of the night was a Junkers 88 which was damaged and set on fire by a Defiant and AA fire over Merseyside. The pilot, Feldwebel Günther Unger, baled out with the rest of his crew, having pointed the aircraft out to sea. Forty years later, to his amazement, he received a letter from an Investigation Group telling him that his aircraft had turned round and flown a further 100 miles before crashing at Wychbald in Worcestershire. He later visited the site.

The second of the 'forgotten' major attacks on Merseyside occurred during the night of 26 April, when 92 aircraft dropped 113 tons of high-explosives and about 15,000 incendiaries in a short raid of 1½ hours from 11.30pm. Little damage was done to port, industrial, or military targets, though there was damage to railways, and to utilities. Only 5 persons were killed – a surprisingly low figure given the tonnage of bombs released.

THE MAY BLITZES

The raids on Merseyside which are most clearly remembered are the May blitzes of 1941, the final sustained effort by the Luftwaffe to bring Merseyside docks to a halt and thereby put Britain's major port out of action. Given that over one-third of the nation's pre-war maritime trade came via the Mersey, it seems inexplicable that this effort was not made earlier and was not sustained intensively. The first attacks in that May seemed to suggest that the enemy was about to remedy this omission.

The raid on Friday 2 May was a major attack: 65 aircraft dropped 105 tons of high explosives and 6,000 incendiaries. This included 13 air mines. The raid lasted from 11.45pm to 2.45am – a comparatively short raid, but nonetheless one in which 110 people were killed, including 10 sheltering in the crypt of St Brigid's Church. The sky was cloudless that night and the damage was widespread. Large fires were started in the raid but were under control by dawn. The Dock Board and White Star Buildings were badly damaged and the Corn Exchange destroyed. Railways and trams were badly disrupted as were gas, water and electricity supplies. Liverpool Diocese lost its records in Church House. Though a major raid in itself, this night's attack heralded Merseyside's heaviest raid of all, which came just 14 hours later.

On the night of Saturday 3 May the raid on Merseyside lasted from 11.pm until 3.30am the following morning (since Double British Summer Time started during the night there has frequently been confusion over the duration and timing of the raid). A total of 298 bombers participated, and claimed to have dropped, 363 tons of high explosive and 50,000 incendiaries. The total bomb-drop was not, in fact, this high: several bombers were tempted to release their bombs in the River Dee, close to the Wirral. One of the decoy 'Starfish' sites (fires ignited by remote-control, designed to simulate from the air the effect of large blazes) succeeded that night in its intended deception.

There had been previously more German aircraft over Merseyside on a single night (324 on 26 August and 299 on 21 December), but in spite of the decoy sites this raid on 3 May was more severe. Visibility was mainly good, but the marker flares dropped by Pathfinder aircraft, and the later bombing of the fires already started, were the main causes of the success of the raid from the Luftwaffe's point of view.

The casualty figures – 406 killed in Liverpool, 57 in Bootle, 16 in Liverpool – demonstrate the severity of the raid. Among the 57 killed in Bootle were 12 WVS women who were preparing meals at a Rest Centre, St Andrew's Church. Twenty-five others, who had taken refuge at the Rest Centre after having been bombed out elsewhere, also died.

Many local people still refer to this raid as 'the night Lewis's went up'. Blackler's departmental store was also gutted and another smaller but famous store 'went up' – Kelly's Tool Shop in Renshaw Street.

Fires were widespread and often extensive: many warehouses were damaged. Efforts to control them were hampered by a shortage of water after mains had been hit. Firemen came in from a wide area of the North and Midlands. If the wind had been stronger, there might have been a firestorm such as destroyed Hamburg and Dresden, where rising hot gases suck in large quantities of cool air to fan the flames.

On the other side of the city the complex of public buildings in William

Brown Street was badly damaged by fire, including the Museum, Central Library, the Walker Art Gallery, and the adjoining Technical College.

Several ships were hit, including the 10,000 ton *Europa*, and 6,500 ton *Elstree Grange* and several smaller vessels. But by far the most serious incident was the blowing up in Huskisson Dock of the 7,600 ton *Malakand* laden with 1,000 tons of bombs. The disaster started with incendiary bombs, most of which were extinguished. Then a barrage balloon which had broken loose fouled the rigging, and the hydrogen gas was ignited, setting the hatch covers alight. With bombs still falling, crew and firemen continued to fight the fire. They tried to flood the hold, but to no avail. The ship had to be abandoned. Crew and dockers sheltered in cargo sheds. The ship exploded 'like an earthquake', causing widespread damage. Sheds simply vanished. A four-ton anchor was thrown 100 yards, sinking a Dock Board hopper, and other vessels were sunk. Steel plates landed 2½ miles away, one killing a married couple travelling along the Dock Road in a car. Miraculously, though, only a few people were killed in this incident. The ship continued to explode for a further 74 hours. The dock was later filled in.

The same night, at Breck Road, Clubmoor, an ammunition train with thirty-two 10-ton wagons was hit. For several hours ten railwaymen, led by Goods Guard George Roberts, shunted wagons into sidings to prevent them burning. They carried on with this task despite the falling bombs and exploding ammunition and incendiaries. George Roberts was later awarded the George Medal. Others were awarded the British Empire Medal, while some received commendations for bravery.

In yet another horrendous incident, a bomb landed on Mill Road Infirmary. Three buildings were wrecked, others damaged and ambulances set on fire, disrupting rescue operations. Three hundred and eighty patients were evacuated but 17 medical staff died, along with 15 ambulance drivers and 30 patients. Dr Leonard Findlay, the medical superintendent, was awarded the George Medal with Gertrude Riding, the Matron, the OBE for gallantry.

The Liverpool Daily Post found itself without gas, water, electricity, telephones or telegraph. Power was quickly restored to the presses but Merseyside's news for several weeks was supplied by the *Manchester Guardian and Evening News*.

There was an air of unreality about that Sunday (4 May) with wreckage and rubble widespread but there was to be no relief. For that night, from 11.55pm to 4.26am, 55 Luftwaffe aircraft returned, dropping 55 tons of high explosives and almost 12,000 incendiaries. Fires still blazing from the previous night in Liverpool guided the Luftwaffe crews. Among the places bombed was the Rotunda Theatre in Scotland Road, which was destroyed by fire.

The 6,800 ton *Silver Sandal*, with a deck cargo of aircraft, was hit by a bomb and set on fire. A fireboat came to her aid and she was towed into Birkenhead.

The following day, Monday 5 May, as people tried to return to work, stock was taken of the situation. The Dock Road was blocked in eight places. Access to the Liverpool and Leeds Canal was restricted due to damage to bridges. To prevent congestion police set up cordons and turned away non-essential traffic. This fuelled rumours of martial law. Only 13% of tram lines remained undamaged. Many routes stopped in the higher parts of the city, unable to reach their usual terminus at Pier Head.

Only Langton Dock's rail link was not blocked by rubble, craters or unexploded bombs. Exchange Station was still ablaze. Troops were brought in to help with the restoration of lines. Amazingly, the huge Edge Hill sidings were hardly affected. It was a near thing, with bombs and incendiaries falling in nearby Wavertree Park and the Botanic Gardens. The volume of rail traffic had been reduced by a half.

Early the following morning – 6 May – Merseyside had its fifth successive raid, when 27 aircraft delivered a sharp attack with 34 tons of high explosive and 6,000 incendiaries. Though there was thick cloud over Merseyside, aircrews bombed through the gaps. There were several fires, especially in Birkenhead. Once again, water was in short supply. A bomb fell on the Anglican Cathedral, passed through the roof and luckily hit an outside wall before exploding. There was a small fire outside in a yard.

A sad loss was the destruction of the beautiful St Luke's Church at the top of Bold Street. The nave and chancel were destroyed but the tower (though not its bell) survived. The gutted church was later taken over by the city and its unrestored shell forms part of a memorial garden. On this night T. J. Hughes's was added to the list of departmental stores damaged in the Merseyside raids.

On Tuesday 6 May, when Glasgow was the main target, Merseyside was attacked once more – an attack similar to that of the previous night. More damage was done to the docks. A Defiant night fighter was shot down by a Junkers 88 near Widnes, but its crew baled out safely. The council chamber in the Town Hall was damaged (scars on a nearby building can still be seen) and meetings had to be held in the Municipal Annexe. The Pier Head was damaged. Brent's Brewery and Cooper's – with its smell of coffee – in Church Street, were set on fire.

The next night, Wednesday 7 May, was the seventh successive raid and, judging by its scale, was possibly meant by Field Marshall Hugo Sperrie (Commander of *Luftflotte 3*) to be the final knock-out blow.

One hundred and sixty-six aircraft dropped 232 tons of high explosives, including 26 mines and 29,000 incendiaries. There would have been more, but owing to an earlier unfavourable weather report 72 aircraft went to Hull instead. The conditions improved, but bombing was erratic. Many houses were damaged, especially in Bootle. The once-famous Metropole Theatre was

Through the eyes of a child

A ten-year-old boy described the raid on Saturday 3 May 1941, in this way:

Long after the all clear that Sunday morning explosions occurred, probably from the 'Malakand', though we didn't know that then. We kept getting out of bed thinking the raid was starting up again. After the umpteenth time my father said we were up and down like a bunch of . . . marionettes and even though we didn't know the cause of the explosions we went back to bed and slept.

Later on that Sunday and for the next few days the ground was covered with white ash – it looked like snow – in May. We later found that it was from the burning Central Library even though we lived about three miles from it.

Later raids on Merseyside

After the blitzes of May 1941 the Luftwaffe attacked the Merseyside region intermittently during the next 15 months:

Thursday 29 May 1941: 3-hour raid but little damage.

Saturday 31 May 1941: Bombs fell near Stanley Park, damaging water and electricity mains. Incendiary-damage at the docks.

Tuesday 24 June 1941: raid on Birkenhead and Wallasey, and the following night on Liverpool. Houses damaged and destroyed: six people killed.

Wednesday 23 July 1941: Birkenhead, where there were some casualties.

20 October 1941: much-bombed Bootle attacked; gas-holder at Linacre Road blown up.

Saturday 10 January 1942: bombs dropped in Stanhope Road and St Margaret's Princes Road: 15 killed.

9 August 1942: siren at 11.59pm, flares dropped, but no bombs. At 1.19am the All Clear sounded, and though it was not realised at the time, this was the last All Clear of the war for Merseyside. The last 'incident' occurred when a barrge balloon exploded in Kirkdale, making 70 people temporarily homeless.

destroyed by fire, so becoming a fellow-victim along with joining the Argyle in Birkenhead, and the Rotunda and Olympia in Liverpool.

There was an unsuccessful attack with parachute mines on the Eastham Lock Gates of the Manchester Ship Canal. Factories bearing famous industrial names were gutted, including Harland and Wolff, Johnson's Dye Works, Scott's Bakery and Bryant & May's Match Works.

It was a bad time for the ferries. The New Brighton ferry boat, *Royal Daffodil II*, was sunk at Seacomb Landing Stage. The *Claughton* was hit by a bomb and the *Bidston* was damaged by falling masonry

A Bootle housewife searches for family belongings in the rubble outside her home

Two out of three Merseyside houses were either completely destroyed or damaged in the Blitz

at the Pier Head. Many other boats were sunk or damaged, but the records are confused, as some were hit several times during the raids.

RAF night fighters were, however, becoming more effective, especially with their airborne radar. Three Heinkel 111's were shot down, crashing at Bagilt, Wrexham and Maplas.

But there could be no doubt about the serious consequences of this raid, especially in the docks. On the morning of Thursday 8 May, it became clear that 70 out of 144 berths were out of action and cargo handling was reduced to 25% of normal. Apart from 80,000 tons of shipping sunk or destroyed, access to and from the docks from the river was blocked. And the railways could neither deliver nor collect. Road transport, including horse-drawn vehicles, had to be employed wherever possible.

At this point – just when their attacks were creating maximum disruption – the Luftwaffe virtually abandoned its attacks on Merseyside, a change of tactics never satisfactorily explained. For no raid came on the eighth night. The Luftwaffe transferred its attention to Hull, Nottingham and Sheffield. Why was this so? Did reconnaissance photos make the situation appear worse than it was, incapable of restoration in the near future? Possibly so. And it is true, too, that the Luftwaffe's resources were being husbanded prior to the invasion of Russia, for which its aircraft would be needed.

An ex-Luftwaffe bomber commander writing after the war was angry at the non-continuance of large-scale bombing, especially on Merseyside. There was a view, held at some levels in the Luftwaffe, that the distribution of the raids had not been managed to the best possible effect. There were later small-scale raids on the Merseyside region, but the opportunity of a major, devastating breakthrough was passed by. This was recognised by General Pile, C-in-C, AA Command, who clearly thought that had raids on a heavy scale continued, the port would have been out of action for a long time. The strain was enormous but civilian morale, though low, held.

On Tuesday 13 May, 554 unclaimed and unidentified dead were buried in a communal grave at Anfield Cemetery. In a city whose population then had passionately-held religious differences, the ceremony was conducted by churchmen of every denomination. At a later stage of the war, when the south of England was being bombarded with V1s and V2s, Merseyside became the host to hundreds of evacuees from the south, and it greatly appealed to the Liverpudlian sense of humour that anybody could regard their city as 'safe'.

Counting the cost . . .

Total Alerts	509
Total Raids	68
High-explosive bombs	2,315
Parachute mines	119
Oil bombs	50
Incendiary bombs	100,000
Houses (out of 282,000) –	
Completely destroyed	10,840
Damaged	184,000

Killed or injured
(in brackets, figures for the 7 nights of the May blitzes)

	Dead		Injured	
Liverpool	2,596	(1,453)	4,148	(1,056)
Bootle	460	(257)	1,426	(26)
Birkenhead	464	(464)	661	(44)
Wallasey	355	(3)	909	(19)

Sheffield's Thursday

When the sirens set up their customary wail at 7pm on the evening of Thursday, 12 December 1940, many people in Sheffield shrugged their shoulders and assumed that it was just another false alarm. They had heard air-raid warnings many times before and had allowed themselves to become complacent. Some even believed that German raiders would never find their city, surrounded as it is by a protective ring of hills.

But those in charge of the city's defences on that cold, frosty night knew better. There was a 'bomber's moon', and police and civil defence headquarters in the area had been warned to expect a heavy air attack. By the time the alert sounded anti-aircraft gunners were standing by their weapons, ready to open fire on the first wave of raiders homing in on their objective from bases in France and the Low Countries.

A thousand volunteers manned three squadrons of barrage balloons, 72 of which hovered above the city on the night of the raid. Other defences were in position. Decoy oil tanks and other structures made from wood shavings and tin foil stood on the Strines and Burbage-Ringinglow Moors and in Eckington Woods.

The Cost of Dying

By August 1939 Sheffield was already on a war footing. The Town Clerk had established an ARP Committee which, among other things, ordered 300 coffins at 25/- [£1.25] each, five hundred hessian bags for human remains and many canvas shrouds at 2/6d [12.5p]. After this grisly start, the Committee went on to create an emergency force consisting of thousands of wardens, rescue teams, ambulance men and women, fire services, field kitchen workers and messengers, all of whom were to play a vital role in defending the city and keeping essential services going when the long-awaited blitz started in December 1940.

FROM THE SOUTH-EAST, A SOLITARY PATHFINDER

There were good reasons why this centre for the manufacture of specialised steel products should be singled out by the Luftwaffe as a prime strategic target. There were many components essential to the war effort being made in Sheffield, and in certain cases the city housed machinery not found elsewhere. For example, during the first eighteen months of the war the only drop-hammer capable of forming the crankshafts of Hurricane and Spitfire fighters was at Sheffield, at the United Steel works. If that could be put out of commission the impact on Britain's air defences would be very serious indeed.

Thursday was early closing day for shops in the city centre, so although it was the pre-Christmas shopping season, things were fairly quiet. However, there were plenty of dances booked in halls in various parts of the city that evening, and all cinemas were open and doing a brisk trade. Those in the streets who had decided that business and pleasure as usual remained the order of the day, heard the first drones of an aircraft engine not long after the noise of the sirens had died down. This was their first indication that this was not to be yet another false alarm.

From the south-east there came a solitary pathfinder, a Heinkel, that first released parachute flares to illuminate the target and then dropped incendiary bombs at Norton Lees and Gleadless. Behind this leading aircraft came others loaded with magnesium fire bombs, to attack Moorhead, Glossop Road, Abbeydale Road, Park Hill, Brincliffe Edge and the Woodseats area. One of the first shops set ablaze was the Brightside and Carbrook Co-op, a familiar local landmark. On The Moor the roof of the Central Picture House caught fire, while 400 or so patrons continued to watch the film quite unaware of their danger. The purpose of the opening moves was clear enough: it was to encircle the city with a ring of fire and so create a beacon for the main attacking force, following on with its deadly cargo of high explosive bombs.

Many houses in the Sheffield area lacked proper air-raid shelters, and once the severity of the attack was realised people started to take refuge with friends or neighbours lucky enough to have an Anderson of their own, or made their way to one of the main public shelters. Cellars also provided a haven for many. In some of the larger buildings work had been carried out to reinforce cellar space with steel girders and pit props, offering

18 were killed when this trench shelter in Porter Street was hit by a German bomb

a high degree of protection against anything other than a direct hit. Far less secure were cellars under ordinary dwellings, although even these provided some protection against falling debris, shrapnel and flying glass. Other families took shelter under the stairs, or were reduced to huddling together under a stout table while the bombing was at its peak.

Outside fires started to spread despite heroic efforts to contain them. Incendiary bombs falling on open ground were usually left to burn out, but every attempt was made to deal with those falling on or near buildings. Dustbin lids were used to choke out the flames, or to manoeuvre the bomb into a position where it would do less damage. Some were even rolled into a sewer, where they were promptly extinguished.

At about 8pm the police decided that places of public entertainment should be closed, and sent word to cinemas and dance halls warning of the danger. This was before the heavy bombers arrived, while the fire-raid was still in progress. So when people started to make their way home they were astonished to find the quiet, darkened streets bathed in a glow of light. To those accustomed to the rigorous discipline of the nightly black-out it was a fascinating, almost unearthly spectacle, curiously lacking in menace or threat of danger.

But these initial impressions were quickly dispelled when the first high explosive bombs came whistling down from the night sky. Now thudding explosions rocked the city. The 500,000 citizens of Sheffield started to experience

Greater Love . . .

At about 9pm a bomb fell at the back of some houses in Westbrook Bank. Several people were injured, including a soldier whose legs were trapped. A rescue team was called and led to the spot by the warden responsible for the area. It was soon realised that the only way to free the trapped soldier was to dig a tunnel in order to reach him. A first-aid party arrived together with an ambulance to give on-the-spot assistance.

Rescue work was well under way when, at about midnight, a second bomb dropped virtually on the same spot and destroyed the rest of the house. Some of the rescuers were buried under the debris, and more volunteers arrived to help those who had responded to the first call. Digging continued until 4.30am. By then it had become clear that three members of the original rescue squad had died and three others critically injured. One of the first-aid team had also died, but his body sheltered that of a civilian who survived. The driver of the ambulance was also killed.

A 14-year-old remembers . . .

When my bus dropped me in town, after some detours, I was lost and scared. By then, some of the bombed buildings had been pulled down, and it looked like a barren land. I was relieved to turn round and see the library still standing, and even more glad to go home. What had been a lovely shopping centre on The Moor, dressed up for Christmas two weeks ago, was now a ruin. To a fourteen year old it was a shock.

at first hand the ordeal of a major air attack, something which they had until now only read about in the newspapers or had seen, discreetly censored, on their cinema screens.

One of the more obvious targets for the first wave of German bombers were the large gasworks at Neepsend. Fires burning on all sides made the installation clearly visible to enemy planes circling overhead, and when the heavy bombers arrived they aimed their high explosive bombs at the flames, causing terrible destruction to houses and other properties in Neepsend itself, on Pye Bank and in Philadelphia. The climax came when a parachute mine, one of six to be dropped on the city that night, floated down and with great accuracy exploded between four of the smaller holders. They immediately disintegrated and the gas ignited. A boiling mass of flame was flung into the night sky, and a great blast wave spread outward from the centre of the explosion. The whole valley lit up: it was as if, as one eye-witness put it, a giant flash bulb had been set off.

Sheffield United's stand at Bramhall was among the many buildings destroyed on the night of 12 December 1940. In the city centre (*left*), trams were 'welded to their rails' by the intense heat of fires started by the Luftwaffe

Although for a time other parts of the city continued to function more or less normally – buses and trains were still running out to the suburbs on schedule, for example – the bombers eventually got the upper hand, and fires in the city centre started to rage unchecked. Shelters under public buildings now on fire had to evacuated: some people were led from one shelter to another, only to be moved again after a few minutes. There was little panic, only profound shock and a sense of disbelief at the extent of the destruction all around.

The hospital at Nether Edge received three direct hits, one of which demolished part of a ward, killing five patients. At 9pm a block of flats in Meadow Road was sliced through by a bomb which did not explode until it reached the pub next door. As the dust settled, an elderly couple could be seen standing on a small piece of flooring in the corner of a room which no longer existed. She suffered severely with arthritis and had been unable to take shelter in the reinforced cellar. A relative came to the rescue first by guiding them gently round to the doorway and then by carrying the woman downstairs, with her husband following. They were badly shaken, but otherwise none the worse for their ordeal.

The onslaught reached a peak between 11pm and 1am as the centre of the city came under attack from wave after wave of bombers. Three direct hits on C & A Modes, a large clothing store, brought the front of the building crashing down. The windows were blown out, and the display dummies added a bizarre touch as they lay, stripped of their clothing, on the rubble. The reinforced roof stayed in position long enough for everyone in the basement shelter to be

. . . And a 16-year-old shows them how to do it

According to a report in the *Sheffield Telegraph and Star* a young clerical assistant, aged sixteen, rang up the local authority 'in the midst of the most frantic appeals for help' and calmly informed them that he had commandeered a local cinema and a couple of schoolrooms to house a group of people he was looking after single-handed. From their wrecked houses he had gathered food and clothing to form a central pool. But it had been necessary for him to spend a few shillings without prior permission, which he hoped 'would be all right'.

A freak affect; high explosive blast sliced this Sheffield tram in half. (*right*) Never-more-welcome cups of tea. Well-known voluntary organisations ran mobile canteens to help people cope with post-raid shock

got out safely. Less fortunate were those taking cover in a trench shelter in Porter Street which received a direct hit. 18 people were killed. Others lost their lives when a Church Army Hostel in Campo Lane was hit, but 83 residents were miraculously rescued from the basement of the building.

The greatest loss of life in a single incident occurred when the Marples Hotel, standing at the junction of High Street and Fitzalan Square, was hit just before midnight. The seven storey building collapsed like a pack of cards, trapping about 73 people – staff, guests and casual passers-by seeking shelter – in the basement below. Entombed by fallen masonry and then cremated by a fire which followed, and burned all night, many of the victims could not be identified. Leading off the main cellar was a small bottling store. Part of the ceiling held up, and to the amazement of rescuers seven people were dragged alive from this part of the wreckage the following day.

Major damage was caused at the works of George Senior and Sons – the only industrial casualty resulting from a much smaller raid in the Sheffield area some weeks earlier. In this main attack one of the bombs dropped near the huge chimney which shook, swayed violently from side to side, and then came crashing down on buildings below, killing two fire-watchers in its fall. Next door, staff of the Electricity Department fought a fire startred by a heavy bomb that fell on their workshops. They were able to draw water straight out of the river, using a motor pump.

Fire-fighting crews in other parts of the city were less fortunate. As the raid grew in intensity water pressures dropped, and firemen watched helplessly as their hoses emptied and flames spread to neighbouring buildings.

But from 1am onwards the ferocity of the attack slowly diminished until three hours later one solitary raider remained over the city, dropping a parting stick of incendiaries before making his way back to the Continent. The All Clear sounded at 4.17am. Sheffield had been burned and battered for more than nine hours, without pause.

People started to emerge from their shelters dazed and horrified by the scale of the destruction all around. Piles of rubble made many streets impassable. Trams stood burnt out and welded to the rails by the intense heat. Elsewhere, tramlines were twisted into fantastic, curling shapes by fire and blast. In Heavygate

Counting the cost . . .

During the two fire-blitz raids on Sheffield on the nights of 12 and 15 December 1940, 668 civilians were killed (with a further 92 listed as missing persons) and 25 servicemen. Almost 600 serious injuries were also sustained.

After the first raid only one in four of the rest centres remained in operation, and a total of 37,000 people found themselves homeless after the second attack. Nearly 3,000 houses and shops were totally destroyed, and another 82,000 required major repair work to be carried out. Of business premises in the city, more than 1,200 were demolished, and a further 3,700 rendered unusable.

Road the gas main had burst, and the whole road was covered in small jets of fire as the gas seeped through the asphalt surface. Rubble and broken glass slashed shoes to pieces as people clambered over the debris, desperately searching for family and friends. Many made their way homewards, not knowing what to expect when they got there, fearful of finding nothing more than a smoking gap where their house once stood.

A reluctant mid-winter dawn slowly revealed the full extent of the destruction, and the size of the task confronting the people of Sheffield. It was too early to think about repairs and reconstruction, other than the simplest of emergency works to make buildings wind and water-tight. The first thing that had to be done in the cold, hard light of day was to press on with the search for survivors. Rescue teams worked on like men possessed, ignoring all the obvious hazards presented by fractured gas pipes, exposed electrical wiring and unsound masonry.

The second most important task was a clearing-up operation on a Herculean scale. Soot was everywhere. Most houses were heated by open coal fires, and even distant explosions loosened soot in the chimneys and sent it cascading down to billow out over carpets and furniture. As buildings crumbled under the attack, huge clouds of brick dust formed, and ash from the fires dropped like dirty snowflakes everywhere, swirling in the wind, seeking out gaps in houses that had survived more or less unscathed, perhaps with only a broken window here and there, or a door ripped off its hinges. In the streets, oily water from the fire hoses drained into the many craters left by the bombs, to form dark and stagnant pools. Burst mains gushed water that ran until it found its own level, and then froze into a muddy slush.

The emergency services swung efficiently into action. As a precaution against water pollution standpipes were erected in many of the streets, and drinking water supplied by tanker lorries. Mobile canteens provided hot drinks and snacks to the homeless and to the many volunteer workers: 60,000 emergency meals were prepared and served during the first twenty-four hours. Roads were cleared of rubble and paths were cut through the piles of debris to get the city moving again. Street by street, essential services were restored, albeit on an emergency basis in many cases. Families were reunited and the fabric of everyday life was replaced as quickly as possible, for as many people as possible.

Three nights later, on 15 December 1940, the Luftwaffe struck again. Probably more industrial damage was caused during this second attack than in the earlier raid but, remarkably, the city's steelworks came through both virtually unscathed. So despite the ferocity of the German onslaught, Sheffield's contribution to the national war effort was not greatly affected.

Nor was the morale of her citizens. 'Reserve between neighbours has been broken down, and even complete strangers have started talking to each other – something quite unheard of in Yorkshire,' said one survivor. 'We know the worst Hitler can do now,' said another. 'We're not afraid of him any more.'

22.XII.40

Prime Minister to Lord Chatfield:

I am grieved to find how very few George Medals have been issued. I had hoped there would be ten times as many. The idea was that you would go about and get in touch with local authorities where there had been heavy bombing, and make sure that recommendations were sent forward which could be sifted, and that you would stir the departments on the subject. Can you not do something more in this direction?

Heroism Under Fire

Charles Taylor, a valveman, was one of many workers on duty at the Neepsend gasworks on the night of the raid. As soon as the incendiary bombs started to fall, they realised that they would have their work cut out to save the installation from total destruction. Fires broke out on top of the gas holders, while the crown of the largest holder had been pierced by one of the bombs, igniting the gas and sending a huge spurt of flame into the night sky. Taylor climbed 45ft with a supply of wet clay in an attempt to stop the hole. Only when he got to the fire did he realise that he had not brought a sufficient supply of material. Nothing daunted, he climbed down to gather more wet clay and on his second ascent was joined by another volunteer carrying asbestos rings. Even these efforts were not enough, and a third hazardous climb had to be made before the fire could be brought under control.

Taylor then noticed another fire on top of a smaller holder and, with his companion, climbed 60ft to put this out as well. So absorbed were they in their task that they did not realise that one of the enemy planes had started to machine-gun them, much to the horror of those watching below.

Charles Taylor was later awarded the George Medal for his bravery.

'Glasgow Houses Are More Solidly Built . . .'

'It is unlikely that Glasgow will be attacked from the air in the same way as London. The physical reasons for this are obvious. Aviation experts point out that German planes cannot carry the bombs so far north because of the difficulty in getting fighter escorts; heavier bombs can be used in the attack on London and other southern towns than on Scotland; Glasgow houses are more solidly built than those collapsed from concussion in London.'

These sentiments, subsequently edited from a statement first made in September 1940, were expressed by no less a person than the Lord Provost of Glasgow, Sir Patrick Dollan. They are evidence of the extraordinary degree of complacency at very high levels before the onset of the German air attack. When it came, that onslaught was no less fearsome, or effective, than other major strikes by the Luftwaffe against Britain's major ports and cities.

> **The Blitz reaches Glasgow**
>
> *. . . for the first time the word 'Blitz' has come into ordinary conversation. I know myself that I used to regard the word as a journalistic affectation, and had no idea, until I visited London in January, that people really did talk about 'the Blitz' in a natural and unselfconscious way, in their everyday talk. But until now the word had not reached Scotland at all, and even now I have only heard it in Glasgow.*
>
> A student of Edinburgh University who volunteered to work with Clydeside 'clean-up' parties. 13 April 1941

But to be fair to the Lord Provost, he was by no means alone in his assessment of the situation. A survey undertaken by Mass Observation in the area early in March 1941 indicated that 70% of those interviewed considered that heavy attacks by the Luftwaffe on Glasgow and Clydeside were most unlikely. Some people said that because of the surrounding mountains the approach was too difficult for enemy bombers. Others expressed the view that Glasgow was too far from Luftwaffe bases to be in any danger of a sustained attack. Still more said that the whole region was too well guarded with anti-aircraft guns. It was even suggested that the Germans were not really 'antagonistic towards Scotland'.

Not everyone shared these comfortable delusions. John Harkness, in a letter to the editor of the *Clydebank Press* in January 1941, had this to say:

> Sir,
>
> If Clydebank should be marked down for an attack some evening by the German Luftwaffe . . . the Town Council must share the blame with the government if thousands are killed . . . for no attempt has been made . . . to get tunnels dug into the Old Kilpatrick Hills or to have bomb-proof shelters built in the town.
>
> Why this wait-and-see attitude? Have Coventry, Sheffield, Birmingham, Southampton, London and Manchester not taught their lessons? . . .
>
> One has no shelter to go to, for the street shelters are not to be thought of. Few tenements in Clydebank have any protection . . .

Whatever reservations officialdom may have had about the vulnerability of Glasgow and Clydeside, there can have been no doubt at all about the suitability of the area as a prime target for aerial bombardment. First, there were the many shipyards along the Clyde. Then a large number of ordnance factories and engineering works of all kinds. These in turn were supported by many ancillary industries and workshops, together with all the essential services to keep them going. In sharp contrast to the Depression years of the 1930s, the whole region was now working flat out to sustain Britain's war effort. There can have been few targets more tempting to the German marauders, which makes the attitude of 'it can't happen here' all the more surprising.

INADEQUATE PROVISION

Fortunately there was another side to the picture. In common with all other major centres throughout the kingdom, the authorities in Glasgow had made some contingency plans before the war to protect their 1,250,000 inhabitants. The ARP Committee, established in 1935, had trained up to 7,000 people, and existing programmes in the fire, medical and police services had been significantly increased. First aid posts, rest centres and emergency feeding arrangements were set up, and stand-by demolition and rescue squads were formed. Information was provided to the general public telling them how best to protect themselves in

Rescue workers search for survivors in the wreckage of a Scotstoun tenement building

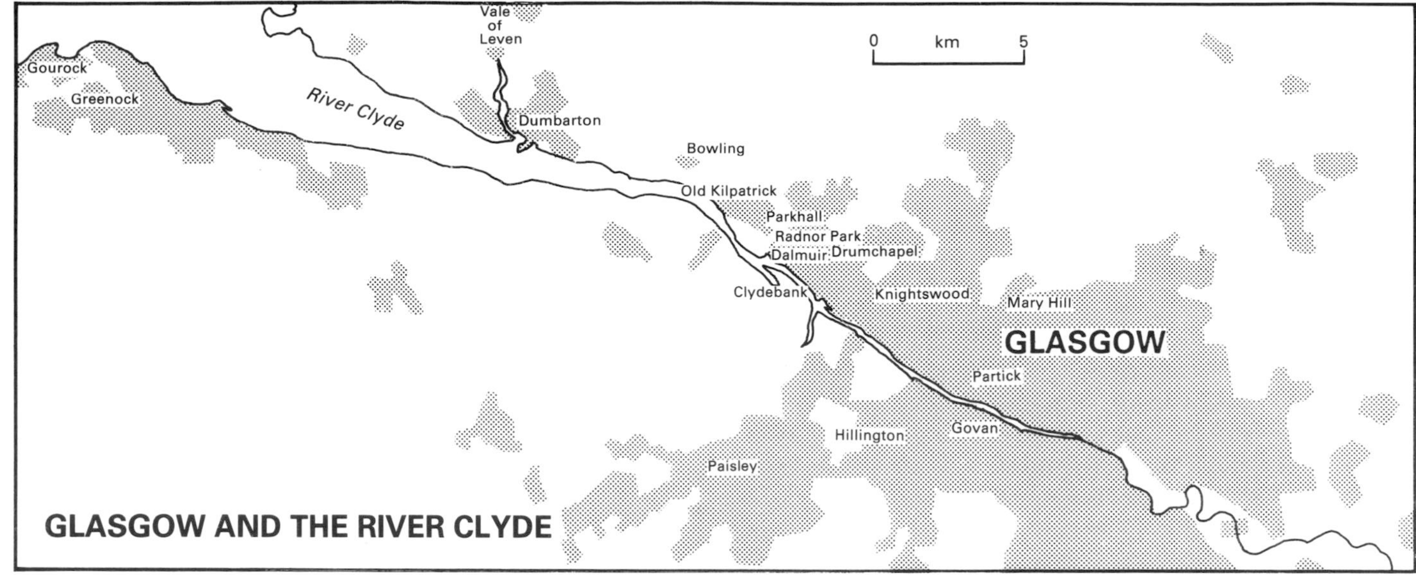

the event of an attack, but it remains true that the provision of air-raid shelters was inadequate compared with that in many other urban centres. There appears to have been not sufficient determination to overcome the very real difficulties of finding suitable locations in Glasgow's densely built-up areas, and it was not until 1942 that the city's population could be said to have adequate provision. And this was only achieved by virtue of the fact that 20% were migrant – people moving out of the city by night to return to their places of work the following morning.

None of the shortcomings was of any importance during the early stages of the Luftwaffe's campaign against Britain, for the premonitory raids, such as they were, were on a very small scale indeed. The first of these took place in daylight hours on 19 June 1940. Further sporadic attacks followed, including one on 18 September when George Square was hit. In the same assault a bomb pierced the upper two decks of HMS *Sussex*, in Yorkhill basin, and exploded amidships. Nearly two months later, on the night of 4 November 1940, the Germans sent 35 planes over the North Sea to attack several parts of Scotland. Bombs were dropped in places as far afield as Aberdeen, Perth and Dundee as well as a few on Glasgow itself. This apparently random pattern was repeated a month later, a few days before Christmas.

Hogmanay was celebrated, and 1941 was welcomed in as traditional a manner as wartime restrictions and Scots resourcefulness would allow. January passed, and then February, almost without incident. Then, at 9pm on the evening of Thursday 13 March the air raid sirens wailed their Alert throughout the Clyde valley. Within minutes the air was filled with the sound of approaching aircraft, a distinctive sound which one witness described as 'a strange vibrating drone that seemed to come and fade, come and fade almost as if their engines were going to cut out . . .'

As seen from London . . .

The London correspondent of the Glasgow newspaper *The Daily Record and Mail*, had this to say to his fellow countrymen:

Little did I think, commenting last night on the desire of Scots MPs to have a full-dress debate in Parliament on Scotland's defence plans, that Clydeside would so soon be the first area in Scotland to be attacked by the same considerable force of German bombers that London and other English cities have already endured.

Local authorities have had plenty of warnings and time in which to prepare themselves. To be quite frank it was inconceivable to imagine, as apparently certain prominent people in Glasgow did, that Clydeside would be left alone. What has happened in Clydeside is likely to happen to any Scottish area or to Clydeside again. Be prepared.

Elsewhere in the same issue there is a report covering the activities of local businessmen cornering the market in such commodities as toiletries and clothes pegs, morale-building pieces on the successful British campaign in Italian Somaliland and the effect of recent RAF attacks on Berlin, speculation about the 'new devices' being used to bring down German raiders, and a letter from a bemused local resident pointing out that in the House of Commons the Parliamentary Secretary to the Food Ministry, Major Lloyd George, son of the famous Welsh leader, recently told the people of England that he could not allow them extra sugar for their Scotch porridge.

PATHFINDERS ARRIVE

Very soon the advance Luftwaffe party arrived – the *Kampfgruppe 100* pathfinders, releasing the first of the more than 59,000 incendiary bombs to fall upon Clydeside that night. The fires which their drops started then acted as markers for the follow-up bombers. The targets they were attempting to identify were the shipyards and installations, including oil tanks, along the Clyde and industrial objectives in Glasgow. The attack was to be concentrated on the north side of the River Clyde, from west and north-west districts of Glasgow to Old Kilpatrick, some ten miles downstream. Specific objectives included the oil tanks at Old Kilpatrick and Bowling, and the shipyards and ammunition depot at Dalmuir. The greatest ferocity of destruction, however, would fall upon Clydebank, a town of about 50,000 whose population had swollen by a further 10,000 with the influx of war workers. Seven miles from

Glasgow, the southern end of the town consisted mainly of small streets leading down to the river, and its docks and factories. The northern part of the town lay on the far side of the Glasgow-Dumbarton road which intersected it; in that part were the districts of Parkhall and Radnor Park with their terraces of small houses and tenements. In the northern part of the town was located Singer's Works, then, like many factories, converted to war-production; in this case, munitions.

Following the pathfinders were the remainder of the 236 aircraft assembled from bases in France, Holland, Northern Germany, Denmark and Norway. The weather conditions were so good that the German bomb-aimers were able to target their objectives visually. In wave after wave Heinkels and Junkers pounded Clydeside through the night for almost 8½ hours. During that time 272 tons of high-explosive caused severe and widespread destruction.

The first incendiaries on Clydebank fell in its centre and upon Singer's timber yard. Here a huge fire was started, a fierce blaze which could not be controlled and acted as a marker for subsequent waves of bombers.

At Yoker a distillery was hit; it flared up in a moment. Again, there was little to be done to staunch the blaze. The brightness attracted more bombers – 'they were on us like wasps,' said one man, 'and then everything came down.' There were two major fires at Rothesay Dock. High-explosives followed the incendiaries and oil-bombs. One resident spoke of the descent of a high-explosive bomb as being 'like an express train coming out of a tunnel'. Unopposed, the raiders crossed and re-crossed the whole area. Parachute mines added to the immediate destruction and to the blast-effects of damage. Houses crumbled in the assault as bomb after bomb exploded. Buildings shook. The Radnor Park area of Clydebank was reduced to a skeleton consisting of walls but little else.

In some districts there was a momentary lull in the assault, to be resumed with further drops of incendiaries, some of them of the explosive type, followed by yet more high-explosives. Fresh outbreaks added to the menacing glow in the sky and were visible along many miles of the Clyde, mostly on its northern bank. There were particularly large fires now raging at Dalmuir and Yoker, whilst a number of warehouses on the south bank of the river had also been ignited. At one point more than 100 fires were visible in the affected parts of Glasgow alone. One dockyard shelter at Yarrows received a direct hit, killing 80 workers within. Amidst all this, the ferry at Yoker continued to operate throughout the night. One of the ferrymen told the story:

> We were at the north bank when they started. We got a load of incendiaries right around us, and my mates and I got to it right away. We had just finished putting them out when a shower dropped on the other bank. So over we went – and we've been doing that for hours. We've snuffed a good few tonight.

Bombs fell either side of the ferry as it crossed the river, and although the boat was not hit directly the blast of explosions threw men about on her deck, one man being hurled down the stairs.

At Clydebank the Communications Centre had itself been hit; coordination of fire-fighting and rescue services ceased. Individual units had to make their own decisions on the spot, their efforts hampered – and in some cases made completely impotent – because of failures in the water supplies, a number of mains having been damaged.

When the people emerged from their shelters many found only a pile of rubble where their homes had been. Some tried to retrieve their possessions, and one survivor later recalled:

> You met dazed silent people walking about in the most ridiculous garbs – fur coats and carpet slippers, carrying canary cages.

Following the raid many fires were still burning in the morning, including one at the Rothesay Dock which was, in the words of the official report of the Regional Commissioner of Scotland, 'completely unattended'. Among the buildings damaged in Glasgow was the University, a hospital, and Bankhead School. Houses, shops, schools, were among the buildings totally destroyed. As darkness fell that night, Friday 14 March, 'there was still' (in the words of the same report) 'a large number of fires out of control . . .' when the raiders returned to Clydeside.

203 aircraft resumed their attacks upon the objectives identified the previous evening, together with the Rolls-Royce aero engine factory at Hillington, between Glasgow and Paisley. The same pattern of attack as on the previous night

All that remained of a passing tram after nearby buildings in Nelson Street, Glasgow, received a direct hit

Radnor Street, Clydebank

ensued, baskets of incendiaries first being dropped – something over 28,000 incendiary devices in all over the target areas during the course of the entire attack. In a graphic phase one of those who lived through the Clydeside blitzes said of the incendiaries that they 'seemed to unroll on the ground like a fiery carpet'. High-explosives, including parachute mines, amounted to 230 tons. Again, most of the Luftwaffe crews were able to identify their targets visually in a bombardment starting at 9pm and continuing throughout the night until the early hours of the following morning. Some of the later Luftwaffe arrivals, however, did experience difficulty in spotting their allocated target-points because of the billowing of rising smoke ascending from the many fires. And many survivors spoke of the increased anti-aircraft activity throughout this raid. Although the actual number of rounds fired from the heavy guns showed little difference between the two nights, the fact that the second raid was more concentrated in time accounts for the effect of greater activity.

One of the conflagrations was at the oil tank installations at Dalnottar and Old Kilpatrick, where an explosion sent smoke to a height of 3,000 feet. Of the 70-plus tanks installed, three had already been hit on the previous night, one of which had been set on fire. Still burning on the second night this attracted further drops from the Luftwaffe bombers. Ten more tanks were set ablaze – eight at Dalnottar and two at Old Kilpatrick. Other tanks were fractured but did not ignite. Nonetheless the fires at these tanks were not finally controlled until five days after the second raid. Other large fires started the second night included those at the power station at Yoker and in the Princes Dock at Govan. Fires were started also at the prime objective – the Hillington Rolls-Royce factory.

The glare of fires which, from a distance, merged into one huge glow, could be seen from miles around. Indeed, some of the men on duty at Dyce aerodrome in Aberdeenshire, 100 miles away, claimed to have seen the burning of Clydeside.

Once more the shipyards, docks, and riverside factories were pounded, where industrial damage was considerable though not, in the event, crippling to production. The worst damage was to housing, whole streets and tenement blocks being blown apart and collapsing in heaps of rubble, sending clouds of dust

Women in a Man's World

The intensification of enemy bombing on Clydeside coincided with a growing shortage of skilled and unskilled labour in the shipyards, where the number of new keels laid grew month by month and more and more men were called up for military service.

Employers were repeatedly urged to recruit women, and even in this most masculine and conservative of industries, growing numbers of them were to be seen handling the heavy equipment and performing the toughest of tasks alongside their male counterparts.

One local worker said: 'We had girls driving mobile canes and doing electric welding, painting and electrical wiring and . . . they fitted in as if they had always been there.'

On the other hand, after women were allowed to form their own pump crews in Glasgow's auxiliary fire service the experiment came quickly to an end when, of their own accord, they came to the conclusion that they did not possess the necessary stamina to manhandle hoses at high pressure.

upwards and outwards as they folded. Buildings which remained standing in Clydebank were now hit, and others – rocking and swaying in the blast – also came crashing to the ground. The Radnor Park district was completely gutted, and other estates very heavily damaged by high-explosives and parachute mines.

DISASTER IN KULMIN STREET

This night, however, there was also devastation within Glasgow itself. Being a large city the damage, for the most part, appeared to be less concentrated than in the comparatively small limits of Clydebank, which had borne the brunt of the first intensive raid. The most badly-damaged areas of Glasgow were at Govan, Tradeston, Partick, Yoker, Knightswood, Drumchapel, and Maryhill. It was in this last district that the single most destructive event took place. A parachute mine, though it exploded in a field, wrecked a school and did very considerable blast damage to houses around Duncruin Street. A second mine at the rear of a four-storey tenement building, nos. 32-36 Kilmun Street, demolished it totally. Other buildings in the street and around were destroyed also. From this one explosion and the resultant fires something like 1,000 persons were made homeless. From the piled debris 83 bodies were eventually recovered, the last of them not retrieved until 28 March, two weeks after the disaster.

As on the previous evening, it was the residential districts which showed the greatest measure of destruction and damage. Estimates of the number of casualties, not publicly released immediately for 'security reasons', were low in relation to the manifest and visible destruction which the people could see for themselves. Speculation gave rise to rumours of numbers far in excess of the real total. Though even today there can be some discrepancies in the tally of figures it would appear that as a result of this two-night blitz on Clydeside 1,085 men, women, and children were killed, and 1,603 seriously injured. Many of the Clydebank dead were buried in a communal grave at Dalnottar Cemetery in a service conducted jointly by Roman Catholic and Church of Scotland clergymen. The burial ground was itself littered with the burned out cases of incendiary bombs. In two consecutive days 121 bodies, wrapped in white sheets, were buried here.

Of the total Clydeside dead, 647 people were killed in Glasgow, a number of deaths which reminds one forcibly that the Clydeside blitz should not be thought of as synonymous with the almost total destruction of the town of Clydebank, the principal zone hit on the first night-raid. Glasgow itself suffered a greater number of casualties than Clydebank, though the physical signs of damage were far more scattered in the city than within the concentrated destruction of Clydebank. It must be acknowledged that as a consequence Clydebank has its own very particular claims to attention. It was to Clydebank, after all, that the sightseers of Glasgow went to see the full effects of blitz bombing. For the town was indeed a wasteland of debris, bricks, mortar, beams, and glass . . . glass everywhere. And soot from the chimneys which settled on everything and everybody, so that people walked the streets with blackened faces.

Very heavy damage caused by the first raid had been turned into devastation by the second. Of the town's housing stock of about 12,000, only eight houses were left completely undamaged by the raids. Almost 3,000 houses were either totally

ONLY EIGHT HOUSES LEFT UNDAMAGED

destroyed or damaged beyond repair. In Clydeside as a whole, and mainly in the Glasgow area, a further 6,000 homes had been damaged, of which nearly 600 were either destroyed or damaged beyond repair. In all, as a result of the two consecutive raids, 55,000 people had been made homeless in the Clydeside region.

During the latter part of 1939 most of the women and children of Clydebank had been evacuated, but the vast majority of these had returned to the town as the threat of serious bombardment seemed to recede. After the first raid on Clydebank, however, 3,000 people left the town the next day, most of them making for the Vale of Leven. Throughout the day another 10,000, and perhaps as many as 12,000, were officially evacuated to rest centres in the counties of Dunbarton, Lanark, and Renfrew. Thousands more simply left the town, making their own way and their own arrangements, some to stay with folks in Glasgow or other parts, and some even camping up on the moors. It has been estimated that during the course of that single day at least 40,000 people left the town of Clydebank. By the following month the total population had dropped to just 2,000.

From the Glasgow *Daily Record & Mail* of 15 March 1941

Dumbarton Road, Dalmuir, Clydebank

Many workers trekked back daily to their workplaces which, for most of them, were the John Brown shipyards, or Singer's, or the Ordnance factory. Gradually people moved back into the town as houses were repaired; but even at the end of the war the population figures remained far below pre-war levels.

Damage to industrial premises and the consequent effect upon war production was, in the light of the devastation along Clydeside, comparatively slight. In most cases production was reduced temporarily because of the failure of utilities, though many firms were back to almost full production within days. And the figures show that most of the workforce returned with very little delay to their various places of employment, hundreds making daily journeys from outside the area.

Though the devastation of March 1941 was not to recur in subsequent raids by the Luftwaffe, Clydeside had to undergo yet more bombardments by the German raiders. In the following month, which saw the heaviest bombing yet against Britain as a whole, Clydeside remained a major target zone. On the night of 7 April, for example, when almost every area of Britain was under air-raid alert at one time or another, Greenock, Dumbarton, and Hillington were among the designated targets of a massed force of long-range bombers. Many of the planes destined for the Clydeside region failed to reach their target areas – some of them released their loads over Bristol and Liverpool instead. Nonetheless, 97 raiders reached Greenock, 30 bombed Dumbarton, and 52 reached their target at Hillington. In all they dropped over 200 tons of high-explosives and 26,000 incendiaries. Though shipyards were again hit the damage was slight, the fires brought quickly under control. Several thousand people were made homeless in the Glasgow region as a consequence of these raids, in which 64 people lost their lives.

Early May brought another double assault upon Clydeside, during which month the German High Command was beginning to pay increasing strategic regard to the eastern front and the opening up of operations there. By the end of the month, though the bombing across Britain would continue, the intense night-time assaults by large fleets of bombers came to an end.

The major target area selected by the Luftwaffe for the night of May 5/6 was again Clydeside, including the Glasgow area, but extending also to Dumbarton, together with Greenock and Gourock further down the estuary. Just after midnight the attacking force, numbering over 280 in total, arrived over the Clydeside region where they pressed home their attack for as long as three hours. The shortest bombardment was over the Greenock and Gourock area where 80 aircraft delivered 112 tons of high-explosives and 8,000 incendiaries in a

'No Praise Is Too Great . . .'

The following entry about the blitz on Clydebank is from the diary of J. P. McHutchison, local Director of Education:

It was all too pathetically evident that terrific damage to houses had been done, especially in the Parkhall and North Kilbowie Housing Schemes, and in the poorest working-class areas of Crown Avenue, and First and Second Avenues, in which streets the miles of four-storey tenements had been completely gutted by fire; some parts were still blazing and hundreds of the tenants watching from piles of saved furniture from the holocaust of their homes. Long queues of now homeless folks awaited the buses that would take them away, and Drumry Road was black with men, women and children waiting at the church Rest Centre for food and guidance. It was a sad, sad sight, relieved however and glorified by uncomplaining fortitude and brave resignation . . .

The contrast between the ugliness of ruination by man's hand and the beauty of warm Spring days will live ever in one's memory, as will the grand courage of so heavily stricken people; not a sign of panic nor hysteria anywhere, though almost all were now homeless and thousands had lost their all.

Clydebank has had a bad knock, probably severer than Coventry or any English town, since the whole town 'got it' and no single area or district escaped. It is quite plain that the object was to block out the whole place and therby close down all work at Browns ROF (Royal Ordnance Factory) and Singers. But that object has not been achieved, for early in this week Browns and Singers have been almost as busy as before, and folks are beginning to trickle back to the less severely damaged houses, and windowless and battered shops to commence trading. No praise is too great for the people . . .

little over two hours. Fires were started among the shipyards and docks along this part of the south Clyde – as they were on the north side of the river at Dumbarton, attacked for 2½ hours by 103 bombers. Here five large fires were reported and many smaller ones. Similar explosive and fire damage was caused within the Glasgow area where a further 103 aircraft launched 130 tons of explosives and about 2,000 incendiaries upon the shipyards and industrial areas. Fires and explosions caused damage to Rothesay Docks, and the John Brown shipyards at Clydebank. This Clydeside raid inflicted considerable damage, and industry was again affected, both directly and through interference with utility supplies. Work at some docks was also retarded because of damage to rail supply lines.

On the following night the damage was compounded by a repeat raid on Glasgow and Clydeside made by a total of 232 long-range bombers. Again, starting just minutes after midnight, 155 of these aircraft ranged over the western stretches of the Clyde, from Dumbarton onwards. In 2½ hours more than 170 tons of high-explosives and 38,000 incendiaries were dropped over the area. Among the damage caused was that at Greenock gasworks where a massive explosion occurred. The remaining 77 bombers concentrated upon a large zone including and around Glasgow, releasing almost 100 tons of high-explosives and over 2,000 incendiaries.

Again, damage to dockyard workings and to industrial plants was heavy, but the greatest destruction was to housing properties. Greenock, and neighbouring Port Glasgow, suffered especially. The total loss of life in these two Clydeside raids was more than 300. They were, however, the region's last serious aerial assault.

Although the Luftwaffe's campaign was not as protracted as those against many other important centres, notably London and Hull, the results were no less severe. In fact, the almost total annihilation of Clydebank must rank as one of the worst of all of the home-front experiences during the Second World War.

ELSEWHERE IN SCOTLAND

Though the Glasgow and Clydeside region of Scotland received by far the greatest pounding during the Second World War, it should be remembered that many other parts of Scotland were also bombed – and some of them were among the first in the British Isles to be visited by the Luftwaffe.

From the declaration of war onwards, during the so-called 'phoney' phase, enemy aircraft were seen at many points, from the Shetland and Orkney Islands, to the north, and along the whole of the eastern flank of Scotland. It is true that many of these sightings were of reconnaissance sorties, but others were of attacks on coastal shipping. In the early months of the war there was a marked reluctance by both sides to engage in the bombardment of the other's towns and cities.

Nonetheless, hostile actions did take place. Among the first of these was the one over Lerwick North Harbour, St Magnus Bay, in the Shetlands, during which a seaplane was set alight by machine-gun fire. Raiders also visited the Orkneys, whose harbour defences at Scapa Flow U-boat commander Günther Prien had penetrated on 14 October 1939, and there successfully torpedoed and sunk HMS *Royal Oak*. Then, on 16 March 1940, several Luftwaffe planes returned to bomb the harbour at dusk, causing the very first British civilian casualty of the war when a cottage at the

'Makeshift and interim . . .'

Churchill noted 'another change in the policy of the German offensive' early in November 1940. Although London remained the main target, widespread attacks were now to be mounted in an attempt to cripple British industrial output. Crack Luftwaffe squadrons, equipped with new navigational aids, were specially trained to attack specific targets, one of which was the new Rolls Royce aero-engine works at Hillington, Glasgow.

All this Churchill described as 'a makeshift and interim plan' filling the gap between the virtual abandonment of 'Operation *Sea Lion*' and the forthcoming attack on the USSR. The remaining months of that winter were to be a time of trial and experiment for the Luftwaffe, using new devices and techniques in their attacks on British shipping and her industries. 'They would have done much better,' Churchill declares with grim satisfaction, 'to have stuck to one thing at a time and pressed it to a conclusion. But they were already baffled for the time being and unsure of themselves.'

Like their colleagues all over the country, Clydebank rescue workers and demolition teams worked day and night, often in conditions of extreme danger. One Clydebank man was rescued after being trapped for nearly eight days in the rubble of what was once his home

Bridge of Waithe was bombed, and a man was caught full-on in the blast.

Several towns along the east coast of Scotland, from Wick to Arbroath, received occasional attention from the Luftwaffe – some of it very minor, or conducted just offshore against shipping. Where actual raids were made, from 1940 onwards, they tended to involve only a small number of aircraft, sometimes a lone raider. There were few, if any, casualties.

Apart from these 'nuisance' raids on cities such as Aberdeen, the Luftwaffe carried on with its mine-laying operations in coastal waters and with its reconnaissance flights.

This pattern of intermittent and minor attacks was suddenly broken on 21 April 1943, taking Aberdeen by complete surprise. A regrouped Luftwaffe unit in Norway mounted a special raid upon the industrial town and its port. Flying low across the North Sea, 29 aircraft approached the coast, six of them maintaining altitude at about 500 feet to close on the town from the north, bombing and machine-gunning on their way. The remaining aircraft climbed to between 3,000 and 10,000 feet for their bomb-drops. Though some bombs fell in open countryside, the damage done to the city was considerable, and 13 fires were started. In all 98 civilians were killed in the raid, and 27 Servicemen stationed at the barracks just to the north of the River Don were also killed.

In the earlier months of the war, the Firth of Tay further south attracted raiders to Dundee and Perth. The first of these towns – though deemed to be 'of limited capacity, and for certain types of cargo only' – was nonetheless specifically mentioned as a target in Hitler's Directive No. 9 for the Conduct of the War (29 November 1939). On 4 November 1940 the Tay region, including both Dundee and Perth, received attention in a series of wide-ranging Luftwaffe sorties carried out by about 35 aircraft, which stretched as far north as Aberdeen. Little damage anywhere was caused.

The Firth of Forth also attracted the Luftwaffe, and recorded the very first air attack made by the Germans upon British territory. On 16 October 1939, for just over an hour in the afternoon, nine Junkers 88s attacked shipping in the Firth of Forth – and succeeded in damaging three Royal Navy ships: the cruisers *Southampton* and *Edinburgh*, and the destroyer *Mohawk*. Two of the Junkers were shot down by two Spitfires.

On the night of 5/6 May 1941 – while a major raid was being launched against the shipyards and industrial targets of the Clyde – the docks, shipyards, and dry docks of Leith, just outside Edinburgh, were bombed. Ten Luftwaffe aircraft took part in the raid in which 20 tons of high-explosive were released. By this stage of the war there were no interdictions upon targets: the Luftwaffe pilots of the October raid of two years before had been specifically ordered to avoid dry docks for fear of causing civilian casualties.

Stray bombs often fell on inland areas of Scotland as Luftwaffe pilots roamed the countryside looking for targets of opportunity, or had missed altogether the pre-selected target of their raid. The west coast docks and shipping traffic lanes also witnessed occasional, but again not severe, attacks from the Luftwaffe. Throughout the war most parts of Scotland, including its isles and inlets, were crossed and recrossed by German aircraft. But nowhere in Scotland were the Luftwaffe's attacks on towns and cities nearly so concentrated, or nearly so severe, as the devastating massed raids along the length of the river Clyde, from Glasgow to the mouth of the estuary.

Manchester – the Luftwaffe's missed opportunity?

That Greater Manchester would be singled out for attack by the Luftwaffe was clear and obvious for several good reasons. It stood at the hub of England's great industrial centre in the North-West, the home of a number of production plants vital to the war effort. With its 35 miles of Ship Canal from the Western Approaches to Salford Docks, themselves an important target, and its road and rail network, Manchester was clearly of enormous strategic significance.

By well-directed attacks the Luftwaffe could expect to wipe out several leading aircraft and munitions factories, as well as a number of important operational and training centres. At Heaton Chapel there was Fairey Aviation, makers of Beaufighters and Halifax bombers. At Ringway, A. V. Roe assembled the first prototype Lancaster (which later went into large-scale production there), and York bombers operated from the airfield. At Ringway, too, was the home of the Parachute Training School, where tens of thousands of paratroopers were trained, and also somewhere in Ringway was the 'school' for secret agents, such as the famous Odette. At Woodford, Metropolitan Vickers assembled Lancasters and Avro assembled other aircraft, including the Manchester Bomber. At Trafford Park were Metropolitan Vicker's works producing Lancasters as well as tanks and tank equipment. At Manchester City Hall, among other places in the area, most of the country's barrage balloons were made.

Winston Churchill acknowledged Manchester's great importance to the war effort, especially for its engineering production when, as First Lord of the Admiralty, he visited the city in January 1940 in order to call for an expansion in production and for a substantial increase in the number of factories and workers.

To defend a centre of such crucial importance anti-aircraft guns and barrage balloons had to be stationed all over the area – in the city of Manchester itself almost every open space in parks and fields, for example, was pressed into service. The likelihood of major Luftwaffe attacks also meant that evacuation procedures had to be taken seriously. In the last days of the summer of 1939, therefore, evacuation plans were well advanced. The planners estimated that no fewer than 80,000 children would need to leave the city. The first evacuation, by train and bus, took place on 1 September 1939, the day that Hitler's forces invaded

City buildings crash to the ground at the corner of Deansgate and St Mary's Gate

> **'Jairmany Calling' Manchester**
>
> The British traitor popularly nicknamed 'Lord Haw-Haw' who regularly introduced his propaganda messages on German radio (then known as 'the wireless' to most people in Britain) with 'Jairmany Calling! Jairmany calling!', would often attempt to undermine local morale by announcing a forthcoming heavy air raid – sometimes showing surprisingly accurate local knowledge. The Manchester suburb of Hulme, for example. 'Are you listening in Hulme? We'll soon get rid of all the vermin there – when all those old houses are bombed away.' And, as one woman there said, 'They had a good try.'

Poland. The full evacuation from the Manchester area eventually accounted for 72,000 children and 23,000 adults.

The preparations which Manchester had made were first tested on 20 June 1940, when the first Alert (a false alarm) was sounded in the area. The first bombs did not fall until the end of the following month, in Salford. But, as in many other parts of the country, while people lived under a continuous threat of air-raids during the summer and autumn of 1940, their worst fears were not realised. During the Battle of Britain, when as many as 250 enemy aircraft might be over various parts of Britain at any one time, the Manchester area recorded raids, including several on suburbs of the city. There were scattered raids throughout September, and on the night of 2/3 October serious damage was reported in Salford. Bombs were dropped over many parts of the town and a large-scale fire was started in a four-storey warehouse in Salford goods station when oil bombs tore through its roof. A part of the Town Hall was demolished by a high-explosive bomb. The raid signalled a stepping-up of Luftwaffe activity in the region for six more raids followed during that month, in which damage or casualties occurred. Hume, Salford, Stretford, Sale, Didsbury, and several Manchester districts were all hit. Further attacks, including a sharp raid on the Ancoats district in which two public houses were seriously damaged, followed in November and December. All of these were precursors of the saturation blitzes to which Manchester was about to be subjected – blitzes which those Mancunians who knew about the pounding of Liverpool and Merseyside to the west, expected day by day.

On Saturday 21 December Manchester was busy with Christmas shoppers, and most people were looking forward to their Sunday rest. That afternoon, however, 270 Luftwaffe aircraft – mainly Heinkel 111s and Junkers 88s, but with a few Dornier 17s – assembled at various *Luftflotten* 2 and 3 airfields in

The Shambles and Market Square

Northern France, Belgium, and Holland, in preparation for a major attack. Radio intercepts clearly showed the intended target.

At 6.28pm the Alert – the 'Moaning Minnie' siren wail – was sounded throughout the Manchester area. Most of the Luftwaffe aircrews were able to sight the target-zone visually that night, though some used radio navigational aids. Guidance to the area was assisted, too, by the fires still burning in Liverpool and Birkenhead from bombing the previous night. Specific targets had already been identified by German Intelligence following a photographic reconnaissance flight over the area in the first days of October 1939. The city centre was to be the focus of the bombing runs, though the importance of the Ship Canal also meant that succeeding waves of bombers would concentrate on the west of Manchester.

Having been alerted, Manchester's defences went into action, and the raiders were harrassed by anti-aircraft fire. Two German aircraft fell victim to their shells, one crashing in Trafford Park, and another falling into the sea off Blackpool.

37,000 INCENDIARIES

The first wave of bombers released showers of incendiaries just two minutes after the Alert had first sounded. Among the places where the first batches fell were Albert Square, the Royal Exchange, the old Victoria Buildings, and Cathedral Yard. Within half an hour of the incendiaries falling the city centre was dotted with fires, and soon the entire city centre was emitting a huge red glow – a magnet for succeeding waves of Luftwaffe crews. Warehouses and their contents added fuel to hundreds of separate fires. By the end of the attack, 37,000 incendiary bombs had been released over the target – an area which spread outwards from the initial concentration point to include Salford and Stretford and other districts surrounding the city. 'They simply plastered us with them', as one man recalled. At one wardens' post in Manchester a warden arrived carrying a sackful of incendiaries and dumped them on the floor. A little later another warden arrived, bringing a live incendiary which he banged on the desk, asking what he should do with it. As one of the men on duty put it, 'Nobody spoke . . .'

Devastation in the Cannon Street area

The Manchester district was short of firefighters – 30 pumps and 200 men had been sent previously to assist in Liverpool. Salford and Stretford brigades were fully stretched coping with fires in their own districts. Reinforcements were brought in from further afield. Firemen had to contend with high-explosive bombs, with which the Luftwaffe followed up its first incendiary drops, and which were now crashing into the target area of rapidly-spreading fires. The Piccadilly part of the city was an inferno. Property of all types was destroyed as 270 tons of high-explosives dropped on the city and surrounding towns and districts. Docks and commercial areas were badly hit.

Throughout that long night tens of thousands huddled in their shelters, and ARP wardens, firemen, and rescue squads worked on. Very occasionally the tension lifted, as when one old lady asked a warden: 'Are they still dropping them indecency bombs?'

When the All Clear was sounded just before 6.30am the following morning people emerged from their shelters to see the extent of the devastation, to return to their homes, and many to go to work. Many residents found that their usual few minutes' walk now took half an hour or more, as they were forced to make detour after detour and to clamber over the debris filling the streets. Particularly badly affected were the centre of

Royal Exchange

Manchester and the north-eastern districts, including the industrial area of Trafford Park. Rescue teams were still trying to dig through debris and smouldering ruins to reach the trapped, and firemen were still fighting to bring some of the largest fires under control. By noon they had succeeded – though some of the largest fires could not be left unattended since the intense heat at their centres meant that they could burst into flames again at any time.

HALF THE STORY

That Sunday night attack, however, was only half the story. For, as in the pattern frequently adopted by the Luftwaffe, the saturation bombing of Manchester was to be a 'double-blitz'. On that same night, even as rescue work was still continuing, the Luftwaffe returned. 171 bombers of *Luftflotte 3* arrived to deliver the *coup de grâce*. This time they released some 7,000 incendiaries and nearly 200 tons of high-explosives over the area – the first waves flying over Manchester shortly after 7pm in a raid that lasted for five hours. This raid followed the same pattern: incendiaries were sown across the target area followed by high explosives to capitalise on the fires' hold on buildings. And once more the Luftwaffe, which had again chosen the centre of the city as its concentration point succeeded in their aim. Cloud and haze made navigation a little more difficult than before, though the target zone became visible to some of the raiders during the attack, as the glow of newly-started fires could be seen through the cloud.

About three hours or so into the raid a strong north-easterly wind sprang up, making control of fires on the ground much more hazardous. Burning embers and showers of sparks were carried in the wind, threatening adjacent buildings. The warehouses around Parker Street and George Street, having been set alight, became a major blaze, the stores they contained adding fuel to the fire.

The greatest conflagration of the night was around Piccadilly, where buildings were gutted, their angular façades silhouetted against the bright reds and yellows of the fires burning inside. Sapped and buckled by the heat, sides of buildings toppled and fell whilst some buildings had to be demolished in order to prevent the spread of the devouring flames. With the exception of York House, containing the telephone exchange, the area around Piccadilly was completely destroyed. Had firemen not succeeded in saving York House, the consequent loss of telephone communication would undoubtedly have added greatly to the general confusion.

Of the city's ten hospitals, four were put out of action completely, including the Jewish Hospital on the previous night's raid. A wing of the Royal Eye Hospital was shattered; Cheetham's Hospital and the Cathedral were both badly damaged. The crowded huddle of shops and pubs of the Old Shambles had been reduced to a literal equivalent of its name, the devastation there stretching as far as Cannon Street. It was calculated that within a one-mile radius of Albert Square 31 acres of the city had been reduced to ruins and piles of scatttered debris. Nor was damage and destruction confined to Manchester itself. Salford, Stretford and Stockport took their share of the pounding. But the major cost throughout the area was in lives lost and private homes destroyed. Some idea of the savagery of the double-blitz upon the Manchester area is gained from the facts and figures relating to this pre-Christmas bombardment.

Across the area during those two nights 1,300 separate fires were started: 3,000 extra firemen, and 400 appliances from outlying areas were called in. Manchester's dead for the two nights numbered 363, with 455 seriously injured. The death toll in Salford was 197, with 177 sustaining serious injuries. The equivalent figures for Stretford were 106 and 87 respectively. There were fatal casualties, too, among civilians in other districts; and to the total deaths must be added the 64 police, fire, and civil defence fatalities sustained throughout the area.

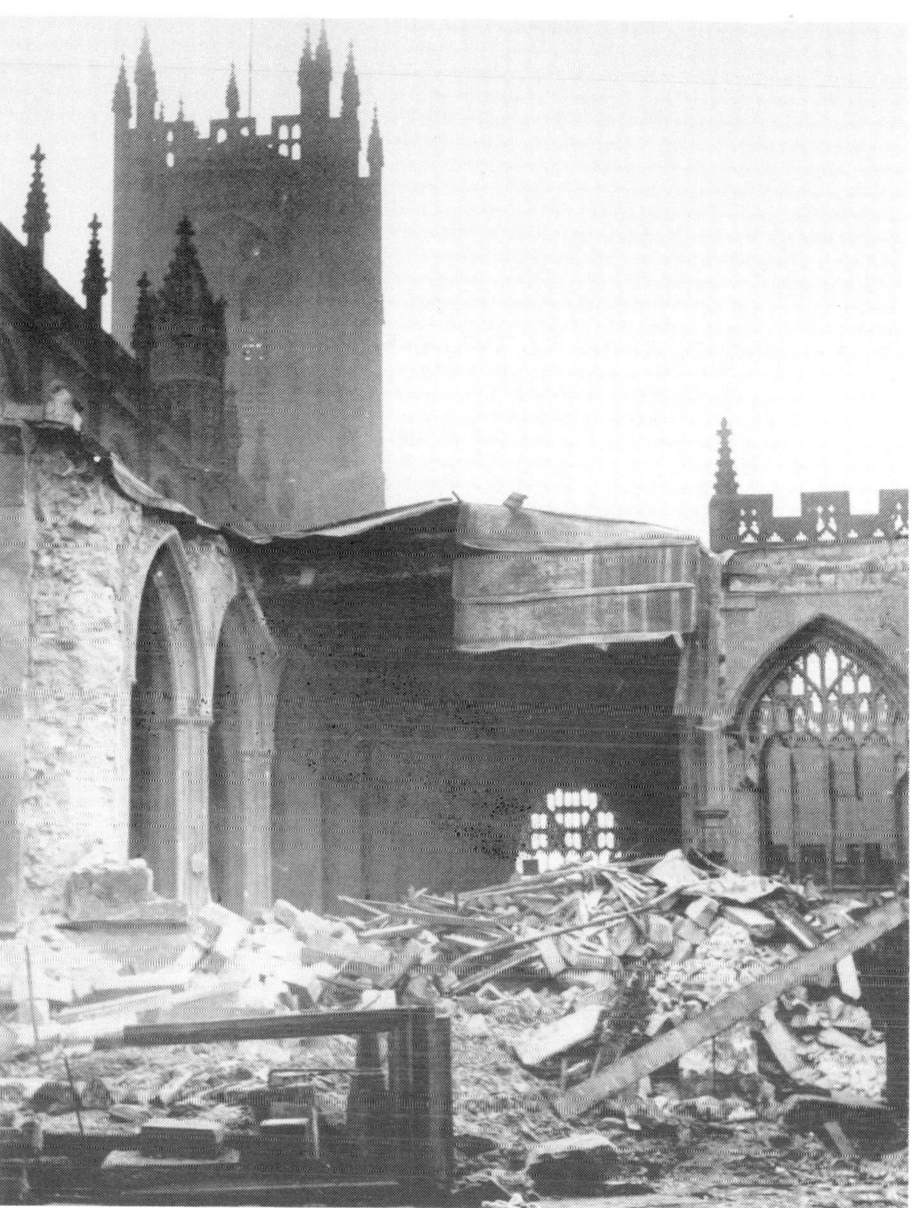
Manchester Cathedral

Bombed at Birth

'My little son was born on 19 March 1941 . . . he arrived as they dropped an unexploded bomb at the bottom of the garden,' recalled a Manchester woman. As she was having a blood transfusion and was too ill to be moved when everyone else was evacuated from their homes, she was left where she was, with a young doctor to look after her and her baby. There was a sudden enormous explosion, and all the windows were blown in. When she opened her eyes she saw that the doctor's cheek had been cut by flying glass, but her new baby was fast asleep in his arms . . .

In Manchester almost 30,000 houses sustained varying degrees of damage, and 5,000 people were made temporarily homeless – a figure which the civil authorities reduced in under two weeks to about 1,500 by the speedy repair of damaged houses. In Salford more than 4,000 were made homeless, and approximately the same number in Stretford.

In the city centre of Manchester, the heart of its concentrated fires, 200 business premises were destroyed, together with 165 warehouses and 150 offices. Hundreds of other business and commercial premises were damaged to some degree.

The Luftwaffe succeeded in inflicting considerable industrial damage. The Trafford Park industrial complex was badly hit, over 100 firms reporting damage of varying degrees. The American Oil Company, for example, suffered the destruction of two storage tanks and two warehouses. The Trussed Concrete Steel Company reported heavy damage, 50% of its works having been destroyed. The Metropolitan-Vickers aircraft factory experienced both physical damage and a blow to the morale of the personnel. Just three days before the second raid the workers at the factory had celebrated the

Miller Street

completion of the first of the bombers named after the home city, the Manchester. On that day it had passed all its inspection tests so that it was ready to be put into operational service. A direct hit from a high-explosive bomb on that part of the factory, where the craft was assembled, destroyed both building and bomber. Another twelve Manchesters which were nearing completion were also destroyed. Production of the Metropolitan-Vickers bomber was put back six months. Tarpaulins draped over the roof of the factory as a temporary measure enabled some work to proceed, but the permanent replacement of the roof was achieved only through a rather imaginative scheme. Roofsheeters were gathered from all over the country to carry out the work, but because of the lack of housing caused by the local destruction they had nowhere to stay. Several carriages of the London, Midland and Scottish Railway were shunted into the Work's sidings, heating was piped from the factory to the carriages, and they became temporary homes for the specialist roofers. The luggage compartments of the coaches were converted into canteens for the men.

At School in the Blitz

At the start of the war many thousands of schoolchildren were evacuated, and by January 1940 ten per cent of schools had been requisitioned. By the time the Blitz came many children were only attending school part time – or were not being taught at all. By the end of the major Blitz, in July 1941, some 3000 State schools in England and Wales had been badly damaged and about 1000 destroyed. And it is hardly surprising that 10% of Manchester schoolchildren were absent in the Christmas term for most of the time, and 75% for a quarter of the time – it seems surprising that they managed to attend at all.

The approaches of the Ship Canal and its terminus at Salford Docks were also bombed by the Luftwaffe – even though ships in the basin had belched out dirty smoke in an attempt to provide a screen. Warehouses and factories around dockland were hit, some burning down to a heap of debris. Part of the railway complex at the docks was severely damaged, as were ships at their moorings. There was a miraculous escape from a parachute mine which came down onto the Canal. In fact, it landed on the *Firefly*, the Canal Company's fireboat. The parachute was caught in its descent in the rigging of the vessel. The bottom of the mine rested on a coil of rope beneath, and the impact which would have detonated the explosive was thereby avoided.

Elsewhere, throughout the bombed Manchester area, there were many unexploded mines to be dealt with in the aftermath of the blitz.

A heavy bomb penetrated Sunlight House in Quay Street, where it went through to a swimming pool in the basement and broke up into large lumps of a substance closely resembling alabaster. One of the wardens on the scene picked up a lump and suggested hitting it with a hammer to find out what it was. Fortunately his suggestion was not taken up: what he had found was 'sympathetic' TNT. Had it blown up it would undoubtedly have set off other explosives in the vicinity with devastating effect.

In the two nights' blitz over 800 high-explosive bombs were released and 32 huge one-ton parachute mines. One of these shattered part of Hulme Town Hall in Stretford Road, Manchester, giving rise to the local belief – which persisted for many years – that dozens of people had been trapped and had died in the shelters in the basement of the Hall.

The rumour was completely false, though some people were trapped there, but they were successfully rescued.

The blast tore away a huge section of the wall on the Trafford Street side of the building. Wardens entered the wreckage and started to tap in the inner walls to see if there was anybody trapped inside. Their taps were soon answered, and the task of reducing the pile of rubble safely was begun. Eventually a hole was made into which a torch was lowered, tied to the string taken from the

Bomb damage at the Jewish Hospital

underpants of one of the rescuers – ordinary rope being too thick for the purpose. However, there was so much dust that the light beam only penetrated to a distance of about 15 feet. So one of the wardens prepared to be lowered into the tunnel and gave a warning shout, 'Keep clear below, I'm coming down.' 'Don't you dare come down here,' a woman answered in a voice distinct and firm, 'I'm not properly dressed.' Happily, the three people trapped in the Town Hall rubble – the caretaker, his wife and their married daughter – allowed themselves to be rescued and were eventually brought out safely.

Recovery from the saturation bombing continued throughout the following weeks and months. Gradually sites were cleared of rubble and normal wartime routines were resumed. Fortunately, the Luftwaffe did not return immediately or in force. The Manchester area continued to be bombed but not in such a concentrated manner. The next raid of any size occurred on 11 March 1941, when in the course of a three-hour attack bombs were dropped on Hulme, Salford and on Stretford, where they fell in the vicinity of Trafford Wharf and Pomona Docks. A gas main was ruptured and set alight; this and the glare from a burning laundry attracting raiders to the neighbourhood. Also hit during this raid was Manchester United's football ground. Damage there was estimated at £50,000, the main centre stand being burned out completely, the dressing rooms and a medical room destroyed.

Smaller raids followed until the night of Whit Sunday, 1/2 June 1941, when the heaviest blow since the pre-Christmas two-day onslaught fell on the Manchester area. It was estimated that 110 aircraft were used in a raid that started soon after midnight, and lasted 1½ hours. Major fires were concentrated in Manchester's city centre and in the Cheetham district. The Assize Courts were hit, and the Gaiety Theatre, the YMCA, the College of Technology and the Manchester police headquarters in South Street were damaged in the raid. Bombs also fell on Stretford, but the worst single incident occurred at the Salford Royal Hospital, where 14 nurses sheltering in the basement of their quarters at the hospital were killed in a direct hit.

After that Whitsun raid in 1941, Luftwaffe activity over the North West became sporadic. Many separate raids were recorded and the area was later affected by the V1 campaign but the days of heavy, concentrated attacks were over. The last raid took place in March 1945, when after more than 300 alerts during the war the air raid sirens sounded in the Manchester area for the last time.

One man's abiding memory of the major blitz may well express what many felt at the time. He vividly recalled seeing the scenes of destruction and devastation and finding that the streets 'were like a glassworks. Glass was everywhere, buildings were all over the place, and the smell of burning was sickening.'

But in spite of all the deaths and devastation caused by the Blitz, and in spite of the undoubtedly heavy damage to industrial plants and the dock areas, the Luftwaffe can hardly be said to have taken effective advantage of the targets offered by Greater Manchester. The docks continued to operate, the factories to produce, the railways to run and Mancunians to live and work – if not exactly as before, certainly unbroken in spirit.

Carry on Manchester

The *Manchester Evening News* – one of the most highly respected of all local newspapers in Britain – consistently opposed Chamberlain's policy of appeasement before the outbreak of the Second World War, and demanded much stronger responses to Hitler's diplomatic bullying.

When war came, stirring editorials and calm, clear advice on emergency precautions helped to maintain local morale. Although the expected bombs did not fall on Manchester at once, the paper 'stayed on its toes, reminding readers of the historic times in which they lived, imploring them to "carry on".'

Nottingham's Greatest Test

Until one terrible night in May 1941, many citizens of Nottingham were quite convinced that their city was not on the Luftwaffe's hit-list. There had been so many Alerts which had proved to be false alarms, including one on the first night of the war. Unlike London and other major cities, Nottingham always seemed to be by-passed by the Heinkels and Dorniers – as if by order. The first air-raid did not occur until the night of 30 August 1940, and by the standards of the day it was relatively minor. Using whistling bombs, whose blood-curdling screeches could be heard a mile away, the Luftwaffe dropped 18 high-explosive bombs, as well as incendiaries, on the Sherwood and Mapperley areas. This raid produced Nottingham's first air-raid casualty – a baby boy.

Before the end of the year there were three more minor attacks. On 2 September two bombs were dropped, injuring three people, and on the last day of October, a wet and cloudy afternoon, a lone raider circled over the city and dropped four high-explosive bombs and an incendiary – all on Bramcote, to the south-west of the city centre. Two weeks later five bombs were dropped, but there were no casualties.

There were more raids in the first few months of 1941, but their comparatively limited scale seemed to support the view that Nottingham was not as important for the Luftwaffe as those cities which had suffered intense and prolonged attacks. In the first raid of the new year, 15 people were killed and 14 injured. On the night of 4 February one bomb was dropped, causing no casualties, and one woman was killed on 14 March when a bomb crashed through the roof of a semi-detached house in the Ribblesdale Road area. The house collapsed 'like a pack of cards'. On 8 April ten high-explosive bombs were dropped on Beeston Boiler Works, killing one woman and injuring a number of people.

How Nottingham Prepared

Nottingham's defence authorities worked on the assumption that heavy air attacks would certainly come, and were as ready for the test as any likely target in Britain. Shelters prepared included large refuges cut into solid rock as well as old caves and cellars. In all there were:

300 public shelters
1,800 communal surface shelters
3,000 domestic surface shelters
over 24,000 Anderson shelters

Such widespread provision undoubtedly reduced the loss of life very considerably.

'WE HAD THAT EERIE FEELING THAT THEY COULD SEE US LOOKING UP AT THEM . . .'

These infrequent and relatively minor raids reinforced the belief that Nottingham would be spared the sufferings endured by so many other British cities. But for Nottingham and its well-prepared Air-Raid Precautions, the great test was near. It came late on the night of 8 May. It was a clear, moonlit night, and observers could see the exhaust trails of the Luftwaffe's Heinkels passing overhead, apparently on their way to attack Liverpool, just as they had done for the past seven nights. As usual, the Alert wailed its warning, but many people did not bother to take to their shelters – damp, uncomfortable places, and everybody knew that Nottingham was not as important a target as Liverpool. But then the Heinkels were seen to turn and circle, droning over the city. One woman recalled that 'we had that eerie feeling that they could see us looking up at them.' Like many another family that night, hers took a vote whether 'to jump into the flooded Anderson shelter in the garden or go back into the warm house and sit under the dining room table', and like scores of others they voted to stay indoors.

Explosions began to rock the city and its surrounding districts as the enemy bombers flew to and fro in the moonlit sky. Some flew so low that, as one eyewitness said, 'they loomed huge across the face of the moon.' Thousands of incendiaries, and a few oil bombs, cascaded down on the houses, shops, factories, schools, churches and other public buildings below. Adding to the sound of destruction came the boom of AA guns and the clatter of falling shrapnel. By the time the All Clear came at 4.00am, 424 high-explosive bombs (totalling 137 tons) had been dropped by 95 German aircraft.

That night 97 fires were started, 12 of them being classified as 'serious' and 40 as 'major'. More than 200 houses were totally destroyed, a further 150 were so

The Lace Market

seriously damaged as to be uninhabitable, and 4,000 more were only 'slightly damaged'. But for the energy and efficiency of Nottingham's fire-fighters the damage would certainly have been greater.

In this one raid, 159 people were killed, 274 injured, and hundreds lost their homes. Six rest centres were opened for those who had been made homeless, and in some districts mobile canteens served food and drink to survivors and ARP workers. The death toll was particularly heavy in West Bridgford which had been hit by many high-explosive bombs, and a number of lives were lost when a public shelter near Black's lace factory in Dakeyne Street received a direct hit.

The greatest loss of life occurred at the Nottingham Cooperative Bakery in Meadow Lane, where two high-explosive bombs exploded inside the building. One of them cut through to the shelter beneath the bakery, tearing apart the roof and bringing down machinery and hundreds of tons of flour – killing 49 people and injuring 20 others.

But there was at least one remarkable escape at the Cooperative Bakery in Meadow Lane. Looking out towards the suburb of West Bridgford, members of the night shift saw parachute flares descending, and as the blast of high-explosive bombs came nearer and nearer they went down to the shelters in the basement – one under the bread bakery and the other below the confectioney department. The cellars were lined with sandbags, and there were blast walls at the entrances. Incendiaries fell on the bakery roof, and then came the first of the high-explosive bombs, cutting through two concrete floors above the confectionary shelter. One of the survivors recalled what happened:

> (The bomb) hit the floor of the shelter at an angle and skidded away from me to a corner. It looked like a dustbin coming through to me. As it hit the ground there was a terrific flash. The blast blew me about three yards under the chlorinator which had recently been installed on the wall . . .

Bomb disposal experts later established that a fault in the casing of that bomb had prevented some of the explosive from detonating.

There were other remarkable escapes. Members of a family were in their Anderson shelter in Eastville Street when a bomb fell in their garden – only a few feet away from the shelter. 'It seemed to lift the shelter into the air,' said one of them, 'and then replace it again.' The whole of the shelter had, in fact, been moved nine inches by the blast.

TO THE GLORY OF GOD
AND IN MEMORY OF THE 48 EMPLOYEES
OF THIS BAKERY WHO LOST THEIR LIVES
THROUGH ENEMY ACTION
ON THE NIGHT OF MAY 8TH-9TH 1941

J. ADDIS
E. ARMES
A. AYRES
C. BELL
W. BILSON
N. BIRCH
G. BREAM
J. BRISTER
F. BOURNE
H. BUTTON
W. CHAMBERS
J. CONNOR
L. CONWAY
R. COWLISHAW
W. CULLEY
H. DAVIS
N. DAWBENEY
C. GAMBLE
E. HICKLING
J. HILL
F. HOWMAN
MR & MRS C. P. JUDD
A. KEETLEY
J. KNOWLES
W. LEVICK
G. MARSHALL
T. MILLER
G. MORRIS
W. NAYLOR
A. PARKES
J. PAUL
J. PEACH
L. PERKINS
A. PULFREE
W. RADFORD
E. ROBERTS
J. ROBINSON
V. J. SANDS
E. SAUNDERS
B. SMITH
P. STANTON
F. STEPHENSON
H. TATE
A. TAYLOR
S. THEAKER
J. WARRENER
T. WHITCHURCH
E. WOODWARD

THEIR NAMES LIVETH FOREVER

This facsimile records the names of those who died at the Meadow Lane bakery of the Nottingham Co-operative Society

'A HUGE PILLAR OF ANGRY RED FIRE AND BLACK SMOKE . . .'

The sun came up on a terrible sight: a huge pillar of angry red fire and black smoke towered up over the city, where several buildings were still ablaze.

With the All Clear at 4am came the daunting tasks of rescuing trapped persons, clearing the rubble, repairing broken pipes, controlling still-burning fires, counting the cost in lives and damage. The air was filled with dust and smoke, and wherever the repair gangs turned there were wrecked buildings, huge craters, piles of debris, smouldering ruins. In the words of a local reporter in West Bridgford:

Most parts of the city were hit. Two of the city's churches were completely destroyed, and a third, the city's mother church of St Mary's, was only saved when firemen operating on a high turntable succeeded in dowsing the fire when its roof was set ablaze. But all that remained of St Christopher's in Colwick Road were the walls, pillars and arches. The almost 100-year old church of St John's at Leenside, built in 14th century style, was almost completely burnt out, its wooden roof offering an easy target for nearby fires.

University College also sustained major damage. The west side received a direct hit from a high-explosive bomb. The mining department and part of the textile department were destroyed, and a great deal of valuable machinery and equipment was lost. Among the famous Nottingham buildings destroyed or severely damaged were the Moot Hall, the Lace Market and the Masonic Hall. A high-calibre bomb crashed through the roof of the Masonic Hall, but although the Steward and his family were in the top flat at the time, all escaped unhurt. One of the biggest and fiercest fires that morning raged in and around the Lace Market, where several premises were burnt out.

Nottingham's sports grounds also suffered severely, including the famous Trent Bridge Cricket Ground, scene of many Test Matches. The practice hall and other buildings were destroyed and damage to the field itself included a large crater on the Fox Road side. Five bombs made sizeable craters in the Notts

Where's the Fire?

Accidents in the black-out and such things as falling anti-aircraft shells were by no means the only hazards arising from Britain's determined efforts to defend her cities from Luftwaffe attack. During the early weeks of the war smoke screens, whose existence was a closely-guarded secret, were used in an attempt to confuse the enemy.

Nottingham was one of the places defended in this way. On the outskirts of the city large numbers of metal drums containing cotton waste soaked in oil were set on fire, producing clouds of oily black smoke that smothered everything, seeping through doors and windows and contaminating every surface with which it came into contact.

The outcry from housewives and others was such that the authorities decided that the cure was worse than the disease, and the use of smoke screens as a means of throwing German raiders off the scent was thankfully abandoned as a routine defence measure.

The Moot Hall

Nottingham University College

It Gives Me Great Pleasure

No single organisation did more to hold the fabric of British social life together during the worst days of the war than Women's Institutes up and down the country. Among their many activities, which included cookery lessons showing how to make the best of frugal wartime rations, first-aid demonstrations, make do and mend sessions, endless fund-raising for various aspects of the war effort as well as voluntary social work of all kinds, they still managed to find time for their more normal type of programme – the guest speaker.

One of the most sought-after of these was Wing Commander 'Guy' Gibson, VC, the famous dam-buster who was killed in action not long before the end of the war. On being invited to address a branch of the WI in Nottingham he was highly amused to hear himself being introduced by the chairwoman, the wife of a local headmaster slightly overawed by the occasion, as the 'celebrated bomb-duster'.

Taking his cue splendidly Gibson produced a handkerchief and solemnly proceeded to dust an imaginary bomb with the utmost care, before going on to describe the May 1943 raid on the Möhne and Eder dams.

County Football Club ground, and a dressing-room was also damaged. In an earlier raid, a bowling green in the Ribblesdale Road area was damaged so badly by a bomb that it was unlikely that it could be used again that summer – to the great indignation of the members. Nottingham Central railway station did not escape the attention of the Luftwaffe, which left 26 coaches burnt out and 70 others damaged.

The night after this heaviest of all Nottingham's air-raids, the sirens

Chicken Surprise?

After the war it became known that the raid which devastated Nottingham on that terrible night of 8 May 1941 had in fact been intended for Derby, where the strategically-vital Rolls-Royce works were situated. The plan was for the first wave of bombers to put these out of action, leaving the city of Nottingham to be dealt with by a second wave later on. German records at the time make this quite clear.

But British scientists had by then developed a technique for deflecting the radio beams which the Luftwaffe pilots followed in order to pin-point their targets. The result was that the first wave of bombers attacked Nottingham instead of Derby, while the second wave, intended for Nottingham, were deceived into making a similar navigational error and actually dropped their bombs on the Vale of Belvoir, to the east of the city.

In the third volume of his history of the Second World War, Churchill describes the action in these terms:

"The German communiqué claimed the destruction of the Rolls-Royce works at Derby, which they never got near. Two hundred and thirty high explosive bombs and a large number of incendiaries were, however, unloaded on the open country.

The total casualties there were two chickens."

sounded again. This time nobody waited to see what would happen – all made straight for their shelters, fully expecting a repeat of the previous night's raid. But only one German aircraft appeared. It dropped three bombs, wrecking the Cremorne Fair Ground (which was then located near Wilford Bridge) and killing two members of the family who owned the business.

The final raid on Nottingham in 1941 was four days later, when another lone bomber dropped three high-explosive bombs, causing three casualties. In the following year, 1942, there was only one raid (though there were 20 Alerts). Shortly before midnight on 24 July a lone aircraft dropped four high-explosive bombs on the Sneinton Dale district and scores of incendiary devices over a wider area. One of the bombs failed to explode, but a fire-watcher was killed and three other persons injured by the explosion from the bomb which failed to detonate. Nottingham had experienced its last air-raid.

Counting the Cost . . .

Air Raid Alerts	225
Shortest (15 Nov 1940)	1 min
Longest (21 Dec 1940)	9 hrs 36 min
No. of Attacks	11
Killed	181
Seriously injured	350

The Poor Law Offices, Shakespeare Street

Everyone knew it was Hull

All news bulletins issued by the Ministry of Information during the Second World War were carefully censored to avoid the risk of revealing any information which might be of use to the enemy. As a result, bombed cities and towns were rarely mentioned by name unless it was quite clear from German propaganda that they knew where their bombs had fallen. One example of this was Hull, which was usually referred to as 'a North-East town'.

In his memoirs, Herbert Morrison, the wartime Home Secretary, expressed sympathy with the people of Humberside for having to endure great hardship and suffering under such a cloak of anonymity throughout the war, and expressed the view that Hull probably suffered more at the hands of the Luftwaffe than anywhere else in the United Kingdom.

This form of censorship probably did not deceive the Germans at all, especially as they always carried out photographic reconnaissance after their major raids. And for people living in the North-Eastern region and in East Anglia the use of these vague geographical generalisations became increasingly meaningless. Whenever, as happened frequently, they were heard on the radio or seen in the press, everyone knew it was Hull that had been attacked yet again.

Despite its great strategic importance, the city was the last major centre to be singled out for special attention during the intensive bombing campaign of 1940/41. It also shared with London the dubious distinction of being one of the last places to be attacked as the war in Europe drew to a close. Unfortunately for its people, as a major port it was not only a primary target in its own right, but was also on the flight path of German raiders bound for Liverpool and other destinations in the North-West. Any Luftwaffe pilot who discovered that he still had some left-overs in his bomb bays after carrying out his main mission, saw Hull as a tempting and convenient last target before making his final dash for home across the North Sea.

The authorities were well aware of the city's vulnerability to air attack, and took great pains in drawing up their emergency plans. Some of the earliest of these, dating from 1937, provided for the evacuation of 100,000 civilians, including 30,000 schoolchildren. On each of the first three days of September 1939 batches of evacuees did, in fact, leave the city. But, by the end of the year, it was apparent that less than one-third of the total numbers planned for had actually moved out, largely because no bombing raids took place during the early months of the war. When the main attacks came in 1941 further evacuations were carried out but, as elsewhere in the country, many Hull evacuees later returned to their homes, risking the dangers in order that families could live together.

At a cost of £1.5m air-raid shelters were made available in large numbers. More than 18,000 communal, public and Anderson shelters were provided together with 21,000 domestic surface shelters. Almost 2,000 indoor domestic

Tourist trap

Soon after Allied forces liberated Belgium in September 1944 a large store of maps, diagrams, photographs and plans was found in the German Army Headquarters in Antwerp. These were of considerable interest to British military intelligence because they showed street plans of Hull, with all the main buildings, factories, bridges, utilities, dock and harbour installations clearly marked.

Some of this information had been put together from aerial photographs taken by the Luftwaffe on reconnaissance missions early in 1941, but there was little doubt that much of the material had been gathered before the war by Germans visiting the city. In all probability this was the work not of full-time agents, but of businessmen and tourists quite prepared to do a little spying on the side for the Third Reich.

The mass of data they obtained confirmed British suspicions that Humberside had been chosen as a suitable landing zone for the second wave assault to follow a successful invasion across the English Channel. But, unknown to the Germans, well-prepared defensive plans had already been drawn up by the time war broke out.

Elevated bridges across the River Hull were to be raised and then immobilised. Swing bridges were also to be made useless by removing essential mechanical parts, to be hidden outside the city. Stocks of fuel were to be destroyed and all vehicles put out of action. There were also plans to flood key roads leading out of the city, and to sink the pontoon of Victoria Pier in order to delay any enemy force.

Crystal, one of the many Humber trawlers lost in action during the Second World War, sank on 26 June 1942 after hitting a mine off Scarborough

shelters were also delivered. In addition, elaborate plans were prepared to set up casualty stations, rest centres, welfare and emergency feeding facilities, together with reception centres of various kinds and billeting arrangements. Auxiliary rescue, fire-fighting and demolition services were also established, as well as a Special Information Centre to handle enquiries about missing persons, and deal with the immediate problems of those made homeless by the raids.

Barrage balloons played an important part in the city's defences. Some were carefully positioned at Spurn Point to prevent enemy raiders making a straight descent in bombing runs from the mouth of the Humber to the city centre. Others were placed at various strategic points elsewhere to keep the Luftwaffe at a height to make pin-point bombing difficult, if not impossible, to carry out. Anti-aircraft units were also in place, and were to claim several 'kills' in actions over Humberside. They were supported by searchlight batteries, two of which were installed on barges moored in the Humber, the *Humph* and the *Clem*, which were also equipped with Lewis guns.

The Trawlermen of Hull

The seamen of Hull played a crucial role not only in the defence of their home port but also in many other theatres of the war at sea. Early in September 1939 all trawlers were requisitioned: many of them were armed and put to war service, mainly on escort and minesweeping duties. For the duration the crews were seconded to the Merchant Navy, a move which did not go down at all well among men unused to service discipline or to the accents and mannerisms of naval officers. However, they acquitted themselves with great distinction in the grim struggle to keep Britain's vital sea lanes open. Over 100 of these Hull-based trawlers were lost in action, many of them far away from their home waters.

ESSENTIAL SUPPLIES

It says a great deal for the ability and foresight of those responsible for the planning of Hull's defences that when the almost unceasing air attack was finally launched, the port was not put out of action for a single day. Along the 12 miles of quays, and 600 acres of storage space, open and covered, essential war supplies continued to be landed and then stored before being moved on to many destinations inland. The flow of essential goods, from basic foodstuffs for the civilian population to the most sophisticated military hardware for the fighting forces, was maintained despite all the efforts of the German raiders to bring the docks to a standstill.

This could not have been achieved, of course, without the steadfastness of men and women who were prepared to work throughout the blitz, remaining in the city despite the widespread destruction and the risk of injury or death. Others stayed with friends or relatives in the suburbs and surrounding villages overnight, and came in to the city and dock areas every day to work.

Even this routine was not without its hazards. One worker recalled being 'machine-gunned by a low flying aircraft in Cottingham on a clear moonlit night, so we decided to stay in Hull on a night and take our chance along with everyone else.' His attitude was typical of most of the people of Hull. As the bombing intensified, so did their determination.

The first Alert sounded on the day after the declaration of war and was followed by many other false alarms until the night of 19 June 1940 when, just before midnight, a few incendiary and high-explosive bombs fell on Buckingham and Victor Streets in East Hull, causing minor damage.

The first serious incident occurred a few days later, at 5.30pm on 1 July. A single bomber attacked some barrage balloons and then released a number of bombs over oil installations at Saltend. Many of these exploded beyond the actual installations, but flying shrapnel ruptured one of the tanks, holding about 2,500 tons of petrol.

Hull's firemen averted disaster. Despite the billowing clouds of dense black fumes and the hazardous conditions, they brought the fire under control and managed to save most of the stock of precious fuel as well. No fewer than four men were awarded the George Medal for their heroism on that night.

The remaining months of 1940 saw a number of minor raids and there were well over 100 Alerts. But one serious incident in October occurred before the Alert had sounded, when two parachute mines were dropped. One fell upon houses at the end of Strathmore Avenue, close to the River Hull, causing – in the clipped language of the official report – 'extensive' damage. In fact, hundreds of homes caught in the power of the blast were affected. A local history of the times, written by Thomas Geraghty, reports the experience of one fortunate survivor. As he was getting dressed in his bedroom he was suddenly 'lifted to the ceiling' and then 'found himself on his bed in the front room downstairs. The blast had stripped him of his pyjamas.

Despite incidents of this kind, the citizens of Hull reckoned that by the end of 1940 they had come off lightly compared with people living in other major cities. The situation remained unchanged during the early weeks of 1941, although the Alerts hardly ever stopped sounding. On one occasion the sirens set up their mournful wail no fewer than six times in the space of 24 hours, and concern was expressed by the authorities about the added stress and loss of sleep caused by these constant, and largely pointless, warnings.

But when February arrived the anxieties became real enough as the enemy intensified his attack upon the city. There were six separate raids during the month, in which four German aircraft were brought down by anti-aircraft fire. Oil mills and warehouses were damaged, the lighters *Monarch* and *Brakeln* sunk at their moorings in Alexandra Dock, and a number of homes destroyed. Six parachute mines were dropped in these raids.

March 1940 opened dramatically when two of these powerful devices, each containing a ton of high explosive, descended on James Reckitt Avenue in East Hull, destroying many houses and killing or wounding civilians. Worse was to follow on the night of the 13th. The Bridge Approach to Stoneferry, the intended target, was damaged. A school in the area was also hit, and a large fire started at the Sissons' paint factory. Eleven tons of high explosive bombs were dropped during the raid, which caused 38 deaths and 79 serious injuries.

The month ended with a general raid on various parts of the city in which flares, high explosive bombs and more parachute mines were dropped, bringing the total for the month to 23. A landmine totally destroyed ARP Headquarters; water mains were smashed; 31 separate fires were started and the streets littered with rubble. 500 homes were destroyed and a further 2,000 damaged. 52 persons lost their lives.

The severity of this attack represented a deliberate stepping-up of activity against Hull on the part of the Luftwaffe, and proved to be a grim foretaste of the night blitzes to follow in May. Actual raids during the intervening month of April were, however, less severe. Apart from a direct hit by a parachute mine on a public shelter in Ellis Terrace, in which more than 50 people perished, and the accidental destruction of two houses in St George's Street and Glasgow Street by falling anti-aircraft shells, the damage to the city was comparatively minor in scale.

But the frequency of the Luftwaffe's visits was an unpleasant reminder of the city's strategic importance. The sirens continued their wail almost every night, so that when another Alert was sounded shortly after 11pm on the night of 7 May it came as no surprise. In brilliant moonlight a few searchlights beamed their way across the night sky, and for a time it seemed that the city might escape without being bombed. An hour passed, and then flares began to fall, followed quickly by incendiaries and high explosive bombs – the opening blows in a raid of major proportions which was to last for nearly six hours.

Soon reports started to come in from all parts of the city reporting direct hits on buildings, and the outbreak of many fires. That night the fire-fighters started their formidable task at a great disadvantage because many mains were damaged early in the raid, and water in the river was at a low level. No fewer than 464 fires were started, many of them major conflagrations that raged virtually out of control destroying everything in their paths. Soon the moonlight on the surrounding hills was outshone by the glow of the burning city, a glow that was seen in the western sky by RAF pilots flying near the coast of Denmark.

In the heart of the city King Edward Street was reduced to rubble, and at Riverside Quay whole timber yards were set ablaze. Oil mills, factories, stores and warehouses provided still more fuel for the engulfing flames, while tons of explosives laid whole areas to waste. Shattered buildings blocked the streets with bricks and girders and debris of all kinds.

The commercial centre of the city, consisting of shops, offices and other buildings, was smashed, and the City Hall was badly damaged. The night before the raid the London Symphony Orchestra gave a concert there under its conductor, Basil Cameron, in a programme consisting entirely of works by German composers. The distinguished pianist Myra Hess, renowned for her lunchtime concerts at the National Gallery in London throughout the war years, was the soloist in a performance of Beethoven's 4th Piano Concerto.

Present in the audience on that occasion was Philip Chignell, who later returned to Hull to see the ruined city centre and wrote the following description of the City Hall:

> The . . . walls of the Hall remain, the roof has fallen in, the floor is a mass of debris, broken and half burned beams, charred seats, broken glass, muck and filth everywhere. A sorry sight. The piano used by Myra Hess . . . has not been removed. It will never sound again . . . although escaping the flames and utter destruction, the piano had its back broken by a fall from the roof, and the beautiful ivory keys were black with dirt and dust and looked as though some evil giant had hit them here and there with a big hammer.

In many residential districts the devastation was no less complete than in the centre of the city. Entire terraces, such as those in Buckingham Street, were totally blasted, leaving only the dividing walls, the flues and the chimneys standing. Such scenes were repeated in many streets throughout the city. Houses, schools, shops, garages, workshops, factories and warehouses were gutted, demolished or damaged beyond

Old Charlie

Old Charlie had a bomb at his front door the other night [27 May 1941]. An old retired sea-going man, who now lives in a small boat drawn up on the Humber bank, which the water reaches only at high tides, Charlie was a watchman in Hull on the blitz night, 7 May. His burnt clothes testify to this fact.

Some nights after this raid, Jerry came round our way. Not far from Charlie's little boat is an old derelict river steamer lying on the riverbank, practically a wreck. Jerry evidently spotted this larger boat, had a shot at it, missed and nearly sent Charlie to kingdom come. The bomb dropped in the Humber mud between Charlie's little house boat and the river. It sent tons of mud into the river and left a big crater-like gash in the Humber bank . . .

Charlie still sits on his boat side, calmly smoking the pipe of contentment. A miss is as good as a mile.

Philip Chignell
in *From Our Home Correspondent*

Tons of precious foodgrains were lost when warehouses in Hull's docks were attacked by the Luftwaffe during the two-night blitz early in May 1941

repair. Broken pipes bubbled water into the streets, where it trickled through the piles of debris, seeking its natural level. There was an all-pervasive smell of gas, brick dust, damp and death. In this one raid 203 people died and 165 were seriously injured.

Unknown to the people of Hull at the time was the other side of the account. No fewer than 23 German aircraft were shot down during the attack either by anti-aircraft fire, or by RAF night fighters, some of them equipped with a brand-new intercept radar system. Although still at an early stage of development, this device certainly showed its future potential on that night of violence and destruction. Indeed, it proved to be a decisive factor in the campaign against the Luftwaffe's night attacks on British cities.

After the first attack a witness was rash enough to say that there was nothing left to burn in the city, but he was proved wrong within a matter of hours. For on that following night, just after midnight, the raiders returned to give the people of Hull no respite from the terror and the authorities no chance to re-muster their over-stretched resources.

This second bombardment before dawn on 9 May 1941 lasted five hours and was concentrated on the King George, Alexandra and Victoria Docks, together with parts of East and North Hull. Among the many warehouses destroyed in the dock area were some containing grain: as they burst open they discharged thousands of tons of their precious contents into the River Hull. The raid was no less ferocious than that of the previous night, with a total of 375 separate fires recorded by Control HQ. Once again, many of these were major outbreaks that could be seen up to 50 miles away. They had to be contained at all costs, but other minor fires were simply left to burn themselves out. More homes, cinemas, churches, hotels and shops were destroyed. Many familiar landmarks disappeared and fresh piles of rubble were strewn over areas which many men had laboured long and hard to clear the day before. Bare walls were left standing or propped against each other, many with roof structures leaning against them at odd angles. Fresh damage was wrought upon the main services, and many temporary repairs made a few hours earlier were rendered useless once more.

The widespread destruction of property of all kinds was matched by the toll of human suffering, for this second raid added 217 to the fatal casualties, and 160 to the list of those seriously injured. Some 200 people who lost their lives during the two nights of bombing were so badly mutilated that they could not be properly identified, and were buried together in a communal grave in a quiet, unpublicised ceremony that took place on 12 May.

Some idea of the scale of these attacks can be had from the cold record. 300

'Dear Rescue men,

Just a few lines thanking you for what you did on July 14th . . . How you helped to get my mother out, and to get my two brothers which was dead, how you help me to get to shelter when I hadn't any shoes on my feet.'

– Letter from a schoolgirl in Hull, 1943

> **Lights out for Violetta**
>
> One opera-lover in Hull remembers how she picked her way through the bombed city centre to reach New Theatre, where *La Traviata* was playing. When she got there she found warnings everywhere about unexploded bombs.
>
> All went well until the last act, when the lights went out as Violetta was dying. A lamp had to be brought on stage 'so the poor lass could die and finish the story. Many may think the situation hilarious, but it wasn't for people at that time.'

high explosive bombs, totalling more than 120 tons, were dropped on the city during the two raids. An unknown, but substantial number of bombs of all kinds fell on nearby villages and outlying areas. 3,000 houses were destroyed and many more severely damaged by blast. Railway lines were hit and gas supplies to East Hull were cut off: scores of gas mains were damaged, while others were flooded. Many warehouses and other commercial properties were burnt out, and the Riverside Quay was destroyed from end to end. Around the city centre the devastation was extensive, particularly along King Edward Street, Prospect Street and Jameson Street. It was in this area that most of the shops, restaurants, hotels and offices were destroyed in one huge fire. The Corporation bus depot was also set alight and a large number of vehicles destroyed.

The terror visited upon Hull during these two days prompted a further evacuation from the city, but on a fairly modest scale; about 8,000 people were involved. The great majority of the inhabitants stayed put and steeled themselves against the possibility of a further attack on the third night.

In this respect Luftwaffe tactics had undergone an important change. During the earlier stages of the blitz on Britain, there appeared to be no consistent plan of attack on cities outside London. Major raids were certainly carried out, as we have seen, but were not followed up in many cases. This gave everyone valuable breathing space and meant that all the emergency and support services could regroup and re-equip ready for the next attack, whenever it came.

But large-scale onslaughts on successive nights, as in the case of Hull, put a

PATTERN OF FIRE

severe additional strain on these services, already stretched to the limit of their endurance. Who could say what might have happened had the Germans kept up their pressure on the third successive night, as many people in the city feared they would?

In the event, this pressure eased slightly because subsequent raids were on a smaller scale, involving not more than 50 aircraft at any one time. This, in all conscience, was bad enough, but at least nothing to compare with the 7/8 May raids was seen until 18 July, when a fiercely concentrated attack was launched once more upon East Hull and the Victoria Dock. The first bomb fell just two minutes after the red Alert was given, and the familiar pattern of fire and destruction soon followed. A gas holder was hit and caught fire, sending a huge sheet of flame into the sky. Large fires did considerable damage to the works of the well-known firm of Reckitt and Colman, and to those of Spillers, the grain merchants.

At one point, a huge grain silo was threatened, and there was a real danger that many more thousands of tons of valuable food grains would be lost. Using water to kill the grain fire carried the risk of making it swell and so bursting the walls of the silo. So it was decided to let the fire burn at the top, just damping it down, while 'leading off' the unaffected grain from the bottom of the storage silo.

In all, about 36 tons of high explosive came down that night, causing large-scale destruction and adding another 140 dead and more than 100 seriously injured, to the casualty figures.

With the advantage of hindsight we can see that the turning point in the Luftwaffe's sustained bombing campaign came in the summer of 1941, when Hitler committed the fatal error of attacking the USSR and recklessly diverted his resources to an eastern front. Not many were able to recognize it at the time, but the people of Hull came to regard the two-night blitz on 7/8 and 8/9 May as the peak of the onslaught, against which all later raids were measured.

There were many of them, some merely 'tip and run' operations, others of a more serious nature. By March 1944 operational standards in the Luftwaffe had fallen to such an extent that when yet another major raid was planned against Hull, very few German aircraft actually found the city. It was also very apparent that the new generation of pilots were reluctant to press home their attacks in the face of heavy, and increasingly accurate, anti-aircraft fire.

Nevertheless, Hull was never allowed to forget that it was in the front-line. German bombs continued to fall almost until the end of the war in Europe. The final raid, in which 12 people lost their lives, took place on the night of 17/18 March 1945, by which time the US 1st Army had crossed the Rhine and was operating well inside Germany itself. Victory in Europe was in sight, and when it finally came the people of Hull had good reason to celebrate their deliverance, before turning their minds and their muscles to the formidable task of removing the many stains of war from their city. For many who lived through those times, however, memories could not so easily be cleared away. Forty-five years later one woman, near whose family home an enemy bomb exploded, recalled for the *Hull Daily Mail* '. . . I have only to smell soot and snuffed-out candles to remember the Blitz.'

> **Counting the Cost . . .**
>
> | | |
> |---|---|
> | Air Raid Alerts | 815 |
> | (*totalling over 1,000 hours*) | |
> | Raids | 82 |
> | High Explosive Bombs (tons) | 400+ |
> | *and thousands of incendiaries* | |
> | Persons killed (approx) | 1,200 |
> | Persons seriously injured (approx) | 3,000 |
> | Homes | |
> | Destroyed | 1,472 |
> | Seriously damaged | 9,260 |
> | Damaged | 75,983 |
> | Undamaged | 5,945 |
>
> Of the seriously damaged homes, many were bombed more than once. Among the many buildings totally destroyed were 120 communal shelters and 250 domestic shelters.
>
> Such was the devastation within the city limits that no fewer than 7,500 tons of iron and steel were recovered from the rubble, together with 610 tons of lead and other non-ferrous materials. All this salvage was re-cycled and put back into the industrial war effort.

Leicester – the Luftwaffe's error?

Leicester made preparations for air bombardment in much the same way as other British towns and cities, but also prepared to receive thousands of evacuees. As a largely rural county, Leicestershire took in more evacuees than any other region of the country. In the weekend after the declaration of war on 3 September 1939 no fewer than 30,000 schoolchildren, most of them from London and Sheffield, travelled to new homes throughout the county. When the Blitz began to hit the larger industrial centres in 1940, a new stream of evacuees was added to the steady flow directed into Leicestershire since the first influx. The warmth with which local people welcomed these children – and with them many of their mothers – into their homes and hearts has been claimed to be the most significant contribution which Leicestershire made to the war effort.

When King George VI visited Leicester in October 1946 he made a special point of acknowledging this act of sustained generosity:

> . . . I would like to express my sincere appreciation to the householders of Leicester who welcomed in their midst refugees and evacuees from the areas which were subject to heavy bombing attacks.
>
> This was a work of practical sympathy which was particularly close to the heart of the Queen . . .'

Though Leicester was designated as one of the 'safer' places in England, there remained a feeling that once bombing began, the city could expect to be attacked. So in line with other centres throughout Britain air-raid shelters were constructed, public and private. Anderson shelters were installed in private gardens, entrances to public buildings were sandbagged or bricked up, and windows were taped as a protection from blast.

Towards the end of August 1939, when war seemed unavoidable, the city of Leicester suffered an outbreak of attacks on its telephone kiosks. A trail of destroyed kiosks from the city centre to Uppingham Road was generally held to be the work of the IRA. Whether or not these acts were intended to show sympathy with the Nazis, they certainly proclaimed an anti-British feeling.

On the outbreak of war Leicester, like the rest of the country, waited for something to happen. Air-raid precautions continued, such as the construction of a public shelter in Town Hall Square. The wail of air-raid sirens became a familiar sound; alerts were signalled, but no bombers appeared. As the months went by many Leicester residents began to think that their city might escape the attentions of the Luftwaffe.

This illusion was shattered at 10am on Wednesday 21 August 1940 when a single Dornier 17 broke through the morning cloud, and released eight high explosive bombs over the gasworks in Aylestone Road. All missed their target but hit houses and shops and ruptured gas mains along a 300-yard stretch of Cavendish Road. Of the hundred houses affected, eight were totally demolished, 14 seriously damaged and all the rest suffered some slight damage. Six people were killed and 24 injured.

Leicester's first air-raid took place on a day when the Luftwaffe made a large number of such raids employing one or two aircraft. Most of these were attacks on airfields in the east and south-east of England as part of the Luftwaffe's attempt to knock out the RAF. Since Leicester was not a primary target in this campaign, nor even a secondary target (as were docks and aircraft factories), there seems to be no clear explanation for this raid. It may have been part of the Luftwaffe's intention to confuse British defences – or it may have been an opportunist attack.

Nimble fingers at work in one of the many factories in Leicester requisitioned for arms production during the war

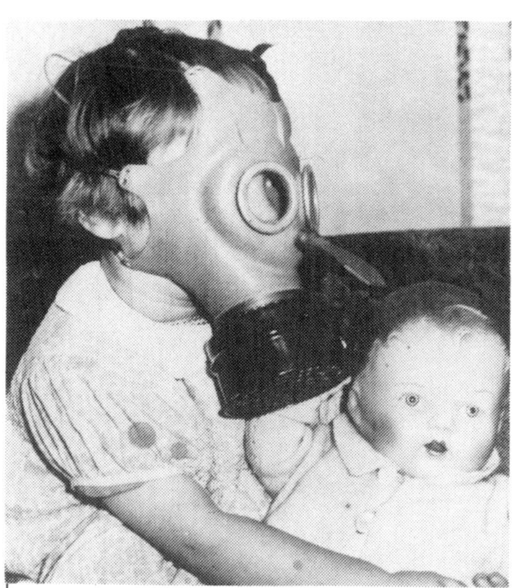

Hitler will give no warning – always carry your gas mask

So ran the poster. Before the war it was assumed that the Germans would use poison gas, and 38 million gas masks were issued to the civilian population during 1938. In the city of Leicester itself more than 120,000 masks of various types and sizes were issued to men, women and children, including infants, and the local ARP Committee arranged demonstrations showing how to detect various kinds of gas, and the best forms of protection against them. As war approached, more emphasis was placed on teaching people how to put on respirators quickly and efficiently in the event of a gas attack.

For local schoolchildren, wearing gas masks became a playtime ritual, as in Leicester's Catherine Street Infant School, , whose headmistress thought that regular wearing of the masks would banish any fear of them. 'If the gas rattles sound, put on your gas mask at once wherever you are, even in bed,' said the official leaflets.

When war came, at first everybody did what they were told and carried their gas masks with them everywhere. But as the weeks went by and there were no gas attacks, they began leaving them at home. By the end of the so-called Phoney War nobody carried a gas mask – except Service men and women who had no choice in the matter.

One of the more unusual precautions taken against the possibility of gas attack was painting the tops of pillar boxes with a special khaki-coloured paint, which was sensitive to gas in the atmosphere and changed colour if any were present. The drawback of this scheme was that fumes from factory chimneys produced much the same effect, and the idea was quietly dropped.

The people of Leicester had now been warned that they might not escape with as 'quiet' a war as many had come to think. The Luftwaffe was not inactive over the county, but no more bombs were dropped on the city until Saturday 14 September when another single raider released a number of high-explosive bombs in the St Ives Road and Ireton Road area. The rest did no damage.

On 14 November 1940 the Luftwaffe signalled its change in tactics to intensive night bombing with a devastating raid on the city of Coventry. While the full weight of its attack was concentrated on that city a number of other towns suffered limited bombing on that same night, including Birmingham, Chester, Crewe, Derby, Sheffield – and Leicester. Two aircraft dropped twenty high-explosive bombs on the area from Hinckley Road to Aylestone Road. Two people were killed and several injured.

Five days later Leicester suffered its longest and most concentrated raid. On the night of 19 November Birmingham was the Luftwaffe's principal target, though many crews did not reach it. Bombing was reported in many widely scattered regions of the country. After Birmingham, Leicester was the worst hit area that night. From shortly before 8pm until 2am the following morning, some 100 Luftwaffe aircraft flew to and fro over the city, dropping showers of incendiary bombs followed by 150 H.E. bombs. explosive bombs.

The first incendiaries fell across the city from the gasworks in Aylestone Road to the railway station in Belgrave Road. With the follow-up high-explosives fires were started in the factories of Grieve and Company and Faire Brothers Limited, and the blaze at Freeman, Hardy and Willis' warehouse in Rutland Street could be seen in the night sky for miles around. Residential properties in a wide area were blasted, and parts of Highfields Street, Tichborne Street, Humberstone Road and many other streets were reduced to rubble. Landmines caused particularly severe damage. One totally demolished several houses at the corner of Knighton Road, while another exploded in Sudeley Avenue, destroying 12 houses and damaging another 400. Among the worst hit areas were Stoneygate, Highfields and the city centre – but there a bomb failed to explode after it crashed through the roof of the Town Hall and fell into the basement.

Saucepans for Spitfires!

'We will turn your pots and pans into Spitfires and Hurricanes', said Lord Beaverbrook, Minister for Aircraft Production in 1940, appealing for aluminium, as part of his drive for more fighter aircraft in the Battle of Britain. The result was – mountains of pots, pans and kettles, mostly collected by the WVS, whose chief, Lady Reading, broadcast an appeal to housewives: 'We can all have the tiny thrill of thinking . . . perhaps it was my saucepan that made a part of that Hurricane!' In sober fact, it seems that there was enough scrap aluminium anyway. But the campaign to salvage scrap metal carried on relentlessly, and iron railings from parks, squares, churchyards and houses provided over a million tons of metal – sadly most of it never used. There were many appeals for salvage of all kinds – paper, books, rags, bones, tins, bottles, old clothes and many homes kept several dustbins, one for each class of salvage. Whatever its real value to the war effort, collecting salvage undoubtedly gave many people the feeling they were doing something to support those who were doing the fighting.

On the night of 19-20 November 1940 the spectacular blaze at the warehouse of Freeman, Hardy & Willis – the well-known shoe firm – could be seen for miles

There were other lucky escapes. When bombs fell close to Hillcrest Hospital all the lights went out and flying glass from the windows covered the beds in the wards, but the patients and staff escaped serious injury. At Highfields a man also escaped injury, if not death, simply because the raid started before his bedtime, as his son explained many years later in the *Leicester Mercury*:

> My father always said he was not going to get up in the middle of the night to go into the air raid shelter built in Welland Street.
>
> Luckily for him the raid started well before bedtime, for a large lump of masonry crashed through the roof and landed on his pillow.
>
> He also received a churned-up silver sugar bowl, unaccompanied needless to say, by its sad owner's sugar ration . . .

Other survivors spoke of the vivid, brilliantly-contrasting red and blue of the night sky as the glow of fires burned

A Leicester rescue team searches for possible survivors in the ruins of a terraced house near the city centre

This scene of devastation in Leicester was one of many photographs suppressed by the censor during the war. It was considered that publication of material of this kind would have a bad effect on morale

into the darkness. Such sights greeting those who emerged from basements and shelters concealed the true horror of that night of devastation. There were many victims. In the worst incident of the night – the destruction of houses at the corner of Tichborne and Highfields Streets – 41 lives were lost, and 13 people were killed when houses and the Methodist Church were destroyed at the junction of Saxby and Sparkenhoe Streets. A direct hit killed five people in a shelter beneath Grieve's factory in Southampton Street. The final casualty list showed that the raid had killed 108 people and injured 203.

Hundreds who had been made homeless were taken to rest centres until they could be found temporary accommodation. Rescue and demolition work continued until all those trapped in wrecked buildings had been released. The last person to be rescued alive was a man who was not freed until three days after the raid. The night after Leicester's blitz a solitary raider flew over the city, producing a natural fear among the population. But this time there were no casualties, although some properties were destroyed at Highfields and Evington.

That solitary raider heralded a return to the comparatively fleeting attention which the Luftwaffe had given Leicester before its single night of devastation. On 20 November – when Birmingham suffered another major raid – Leicester was among the targets for the widespread minor bombing attacks being made the same night. Two parachute mines caused extensive damage – one to the houses surrounding the badly damaged pavilion at Victoria Park, the other to the Steel Busks Engineering Works. More than 20 people were injured by the explosions, but no one was killed.

As Leicester did not appear to be a major target in the Luftwaffe's pattern of raids, it seemed as if the devastating raid of 19 November was an aberration. The question then began to be asked: had it been made in error? Perhaps Leicester's bombs had been intended for somewhere else? No definite answer appears to be possible. Not all the *Luftflotten* 2 and 3 crews assigned to Birmingham, the principal target for that night, managed to arrive at the drop-zone. Bombs fell that night on Northampton, Coventry, and Grantham, as well as in counties to the south and east. Leicester may have become a secondary target for pilots who failed to locate Birmingham.

In support of this view one authority claims that the raiders were attracted to the city by the glow from an accidental fire started that same evening at Lulham's factory in Northampton Square, assuming it was caused by their own incendiary bombs. On the other hand, the Germans were certainly well aware that Leicester's industries were making a big contribution to Britain's war effort. Textile, engineering and footwear firms in the county and city had switched to the production of munitions and essential equipment. The Germans' pre-war information-gathering, as well as their efficient aerial reconnaissance photography, enabled them to plot important industrial and other targets in Leicester. It is clear enough that Leicester was a *marked* target, but whether it was a *scheduled* target for that night is open to question.

The few remaining raids on Leicester seemed to suggest that the Luftwaffe regarded it as a target that required nothing more than occasional attacks, and even these may have been opportunist raids rather than planned missions. Leicester was passed by on 4 December, for example, when bombs were dropped on other parts of the county. On the night of 9/10 January 1941 it was reported that flares were dropped over Leicester, among many other places, but there was no follow-up bombing. No more high-explosive bombs were dropped on the city until the night of 8/9 April 1941, when a single raider dropped several bombs in the Ash Street area, and hit the Co-operative food warehouse in Unity Avenue. A few people were injured, but no one was killed.

There were similar raids by lone aircraft in the early hours of 17 May and on the night of 14 July. In the first of these two bombs hit the Braunstone estate, causing one death. In the second, ten high explosives fell in a line from London Road station to Worthington Street, and one person was killed. This was the last occasion on which bombs fell on Leicester.

Counting the cost . . .

People killed on 19/20 Nov. 1940	108
in other raids	14
in Leicestershire	21
Seriously injured	284
Houses destroyed	255
badly damaged	450
superficially damaged	5000+
Industrial premises hit	100+
completely destroyed	50

The casualty figures show that Leicester's blitz was in effect a one-night event. Of the 122 people who lost their lives in raids on the city throughout the war, all but 14 were killed on the night of 19/20 November. A further 21 people died in the 50 raids suffered by the small towns and villages of the surrounding county (in which 1,000 bombs were dropped). Given Leicester's important contribution to the war effort, it seems remarkable that it escaped so lightly – although 'lightly' is a word that can only be used in comparison with the destruction suffered in other parts of the country.

The corner of Highfields Street and Tichborne Street, where 41 lives were lost on the night of 19-20 November 1940

Plymouth: indestructible city

For centuries Plymouth played a prominent role in Britain's role in Britain's wars. Her seamen fought in sea battles with the French, the Spaniards, the Dutch, the Germans, and her citizens watched famous ships and sea captains come and go – from the days of Sir Francis Drake and the Golden Hind to the return of HMS *Exeter* from the battle of the River Plate early in 1940. This proud West-country city, with its splendid harbour, its dockyards and naval station, its garrison and its fine buildings was clearly destined to be a prime target.

Showers of incendiary bombs were released by the German raiders followed by high explosives, which killed many Plymouth firemen and rescue workers

'What was different about the Second World War,' according to Keith Scrivener in his *Plymouth at War*, 'was that the battlefront was brought to the very door of Plymouth, closer than ever before.' And that, of course, is what the Blitz meant for most of Britain. But even when war was declared, it seemed to be something that was happening far away from Plymouth, as it almost always had. This, too, was the experience of most of Britain in those strangely unreal months of the 'Phoney War' – although Plymouth people probably knew more than most about the ships and men lost in the Battle of the Atlantic.

All this changed with the fall of France in June 1940. Barely a month later the Luftwaffe dropped its first bombs in the area, killing a man, a woman and a boy in Swilly Road, Devonport. From then on Plymouth endured many daylight raids, and with the coming of winter the raids increased and the townspeople spent many a night in the shelters. 'Because of these raids,' recalled one observer, who was 16 at the time, 'there was much damage in the town, but shops were still open with their shattered windows boarded up, with signs written on them saying 'business as usual', but of course goods were in even shorter supply then . . .' But it was on 20 March 1941 that war came closer to Plymouth than ever before, for on that terrible night the town had its worst air raid so far, and its citizens experienced the full horror of the Blitz.

'WE FELT SURE EACH BOMB WAS FOR US'

'On that Thursday,' recalled the same observer, 'the King and Queen had visited Plymouth, they had toured the town looking at bomb damage from previous raids, talking to people who had been bombed out. Their train left only two hours before the raid started.' The attack was made by 125 aircraft of *Luftflotte 3*, beginning before it was fully dark and lasting four hours. As usual the raid opened with flares and incendiary bombs – nearly 32,000 of them, followed by nearly 400 high-explosive bombs. Most of the bombs fell in the harbour area and the docks, but the town was also badly hit. The same 16-year old many years later wrote a vivid description of what it felt like that night:

'. . . I think it was soon after eight o'clock that the siren went, and almost immediately there was terrific gunfire, then the bombs began to fall. It was a terrible sensation to sit in the shelter and hear the whistling of the bombs, the whistling getting louder and louder before exploding with a terrific crash. The whole world seemed to be shaking and reverberating around us, we felt sure each bomb was for us. This raid went on for hours, longer than any previous raid, it seemed endless. Eventually there was a lull for quite a while before we heard the All Clear. We returned to the house to find it had surprisingly escaped any damage, but the red glow in the sky told us that not many streets had been as lucky as ours . . .'

A panoramic view of the North Hill district of Plymouth, after three days of intensive bombing

The following night the attack was repeated – with rather more bombers, and over 36,000 incendiaries were dropped, accompanied by 187 tons of high explosive. For about three hours from 8.43pm wave after wave of bombers flew relentlessly over their target, tearing out the heart of the city. In those two raids, the centre of Plymouth was virtually flattened, and for once the BBC radio news bulletin gave the name of a bombed town, announcing that Plymouth had been 'Coventrated'. The commentator described blazing department stores with models in the windows melting in the terrific heat, giving the impression of writhing human beings, and firefighters standing helplessly to watch the old Guildhall burned down because there was no water for fighting the fires – the water mains had been fractured by bombs.

A Night at the Cinema

'I remember going to the cinema one night,' recalls a Plymothian who was 16 in that winter of 1940, 'to see a film called *The Hunchback of Notre Dame*, starring . . . Charles Laughton . . . I thought it a very dreary, boring film, but . . . just before the end of the film, the Alert sounded, so we had to stay in the cinema. It turned out to be a long raid, so to take people's minds off the bangs outside, they ran the film over and over again, I lost count of how many times. I still feel I never want to see the story of Quasimodo again . . .'

On the first of those two dreadful nights there were many who claimed to have heard the beating of Drake's Drum to announce an impending disaster – according to an old legend. True or not, the disaster certainly came, and old Plymouth and most of its familiar landmarks vanished in flames and smoke. An area of 600 yards radius around the Guildhall was reduced to 'a brick-pitted desert', showing only the remains of once-great buildings, like some archaeological site. Medieval buildings such as The Guildhall, the old Guildhall, the Library, the Post Office and the City Hospital, as well as the municipal offices (including the ARP control room), were gutted, and the shopping centres of Plymouth and Devonport were no more. Well-known department stores such as Costers, Spooners, the Co-op (with its familiar clock tower) were destroyed beyond repair. Two clocks that had given the time to generations of Plymouth's residents and visitors – the Guinness clock at Drake Circus and Derry's clock – were smashed, although Derry's tower remained unshaken. Another landmark for visitors, the splendid Victorian Promenade Pier at the Hoe, became a mass of twisted metal – as did the stands at Plymouth Argyle's football ground at Home Park.

Many other public buildings suffered damage or were totally demolished during these two raids in March and the five

BABIES IN THE DEBRIS

more to come in April. Several large hotels and 150 pubs were hit, as were almost all the hospitals in the area, including the City Hospital, the Royal Naval Hospital, the Devonport and Lockyer Street Hospitals, the Isolation Hospital at Swilly, the Royal Eye Infirmary at Mutley and the Stoke Military Hospital. The Maternity Ward of the City Hospital received a direct hit on the night of 20 March, and 14 babies and three nurses were killed. Oblivious of the falling bombs, a few babies got themselves born among all the debris.

Amid all this destruction, Plymouth Dockyard – presumably a major objective of the raids – suffered comparatively little damage, and it never stopped work. In this respect it was similar to Portsmouth and Clydeside, where intensive bombing had scarcely any significant effect on production in the shipyards.

Nearly 50 of Plymouth's churches were so badly damaged that they had to be pulled down. But some were preserved and restored. Among these was Plymouth's 'mother church' of St Andrew's, on the site of which a church had stood for nearly nine centuries. On 20 March a bomb burst near the main door, causing serious damage, but not to

Firemen remained on duty at Drake's Circus to deal with the aftermath of a night's heavy bombing

the main fabric of the building. The next night incendiaries and heavier bombs destroyed the roof and left only the walls standing. Undismayed, the parishioners cleared the rubble and laid out the grounds as a garden, and services continued to be held in the ruins. The remains of another well-loved church in the city centre, Charles Church, were preserved much as they were the day after the bombing, as a memorial to those who died and as a reminder of the horrors of war. It may still be seen today. Weddings in churches were not cancelled because of the blitz, and in one burned-out church the wedding party had to wear goggles to protect their eyes from the smoke from the still-smouldering ruins.

The human cost of those two nights was horrific. The total civilian deaths alone amounted to 336 men, women and children, and 18,000 houses were destroyed, making 30,000 people homeless. Few families were unaffected by death, injury or loss of their homes. The dead had to be buried in mass graves with clergy of all denominations conducting the funeral services. The homeless were accommodated in temporary rest homes or with relatives – or they fled to the edge of Dartmoor outside the city.

'The civic and domestic devastation exceeds anything we have seen,' reported two Mass Observers. In a more homely way, the Plymothian observer already quoted, said: '. . . how much damage had been done in the town centre . . . (was) brought home to us by the fact that we had no water or gas; water tankers used to come round the streets delivering water every day. For a few days we had to cook the best way we could on open fires, people with electric stoves were very popular as the electricity supply was alright . . . the spirit of the people was wonderful, taking all the inconveniences in their stride, but the stories we heard were horrific . . . of people who had been trapped in the town when the raids started and unable to get home until next morning (only) to find their homes gone and all the families killed . . .'

'SURELY WE HAVE REACHED THE LIMIT'

'Rest centres,' he continued, 'were opened up all over the town for people who had been bombed out and emergency kitchens were set up amidst the rubble and debris, life went on, we had no bad raids for a while, but people still left the town every night, going on to the moors in whatever transport they could find. A lot of firms allowed their lorries to be used to take people out on the moors . . .'

Those 'going out to the moors' numbered some 50,000 a night, and they would sleep in churches, barns, tunnels, under hedges and in ditches, and of course with any people who would take them in. Probably not many of them got much sleep, but at least they felt safe. There were complaints that there were no plans for evacuation, even after the first heavy raid. Plymouth, like Bristol, had been designated a 'neutral' area for evacuation – it is hard to see why – and not even children could be evacuated, unless their parents could afford it. Not all observers were as buoyant as our 16-year old. One journalist noted in his diary: 'One wonders how much longer the mental and physical strain can last? Surely we have reached the limit.' Although Plymouth had a tradition of toughness and its citizens felt they could take it better than anyone, under the bravado there were deep feelings of fear and shock. The Cabinet, particularly the Home Secretary, Herbert Morrison, had

The Guildhall lost and restored

Most of Plymouth's fine public buildings were destroyed or severely damaged by the raging fires of the Blitz, including nearly 50 churches, the municipal offices and the magnificent Guildhall, under which was an underground bunker for the city's main air raid control centre. The Guildhall was left a burned out ruin after the second Luftwaffe onslaught in March. After the war it was restored to its former glory and re-opened in 1959 by Field Marshal Viscount Montgomery.

Spooner's Corner and Old Town Street devastated after one of the heaviest raids

The Luftwaffe passed this way . . . Terrace houses in the Mutley Plain district of Plymouth

serious doubts about morale in the bombed cities, and one writer noted that 'he keeps underlining that . . . people cannot stand this intensive bombing indefinitely and sooner or later the morale of other towns will go, even as Plymouth's has gone.'

It is not easy to see now how Plymouth's morale had 'gone': its citizens might have agreed with the man who said 'people who have lost friends and relatives, they don't go around grinning.' There was undoubtedly much bitter criticism of the civil defence (even though the city could rely on 90% of its wardens being on duty in a raid!) and post-raid services – criticism forcibly expressed by the Mayor himself, Lord Astor, and even more powerfully by his wife, Lady Astor, who was the MP for Plymouth. 'Everyone knows,' she said in the House of Commons, 'that the first thing a local authority wants to do when a town is blitzed is cover up its mistakes.' Apart from calling for a reorganisation of the fire services (which were at that time so uncoordinated that often one brigade's hoses could not be fitted to the hydrants in another's area!), Lady Astor's special contribution to morale-raising was to organise dancing on the Hoe – which not everybody felt in the mood for after a heavy raid. The post-raid services were indeed basic, and perhaps Plymouth was fortunate in having the Royal Navy on hand to send in parties of able seamen with shovels to clear up the rubble.

In the March blitz Plymouth city centre had been more heavily bombed than Devonport with its naval dockyards. In April 'Lord Haw-Haw' (William Joyce, the British traitor) announced on the German radio: 'Look out, Devonport – it's your turn next!' And on 21, 22, 23, 28 and 29 April the Luftwaffe kept his promise for him and raided Devonport in force. 'After these raids,' recalled our young observer, Devonport was practically wiped out. The main shopping centre was Fore Street, a long street consisting of shops and a great many public houses and some hotels. There was Woolworth's, British Home Stores, Tozers, Marks and Spencers and many other stores. There were also three cinemas . . . in those raids. Fore Street was almost obliterated, the only buildings left were Marks and Spencers and the Forum Cinema, but these were badly damaged. The Royal Sailors Rest . . . at

'I've never seen the like,' said Churchill

Winston Churchill visited what was left of Plymouth on 2 May 1941. As he drove through the ruins, he was clearly saddened and kept repeating 'I've never seen the like. I've never seen the like.' His secretary noted that the destruction in Plymouth was 'far worse than Bristol, the whole city is wrecked.' The Prime Minister's visit undoubtedly raised the spirits of all who saw him, and to them he showed the dogged 'Winnie' they expected to see, telling them 'your homes are down, but your spirits are high,' and shouting, 'God bless you all' from his car as he passed by.

the top of Catherine Street was completely destroyed, as was the rest of Catherine Street. The Royal Hotel was just a pile of rubble, and of course inside the Dockyard there was great devastation. There was not much left of the residential areas of Devonport either – Granby Street and Duncan Street, where we had lived for many years, were among the worst hit areas . . .'

'Plymouth received another battering on these nights,' the account continues. 'One particular tragedy was in Portland Square (which is next to the Library and Museum) . . .' On the night of Tuesday 22 April a large shelter in the square 'was packed with people, and during that raid the shelter received a direct hit, killing

Carrying on where the bombers left off, demolition workers make safe dangerous buildings at North Hill (*below*) Bomb damage near the Plymouth dockyards, an obvious target for attack by Göring's Luftwaffe pilots

72 people; entire families were wiped out, many were seriously injured . . .'

These five April blitzes were the last of the heavy and concentrated raids on Plymouth, and the city could now dispute with Coventry, Southampton, Portsmouth, Bristol and Clydeside the unenviable title of 'most bombed city' (London, though most often bombed, being too big to be in the running). But it had by no means seen the last of the Luftwaffe. There were fairly frequent attacks during the rest of 1941 and into 1942 – daylight raids in the summer, night raids in the winter. 'But the raids were not of the intensity of the March and April 1941 blitz,' commented our on-the-spot observer later, 'there was no point, the Germans had achieved their object of flattening Plymouth and Devonport.' However, people were still being killed by high explosive bombs until late in the war. The last bomb to be dropped on Plymouth fell at Princes Rock on 30 April 1944 and the last Alert sounded on 30 May of that year.

INSCRIBED IN GRANITE

Long before this, the worst of the war was over for the people of Plymouth and Devonport, and the work of restoration began. Roads were cleared of rubble, dangerous buildings pulled down, unexploded bombs defused, bomb sites tidied and temporarily laid out as gardens. The spirit of all this urge to rebuild the city was well expressed by the word written in chalk on a piece of charred wood fixed to the door of the ruined St Andrew's Church – an inscription which can still be seen today over the North door of the rebuilt church, though now it is in granite. It simply says: RESURGAM, that is, *I will rise again*.

Counting the cost . . .

Alerts	602
Raids	59
Civilians killed	1,172
Note: many service men and women were also killed.	
ARP wardens killed	11
People injured	2,177
seriously injured	1,092
Houses destroyed	3,754
seriously damaged	18,598
slightly damaged	49,950

Secret witness

Armed with a humble box Brownie camera, Reg Mumford produced a unique and moving record of the death of a city.

Patrolling the streets as an air raid warden, Reg surreptitiously photographed Plymouth's agony – and his photographs today bear silent witness to the city's suffering.

'I wasn't supposed to do it, of course,' said Reg. 'We were not allowed to take such photographs during wartime, so my girlfriend Edith used to stand look-out for me.'

Reg became an air raid warden in February 1941, just before the worst of the air attacks on Plymouth.

He lived opposite Plymouth Argyle's Home Park ground where the vehicles were based which used to travel the city streets at night belching out black smoke to obscure the target.

Night after night the bombs and incendiaries rained down on the stricken city, and Reg was in the thick of it.

'There are many terrible memories,' said Reg. 'Many people were killed in Scott Road when a bomb scored a direct hit on an Anderson shelter.'

But the fighting didn't all go one way: 'One night we saw some tracer bullets going across the sky.

'One of our night fighters was after Jerry. We saw the German plane catch fire and crash in the St Budeaux direction, then our plane was up there doing the victory roll. Everybody on the ground was cheering.'

Milehouse bus station

Yarmouth on constant alert

'Come to Sunny Yarmouth' was the invitation issued to holiday-makers during the 1930s in press and poster advertising to promote this East coast resort. Starting in the summer of 1940 the Luftwaffe accepted the offer with enthusiasm, and they bombed the Great Yarmouth and Gorleston area 96 times during the war. This figure represents only those raids which caused damage to life or property: there were many other occasions when bombs fell harmlessly into the sea or on the surrounding marshland. As a front-line port Yarmouth was an obvious target, but it was also situated on the bombing route to and from many other targets in the Midlands, and consequently it had to endure more air raids than any other area of Britain.

The first raid on Yarmouth took place on 11 July 1940. Four people were killed in an attack by a single Dornier on a weather reconnaissance mission. After releasing its bombs it was chased off by two Spitfires and was shot down over Cromer by Douglas Bader. He was, of course, the distinguished fighter pilot, who managed to re-join the RAF at the beginning of the war despite having two artificial legs. The last raid on Yarmouth was on 1 June 1944, only five days before the D-Day landings in Normandy. So Yarmouth was under virtually continuous attack for nearly four years. German plans for this onslaught were laid well in advance as an Ordnance Survey map, recovered after the war from Luftwaffe records, reveals. Prepared on 9 April 1939, well before the outbreak of the Second World War, the map shows the eastern parts of the town with strategic bombing targets clearly marked.

3,900 alerts!

The sirens sounded so frequently in the Great Yarmouth area (there were 2,046 'normal' alerts during the war) that in order to keep life and business going the authorities instituted what were called 'Crash Alerts'. These were sometimes made during a normal Alert when the threat had reached the 'Red Alert' level. This allowed all those involved in the war effort to continue working during an Alert. Only when the situation was considered to be particularly dangerous was the Crash Alert sounded, warning war workers to rush to the shelters or take up their civil defence roles. In an announcement in the local press the Chief Constable explained that Crash Alerts would be made by sounding the steam hooters of industrial premises for two minutes. These warnings would consist of a succession of intermittent blasts of about five seconds separated by silent periods of three seconds. The 'raid over' message would be a steady-pitch signal for two minutes. Locally, these Crash Alert warnings came to be known as 'The Cuckoo'.

Sometimes raiders making their way across the North Sea could not be detected until the last moment, and Crash Alerts were used to signal imminent danger when no normal Alert had been sounded. There were no fewer than 1,854 Crash Alerts, and adding these to the figure for normal Alerts gives the staggering figure of 3,900 Alerts in the Great Yarmouth area.

Undoubtedly the worst of the four years was 1941 during which there were 167 raids, including some in which no direct damage was caused. 102 people were killed and 329 seriously injured that year, when 767 normal Alerts and 1,328 Crash Alerts were sounded. It is obvious from the detailed records that the town was virtually under siege, and the threat was ever present that the enemy would appear, with little or no warning, to create more havoc at any time he chose.

NIGHT AFTER NIGHT

Yarmouth was one of the targets bombed by the Luftwaffe on successive nights so that the cumulative destruction of property and services would put so severe a strain upon the civil defence system, that it would eventually fail. Following this scheme of attack, German bombers hit Yarmouth on 8, 9, 10 and 11 April 1941. The most severe of these raids was on the first night. The raiders first flew over the town dropping flares, followed by a large number of incendiaries. Shortly after midnight the first high-explosives were dropped. At 12.32am two parachute mines drifted down on the Collingwood Road area, to the north of the borough. Two people were killed and seven injured: casualties might have been much worse had not large numbers of people been evacuated. At about 1am explosive incendiaries were dropped over a large area extending from Market Place to Gorleston, and fires were started in many places. By two

The sea-front at Great Yarmouth under attack by the Luftwaffe

o'clock it became necessary to call for fire-fighting assistance from Lowestoft and Beccles. Later on, more reinforcements were called, this time from Cromer and Norwich. Despite all this support, and the efforts of local services, fires gained the upper hand, and attempts to put them out were hampered by continuing attacks from enemy aircraft raining down even more incendiaries. By the time the raid came to an end, at 6am, Luftwaffe bombers had created scores of fires. The *Yarmouth Mercury* issue published at the end of the week of this raid reported: 'The whole town was lit up and a newspaper could be read a mile away from the centre of the blaze'. In the town centre itself, however, the density of smoke reduced visibility to about twenty feet.

High explosive bombs produced huge craters in Southtown Road, closing the strategically important communication route between Yarmouth and Gorleston. Bombs had also fractured mains, so reducing water pressure for the fire-fighters to a dangerously low level.

Just after 5am, two more parachute mines fell – one at the junction of Blackfriars and Queen's Road, and the other at the south end of Middlegate. The first killed five special constables, and the second caused havoc to properties in the centre of town. Many shops were seriously damaged or gutted by fire, including Rose's Fashions, Boots the Chemist, Hill's Restaurant, Marks and Spencers, Kerridges, the Maypole Dairy, Greens and Halfords. Johnson's clothing factory, Mason's Laundry and the Seagull Garage were among the commercial properties destroyed. Three rescue teams arrived from Norwich to help deal with

Helpful hints on dealing with incendiary bombs

One of the greatest threats during the raids on Great Yarmouth, as in all heavily bombed areas, was the huge numbers of incendiary bombs that were dropped. These could cause immense damage if not dealt with very quickly. A contemporary local newspaper, like many others throughout Britain, carried an article explaining how these bombs worked and offered the standard suggestions for dealing with them: '. . . if behoves every occupier to keep on the top floor of (their) premises a quantity of sand, either in a bath or a bucket, and a long-handled scoop or a household coal shovel with a broom handle attached to enable them to deal effectively with any incendiary bombs that may penetrate the roofs of their premises . . .' In one respect, however, the location of Great Yarmouth enabled the authorities to be rather more directly helpful, as the same article adds: 'The inhabitants of the borough have permission to take sand from the beach where fine sand is available . . .' Many residents needed this advice during the raids. A similar article advised on another danger under the heading: 'Gas-proofing a room. A few hints', outlining the methods by which people could remain alive for up to twelve hours in an area engulfed by poison gas. Luckily, this advice did not have to be put to the test.

over 65 major fires which raged in the borough. There were also some 200 minor fires, and it seemed that the centre of town and South Quay would be reduced to a smoking ruin. But by magnificent efforts complete disaster was averted, despite an estimated 4,000 incendiary bombs dropped that night. Casualties of the raid were 17 dead, and 68 injured.

The next day was spent clearing roads and dealing with the most dangerous structures. The people of Yarmouth suspected that the following night would bring further attacks and that they would need to be prepared, as best they could, to face a further ordeal. They were right, but fortunately the raid was not very well aimed, and most of the bombs fell into the sea or the Yare River. However, three high explosive bombs fell on houses in Upper Cliff and Nelson Roads in Gorleston killing six people and injuring five others.

The raiders were back again the following night with two major attacks. At 12.17am on 11 April, Good Friday, four heavy high-explosive bombs were dropped and a communal Anderson shelter in the George Street area received an almost direct hit, which killed seven of those inside. That night thirteen people died in all and twelve were injured. The town then experienced several nights of peace until the morning of Tuesday, 16 April when it was attacked for over five hours in five major raids. The worst incident occurred when a large parachute mine fell at the junction of Palgrave and Alderson Roads. These raids, following the repeated attacks that had preceded them, had so exhausted the local police that it was agreed that the following day their normal duties should be taken over by units of the Norfolk County Police, while local police caught up on desperately-needed sleep.

NO RESPITE

But there was no respite and the nightly attacks recommenced immediately. On 17 April, Beccles Road, Gorleston, was hit, and on the next day Coronation and Elsie Roads in Cobholm were hit by two heavy high-explosive bombs, which killed 12 and injured 13 persons.

So the pattern continued throughout 1941. The attacks were so frequent that few could have slept well even on the nights when there was no activity. Yarmouth people dozed fitfully with one ear cocked for the sound of the air raid warning, the crash alert, or the drone of enemy aircraft engines.

Sadly, Yarmouth lost many historic buildings during the blitz. In the frenzied attacks in April 1941, the Tollhouse in Middlegate Street, the Science School on South Quay (one-time home of Sir James Paget), the Institute of the Missions to Seamen and the British Sailors' Society buildings were all destroyed. The Tollhouse Museum was one of Yarmouth's most treasured buildings, for throughout the centuries it had been linked with the history of the town. It was originally a collection place for tolls, then a gaol, a court of justice, an assembly hall and lastly a museum. The principal exhibits saved from the wreckage were the collections of Early English drinking glasses, the Yarmouth glass and pottery collections and the Lowestoft ware. These were stored in the dungeons. But most of the town's historical records were destroyed.

Like almost every other target area in Britain, Great Yarmouth could not be defended against air attack: the effects could be minimised, but they could not be averted. The town was defended by anti-aircraft batteries on land and also by guns on boats moored off-shore. These were particularly effective in the early months of 1941, when day raids were far more frequent. Low cloud cover assisted the raiders on one day in February, when daylight activity was at its worst. Early in the morning the Aquarium public house was wrecked and throughout the morning there were more raids. On one occasion an enemy plane roared over the town so low that it narrowly avoided crashing into the roof of the town hall. The attacks continued during the afternoon, and there were many casualties in the Kings Street and Apsley Road area. A few days later, the Regal Cinema received a hit shortly before the end of the evening performance. Though the

cinema was fairly full only four people were injured, one woman dying some weeks later. The bomb entered the roof at an angle but did not burst until it passed through the east wall. The blast created was largely dissipated outside the cinema and numerous casualties were thereby avoided.

With the tension caused by unrelenting air raids and the consequent pressure upon the defences, it was perhaps inevitable that some dreadful mistakes were made. On 21 October 1942, five Stirling bombers took off from Oakington, in Cambridgeshire, to lay mines off the coast of Holland. Among them was Stirling BF390 captained by Flying Officer Brady and his crew, which included three members of the Royal Canadian Airforce. It is not clear whether the plane was hit by anti-aircraft fire from a 'flak ship' or by fire from a German fighter plane, but its tailplane was reduced to a mass of mangled metal. The crew signalled for help and were given a direct course back to Britain over the north Norfolk coast. But, probably because of the damage to the tailplane, BF390 drifted 30 miles to the south to make landfall over Yarmouth, where a raid was already in progress. Two raiders had already attacked the town and departed. At 9.40pm the noise of another aircraft was heard approaching from the east. Swiftly the anti-aircraft gunners traversed their weapons ready to aim at this new target, which was picked up by a searchlight over the Britannia Pier. Soon other searchlights trapped the stricken RAF bomber in a web of light. The guns opened up and the plane shuddered as the shells struck it. The pilot tried to take avoiding action, but at only 500 feet he was well within range of most of the guns. Yet no one recognised that this well lit-up target was one of our own aircraft. The pilot's attempts to find safety merely brought his plane within range of more guns both on shore and mounted on ships. The plane dropped two sets of recognition Verey lights, but possibly because of the effects of tracers and searchlights, neither appeared to be the correct colours of the day.

Finally, pursued by streams of gunfire, the bomber turned back towards the sea. Only seconds after it had disappeared into the darkness the roar of its four aero engines ceased abruptly. Stirling BF390 crashed only about half a mile offshore, opposite the pleasure beach.

Gorleston lifeboat was launched to search for survivors but none was found. But it did return with part of the fuselage, that clearly identified the plane as a British craft. In the town's air raid record book an entry was made: 'Reliable evidence has been obtained which would indicate that the plane referred to as having been brought down in the sea was friendly'. Later a court martial inquiry resulted in a new officer being appointed to command the Yarmouth area gun defences. The families of those killed in BF390 were merely told that they were 'Missing – no known grave'.

BELOW THE RADAR

Throughout 1943 the pressure on Yarmouth was maintained. On 7 May, for example, the borough was attacked for the first time by Focke-Wulf 190 fighter-bombers, which were particularly effective in raids on seaside towns. Their pilots were trained to fly at low altitudes to get below the radar screens, and so arrive at their target without warning. As the sun came up, 20 of these aircraft came screaming over the rooftops, each dropping a single 500kg bomb. One of these, which failed to explode, severed a passenger coach at Southtown Station and came to rest between the lines near a platform on which, as chance would have it, a naval bomb disposal officer was standing. He leapt down on to the track and defused the bomb immediately. Another bomb, also released from low altitude, bounced off the railway lines, tore through two coaches, and finally exploded in the station forecourt. Elsewhere there was much damage, including a direct hit on the Burroughs public house in Market Place. One firewatcher described the scene:

> I saw the planes sweep one after the other, firing their cannons at the street and releasing their bombs which seemed to glide away and almost travel like aeroplanes themselves over the roofs until they hit and exploded. It was, without doubt the fastest raid we have ever had.

Four days later the pattern was repeated when about twenty FW190s dropped eleven bombs. They arrived so suddenly that the first bombs fell as the warnings sounded. The raid took place shortly after a squad of ATS women had returned to their billet after a night on duty. The building received a direct hit and burst apart. The planes were so low that their black crosses were plainly visible. It seemed that they had to climb sharply to clear the rooftops, as they screeched over the town, machine-gunning as they went. Rescue teams were soon at work on the billet but 24 women and two soldiers died in the wreckage. Some of the bodies were later buried together at Caister with full military honours while others were sent home to their families.

A ten-year-old boy watched the Focke-Wulfs clear the rooftops, and in his own words:

> I saw a bomb leave one of the planes and it fell at the back of some houses not far from me. The next thing I knew I was covered with feathers from chickens that must have been killed in one of the gardens.

By this stage of the war the Luftwaffe was becoming increasingly short of aircraft and only two more raids causing damage were mounted on the Yarmouth borough. It remains a fact, however, that of all the British targets that came under Luftwaffe attack during the Second World War, only one suffered more air raid warnings than Yarmouth. And that was the island of Malta, which was awarded the George Cross for bravery under sustained bombardment.

Two inside stories

Reports of air raids in the press were naturally heavily censored during the war. But Miss Rosa Bull, who lived in Litchfield Road, Southtown, was undeterred, and carefully collected such reports – to which she attached details of the locations and buildings which had been hit. She also noted information about the people who had been killed or injured. Keeping such a record was actually illegal at the time because it might have helped the enemy if it had fallen into the wrong hands, but Rosa Bull's careful notes have preserved invaluable first-hand evidence of the Blitz in Great Yarmouth.

In addition, Charles Bull, the Chief Constable, who was in charge of Civil Defence, kept an Official Diary of the events, and this was published after the war as *Front Line Town*. Both these documents show how the pressure of the unceasing succession of raids affected the morale of the people of Great Yarmouth.

Belfast – the unprepared city

Belfast was totally unprepared for the blitzes that devastated the city in April and May 1941. Although the Prime Minister of Northern Ireland had declared on the outbreak of war in 1939 that 'we are prepared with the rest of the United Kingdom and Empire to face all the responsibilities that [it] imposes,' the general feeling seemed to be that Northern Ireland was so remote from the theatre of war that the Province would scarcely be affected. Even when an Independent Unionist MP pointed out in parliament that German bombers could reach Northern Ireland in two-and-a-half hours, no one took him seriously.

A corvette under construction at the Harland and Wolff shipyard was badly damaged in the 15/16 April 1941 raid

Throughout the Phoney War, the Battle of Britain, and the Blitz on the mainland, life in Belfast went on much as usual. True, there was the black-out, food rationing, and evacuation plans – but less than half the schoolchildren enrolled for evacuation turned up on the appointed day. A Local Defence Force (the Northern Ireland equivalent of the Home Guard) had been set up, iron railings and gates had been collected for turning into fighter aircraft, and there were posters everywhere urging people to 'carry your gas mask', 'dig for victory', and 'support the war effort' in all sorts of ways, but the authorities and the general public remained quite unready to meet any type of enemy attack. There were only two dozen AA guns in the entire Province, *no* searchlights, only a small, almost token, balloon barrage over Belfast docks, and very few air-raid shelters.

Local authorities in Northern Ireland took advantage of this lack of leadership shown by the Government by doing nothing, or very little, on their own account. It is true that a Ministry of Public Security had been set up, but it is doubtful whether the Minister appointed had the full support of his colleagues, and to many observers the move seemed little more than a public relations exercise. Others were even more critical and dismissed the initiative as a complete failure.

It should have been obvious to those in authority that Belfast was an inevitable target for German bombers. St George's Channel, south of the Irish Sea, separating Ireland from the rest of the British Isles, was closed to merchant shipping, which meant that Belfast had become an increasingly important supply port. The situation has been described by a former naval expert and reported in *Rooms of Time*:

> The ports of Belfast and Londonderry were the last outposts for British shipping. This was because the ports of the south of England had all been closed as a result of heavy bombing by German aircraft. All shipping – liners, cargo vessels and oil-tankers – came round the North Channel. There was no entry to Glasgow or any other British port. Naval vessels came into port along with liners and cargo ships, sometimes a hundred at a time and anchored off Bangor . . .

The 'defences' of Belfast were first broken on the night of 7/8 April 1941 in a sharp attack which killed eighteen persons. It was a warning that the Luftwaffe was indeed prepared to commit aircraft to the round trip of 1,000 miles or more from their bases in France. But it was too late to bolster defences for the return massed, devastating raids which followed one week, and then two weeks, after the warning bombs had been dropped, when first 180 and then 200 German bombers returned to Belfast and its surrounding areas. The basic facts about these two Belfast blitzes are recorded in *A Chronology of Irish History since 1500*:

> 15/16 April:
>
> Nearly 300 German bombs drop on Belfast, killing 475, injuring 1,500; 1,600 houses completely destroyed, and over

Wrecked trams balance precariously on the edge of a huge crater at the entrance to their depot

28,000 severely damaged; 40,000 accommodated in rest centres, and 70,000 fed in emergency centres. De Valera despatches 13 fire engines from Dublin, Dun Laoghaire, Drogheda and Dundalk to aid Belfast.

4/5 May:

Belfast again bombed by German planes; shipyards and Short's aircraft factory badly damaged, as are harbour Power Station and York Street railway station; 150 killed and 157 seriously injured.

The routine followed in the Belfast Royal Victoria Hospital during the first of the blitzes is evidence of the casual attitude which had been adoted towards enemy air raids:

> When the sirens sounded the juniors in the new home rose, dressed (by torchlight) in full uniform, and carrying a rug, torch, change of clothes, identity card and money (if any) – all normally kept ready in a small suitcase – went to the basement shelter, which was guarded by Sister Lynas. Having satisfied herself that each nurse's uniform was correct in every detail (and sending her back to her room to repair any omissions if it was not) she issued them with palliasses on which they tried to continue their broken night's sleep – bombs and gun-fire permitting Senior staff went to their wards. On the night of one of the major raids, a nurse, obviously and understandably terrified, in an effort to bolster her failing courage, began to sing to herself, a sound virtually inaudible amid the cacophony of the raid. It was audible, however to Sister Brown, who greeted her arrival in the ward with a stern, 'Nurses do *not* sing on duty'. If Sisters Lynas and Brown were going to have anything to do with it, Royal nurses would face anything Hitler had to offer, dressed correctly and behaving with proper decorum. (P. Donaldson, *Yes Matron*).

People could not really believe that the city was being bombed. When the siren sounded on the night of the first blitz, most people just went on doing whatever they were doing, as this man remembers:

> Many people were at dances that night and when the air-raid siren went they just ignored it and kept on dancing; one dance band, I think it was The Plaza, had just begun to play *Who do you think you are kidding Mr Hitler?* when there came a great 'carrummppp' and the building shook.

Everyone suddenly realised that this was for real and began to think about getting home and they hoped to safety . . .

There was an Easter Ceilidhe in the Ulster Hall and the guest artiste was Delia Murphy, the well-known Irish ballad singer. There must have been about 800 people there that night. When the siren sounded the air-raid Delia Murphy just went on singing and the crowd stayed listening. Either she was a very brave woman or else she was unaware of the danger of the situation. In any case the audience did not leave the Ulster Hall until five a.m. – after the all-clear had sounded.

Up to that time the people of Northern Ireland had only known about air-raids from the newsreels in the cinema, or from newspapers and the radio. When the first flares or Verey lights dropped on Belfast on the night of Easter Tuesday 1941, people stood around in amazement (and amusement) at the brightness of these strange lights. It was almost like watching a fireworks display. One man remembers being in a group of fellow university students reading the *Belfast Telegraph* in this new light. But study of the newspaper was short-lived when there came a piercing whistle followed by a great explosion. They quickly realised that the brilliant Verey light was the harbinger of a bomb. Before they reached the air-raid shelter more bombs rained down. Fortunately, they did not fall too close: they found out later in the night – when helping relief teams – that these first bombs had fallen on the Antrim Road area.

PLASTIC HELMETS

It was only after the first bombs fell on the city that Belfast began to take some precautions. A man who was a University student at the time recalled that at night oil was burnt in huge bins in the harbour area in order to create a smoke screen to hide the shipyards from enemy aircraft, and people in houses nearby had to keep their windows shut because of the noxious fumes. A number of students became temporary air raid wardens, taking turns at fire-watching at night. They were issued with plastic helmets, not metal ones like the full-time wardens, 'but we wore them anyhow and felt safer with them on'.

Another Belfast resident at the time recalls the morning after the Easter Tuesday blitz:

. . . five or six of us went down into the centre of the town to see the damage. It was difficult walking as the streets were littered with broken glass, bricks and coping stones which had been blown off the tops of buildings. The shop windows were gaping open and all sorts of goods were scattered along the pavement; torn sunblinds and awnings were flapping in the breeze. There was a big double bed up on the roof of a house with its legs sticking down through the slates and it looked so incongruous.

When we reached High Street, firemen and soldiers were trying to break the sixth-floor windows of a big store – I cannot remember now but I think it was either Arnott's or else the Athletic Stores, just about where River House now stands. They wanted to break the glass so that they could get water into the top of the building and so quench the flames which had been started by incendiary bombs in the roof and were coming down through the floors. We were amazed when they asked us to join in; I thought 'This is crazy' – it was the first time anyone had ever invited me to break windows. Many's the thumping I got for doing that when I was a boy.

We set to with a 'heart and a half' but the windows were so high up that by the time the stones reached the glass they were at the top of their parabola and so were really a spent force. The fire brigades were not sufficiently well equipped to deal with the fire on such a large scale. They had very few turntable ladders and monitor guns seemed to have been unheard of in the city.

'Like a bad dream . . .'

'When the bombing started it all seemed to be overhead', recalled two retired Belfast nurses. 'Our first casualty on Easter Tuesday night was a Dr Frank McCloskey from Carlisle Circus, a short distance away from the Hospital. He was working in England but had come home for Easter. He was on his way to the Hospital to render assistance, when the blast from a bomb smashed a plate glass window as he was passing. A sliver of glass pierced his jugular vein and he died about ten minutes after admission to the theatre.

Shortly after we started work the Nurses' Home which was next to the Hospital went up in flames and we lost all our belongings. The gas mains had been fractured and the electric lines were down. Our only light was from candles. The wounded and dead were carried into the Out-Patients' Department. Medical students carried the injured upstairs on stretchers; hundreds of them, some moaning, some yelling, some unconscious, some dying. They were mostly covered in lime-plaster, dust and blood; some with a foot hanging off, half a face gone, blood everywhere – it was awful. That scene will be with us until the day we die. You can imagine our shock when we saw a fellow, whom we had seen earlier at the dance, lying dead on a stretcher. All had labels tied to their wrists or ankles; the labels carried names like Lonsdale St., Fairfield St., Antrim Road, Lincoln Avenue and other streets, which we don't now remember.

Next morning gas and water mains were all fractured around the Carlisle Circus area. The main meal at the Hospital was green peas, heated on oil stoves. We didn't even manage to get any; it is doubtful if we could have looked at food!

The morgue was packed with dead bodies and outside on a sort of platform lay six or seven soldiers, still wearing their helmets and with hardly a mark on them; they had been killed by blast. It must have been a warm day as the stench was beginning to rise, but as it was out of bounds for us, we never went back, so I don't know how long they lay there. There were two little girls of about nine and ten in their nighties, with their arms around each other – it was heart-rending.

An old man who lived in York Street was thrown against the open fire and his arm was burnt right to the bone. It was almost like a well-cooked leg of lamb. He was made of steel!

We were on duty in the theatre but one of us was just kept busy dealing with admissions; the main corridor was packed and by this stage, the wards were all full. While we were dealing with the injured, we were told to lie on the floor as a land-mine was seen drifting in our direction. We crawled under a table and waited. In the event the land-mine drifted past and demolished a street of houses at the back of the County Courthouse on the other side of the Crumlin Road.

To us it was all like a bad dream. The Easter Tuesday night was the worst but as we were not allowed down into the city, we only know what happened in the Crumlin Road area. Being young, we did not realise the gravity of the situation and the terrible destruction which had occurred.

Then there was one harrowing aspect – people coming searching for their loved ones, the terrible confusion and the feeling of exhaustion which we all experienced.

(*top*) Firemen keep their hoses trained on the smouldering remains of a collapsed building in Victoria Street
(*below*) Belfast's High Street, with the Albert Memorial just visible in the misty background, as it looked after the 15/16 April raid

For no obvious reason the Belfast Waterworks on the Antrim Road were given special attention by the bombers. It is not clear if they had been mistaken for part of the docks. On the other hand it may be that the Germans intended to inflict maximum inconvenience, by crippling the city's water supply. Probably because the Waterworks were still clearly marked on modern maps, the Germans did not seem to be aware that they had ceased to function as Belfast's main water supply in the late 1880s. On the other hand, from a high altitude, the Waterworks may have looked remarkably like a dock.

On the morning after the Easter Tuesday blitz, it became clear that the city's normal morgues were totally inadequate for the numbers of dead, which were increasing by the hour. To add to the problem, one of the largest firms of undertakers, Wiltons on the Crumlin Road, had been bombed, so their mortuary facilities were out of commission. The Corporation officials saw that there was nothing for it but to use the public baths on the Falls Road and at Peter's Hill. It was thought that there was sufficient space around the sides of the baths for all the coffins, but as more and more bodies arrived, it became obvious that the baths would have to be drained and used. Eventually the procession of coffins began to thin out but they were followed by stretchers containing arms, legs and bits of mangled bodies. Some bodies were wrapped in bed-clothes or curtains; in fact, in anything which gave them an appearance of decency.

One survivor recalls a doctor and his family who lived in a big house on the Antrim Road. Most of the family had gone to stay in a cottage in Ballycastle for Easter, the doctor and his wife remaining at home. When the sirens sounded the doctor went at once to help out at the Mater Hospital. When he returned next day his house was a pile of rubble. He began to panic, knowing his wife would not have left the house. After working an

Rubble clearance reveals the full extent of the devastation caused at the junction of York Street and St Patrick's Street

hour or so to clear the rubble, the rescue-workers found his wife, her maid and the dog safe and sound – under the big solid-oak dining table.

Many horses were killed in the Belfast blitzes, for in the 1940s much of the city's heavy transport was horse-drawn. The Reynolds were a well-known firm of carriers who brought goods from the docks to the shops and warehouses. Their stables were in Canning Street not far from the Docks. Since most of the action was concentrated on the Docks area the stables were badly damaged and most of the horses were killed. Some 25 horses were lost on that night. Wiltons, the funeral undertakers, lost many fine black Belgian hearse-horses in the same way.

Incendiary bombs were the cause of the fiercest fires ever seen in Belfast and they probably destroyed more property than the high explosive bombs. It was claimed that on 5 May 1941 the flames from the 200 fires rose so high that they could be seen as far away as Liverpool. A fireman interviewed in the *Irish Times* of 6 May 1941 claimed that: 'The first incendiary bombs were quickly dealt with, but we did not have a chance . . .' simply because the Luftwaffe continued to pour thousands of incendiaries all over the city centre. Areas in the centre of the city which had escaped damage in the earlier raids were subjected to a fire-blitz beyond belief:

> I was a part-time fireman and going to a fire you hung on to the outside. Some of the drivers were mad: they drove at tremendous speed and they went round corners so fast that if you didn't cling on to the rails you'd be thrown off. I only saw one floating bomb which came down in York Street but I did see a lot of incendiaries . . . I saw those coming down in dozens; some of them fell on the roads and did not damage but others fell into houses and led to fires. Actually one of the places I was at that night belonged to the *Belfast Telegraph* – it was a store with great big rolls of paper. The incendiaries fell on to the paper and set the place alight; to make matters worse our water supply failed because the bombs had hit and fractured the water mains; and we were helpless then.

Around about 2am it was evident that the Belfast City Fire Brigade was unequal to the task of fighting this conflagration, and an appeal for assistance was sent to Eire. Despite the fact that Eire was neutral, De Valera, the Taoiseach, responded generously, and fourteen units were sent from Dublin, Drogheda and Dundalk. Help was summoned from other Northern Irish towns, and units from Derry, Coleraine, Ballymena, Enniskillen, Carrickfergus, Ballymoney and Ballycastle turned out to assist their city colleagues.

The gas mains were fractured, so there was no gas for cooking; the electricity lines were down; hot meals were out of

Legitimate targets

Official bulletins issued after the raids on Belfast laid stress on the widespread damage done to residential properties, but admitted that a number of 'industrial targets' had also been attacked. Among the most important of these were the Harland & Wolff shipyards, working to full capacity to build vessels for the Royal Navy, the Harland & Wolff aircraft factory and the Short & Harland works. All three targets received direct hits during the Luftwaffe raids in April and May 1941.

the question. The bombing hit not only the water-mains but also the main sewers with the result that the water was contaminated. Every day loud-speaker vans patrolled the Co Antrim half of the city announcing 'All water on this side of the river must be boiled'. Boiling may have killed any bacteria present, but it did not improve the taste of the water. Tea was virtually undrinkable.

Another survivor, a university student at the time, recalled:

> A couple of days after the first blitz on Belfast I was sent out with other university students to help to clear up the rubble left where houses had been bombed. We were working in Lonsdale Street and I got an awful shock. As I was shovelling rubble into a lorry I saw a hand lying there: there wasn't a body: just a hand. I felt faint and I must have been as white as a sheet. I wasn't able to work any more that day. I'll never forget it as long as I live.

Other survivors have special memories of air-raid shelters and families fleeing from the city.

> The safest air-raid shelters were underground but they took longer to make and were very costly, so most of the public shelters were simply built with brick above the ground. They were reasonably safe but if a bomb dropped close to them, they collapsed in a heap of rubble. This happened to a shelter in Percy Street and all those in it were killed.
>
> • • •
>
> One night when the Germans were bombing Scrabo Hill, a local inhabitant sat out all night in case his house would be hit with a bomb. He sat under a tree and he had his goat tied to the same tree. He woke up next morning and went back into the town. When he went back later for his goat the tree and goat were both gone. All that was left where the tree had stood was a great deep hole. When the police investigated the matter, they found that he had been sitting on an unexploded bomb all night.
>
> • • •
>
> Every night after the first blitz, people left their houses and went out into the country. You would have seen whole families going up the Cavehill – some of them stayed out all night because the raids were mostly at night. People were terrified by what had happened that first night.
>
> • • •
>
> Crowds of people took to the fields and each evening hordes of people could be seen making their way up the Cave Hill or the lower slopes of Divis Mountain. People were bewildered and did not know what to do. Many of them left the city and went to live in smaller towns where they felt they would be safe.

The following report appeared in the *Irish Times* on 14 May 1941:

> 20,000 SLEEPING IN THE FIELDS
> NIGHTLY ORDEAL FOR BELFAST FAMILIES
>
> The nightly evacuation of Belfast by women and children who sought shelter in the fields and hillsides, was raised in the Northern House of Commons yesterday, following an announcement by the Premier (Mr J. M. Andrews) to the effect that the Government had decided not to hold a secret session of Parliament.
>
> It was stated during the debate that in one district 20,000 people were sleeping out at night, and the fear was expressed that if 40,000 family huts were not provided around the city before the winter, there might be an unspeakable calamity.

Typical of many Belfast buildings at the time this imposing Victorian block, at the corner of Albert Square and Tomb Street, was reduced to an empty shell during the Luftwaffe's attacks on the city

Statistically, Belfast did not head the league-table of most heavily bombed cities. It came twelfth for tonnage of bombs dropped. Nevertheless, its bombing created its own special sense of terror. The fact that the city was almost wholly unprepared, and therefore its citizens equally unprepared, caused tens of thousands of them to become 'ditchers' (known as 'trekkers' on the mainland) and to flee to other parts of the province and even to Eire. For Belfast those two night blitzes brought human suffering and physical loss on a scale which very few people in the city had imagined to be possible.

Counting the cost . . .

The scale of the destruction of Belfast by the Luftwaffe has perhaps not been fully appreciated in other parts of the United Kingdom. In just two massed attacks the Luftwaffe released 440 tons of high-explosive bombs and over 120,000 incendiary devices. The scale of the disaster has been obscured, too, by the lack of definitive casualty figures. First casualty figures for the Easter Tuesday raid, 15/16 April, of 'about 200' were revised to 758, though even this figure has been challenged as being too low, the true figure perhaps being closer to 900. Thus the blitzes on Belfast in total may have claimed close to, or even just over, 1,100 lives in and around a major area with the smallest *per capita* provision of air raid shelters of any UK city.

Portsmouth fire-watchers keep vigil

How Civil Defence Worked

Great Britain entered the war well prepared in at least one respect – civil defence. Indeed, the death and destruction to be expected from air raids was, if anything, over-estimated. In some areas, for example, more hospital wards and coffins were made available than proved to be necessary. But the Civil Defence (originally 'Air Raid Precautions') Service was soundly planned and established over two years before the outbreak of war. By 1939 Air Raid Precautions schemes were in being and Air Raid Wardens appointed throughout Britain. In each area the Town Clerk or other chief officer was the Controller responsible for all local Civil Defence.

At the beginning of the war there were Air Raid Wardens' Posts in most streets, and most wardens had received some training and knew what to do in the event of a raid. Black-outs had been practiced and sirens installed and tested in public. Most important, all the services – fire brigades, ambulances, rescue teams, hospitals, police, etc. – needed for effective operation when an 'incident' (the Civil Defence term for an air raid) occurred, were in place and were trained in their roles. Their general efficiency, despite often justified complaints, was proved when the Blitz actually began.

To understand how the various auxiliary services worked, and who did what, let us see what happened in the event of a raid (or 'incident'). If a bomb fell or a fire started the nearest street warden reported it by telephone, or foot, or by messenger to the Control Centre, which was often at the local Town Hall, or if it was a fire to the Fire Control (local Fire Brigade). The Controls then decided how to deal with the incident and ordered out the necessary services – ambulance, fire parties, rescue teams etc., and informed the police.

Taking cover

The most common domestic shelter was the Anderson. This consisted of six curved steel sheets bolted together to form an arch and sunk 4ft into the ground. By September 1940 nearly a quarter of the population had Andersons, which could withstand anything except a direct hit. Often waterlogged, dark and smelly, the Anderson certainly saved thousands of lives.

Later came the Morrison indoor shelter, which looked like a steel table with wire mesh sides. Anderson and Morrison shelters were supplied free to people with low incomes.

The most common public shelter was the ordinary street shelter, which was simply a long, low brick building with a concrete roof. At first without seating or any other facilities, they were death-traps when bombs hit them direct or exploded close by.

Many other public and semi-public shelters were created by strengthening basements and cellars. But most people felt safest deep underground, which is why natural shelters like the caves at Chislehurst and Dover, disused mines, tunnels and quarries were popular.

The Messenger was usually a boy on a bicycle, a part-time volunteer, and very often a schoolboy. Many of these lads braved extraordinary dangers.

The *Fire Services* undoubtedly had some of the most spectacular, dangerous and 'photogenic' tasks – and the hardest. With hoses and water as their main weapons, they often had to force their way through crater-torn and rubble-filled streets, amid collapsing buildings to deal with fires in buildings filled with inflammable stock. Often, too, they had to serve a pump or stand at the top of a ladder to direct water at a blazing building, while incendiaries and high explosive bombs rained down all around.

The *Rescue Teams* were craftsmen born of the Blitz. They were men who had learned the skills of burrowing into rubble and debris to extricate broken bodies, if possible still alive. Rescue Men knew how to get safely through shifting walls and fallen timber, how to shore up shaky ceilings and deal with burst pipes of one kind or another. Above all, they had to sense exactly where to find those who had to be rescued.

When this house received a direct hit all the people inside were killed. If they had used their Morrison shelter, seen almost intact under the debris they would certainly have survived

First Aid Parties usually consisted of four men and a driver, all trained first aid workers. Their primary job was to help the Rescue Men to release trapped casualties. They then decided who needed first-aid treatment either on the spot, or at the nearest First Aid Post, where there would be a doctor, trained nurse and nursing auxiliaries. They also needed to recognise urgent hospital cases and those who could safely be allowed to go home.

The *Ambulance Drivers* were mostly women volunteers, who had stated their occupation as housewife, secretary, or 'none'. Their job it was to drive the ambulance and attendants from the depot through the streets, regardless of danger, in order to pick up the injured, as well as the dead and the mutilated, and take them to hospital.

The *Police* performed almost all the jobs of Civil Defence as well as their normal duties – reporting incidents, moving people in or out of shelters, diverting traffic, evacuating people from their homes, rescuing the trapped, rendering first aid . . . and even fighting fires. Many of them were Special Constables, serving part-time but fully accepted as professional policemen.

The man rescued by this ARP team was buried in rubble for 14 hours, but was practically uninjured and suffering mostly from shock

An AFS crew manhandling their pumping equipment through the wreckage of bombed buildings in Norwich

The *Women's Voluntary Services* (WVS) were a unique and special service which helped the victims of air raids on the spot and in ways not possible for the official services or even for families and friends. They organised the Rest Centres for the bombed-out and ran Street Kitchens and Canteens. They drove Mobile Canteens and staffed the Queens' Messenger Convoys that drove into towns after a raid bringing hot food and much-needed cups of tea. They helped and comforted people suffering from shock or distress, and gave practical assistance to those who had lost everything. They even ran clothing depots throughout the country to provide for people who had been bombed out and left with nothing but what they stood up in.

The WVS had been formed with State encouragement, and its million members wore a green uniform, or sometimes just an armband with their everyday clothes. There were many other voluntary services doing equally valuable work during the Blitz, including the YMCA, the Red Cross, St John Ambulance Brigade, the Church Army, the Friends' Ambulance Unit, and the Citizens' Advice Bureau. Indeed, it could be said that it was the voluntary, good-neighbour spirit that enabled the British public to survive the horrors of the Blitz.

North-East: Tyneside and Wearside

With the approach of war, the North-East, Tyneside and Wearside, seems to have planned air raid precautions more thoroughly than the Luftwaffe planned to attack the area. For the region was largely spared the concentrated, mass bombing attacks that were visited on London, the Midland cities, Liverpool and other ports. Here were extensive shipyards, an important port, many factories making armaments and other vital war requirements, and major coal-fields – and yet the Luftwaffe never gave the area the kind of attention that it gave to Clydeside. In the 'night-blitz' period of September 1940 to May 1941, for example, Newcastle and Tyneside had only one major attack (defined as one in which 100 or more tons of high-explosive bombs were released over a target area).

Naturally unknown at the time, the Luftwaffe's pre-war reconnaissance had, however, identified specific targets along the Tyne, including its bridges, docks, oil tanks, and the steel works at Newburn. There was a wealth of tempting targets. At Wallsend, for example, the Swan Hunter site covered 80 acres with a waterfront of over three quarters of a mile, and its fifteen berths had an annual shipbuilding capacity of 150,000 tons, building light aircraft carriers, cruisers, destroyers, landing craft, merchant ships etc. At Hebburn, Hawthorn Leslie's shipyard, with nine berths, was also building cruisers, destroyers, minelayers, cargo and passenger vessels. Vickers Armstrong, too, were major shipbuilders, and also produced tanks and field guns. C. A. Parsons, peace-time steam turbine manufacturers, were now also making gun barrels and mechanisms, mobile searchlights, condensers, transformers, and other products required for electricity generation and transmission. Later in the war, the firm made components for Bailey bridges and the Mulberry Harbour.

Although the area was certainly not omitted or overlooked in framing the Luftwaffe's list of targets, it seems possible that the industrial and strategic significance of the North-East was not fully appreciated. Hitler's Directive No 9 for the Conduct of the War (29 November 1939) clearly made the region a lesser target priority – after London, Liverpool and Manchester. Along with the South Wales ports, Newcastle and Sunderland appear to have been identified exclusively with 'the export of coal'. It was undoubtedly a fact, too, that the Luftwaffe's resources did not permit it to attack all targets with equal force.

SERIOUS PREPARATIONS

But Tyneside was not to know this, and in view of the targets it offered, it took its war preparations seriously. Along the length of the Tyne children were evacuated from Gateshead, Wallsend, Hebburn, Jarrow and Newcastle. In the first two days of September 1939, 44,000 schoolchildren were evacuated from Newcastle alone to Cumberland, Northumberland and Yorkshire. But by the end of the following month, no bombing having occurred, a quarter of that number had returned home.

ARP volunteers were in place and prepared for the anticipated bombing – although some householders had not bothered to erect the shelters supplied to them. As in all other places under threat, factories and other buildings were sandbagged. Balloon barrages guarded Tyneside and its shipyards.

The pattern of attack on the north-east of England which ensued has been described as 'drip-bombing'. Though seldom subjected to massed attacks by enemy aircraft, the region experienced repeated and frequent assaults by small numbers of planes, and often by a lone aircraft. Almost every location suffered. Every postal district of Newcastle, a city of a population of 300,000, was hit. And the loss of life and destruction in single incidents was often high.

The attacks on shipping conducted by the Luftwaffe in the early months of 1940 brought the prospect of aerial bombardment to the coast, but inland bombing was not recorded until June. On the night of 21/22 June 1940 a single raider flew in from the North Sea and after a short space of time flew out again over Whitburn. Just before crossing the coast again it released a stick of three bombs. They fell on open ground, and one smashed a stable. The two horses were the first fatalities in the region.

A pre-war fire drill gives auxilliary firemen in Newcastle a glimpse of things to come

On 2 July Newcastle and Jarrow were bombed during the afternoon under low cloud conditions. A single raider flew over the Heaton district of Newcastle and around Town Moor. Spillers' old factory, just yards away from the High Level Bridge (almost certainly the intended target), was hit, as was a residential quarter in Jarrow, where most of the 13 deaths of that day were recorded. During a night-time attack on 28/29 July, when virtually the whole of the country was put on Alert, a string of high-explosives fell across the city of Newcastle. Three people were killed and there was considerable material damage. Several more low-intensity raids followed in the first part of August, including the daylight raid of the ninth of the month when Monkwearmouth railway goods yard was hit.

Then, on 15 August, two days after the *Adlertag* which signalled the Luftwaffe's campaign to swamp British defences and smash the RAF, Newcastle and the Tees were selected for one of the five major actions of that day. The bombing force despatched by *Luftflotte* 5 from Norway and Denmark, consisting of 65 Heinkels and 34 escorting Messerschmitt 110 heavy-fighters, expected to meet little RAF fighter resistance. The Luftwaffe commanders presumed that RAF reserves in the north would have been committed to the defence of the southern parts of the country. In fact, Dowding had not moved his reserves, so the attackers encountered stiff opposition. Sixteen bombers and two fighters of *Luftflotte* 5 were shot down in the actions over the North-East and the total Luftwaffe losses for that day amounted to 75 aircraft. It was a day which significantly altered both the tactics of the Luftwaffe and the conduct of the air war, and it may well have contributed to the relative low-priority given to the region by the Luftwaffe in much of the subsequent aerial bombardment of Britain.

The incoming force arrived in the early afternoon, and it was the Sunderland area which on this occasion bore the brunt of the bombing from one section of the Luftwaffe fleet on its way to a designated target, the RAF Fighter Command Station at Usworth, a few miles to the west of Sunderland. Within just a few minutes about 20 high-explosive bombs were dropped over the town, most of them in the northern suburbs. A number of houses were demolished, and others damaged in the blasts. Three people were killed.

Small raids followed in the remainder of August and in September. Sunderland and Newcastle and outlying districts were all bombed, but there were few casualties. There appeared to be no intensification in these 'nuisance' or 'sneak' raids, as they were variously described. There was, however, cheering in the streets on the night of 5 September when crowds watched a Heinkel bomber brought down by anti-aircraft fire. The plane crashed in Suffolk Street, in the Hendon district of Sunderland, falling on two houses, which were set alight. All the crew members were killed. During the raid Sunderland Central Railway Station was hit and carriages damaged.

New Bridge Street Goods Station, Newcastle, 2 September 1941

A couple of days after this September raid the Luftwaffe's strategy changed and, with it, the course of the war in the air. For on 7 September Göring directed the massed assault against the capital, London, in all-out night attacks which continued unabated for two months. With most of the Luftwaffe's available resources so occupied, the North-East and many other regions were given a respite.

Bombing across a wide area of the North-East resumed on the night of 15/16 February 1941 when raids were recorded in most regions of the country. For several hours Luftwaffe planes crossed and re-crossed the area, many on their way to other targets, and AA activity was intense. Tynemouth and Blyth were among the places where bomb-damage was sustained, though the destruction seemed small compared with the activity of the night. The single incident of that raid, still most vividly recalled locally, was the Heinkel bomber which crashed into Marine Park, South Shields. It struck a barrage balloon cable, causing it to dive out of control. Upon impact it caught fire, and in a short space of time the remaining bomb-load, a mine, exploded. A policeman and two firemen were killed in the explosion. All four of the crew aboard were killed on impact, and the fifth member, who had baled out, was electrocuted when he landed on trolley-bus cables.

Further raids followed, all of a minor character: precursors of the major attack of the night of 9/10 April.

The Luftwaffe's principal target that night was Birmingham, which was attacked by about 240 aircraft. But Tyneside had also been set as a major target. For five hours, from shortly before 11.30pm, about 120 German bombers attacked Tyneside from Newcastle to Tynemouth and South Shields on the coast, north and south of the Tyne, and south of the river to Sunderland on the Wear. In those hours about 150 tons of high explosives and more than 50,000 incendiaries were released over the zone. Scatttered the length of the river, explosions rocked buildings and installations, and numerous fires were started on both sides of the Tyne. Destruction was widespread in Newcastle, Gateshead, Hebburn, Jarrow, North and South Shields, Tynemouth, and Wallsend. Among the scores of fires, timber yards ignited along the north bank of the river to form a mile-long blaze. Additional fire-fighting crews were called in from outlying districts such as Blyth and Newburn, together with 300 troops, but despite these reinforcements the blaze was not finally extinguished until the afternoon following the raid. Smaller fires, amounting to a reported 400-plus, were in the main quickly dealt with. The manager of the North Shields gasworks, assisted by his daughter and the foreman of the works, managed to smother an incendiary bomb which fell upon one of the gas-holders.

Commercial, industrial, and residential properties of all kinds were demolished, burnt out, or damaged in the night's raid. At Sunderland the Town Hall was among the buildings set on fire, whilst the huge Binns departmental store in Fawcett Street was completely gutted. Among the places hit in North Shields was the Lifeboat Station. At Preston the Institution was hit, killing two patients and three male attendants. At South Shields, where about 40 high-explosives had fallen together with some 6,000 incendiaries, there was considerable damage; many houses were demolished, and the Queen's Theatre was gutted. A major disaster was averted, however, largely owing to the bravery of two railwaymen helped by several others. Incendiaries had fallen on a stack of timber pit props at the side of the track. These blazed into a huge fire, threatening a long string of hundreds of loaded wagons. At great risk to their own safety, Robert Hume and John Steele proceeded to shunt the wagons beyond the reach of the spreading flames. With help they moved 274 wagons to safety, for which they were each awarded the George Medal. Most of the wagons were loaded with ammunition.

Across the whole region the total death-toll reached close to 60; perhaps a surprisingly low figure, given the heaviness of the attack, but almost certainly accounted for by the fact that the bombing, instead of being concentrated, was scattered across large areas of the region.

Within a week the raiders returned. On the night of 15-16 April, when Belfast was the major target, 38 Luftwaffe raiders dropped an equivalent tonnage of high-explosives, with several thousand incendiaries, across Sunderland and parts of Tyneside. Dock installations at Newcastle, Hebburn, and South Shields were the targets. A workshop and a store at the Sunderland Forge works were among the buildings hit, and the Victoria Hall (where, in 1883, 183 children had been crushed to death stampeding through a narrow corridor) was completely demolished. Landmines also fell at Whitley Bay, where German bombers had long used St Mary's lighthouse as a navigational fix, and had many times passed over that part of the coast en route for Tyneside or south towards the industrial concentrations of Yorkshire and Lancashire. At Whitley Bay, in the 'Ocean View' affair, as it was known locally, 16 people were killed in the explosions.

Ten days later Sunderland was again the target of the Luftwaffe in the North-East, though not a bomb dropped within its boundaries. Most of the 80 tons of high-explosive bombs and about 10,000 incendiaries fell on districts of Newcastle, with others falling on Wallsend, Tynemouth, South Shields, Hebburn, and Jarrow. Most of the destruction and loss of life that night was attributed to parachute mines, one of which certainly caused the largest loss of life in a single incident, when 35 were killed in Guildford Place, Heaton. One survivor recalled her experience for the *Newcastle Journal*:

> There was just a swish, which must have been the noise of the parachute when it was about 100 feet from the roof tops. Then this overwhelming noise and a sort of . . . disintegration . . . I had the impression of the house falling, the world ending. I found myself lying in the passage eight feet away. My grandchild, who had been wearing pyjamas, was still in my arms but he was naked.

The woman's husband recalled that though the house was a shambles, the grandfather clock still stood in the corner of the room 'ticking loudly', and the wireless 'which had been thrown from its table to the other side of the room, was still playing'.

The spread of fires started across the entire bombing zone that night was, however, very efficiently checked. But the raid seemed to confirm the view that harassing, if not major, raids on the North-East were likely to continue. In

Incendiary bomb damage in the Church of St Michael, April 1941

The 'miracle' of Durham City

Fifteen miles to the south of Newcastle lies the city of Durham, where the splendid Cathedral of St Cuthbert stands proudly on its promontory. During the 'Baedeker' raids Durham, like many other places with a great cultural heritage, anticipated that it might be next on the 'visiting list'. On the night of 30 April 1942 there was a full moon and a brilliantly clear night. Then the sound of Luftwaffe bombers was heard droning towards the city which, it seemed evident, was to be the target for the raiders. In the few minutes which elapsed before their arrival there occurred what, for many years, was referred to as the 'miracle of Durham City'. Suddenly a mist arose from the valley which encircled and then completely draped the cathedral and the city in a swirling white shroud. As the mist covered the city, the German planes passed overhead. For some, the event was divine intervention; for others, a completely natural phenomenon which had often occurred before.

fact, the figures now available show that of the 61 raids involving 50 or more aircraft mounted in the twelve weeks from mid-February to mid-May, three were in the North-East – two on Newcastle, and one on Sunderland.

Indeed, in the first half of May it began to look as though the region might expect even greater attention from the Luftwaffe. On the night of 3-4 May there was again a widespread attack, followed by three more within a week. In the first May attack there were 18 fatal casualties at Sunderland, while the greatest tragedy of the night's raid occurred at the shelter beneath Wilkinson's mineral water factory in North Shields. Here some 200 men, women, and children were taking refuge when the shelter received a direct hit. Seventy-six persons were killed. One 15-year-old boy was rescued from the debris two days after the raid. There were casualties also in Sunderland where 18 persons lost their lives.

Two nights later 12 enemy aircraft roamed over Tyneside for nearly three hours from midnight onwards, searching for their targets in the dockyards to the east of Newcastle. The Shields Road district of the city suffered badly. The Apollo cinema, Byker, was destroyed. In all, the raid claimed 12 lives, most of them at Tynemouth. The same night 28 bombers were sent back to the Tyneside region in an attack lasting about two hours, from midnight onwards. The raid succeeded in starting a number of fires in the docklands of Newcastle, Wallsend, and Hebburn, but these were all contained. The Luftwaffe bombers that night covered a larger target zone, for more bombs were dropped over Middlesbrough and the Tees region to the south, where there was considerable damage to housing.

By this stage of the war German plans to open up the Eastern Front meant that much of its air force was being moved to the east from stations in France and the Low Countries. These new dispositions, and the invasion of the USSR that followed, eased the pressure of air attack over much of Britain. The sole exception in the North-East was the single Heinkel which appeared just before noon over the coast of Roker on 13 August. The three bombs it released landed close together in Mayswood Road, Fulwell, killing four people.

On the night of 1-2 September, however, the Luftwaffe returned to the region in some force when 28 aircraft attacked mainly the Jesmond and Shieldfield areas of Newcastle. In that raid a major fire was started in New Bridge Street, the flare of which could be seen for miles around. Equipment and appliances from several parts of Northumberland and Durham were called up to help bring the blaze under control. Nevertheless it burned throughout the day and the following night and requiring miles of hose before it was finally extinguished.

In the goods station a railway truck in a siding was flung in the air, landing in New Bridge Street upon a parked van. Lengths of sleeper were also ripped up in the blast, some of them flying considerable distances before embedding themselves in the roofs of houses. Scores of trucks, loaded with foodstuffs, were rescued from a warehouse in the goods station – an action that averted a local shortage of vegetables and other foodstuffs the following day. Though a short raid, lasting little more than one hour, 57 people were killed, 100 houses were demolished, and about 1,000 persons made homeless.

SOUTH SHIELDS

At the end of the month, and again on the night of 2-3 October the Luftwaffe returned to the North-East, its bomb drops on these occasions centring on, first, North and then South Shields. There were casualties in both places on each of the nights. The raid on South Shields proved to be one of the most damaging, and most costly in lives, of all the raids in the region. About 50 bombers took part, bombs falling over a wide area. Many fires were started that night and there was considerable destruction. The Market Place, close to the river, was amongst the worst-hit parts of the town. Here, the Town Hall, a department store and a church were among the buildings hit, as were several trolley buses in the square. There was also a direct hit upon a public shelter in the Market Place, which killed 12 people. In all, 51 people died in South Shields that night, a figure to be added to the 19 deaths in the previous attack, two nights earlier.

The 'drip bombing' of the North-East continued throughout the remainder of 1941 and into 1942. The pattern of attack reverted to raids conducted by one or a small number of raiders. Parts of Sunderland received such attention on the night of 7 November during a raid on the general region of the Tyne to the Tees. At the end of the year, however, on the night of 29-30 December, the Luftwaffe sent a larger force, of about 55 bombers, to the North-East. Bombs fell across a wide area, including Gosforth, Jesmond, Dudley, Byker, Newburn, and Newcastle. The greatest damage, occurred in the Matthew Bank area of Newcastle

Guildford Place, Newcastle – one of many residential areas throughout Tyneside and Wearside attacked by the Luftwaffe at the height of the Blitz where four bombs fell in a row along a residential street with the loss of five lives. Since very few people, it emerged later, had bothered to seek shelter, the low death toll appears quite remarkable.

One man, Mr Gibson, who had just come in from Observer Corps duties, was talking about the Alert with his wife who was bedridden with diphtheria. A bomb exploded in the garden. Mr Gibson picked himself up, discovered that the window through which he had been looking was no longer there, and that most of the room, including the bed and his wife, had disappeared:

> Then I wandered out into the garden and I saw the bed. It had been lifted bodily at least ten feet. There it was, surrounded by bricks and boulders, and with heaps of lighter debris on the bedclothes. I forced my way to my wife's side.
>
> She still lay there securely in the bedclothes . . . she had not a scratch . . .

'Drip bombing' continued intermittently throughout 1942. On 11-12 October, for example, there was scattered bombing of Hebburn, South Shields, Tynemouth, Whitley Bay, and Sunderland.

During 1943 the Luftwaffe command was re-organised in preparation for a renewed assault on Britain – the so-called 'Little Blitz' of the first three months of that year. In spite of its depleted forces the Luftwaffe managed to make some fairly substantial raids. Not all of them were successful, as in the case of the raid planned for Newcastle on the night of 11 March, when not a single bomb fell in the city.

Two nights later, however, about a dozen aircraft succeeded in getting through to Sunderland, when the area most hit was around Boldon Colliery. The following night Sunderland was hit again. Among the high-explosives dropped that night were four parachute mines, one of which fell on the New Market. The force of the explosion shifted the entire structure of the Empress Hotel six inches. Shops, business premises, and houses were destroyed. More shops, offices, and the church of St Thomas were destroyed when another land-mine fell in John Street: 17 people died.

Two months later the Luftwaffe again mounted two attacks on Sunderland, each involving about 80 aircraft. In the early hours of Sunday 16 May bombs started to fall across all areas of the town, with Alexandra Park and the Roker Park Football Ground among the first places to be hit. A parachute mine exploded on the railway crossing at Fulwell Road causing extensive damage, dozens of houses being flattened by the explosion and blast. The Kings Cinema, Crowtree Road, was gutted by incendiaries, and the Royalty church had a remarkable escape when a bomb struck the road and bounced over the building, failing to explode where it came to rest. There was extensive damage in the Monkwearmouth district, as elsewhere in this raid, which claimed a total of 71 lives.

In the tangled wreckage of New Bridge Goods Station firemen fight to bring the blaze under control

Just over a week later, on 24 May, the Luftwaffe returned to Sunderland, again in the early hours of the morning, and again with the same mixed cargoes of high-explosives, parachute mines, and incendiaries. It was to be Sunderland's worst night of the year. The bombs fell on all areas of the town and its shipyards. St George's Square was hit by a landmine which fell in the middle of the east side of the square, demolishing six houses, and starting a fire which took eight hours to put out. Almost all the residents were sheltering in the basements of the homes; six were killed. Another tragedy occurred when a communal shelter at Lodge Terrace, Hendon, was partly demolished by a high-explosive bomb, claiming 12 lives. The destruction was widespread, and when the death-toll was calculated, it was found that the fatalities were even higher than in the previous raid, for on this occasion 83 people had been killed.

These two May raids accounted for well over half the total of 267 persons killed in the 35 raids on Sunderland. Less well-known generally is the fact that Sunderland was one of the seven British cities and towns most heavily bombed by the Luftwaffe. Given its strategic importance it remains something of a mystery, therefore, that Newcastle 'escaped' comparatively lightly with 31 raids in which 141 people died.

The Baedeker Raids

In their November 1940 attack on Coventry the Luftwaffe started a large number of fires simultaneously with the intention of overwhelming the local fire-fighting services. It was not the first time such tactics had been used, as Air Chief Marshal Harris had already noted during the earlier attacks on London. Instead of trying to 'knock out' specified objectives, which was the British strategy of conventional target-bombing current at that time, the Luftwaffe deliberately used fire-bombing to destroy homes and factories at random.

Arthur Harris had fought as an infantryman in the First World War before joining the newly-formed Royal Flying Corps. His career prospered, and by 1939 he commanded No 5 Bomber Group. In May 1941 he joined a high-level Service delegation to the USA to negotiate support and discuss overall strategy. On his return to England in February 1942 he took over Bomber Command, making his intentions quite clear in a filmed interview. 'There are lots of people who say that bombing cannot win the war,' he said. 'My reply to that is that it has never been tried. We shall see!'

Harris's blunt views now found increasing support among members of the War Cabinet, who were more prepared to accept the proposition, however disagreeable, that bombing the homes of industrial workers was necessary since it served the double purpose of striking at production capacity and at enemy morale. It was hardly a view supported by evidence at home, where the German bombing of towns and cities had not yet broken civilian morale and where production – though often interrupted, and very badly so at Coventry – had nowhere ceased altogether.

Harris soon created an opportunity to put into practice the lessons he had learned directly from the enemy. On the night of 28/29 March 1942 a force of British bombers took off for the Baltic port of Lübeck. Although it was of little strategic or industrial importance Harris chose this Hanseatic city because, unlike the major industrial centres of Germany, its anti-aircraft defences were very light. Also, it could be approached from the sea, which meant that attacking aircraft did not have to fly over hostile territory.

As Harris later wrote, it was 'better to destroy an industrial town of moderate importance than to toil to destroy a large industrial city.' With typical forthrightness, he added: 'I wanted my crews to be well "blooded", as they say in fox-hunting, and to have a taste of success for a change.'

In the event, of a total force of 234 RAF bombers, 191 actually bombed Lübeck in two large waves: the first started fires which, half-an-hour later, guided the second wave to the target zone. Twelve bombers were shot down in the raid. Lübeck, founded in 1143, was still largely a medieval city of narrow streets and half-timbered houses – 'built more like a fire-lighter than a human habitation', in Harris's words. The two fires started by the incendiaries took 32 hours to extinguish, and 200 acres of the city centre were completely burned out. In the conflagration two thousand of Lübeck's buildings were completely destroyed. More than 15,000 of its inhabitants were made homeless; 312 deaths were recorded.

Two days after the raid Dr Josef Goebbels noted in his diary: 'Eighty per cent of the old part of the city must be considered lost.' In a later entry, having seen a newsreel of the destruction, he wrote:

> It is horrible. Thank God, it is a North German population, which, on the whole, is much tougher than the Germans in the south or the south-east. Nevertheless we can't get away from the fact that the English air raids have increased in scope and importance; if they can be continued for weeks on these lines, they might quite conceivably have a demoralising effect on the population.

BAEDEKER 1: EXETER

Hitler had boasted that any RAF bombing of German towns and cities would be returned a hundredfold by the Luftwaffe. Now he was faced with the destruction of a famous landmark, a part of northern Germany's heritage, a city known for its beauty and ancient monuments. On 14 April, therefore, the Führer gave orders to intensify the air war and to target every city in Britain noted for its architectural interest, and thus to strike at historic locations which, like Lübeck, would not be well defended and would have limited civil defence resources. On the night of Thursday 23 April 1942, in the first of these retaliations, the Luftwaffe despatched 45 bombers to attack Exeter. The attack

Exeter High Street

largely failed, mainly because of cloud cover over the city that night, and most of the bombs went astray. But among the places hit was Devon Mental Hospital, five miles to the south of the city, where nine persons were killed. A further four were killed in the raid, and about 200 houses damaged.

While the Germans were raiding Exeter the RAF attacked Rostock, another Baltic port, 50 miles to the east of Lübeck. The 161 bombers sent that night, however, achieved minimal results: many of their bombs fell several miles aways from the target zone. The raid nevertheless produced a furious response from the German Foreign Office. The Deputy of the Foreign Press Department, Baron Gustav von Stumm, addressing overseas journalists, announced that as reprisals for the RAF's bombing of Lübeck and Rostock, the Germans henceforth intended to choose British targets according to their historic significance. The targets would be selected from the German Baedeker *Handbook for Travellers* guide to Britain. Von Stumm announced: 'We shall go all out to bomb every building in Britain marked with three stars in the Baedeker guide.' Thus was born the phrase 'The Baedeker Raids' to describe the succession of Luftwaffe raids upon the cathedral cities of England. Thus, too, was born the myth of the '3-star' raids. For, as was pointed out as early as May 1942 by a correspondent to *The Times*, none of the Baedeker guide books – from Karl Baedeker's original of 1842 onwards, through all subsequent editions – had ever identified *any* building with three stars.

Following these two unsuccessful raids – the Luftwaffe's on Exeter, and the RAF attack on Rostock – the same targets were chosen by the adversaries for the very next night, Friday 24 April. The RAF sent 125 bombers to Rostock, only one of which was lost, and this time succeeded in locating the city centre, which was heavily bombed. The Germans made their repeat raid on Exeter without loss, and caused severe damage to the city. 60 aircraft were used in the attack, many of which made two round trips from base to target, thus achieving a double wave of bombing.

Incendiaries and new heavy-calibre bombs were targeted on the cathedral and the surrounding area. The cathedral suffered serious structural damage on the south side of the choir aisle, and lost almost all of its medieval glass. Saint James's Chapel and the cathedral sacristy were demolished. A number of medieval buildings were damaged, including St Lawrence's Church and the 14th-century hall of the Vicar's Choral in South Street, as well as the old market hall, a teacher training college, and several thousand homes and businesses. Some of the losses included elegant Georgian crescents and terraces which gave Exeter much of its character. Altogether the raid that night claimed 74 lives, and over 100 people were injured. The raid had certainly been heavy, though it was only a precursor to the most severe bombing of Exeter which took place a few days later in early May.

Exeter Cathedral Chapel

The tit-for-tat bombings continued. On Saturday 25 April the RAF despatched 128 aircraft for the third night running to Rostock, all planes returning from the raid. On that evening the Luftwaffe switched its attack to Bath, mustering virtually the whole complement of its serviceable bombers stationed in the west to make a total of 151 sorties. It was the heaviest Luftwaffe concentrated attack since July of the previous year, and the first of three consecutive Baedeker raids on the city.

Landsdown Place East in the city of Bath: April 1942

BAEDEKER 2: BATH

In an account of the Bath bombings published, most unusually for those times, very soon after the event itself, a local historian, C. Wimhurst, described Bath as a place where –

> . . . the past and the present blend to form a perfect harmony for gracious living. The civilisation of the Romans is to be found round the hot springs . . . a terraced city of Georgian architecture without compare – of noble squares and crescents and broad, spacious streets, all girdled by the green hills. Here, in this small, compact city, have lived the famous in all walks of life – statesmen, soldiers, sailors, divines, artists, writers, actors . . .

Bath was then an undefended city, and indeed had been viewed as a safe haven, 4,000 evacuees having moved into the city and its immediate neighbourhood within days of the declaration of war. By the end of 1939 about 10,000 people had added to Bath's population, including several hundreds employed in a number of important government departments in and around the city.

The district around Bath contained several stone underground quarries. These had been pressed into service as ordnance supply depots, as an aircraft factory, and as an engineering works. In addition, the Admiralty had set up administration offices in Bath – a fact known to the German High Command – with hutments at Foxhill in the southern part of the city.

Nonetheless, only 'the odd bomb' had been expected by the civil defence authorities, an expectation which had been proved correct, despite the great number of Alerts to which the area was subjected. These were largely on account of the proximity of Bath to Bristol, which received repeated visits from the Luftwaffe. By mid-January of 1941, for example, Bath had already had 400 Alerts, and in that month a lone bomber had jettisoned its load over Twerton High Street in order to escape from a pursuing British fighter.

Therefore when the Alert sounded once more, shortly after 11pm on Saturday 25 April, it caused no particular alarm. Even when incendiaries started to fall in the Kingsmead and Green Park areas most people, according to contemporary witnesses, tended to be unconcerned, many of them staying in bed. Then high-explosives started to hit Kingsmead, and the raid increased in intensity. Soon, as one observer noted:

> It was like daylight outside. The sky seemed alight. It would suddenly light up with bright sheets of light. You could see the aircraft coming over. They were machine gunning as they came over Twerton Roundhill. You could see the red tracer bullets flying . . . They seemed to skim over Roundhill and then drop down towards the city centre.

During this first raid on Bath there were at times many aircraft to be seen in the sky and at other times either few or none at all. Most of the bombs dropped were incendiaries, and soon practically the whole of Hungerford Road was on fire. Severe damage was done to the goods yard of the Midland Railway, and a gasworks in the west of the city was also hit. After a lull of a few hours the Luftwaffe returned, shortly after 3am on the Sunday morning, in a second raid which lasted until just before daybreak. Not long after the midnight of that Sunday (the siren sounding at 1.15am) the Luftwaffe bombers returned in a third raid which, though it lasted under two hours (until 2.45am), was even more deadly.

Clearing up after the first raid was still in progress when the second was launched, and similarly the third blow fell while fire and rescue services were still dealing with the destruction caused by the earlier raids. Many buildings of all kinds were damaged: churches, historic buildings, offices, shops, dwellings, workrooms, nursing homes, hotels, factories, and stockrooms. The report, lodged in the City of Bath Reference Library, prepared after the raids by the City Engineer, lists four categories: those buildings which were totally destroyed, those so badly damaged that they had to be demolished, those seriously damaged but repairable, and those receiving slight damage only.

Few buildings escaped altogether. Fire-twisted girders, charred wood, and broken walls were all that remained of the magnificent Assembly Rooms (of 1769-71) which had been renovated just before the war. Four Anglican churches were destroyed, including Holy Trinity in James Street West, which was hit the first night and burned out the next. Blast did substantial damage to Bath Abbey, known as 'The Lantern of England' because of its many fine stained glass windows. Glass blown from the east and other windows was carefully gathered up and stored for future restoration. Three hospitals were damaged, the most seriously affected of which was the Royal National Hospital for Rheumatic Diseases, in Upper Borough Walls, where the west wing received a direct hit. Nothing daunted, as a local and contemporary account tells, a group of 25 redoubtable rheumatism sufferers picked their way through the flaming debris and rubble for their regular visit to the health-giving waters at the Royal Bath on the Sunday morning.

The Circus, one of the most famous landmarks in the city, was spared – one segment only suffering from fire damage – though houses within 30 feet of this elegant terrace were destroyed. The Royal Theatre, the first to be built in the city in its heyday, was badly damaged. Four schools were destroyed, including the Bath School of Art (in which Walter Sickert had taken such an interest) which was burned out. The area of the city which suffered the greatest concentration of bombs was Kingsmead – possibly because, as Niall Rothnie has pointed out in a recent local history, 'the word "Bath" on the original German photo-map happens to be inscribed across Kingsmead'.

The destruction visited upon the city enabled Dr Goebbels to claim, in an attempt to assure Hitler that the Luftwaffe had avenged the RAF's attacks upon Rostock, that 'there was nothing left standing in Bath'. Though this was an exaggeration, the destruction was indeed widespread. More than 19,000 buildings suffered some degree of damage, and the casualty-list was very high. In the successive raids 400 civilians had been killed. Many had remarkable escapes, such as the woman who was reading by her fireside after supper when something tore through the ceiling and carried on diagonally through the floor three feet away from her. It was, in fact, a large bomb which then exited through the front door and buried itself deep in the roadway outside. Rescue workers found many victims buried in the debris, some of whom survived their ordeal. One seven-year-old boy was rescued thanks to the quick perception of an air raid warden. Seeing a cat dart down a bomb crater hole he put his arm down the hole and, as expressed in the *Bristol Evening News* report, 'was surprised to find it grasped by a child's small hand. The little boy was dug out unharmed except for shock'.

Though the loss of life and destruction in Bath was high, these raids conferred little or no strategic advantage on the Germans, just as the RAF's pounding of German civilian centres brought little benefit to the British war effort. For the fact was that heavy bombing had a surprisingly limited effect on war production, and after even the worst raids the threads of living were soon picked up again. But once the policy of bombing British historic and cultural centres had been adopted, the Luftwaffe continued to pick and attack appropriate targets.

On 27 April Dr Josef Goebbels had lunch with Hitler.

> . . . The Führer declared that he would repeat these raids night after night until the English were sick and tired of terror attacks. He shares my opinion absolutely that cultural centres, health resorts, and civilian cities must be attacked now; there the psychological effect is much stronger, and at the present moment that is the most important thing.

'Was this a real raid?'

The most famous rescue story from Bath concerns an elderly lady who had been trapped in one of the houses in the Paragon since the raid on Saturday night (25 April). Rescue workers were still trying to free her on the following Tuesday; they had given her tea to drink through a rubber tube, and a doctor had succeeded in giving her an injection. She was dug out on Tuesday evening, and her story, as written up in a pamphlet issued soon after the raids, won her considerable local fame:

'. . . rescued from the debris of her house, (she) asked for, and got, first her glasses and then her false teeth. She was prevailed upon to enter the ambulance and was driven away. Suddenly she sat up and said to the attendant, "Tell me, young man – was this a real raid or just one of your practice stunts?"'

However, the lady appears to have died in hospital on the Friday.

The last person to be rescued alive after the raid – and again from a house in the Paragon – was a young girl who had been buried in the rubble for over three days. She had sheltered in a cupboard in the house, and her tapping on its sides with a spoon had alerted the rescuers, who managed to bring her out on Wednesday evening – four days after the raid.

BAEDEKER 3: NORWICH

On the night of 27 April 1942 the RAF raided Cologne and the Luftwaffe attacked its next Baedeker victim – Norwich. Following the repeat pattern of bombing the Germans had now adopted, the city was bombed again two nights later.

In one sense, Norwich fitted Hitler's requirements exactly. Its medieval centre contained many buildings closely associated with England's heritage. The Cathedral, built by Bishop Richard Nix between 1501 and 1535, was hit but suffered only minor damage, largely, it is believed because after an earlier fire the old timber roof had been replaced with stone transepts. The Rosemary Tavern, a Tudor house once lived in by Thomas Pickerall, a mayor of Norwich who died in 1545, was partly demolished by fire. A similar fate befell The Boar's Head, built in 1495, in St Stephen's Street. The 19th-century Jewish Synagogue in King Street was demolished. The Quaker Meeting-House, built in 1699, was damaged. This was the burial-place of Amelia Opie and of the Gurney family, one of whom, John Joseph Gurney, was the father of Elizabeth Fry, the prison reformer.

Despite all this damage, especially to the older parts of the city, the local newspaper editor wrote, a few days after the raids, 'If Norwich Cathedral were destroyed, it would be no answer to bomb Cologne Cathedral.' Future events were to lend a certain irony to this generosity of spirit before war with Nazi Germany came to an end.

At the time the severity of the raids on Norwich was not fully appreciated. In large measure this was because the number of deaths was at first very seriously under-estimated. Home Security announced that 53 persons had been killed in the first raid, and 30 in the second. Later it was established that in fact the total death-toll in the two raids was 236. Within a few days the Luftwaffe continued the attack with a third raid on Norwich.

By this time, the effects of Germany's campaign of reprisal on British cities were being widely reported in the world's press and, in a stream of exaggerated claims, Berlin Radio hardly stopped boasting about its success. Experts working for British intelligence did their utmost to find out where the next Baedeker blow would fall so that defences could be organised, and people living in the target area could be given as much advance warning as possible. Codebreakers at Bletchley were now reading German Command signals with some ease, but certain code-words continued to elude them. Codes for Coventry and Birmingham, for example, were well known, but now a new code-name, not previously seen on intercepted enemy signals, started to appear. There was very little time for de-coding the new cypher, with the result that when a force of 40 bombers consisting of Junker 88s and Heinkel 111s assembled on the night of Tuesday, 28 April – between two of the Norwich raids – their target was still unknown.

BAEDEKER 4: YORK

It was, in fact, the city of York, which matched almost exactly the criteria laid down by Hitler and Goebbels for Baedeker raids. Historically, it had been the cultural centre of the North of England, its Archbishopric ranking next to that of Canterbury in the Anglican hierarchy. Its Minster and the walled city, together with its churches, fortifications, and the market town which had grown up around it, had played a significant part in the heritage Hitler wished to destroy. Apart from the city's Baedeker status, a strategic case for selecting York could also be supplied. For it was an east-coast base which, together with its surrounding area, had been the launch-pad for numerous attacks upon Germany, including the Lübeck raid. Furthermore, York lay between the industrial regions of Yorkshire and Lancashire and access to the North Sea; as such, it was an important staging-post in the supply of munitions to Britain's ally, Russia. Lastly, the LNER, Britain's main east-coast railway line, passed through York. For all these reasons, the German High Command considered that a blow struck at York would inhibit RAF attacks upon Germany and disrupt transport and troop movements on the eastern side of the country, as well as hampering supplies via the Arctic convoys to Russia's port of Murmansk, thus easing the pressure on Germany's Eastern Front. Moreover, it was felt that the destruction of so noble a city would deal a very severe blow to British morale.

In the early hours of Wednesday 29 April the Luftwaffe bombers, despatched from their bases the night before, approached York from the east, flying in over the North Sea in order to avoid radar detection. Most of the city's inhabitants were sleeping soundly. After all, York had by that time been subjected to 780 Alerts and nothing much untoward had happened. On the other hand, other parts of Yorkshire, Hull and Sheffield in particular, had been bombed many times.

The London to Edinburgh train had stopped briefly at York station when the first of the two waves of 20 aircraft firebombed the station and then continued to release heavy-calibre high-explosives. The station, rolling stock, the main lines north and south, the marshalling yards, and dozens of surrounding buildings were all damaged.

Among the industrial targets was one of Rowntree's factories. Containing many tons of sugar, the premises burned fiercely when fired. Several schools were hit, including a convent school where

The Guildhall in York blazes during the Baedeker raid on 28 April 1942

some of the nuns were killed. Damage to housing was severe. Women of the ATS worked through the night with local ARP wardens and every available helper to try to free injured civilians from the rubble.

The Municipal Art Gallery was destroyed, as were many streets of shops and the church of St Martin-le-Grand. York Minster itself, however, stood throughout the conflagration. Windows, of course, were broken by the scores of blasts in the surrounding streets, but the irreplaceable stained glass had been removed as a precaution, put into safe storage, and replaced by plain glass.

However, it was not the Minster – York's crowning glory as an ecclesiastical centre – that received the most crushing blow, but the focus of its civic history, the Guildhall. An early casualty of the Blitz had been London's Guildhall during a raid in December 1940. In the following January the Guildhall in Portsmouth had likewise been hit, and two months later the Plymouth Guildhall met a similar fate. Now it was the turn of York's Guildhall, the 500 year-old centre of trade and industry in the city. Since the destruction of London's Guildhall it had become the oldest surviving monument to the medieval system of craft and trade. Showered by fire-bombs the new roof of the building, the cost of which had been raised by public donations in 1939, was soon ablaze and, despite the effort of fire fighters, came crashing down, scattering burning debris throughout the ancient building.

In all, about one-third of the dwellings in the city were destroyed; almost 10,000 houses had been damaged or destroyed and 74 civilians were killed, within the city's limits, in York's bloodiest night since the Civil War. Several Civil Defence personnel and soldiers also lost their lives in the raid.

In the series of raids which so far comprised the 'Baedeker' offensive – the raids on Exeter, Bath, Norwich and York – 938 British civilians had been killed.

EXETER BOMBED AGAIN

The break in the series of Baedeker raids lasted just a few days, though it was beginning to prove difficult for the Luftwaffe to assemble strike forces from its depleted stock of serviceable aircraft in the west. However, on the night of 3/4 May, the Luftwaffe returned to complete its destruction of Exeter, once more mustering about 40 bombers for the purpose.

In clear, almost cloudless conditions the German bombers approached Exeter from the south, moving along the Exe estuary towards the cathedral city. They arrived over Exeter at 2am, and the first planes released incendiaries to fire the target-area. The greatest concentration of incendiaries fell across the city centre and the Heavitree Road district. In the following one and a half hours 10,000 incendiaries fell over the city, to be followed about half an hour later by the first high-explosives. During the raid, 75 tons of high-explosives (160 bombs of all sizes) were released in as many minutes.

Within half an hour of the first bomb 69 major fires were reported throughout the city. Whole streets were ablaze. A major conflagration illuminated Castle Street, Bedford Circus, Sidwell Street, and the High Street. Historic as well as modern buildings were hit. St Luke's College was gutted; the main block of the City Hospital was destroyed, as was the famous Deller's Cafe. Two hotels were demolished: the Globe, in Cathedral Yard, and the Seven Stars, near Exe bridge. Bombs which exploded in the Cathedral precincts did some damage to the buildings, where vaulting was torn away from a choir aisle. The new City Library was burnt out, with the loss of about one million volumes.

Shortly after the raid Nazi propaganda proclaimed: 'This Exeter is a jewel. We have destroyed it'. In the nature of such announcements, it was, of course, a great over-statement. Nonetheless, the damage resulting from this raid was very extensive. About 30 acres of built-up areas in the city had been flattened. Over 400 shops had been destroyed, together with 50 warehouses and stores, in addition to banks, public houses, chemists, and a cinema. Of the city's housing stock of about 20,000 houses, 1,500 were totally destroyed. The death-toll was high: 164 people were killed and 70 seriously injured. Casualties would have been even higher were it not for the fact that, as a result of the previous raids, many people spent their nights away from the city, and that some of the bombs intended for Exeter fell outside the area.

'Let a feller sleep . . .'

In the west of the city a 'near miss' blew out the front of a house, cutting it almost in half and exposing the bedrooms.

On the first floor a bed was perilously overhanging the street. The body under the bedclothes was still.

ARP workers thought they had found another victim of the devastation, but when they shook the form – that of an elderly man – he woke up and said: 'Blast it, can't you let a feller sleep in peace?'

He was stone deaf.

From: the Exeter *Express and Echo*, 4 May 1972.

NORWICH REVISITED

Considerable though the destruction was in Exeter, the previous Luftwaffe assaults upon Norwich had already produced a higher casualty list. In the two April raids upon Norwich 236 people had been killed and over 800 injured. And it was for this return target that the Luftwaffe next mustered a force of bombers from those remaining in the West. Again, some 430 bombers were assembled, a mixed strike force – mainly Dorniers, together with Junkers 88s, and Heinkel 111s. Shortly after midnight of the 8/9 May 1942 the first of the attacking force crossed the Norfolk coast heading for the city in what, on this occasion, was to prove a largely ineffectual mission.

Several factors helped to reduce the effectiveness of this third Baedeker attack on Norwich. For more than an hour the Luftwaffe's approaching bombers had been monitored, even though the German directional radio guidance signal was not positively identified as targeting on Norwich until a few minutes before the first bombs started to fall. Nonetheless, defences had been alerted. The defence of Norwich had also been strengthened in the weeks following the previous raids; most notably, the barrage balloon defence had been augmented. On the night of this return raid one German bomber was definitely accounted for when it ran into a balloon cable. The mere presence of about 30 more balloons was a deterrent to the approaching bombers, making homing in and the accurate release of bombs much more uncertain.

Another defence measure also proved its worth that night. Sited some two miles to the south-east of the city was a decoy

This remarkable photograph, taken from a Westland Lysander, shows the burnt-out shell of Caley's chocolate factory in Norwich after a Baedeker raid on the city

'Starfish' site – mock structures which could be fired by remote control, burning fuel and casting light to suggest, to the crews above, the effect of burning buildings. Shortly after reports of the first bomb-loads falling the site was set on fire, attracting several high-explosive bombs intended for the city.

Lastly, the anti-aircraft defence in and around Norwich was much more effective on this occasion. The barrage was decidedly more hostile, and for the first time in the area large-calibre (3.7 inch) heavy guns joined in the action. As elsewhere when such heavy guns were employed local residents found comfort in the resounding boom of their discharge, feeling, at the least, that the enemy was not being given an easy run.

In the event, the bombing was widely scattered, the combination of defences certainly having succeeded in reducing its effectiveness. The total of 180 high-explosive bombs (of 113 tons), together with several parachute mines and several thousand incendiaries, fell in 21 different localities in Norfolk, many of them in rural locations, villages, farms, and open country.

This Norwich raid confirmed the view that, though potentially destructive, such attacks could be countered. The sense of outrage and humiliation which the Baedeker missions might have achieved had been deliberately played down by the Cabinet, at Churchill's suggestion. All the emphasis throughout the spring campaign against the cathedral cities of England had been put upon the indomitable spirit of the people and – in newspaper coverage – upon those buildings which had remained standing rather than those which had been destroyed. What Hitler had achieved with these missions had so far proved relatively insignificant in its effect on British morale. Compared with earlier concentrated blitz attacks on other centres they were, indeed, on a smaller scale. What they did achieve was a hardening of opinion which persuaded the War Cabinet to give the go-ahead to Air Chief Marshal Harris, who had by now acquired the nickname 'Bomber', for massive retaliation on a major target. On 18 May Harris proposed sending a force of a thousand bombers to attack a single industrial target, and thus saturate the defences by sheer weight of numbers.

One month after the Luftwaffe attacked York, 'Bomber' Harris was ready to mount his 'Arabian Nights' operation. By drawing upon all available resources, including aircraft from training units together with instructors and, in some

Goebbels speaks . . .

On 27 April 1942 Dr Goebbels declared that 'Our task must now be to reply to terror with terror and to respond to the attempted destruction of German centres of culture by razing English cultural shrines to the ground. That is now to be done on the biggest scale possible. The Führer has already given orders for . . . such a plan.

There is no other way to bring the English to their senses. They belong to a class of human beings with whom you can talk only after you have first knocked their teeth out.'

cases, even trainee pilots, he managed to assemble a force of 1,001 bombers.

The original target chosen for this massive operation was Hamburg, but on the night of the raid – 30 May – unfavourable weather conditions over the target zone were reported. So, virtually at the last minute, the attack was switched to the 'reserve' target, the city of Cologne.

As the industrial capital of the Rhineland it was of obvious strategic importance. And as an ancient cathedral city, boasting many fine buildings and a long, proud history, it could also be regarded as an appropriate choice from a cultural point of view – the Baedeker approach in reverse, as it were. And certainly, the British public, as well as members of the War Cabinet, were now prepared to think in such terms after the Luftwaffe's attacks on Exeter, Bath, Norwich and York.

In this first 'thousand bomber raid' 13,000 German homes were destroyed in Cologne, 45,000 of its citizens were left homeless and 469 civilians were killed. Chemical and engineering production was crippled. The results were severe – but, it should be noted, still not on the scale of the German bombing of London in April the previous year.

BAEDEKER 5: CANTERBURY

The effect of the Cologne raid on the German High Command was quite clear. There was a sense of shock, and Hitler himself acknowledged the unprecedented scale of the attack. He ordered immediate retaliation. This time the selected target was Canterbury – "a reprisal for the terrorist raid on Cologne", in the words of the German High Command. So on the night of 31 May/1 June some 80 Luftwaffe bombers attacked the city. Canterbury, the seat of Christianity in England, whose eleventh-century cathedral contains the shrine of the martyr St Thomas à Becket, suffered greatest damage in its eastern parts. Three churches, two schools, and a newspaper office were destroyed. Many houses and shops were also destroyed, as were other buildings, including the Corn Exchange and the City Market. It appeared, however, that the Germans made a specific attempt to destroy the cathedral itself, a number of high-explosives falling close to the great building. In the event, only the cathedral library was destroyed. A few incendiary bombs penetrated the roof but these were dealt with effectively before they could do severe damage. The bombardment cost the lives of 43 persons, and more than twice that number received serious injuries.

In accordance with what had become standard practice for these raids, a repeat attack was mounted by the Luftwaffe two nights later, and another on the night of 6/7 June. In these assaults, large areas around St George's were flattened. In the three Baedeker raids on Canterbury one-third of the city area had been laid waste. As a strategic target the city was without significance, and as a Baedeker strike the raids were failures. As a reprisal, the number of casualties was relatively low, even allowing for the fact that Canterbury's population of 24,000 bore little comparison with Cologne's 772,000.

BAEDEKER 6: IPSWICH

Between the first and second raid on Canterbury the Luftwaffe visited Ipswich on the night of 1/2 June. Though there was some damage to this East Suffolk county town, there were few casualties. Ipswich was not unused to air raids, though on most occasions they were carried out either by single, or just a few, aircraft. Altogether Ipswich was raided on 51 occasions, a total of 40 people being killed.

With hindsight, the Baedeker raid on Ipswich might be seen as the point at which the whole offensive began to falter. It is difficult to see that the later raids in the series achieved any strategic advantage at all. Dwindling resources, especially of trained pilots, forced the Luftwaffe to slow down the frequency of the attacks and, in many ways, to choose less credible targets. Poole, for example, was raided on the night of 3/4 June as part of the continuing campaign. There was considerable damage, but only two fatal casualties were recorded. Southampton was bombed on 21/22 June: again, substantial damage was caused with the loss of 14 lives. Three nights later Nuneaton was bombed for about an hour by 35 aircraft. 16 people lost their lives in this raid, which may well have been intended for Coventry, only five miles away. Norwich was the target once more on the night of 26/27 June in a raid lasting for about an hour, in the course of which 36 persons were killed. Weston-super-Mare was attacked on two nights in succession, beginning the night after the Norwich raid. In the second raid some 70 fires were started, and the casualty list was high with 55 killed.

CANTERBURY AGAIN

About 30 Luftwaffe bombers attacked Canterbury in a daylight raid on the last day of October, when further considerable damage was done to residential properties and 32 people were killed. That night about 35 bombers returned to the cathedral city when the damage reported was on a smaller scale, and only two persons were killed. As with many other attacks it is difficult to determine whether these were intended as a continuing part of the Baedeker programme,

'I'll strangle him . . .'

[Mrs Ware], a resolute lady, emerged from her cellar . . ., her face blackened with soot, Bruce the dog, his coat turned white in a matter of an hour, with her canary singing crazily in the chaos of her living room, to find a Signal Corps captain billeted on her, fumbling wildly with his service revolver. 'What on earth are you doing?' she demanded.

'They say Jerry drops parachutists during the cover of a raid,' the captain explained excitedly. 'I'm going out to shoot them.'

'Put that gun away,' Mrs Ware commanded firmly. She looked around grimly at her shattered room and snapped. 'The way I feel at this moment – if any German parachutist lands here, I'll strangle him personally – *with my own bare hands*!'

From: Taylor and Kessler, *The York Blitz 1942*.

A damaged section of St Augustin's College at Canterbury

or whether they were small-scale attacks on isolated targets. Cromer, for example, was bombed by a single aircraft on the night of 22 July, when four high-explosive bombs dropped near the town centre did considerable damage. Some reports from German sources maintain that the Baedeker campaign continued virtually to the end of 1942 and included such targets as Sunderland, Newcastle, and Middlesborough in the north-east, Swansea in the west, and Colchester and King's Lynn in East Anglia. There can be no doubt that the most concentrated period of attack was the three months of April, May and June. By July the attacks were of a reduced weight apart from three attacks on Birmingham in July (27/28, 29/30, and 30/31) which were on a considerably larger scale than other Luftwaffe raids at that time.

The Dean of York Minster spoke for many in Britain when, at the memorial service for those who had died on the night of 28 April 1942, he said: 'York paid its toll in the defence of our England, our liberty, our race. We do not grudge it. We have not complained. We will be proud of it.'

Many buildings of architectural value and interest were either lost or severely damaged in cities and towns attacked by the Luftwaffe during the Baedeker offensive. But in a number of places schemes were already in operation whereby architects, builders and antiquarians worked together to limit damage before an air attack, and to restore important buildings afterwards. In this way, some irreplaceable features such as early stained glass windows, for example, were removed during the first weeks of the war and stored in a safe place for the duration. After the start of the Blitz, local experts supervised the covering, waterproofing and storing up of important buildings damaged by blast and fire, and advised on demolition where they were no longer structurally sound.

By and large such panels were successful in their salvage and rescue work. The badly damaged Rose Tavern in Norwich was saved and partly rebuilt, and is today the oldest inhabited house in the city. In Exeter the clearing away and reconstruction work unearthed sections of Roman walling, adding to knowledge of the city's history, and the city of Bath still stands as a monument to the grandeur of Regency high society. The bombing of a major portion of the old city of Canterbury enabled archaeologists to trace the story of its occupation from the Stone Age through to Roman and medieval times.

T. H. O'Brien, the official historian and author of *Civil Defence*, summarised the effects of the Baedeker raids in these terms:

> The destruction and damage to vital war industries by the attacks over these four months was small. But from the wider standpoint of the destruction of human life, of the services upon which these various communities depended and of buildings of national significance the enemy's achievements should not be underrated.

And in the context of the whole war it should not be forgotten that the Baedeker raids significantly shifted the British attitude towards indiscriminate bombing of German targets. It was a policy which would not have found favour in the earlier stages of the war but one which, in the event, was to unleash manifold destruction and suffering upon German cities and towns.

Dover and the South Coast

It is with a sense of pride that the people of Dover will tell you that their town has been in Britain's front line for more than 2,000 years. Conquerors and would-be invaders from Julius Caesar onwards have regarded Dover as a prize of the greatest value – a gateway to Britain that, in wartime, has either to be captured or destroyed.

This sense of history, and of the strategic importance of their town and harbour, may well account for the decision taken by Dover Council to introduce ARP as early as 1935. Memories of the First World War were still fresh in people's minds: they had no need to be told how vulnerable they were to attack. On a clear day, could they not see for themselves, on the horizon, the thin outline of a foreign shore? And what if, one day, that foreign shore should fall into hostile hands?

So the authorities set about making preparations with determination and efficiency. A basic civil defence team, recruited entirely from the local population, was established and a network of huge underground cave shelters was made ready. The newly-built police station contained within its walls a specially-designed and equipped gas decontamination centre.

In these and in many other ways Dover prepared for war. But when it came in September 1939 the first thing to happen was the arrival of 426 evacuee children from London. Those responsible for such matters had decided that the town was to be a reception area. The lessons of geography and of more than 2,000 years of history, so clearly understood by the local citizens, appear to have been lost on the authorities in Whitehall. Not until Dunkirk was this folly put right: as the exhausted and defeated BEF disembarked at Dover Harbour, so many of the town's children were quietly evacuated to safer havens in Wales.

BASTION DOVER

With the fall of France and the threat of invasion growing day by day, those who had no need to stay in the town were encouraged to leave. As a result the population fell from 40,000 to less than 10,000. Dover became a military outpost in a top security zone; a bastion against the overwhelming and terrifying power that had now engulfed so much of the European mainland.

At this time German reconnaissance planes were spotted over the south coast, reinforcing the belief that Hitler's invasion was imminent. Also during May 1940 there were false reports of German parachutists landing in the sea: one of many rumours that did little to allay local fears and anxieties. To make matters worse, the first air attack against Dover Harbour occurred on 25 May 1940. Although only one aircraft was involved and there were no casualties from the raid, one of the bombs struck a magnetic mine out at sea. This exploded with a 'terrific' noise, and created a good deal of alarm.

Dover's front-line status became more apparent as the Battle of Britain began to unfold. The Straits of Dover saw some of the most intense attacks of the war against British convoys as the Germans sought mastery of the Channel. The actions, usually savage and costly to both sides, were often witnessed from the heights above the town. As the battle intensified vapour trails filled the skies day after day. The roar of aircraft engines and the rattle of machine-gun fire could be clearly heard. 'Goofing' (watching the action instead of taking cover) became a popular pastime, and 'Hellfire Corner' became known to millions of BBC listeners all over the world.

In the opening (July 1940) phase of the Luftwaffe's bid to destroy the RAF and gain control of the air for Operation *Sea Lion*, their probing tactics included not only daylight attacks on British convoys and ports, but also night raids on Dover and Folkestone. Another and more direct assault against Dover Harbour, which was beaten off by fighters and AA fire, was made by a force of about 40 Stuka dive-bombers on 29 July.

As the Battle of Britain entered its second phase, the Germans brought up long-range heavy artillery to the north-western coast of occupied France with

The first of many

The first bomb from an aeroplane to fall on English soil landed in Mr Terson's garden in Taswell Street, Dover, on Christmas Eve, 1914. His gardener was winter pruning some fruit trees at the time, and he was so surprised by the explosion that he fell off his ladder without, we are told, sustaining any serious or permanent injury.

Marine Station on the Admiralty Pier

the main intention of closing the English Channel to Allied shipping. But the maximum range of the largest of these guns was 34 miles, which meant that both Folkestone and Dover were within reach. It also meant that for the first time British towns could be shelled directly from France. A new burden of war was added to those already carried by people living in this vulnerable part of the South-East.

The first shell, which took about 60 seconds to cross the Channel, ('long enough to put down your pint and take cover', as one resident explained) landed on Edgar Road, Dover, at 11am on 12 August 1940, the day before *Adler Tag* when the Luftwaffe started its major offensive. This opening bombardment brought a vigorous response from the Mayor of Dover, Councillor Jimmy Cairns:

> If the Germans think they can intimidate people here by these tactics they're wrong. Last night's bombardment had precisely the opposite effect.

Two deaths resulted from the attack, the first of many that followed over the next four years. It has been estimated that 2,226 shells fell on the town during the war, killing 148 people and destroying more than 1,000 homes. There is no doubt that the death toll would have been much greater had it not been for the cave shelters, capable of housing 12,000, and the strict enforcement of regulations.

Night shelling often started in the early hours of the morning, presenting an uncomfortable choice of getting out of a warm bed and bundling on clothes to seek the shelter of the caves, or of turning over and hoping for the best. Many people chose to spend every night in the safety of caves, where there developed a great deal of social activity and where a strong spirit of community prevailed. Heating, lighting and cooking facilities were provided, and there were even underground hospitals with their own operating theatres and decontamination centres.

The German army gunners timed their bombardments to disrupt the lives of Dover's inhabitants as much as possible. Shelling activity would be stepped up on Saturday mornings when the shops were at their busiest, or would coincide with the opening times of cinemas and dance halls. And because 'All Clears' were sounded one hour after the last shell, single shots came over at more or less hourly intervals to maintain a state of Alert for as long as possible.

Shells fell singly or in clusters, as on Priory Gate Road in 1944, when a whole terrace of houses was destroyed. Some of the shells that fell on the town were probably 'over-range' shots intended for convoys in the Channel. Bombing raids and shelling attacks sometimes came together, as on 11 September 1940, when both Dover and Deal were the targets. On that occasion seven people lost their lives and considerable damage was done to shops, houses and to Dover Priory railway station.

As they would be the first to acknowledge, it was not only the townspeople of Dover who suffered by being too close to the enemy. During the brilliant late summer and early autumn of 1940, dogfights and vapour trails could be seen in the skies over virtually the whole of southern and south-eastern England. Action was by no means confined to the front line. The Luftwaffe not only attacked Fighter Command stations but also bombed such places as Weybridge in Surrey, where the Vickers Armstrong and Hawker aircraft factories were situated. One of the many hazards faced by people living in the region was the risk of falling aircraft – casualties of the battle, friend and foe alike. Not all came down in open country: some landed in built-up areas with disastrous results.

Even when the focus of the German air attack was switched to London there was little relief for the South-East. Coastal towns were still singled out by the Luftwaffe, as on 26 September 1940, when a number of places between Southampton and Folkestone were attacked. Widespread disruption followed, and railway lines at Eastbourne, Hastings and Bexhill were put out of action for a time. On that same day, Dover was heavily shelled once again, leaving over 50 shops and houses damaged.

In early October, five people were killed when bombing demolished several houses at Folkestone, and on 2 November 1940 Ramsgate recorded its worst incident to date when residential properties and a gasworks were hit, killing eight people. Just over two weeks later, on 18 November, tragedy returned to Folkestone when at about 4am two land mines were released from a single German aircraft flying over the town at about 500ft. They came down almost simultaneously – one in the area of the fish market around Beach Street, and the other at Rossendale Road. In the first explosion, public houses, shops and cafes were destroyed, while in the second, many houses were wrecked and widespread devastation was caused by the blast. The death toll stood at 14, the heaviest loss of life sustained in air raids on the town at that time.

One important region in the South-East became even more vulnerable after the Luftwaffe's change of tactics on 7 September 1940. The whole of the Thames estuary became a huge flight-path, as wave after wave of German bombers followed the river to reach their new target – London. Hardly a place on either bank escaped. The vast Ford factory at Dagenham presented a tempting target: East and West Ham, together with Barking, also came under heavy attack. The GEC factory at Erith was frequently bombed, as were many other places south of the river, such as Dartford and Gravesend. The whole of the Medway area became a target area, and the naval dockyard at Chatham was singled out for special attention. At Rochester, not far away, the Short Brothers aircraft factory was hit and set on fire during a Luftwaffe raid in April 1941.

Other parts of the South-East as well as the Thames estuary were vulnerable to random attacks by German bombers which had failed to penetrate London's defences. As they came under attack from RAF fighters, they would get rid of their bombs to lose weight and so improve

Snargate Street, once one of Dover's main shopping streets, close to the Hippodrome Theatre. On the right is the old Trocadero wine stores

Flashmans furniture workshops and depository were damaged first by bombs in March 1941, and then even more severely by a shell which fell nearby in October 1943

their chances of getting back safely to the network of Luftwaffe bases in France and the Low Countries. Again, many of the jettisoned bombs fell harmlessly on open countryside, but others did not. Virtually the whole of Kent and much of Sussex suffered in this way: Hastings, Margate, Lympe, Worthing, Hythe, Bexhill, Ashford and Maidstone were among the many places hit.

After the 'Baedeker' raids, in the eighteen months from July 1942 to January 1944 (the massed bombing of industrial and coastal targets being almost over), the Luftwaffe adopted a form of attack popularly known as 'tip and run' or 'scalded cat' raids. In these, a few aircraft (often Focke-Wulf 190s), or even just one, made fast, low-level attacks on coastal towns, usually in the South-East. The speed of approach by planes flying at over 300mph and at a low altitude, presented difficult problems for the defences, especially as they were often undetected until the last moment. Indeed, at times the Alert warning of their arrival sounded *after* they had left. These lightning attacks could result in substantial damage and loss of life.

Among scores of 'tip and run' raids in the South-East there is space here to mention only a few. Eastbourne was hit on 26 August 1942 by two Focke-Wulf 190s, each armed with a single high-explosive bomb. A residential district and an electricity works were hit and three people killed. Hastings was attacked by seven planes on 24 September: in that single raid 23 people lost their lives. Brighton's turn came on 12 October, when five people were killed and 20 houses demolished. One of the great tragedies caused by these attacks occurred on 29 September when five raiders roamed across Kent, Sussex and Wiltshire. One of their bombs scored a direct hit on a boys' school at Petworth, West Sussex, and 31 boys were killed – a precursor of a similar disaster early in 1945. Among other South-East coastal towns to suffer from 'tip and run' raids in late 1945 were Dover, Deal, Folkestone, Rye, Newhaven, Worthing, Broadstairs and Margate.

The results achieved by the Luftwaffe by these high-speed, low-level attacks on the south-east corner of the country, and on the south and east coasts in particular, led to a larger-scale attack of the same type in January 1943. On 20 January came the biggest daylight raid on London since the beginning of the Blitz in September 1940. More than 20 aircraft, Focke-Wulf 190s and Messerschmitt 109s, selected their individual targets for attack in south-east London. These included the Surrey docks, where substantial damage was caused. One of the places hit was Sandhurst Road School, Catford, resulting in one of the worst tragedies of this period of the war. Shortly after midday a bomb hit the centre of the school, and the blast and explosion killed 38 children and six of their teachers. The full reports of this event in the press, which was exempted from the usual censorship, aroused massive feelings of outrage.

'Tip and run' raids, though conducted by small numbers of aircraft, could be extremely costly of life, as the Catford disaster showed. But the Luftwaffe was now heavily committed on the Eastern Front, and its dwindling reserves produced a steadily declining scale of attacks in 1943. The estimated tonnage of bombs dropped on the United Kingdom decreased from 3,030 in 1942 to 2,230 in 1943. Before 1943 had ended, however, many severe attacks were recorded in various parts of the South-East, a few examples of which will show that although raids were becoming less frequent, individual attacks could still produce devastating results.

March opened with more shelling of the Kent coast from the Pas de Calais and a sharp air raid on Eastbourne, carried out by twelve German aircraft, in which 21 people lost their lives. On 9 March Worthing and Hove came under attack, to be followed by Hastings two days later. On the 24th, fourteen bombers ventured a few miles inland to bomb Ashford in Kent, where in only three minutes 50 people were killed and widespread devastation was caused. Finally, just before the end of the month, a raid on the Brighton and Hove area resulted in 16 more fatalities.

The effects of 'tip and run' raids of this kind did not go unnoticed by Hitler's Minister of Propaganda, Dr Goebbels. Substantial residential properties were destroyed or damaged by attacks on coastal towns to a far greater extent than in the major cities, with their closely-packed terraces and back-to-back dwellings. Making a virtue of necessity, Dr Goebbels proposed that:

> ... in future we should bomb not slums, but the residential sections of the plutocracy ... According to my experience this makes the deepest impression. The Führer agrees. It does not pay to attack harbours or industrial cities. At present we have not sufficient means for such attacks. The Führer agrees that air warfare against England must now be conducted according to psychological rather than military principles ...

Although this seems not to have been the only policy adopted by the Luftwaffe governing their choice of targets in Britain for the rest of the war, there is reason to believe that pressure exercised by Hitler, directly and indirectly, accounts for the persistence with which some continued to be attacked. The basic strategic value of targets was well understood by the Germans, and they must have been aware that many places along the south coast of England were of little military significance, and others of no significance at all.

However, on 3 April 1943 Eastbourne was attacked yet again: more than 30 people were killed in the raid, most of them in a surface shelter which received a direct hit. On 23 May a twin assault was mounted against Hastings and Bournemouth. In a Sunday lunchtime attack on

The ancient 'Old St James's' Church was repeatedly hit during the many bombardments of Dover

Big Berthas in the bag

Cross-Channel shelling continued until the German batteries at Cap Gris Nez were captured after a combined operation between the US Air Force and units of the Canadian and British armies. On 30 September 1944 the CO of the 9th Canadian Infantry Brigade sent this telegram to the Mayor of Dover:

> *'Greetings from the Brigade and may you enjoy your pint of beer and stroll on the front in peace from now on. We have all of Jerry's Big Berthas'*

In his reply the Mayor thanked the Canadians and told them that the people of Dover would 'not enjoy our beer and stroll on the front to the full until you all can join us in it. We wish you God Speed and all further success.'

Hastings, twelve aircraft made low-level passes over the town and succeeded in destroying 50 buildings and damaging hundreds more, with the loss of 25 lives. The Bournemouth attack was made at the same time, but on an even larger scale. Twenty-two aircraft took part in the raid which caused considerable damage and killed 123 people – 77 civilians and 46 service personnel. On the first day of June a less ambitious strike was mounted against the coastal resort of Margate, in which six people lost their lives during an attack lasting only one minute.

The counties most affected by these 'hit-and-run' raids were Sussex and, to a slightly lesser extent, Kent. Serious as the attacks were, it became clear as 1943 unfolded that their incidence was on the decline. The year started with 80 'hit-and-run' raids in January. By March the monthly total had dropped to 52, and by June to 39. The figures continued to decrease, month by month, until December 1943, when only seven such attacks were recorded.

But the Luftwaffe had not yet done with London and the South-East. During the first three months of 1944 – a period that later became known as the 'Little Blitz' or the 'Baby Blitz' – German aeroplanes dropped 2,350 tons of bombs over the region, a greater tonnage than was delivered during the whole of the previous year. In a renewed show of strength, the Luftwaffe staged night-bombing raids, using aircraft in increasing numbers, and reverting to the saturation-bombing tactics that had characterised the opening phases of the Blitz.

They were met by vigorous anti-aircraft barrages and by RAF fighters, whose ability to stalk raiders at night had been greatly increased. The effectiveness of the defences was clearly shown in a raid on London on the night of 21/22 January 1944. In an attack on a scale that had not been seen since the raid on Birmingham in July 1942, two waves of

Cannon Street, Dover, where in June 1943 a single shell killed a young Wren, 11 servicemen and a child, and left 31 others injured

More than three-quarters of the collection housed in the Dover Museum on the upper floor of the Market Hall was destroyed when a shell landed on the premises in 1942. Among the many stuffed animals lost was half a lion, which was hurled into the street

enemy aircraft, each consisting of about 90 bombers, made for the capital. But AA batteries and the RAF night-fighters put up such a good defence that only 14 bombers from the first wave, and 13 from the second, actually got through. The result was, in the words of the official historian T.H. O'Brien, 'a considerable spill of bombs over South-East England'. So completely was the Luftwaffe's attack broken that most of the 245 'incidents' that night were recorded not in the London area, but in Kent (110) and Sussex (53).

The Steinbock raids, as they were also known, were concentrated on London, though other targets were also selected. South-East coastal towns still came under attack, but much less frequently than in the past. Indeed, had it not been for the intermittent shelling from across the Channel, the air bombardment of the Dover salient and of the south coast generally might be said to have petered out almost completely. And when no more Steinbock raids came after the end of March 1944 it really seemed that the Luftwaffe's onslaught against the South-East had at last run its long and bitter course.

But behind the scenes it was known that an even deadlier attack, using Hitler's much-vaunted secret weapons, was about to begin. The existence of such weapons had been rumoured for a long time, and Hitler had often threatened to unleash them against Britain. Now the time had come for these dark threats to be realised.

In the month of June 1944, a few days after Allied forces landed on the beaches of Normandy, the first of many 'flying bombs' (V1) spluttered their way across Kent on their way to London, leaving behind them a trail of havoc. In due course they were followed by a more frightening weapon – the V2 rocket – which landed in considerable numbers and over a much wider area. These 'revenge weapons' brought more death and destruction to London, the South-East and to other regions, and it was not until all their launching sites were overrun by the advancing Allied armies that the menace of attack by air was lifted from the whole of the country. By the time that point had been reached, the end of the war in Europe was clearly in sight.

The call of the sea

According to the *Dover Express* one local youngster was quite scared when the guns at last fell silent. 'What's that swishing sound, Mummy?' she asked. 'It's the waves breaking on the shingle,' came the reply. 'Nothing to worry about.'

V for Vengeance

By the end of 1942 the Germans were conducting sensitive and top secret experiments with new weapons at Peenemünde on the Baltic coast of Pomerania. Two major new weapons were being developed: an 'A.4' rocket, which would be under control of the Army, and a pilotless aircraft to be operated by the Luftwaffe. In December of that year, the pilotless aircraft had been successfully launched in two modes. It had been dropped from a 'host' aircraft, and it had been launched from a catapult ramp. Both these methods of delivery were eventually employed against England.

The experimental site and testing station had been set up at Peenemünde because the Germans hoped that it would be beyond the range of RAF photographic reconnaisance. They were mistaken. In response to a flow of Intelligence reports of secret weapons being developed, including rockets, the RAF succeeded in flying sorties over the site, and brought back the first photographs on 22 April 1943. These and later photographs revealed rockets and their trailers among the buildings and works.

The problem for British Intelligence was that information received earlier, and during the summer months that followed the RAF photographic reconnaissance, was based on observation and reports relating to *two* types of missile – the pilotless aircraft and the upright rocket. This often caused confusion in interpretation. When a pilotless aircraft, test-fired by the Germans, landed on the Danish island of Bornholm in August, a photograph of the wreckage that was forwarded to London increased this confusion, for what had actually landed was a four-metre-long scale model of the craft under development.

By May 1943 work on the pilotless aircraft had reached the point where a series of demonstrations could be confidently arranged for Albert Speer, Hitler's Minister for Armaments and War Production. What he saw led Speer to give the go-ahead for continued development and production of the weapons.

Within weeks new installations were being built on German-occupied Channel coastal sites, and British Intelligence was beginning to receive reports about them. Some sixty sites were well on the way to completion by the end of September. In that month a Frenchman, André Comps, got a job as a draftsman at one of the sites, where he made copies of the site blueprints. He handed these over to a fellow Frenchman, Michel Hollard, who was a British agent. Hollard managed to smuggle the blueprints through Switzerland to Britain. Using these plans, British scientists made models of the sites, but the nature of the weapon for which they were being built remained uncertain. In November the RAF was ordered to carry out a detailed reconnaissance of the sites in Northern France, as they appeared to house some kind of 'ski' or launching apparatus. Though some interpreters strongly suspected that the sites were associated with a flying device, there was still no firm evidence linking them with the information already obtained.

The Peenemünde site was photographed again by the RAF on 28 November 1943. This photograph, together with a re-interpretation of earlier evidence, enabled Intelligence experts to confirm in two days that a pilotless plane rested on the 'ski' at Peenemünde. Though there was still some scepticism, it was now clear that previous information related to the development of *two* new weapons: the pilotless aircraft and a rocket bomb photographed earlier. Persistent suspicions about German development of a pilotless aircraft were now incontrovertibly confirmed, and previous confusions began to be resolved. The size of the warhead carried by the new weapon, however, was greatly overestimated, the initial calculation being seven tons.

OPERATION CROSSBOW

Now that the existence of the pilotless aircraft had been confirmed, *Operation Crossbow* was launched on 5 December, systematically to bomb 'ski' sites along the north coast of France, as well as research and experimental stations, including Peenemünde. The installations themselves could be concealed, but their supply lines could not. These raids certainly succeeded in delaying the introduction of the new weapons, and perhaps also in reducing the scale of their use. Early in March 1944, for example, direct information from France led the RAF to bomb a German ammunition dump near Creil. Included in the ordnance stored there were 2,000 pilotless aircraft, or 'flying bombs'.

The Fzg. 76 (also known in German military circles as the Fieseler Fi 103) was given another description: *Vergeltungs-*

waffe I ('Revenge Weapon I') or the 'V1' as it was more familiarly known. The description is apposite because it was clear that Hitler and his Staff were determined to inflict on Britain some of the ferocious bombing which German towns and cities had been suffering. But in another sense 'revenge' was only a part of Hitler's design, for he saw the V1 as a weapon of strategic importance in waging the war which he still believed Germany could win. Even after the D-Day landings in Normandy and the Allied advance inland, Hitler expected that sustained V-weapon attacks, supplemented by the introduction of his new jet fighters, would regain control of the air for the Luftwaffe. That achieved, he planned a repeat of the 1940 *Blitzkrieg* tactics, surging again through the Ardennes with an army that would either drive the Allies back or force them to offer peace terms acceptable to the Reich.

When in the middle of June the V1 pilotless aircraft were first directed against England in accordance with Hitler's orders, the new bombardment certainly did not 'open like a thunderclap' as he intended.

The Flazeitlgerät Fzg. 76, or Fieselor Fi 103 (named after the principal engineering contractor) was a pilotless, pre-aimed, small monoplane powered by a pulse-jet engine burning petrol fed with compressed air. Once settled into its flight, the V1 travelled at speeds from 250mph to a little over 400mph. The height at which the weapon flew varied between near ground-level and 8,000 feet, though the vast majority of V1s operated at between 3,000 and 4,000 feet. The craft's range extended to about 130 miles from its land-based launch-site. When air-launched from a Heinkel 111 the operational range increased to over 300 miles.

At 4.13am on the morning of Tuesday 13 June the first V1 to land in England fell harmlessly on open farmland near Swanscombe in Kent. At 4.20am, a second flying bomb landed at Cuckfield in Sussex. The third, and the first V1 to cause casualties in England, came down at Bethnal Green in the East End of London. The fourth V1 fell at 5.06am at Platt near Sevenoaks, also in Kent.

The V1 at Bethnal Green clearly demonstrated the potential destructive force of the new weapon. Six people were killed by its explosion and the blast damaged many houses in the area of the impact point – the railway bridge in Grove Road.

Sometime before midnight on Thursday 15 June V1 attacks began in earnest, as during the next 24 hours the Germans launched 200 of their Fzg. 76s. Fortunately the barrage was reduced because only 144 reached England, 73 of which landed in the London area. In the face of such a heavy onslaught, the Cabinet had no option but to release some general information about the new weapon.

Once the assault had begun, it was maintained with a steady stream of 'flying bombs', night and day. By the end of the first weekend, more than 500 V1s had been launched against England. Not all of them succeeded in landing on British soil, but one hit the Wellington Barracks in Birdcage Walk, the London home of the Brigade of Guards. The bomb struck the Guards Chapel at 11.20am during morning service. The death toll was 121: 63 Service personnel and 58 civilians. More than 60 people were seriously injured in the collapse of the building. This was the worst incident, in terms of loss of life, in the entire V1 bombardment. It occurred, too, during the worst days of the assault – before defences had been re-organised to deal with the new threat.

THAT EERIE MOMENT

Even as barrage balloons, searchlights, and gun emplacements were being re-deployed to counter the attacks, many dozens of flying bombs were leaving their traces throughout the South-East, particularly in London and Kent. Within weeks the public had christened them 'doodle-bugs', partly perhaps in recognition of the buzzing sound made by the engine. (They were also known as 'buzz bombs'.) What everyone who experienced flying bombs recalls most vividly is the silence immediately after the engine cut out. Many have tried to describe that eerie moment and the quality of the silence. First, there was the rattling sound as the V1 passed close by, then a period of silence, perhaps only ten or more seconds, and then the sound of the explosion when the bomb landed. That brief interval of silence has been variously described as 'ominous', 'terrifying', and even 'deafening'.

By the end of the first month of the campaign, 1,600 people had been killed and 4,500 seriously injured. About 200,000 houses had been affected by explosions and blast, many of them seriously damaged and others totally demolished. The sheer unpredictability of V1s – which would arrive at any moment without warning – added to the general anxiety they caused. Many people who lived through the night blitzes in London in 1940/41 claimed that V1s were much more terrifying. The attacks seemed to have no regular pattern, and so there were few effective precautions that could be taken.

They were launched in such numbers that many of them penetrated the three lines of defence: the outer circuit of fighters patrolling from the South Downs to mid-Channel, the thick belt of AA guns to the south and east of London, and the dense curtain of balloons guarding the approaches to the capital.

For a time there was some confusion between the defences, and on occasion pursuing fighters were shot down by their own AA guns. Some RAF pilots developed novel tactics for destroying a flying bomb, even after running out of ammunition. Drawing level with their quarry, they would get a wing tip under one of the flying bomb's wings and flip it. This manoeuvre upset the gyroscopic control mechanism and sent the V1 out of control until it hit the ground. It was reported that these tactics were used late in June, but they were certainly in use early in July.

As the British defences against the flying bomb improved, and the kill-rate rose, the Germans attempted to outmanoeuvre their enemy. In the early hours of Saturday 8 July a V1 was air-launched from a Heinkel over the North Sea, the first of more than 1,100 to be launched against London in this fasion. Though the method at first certainly out-flanked the defensive rings to the south, it was fraught with its own difficulties. The pilot of the carrier-craft had to reach a pre-determined position and altitude, at a speed equivalent to the flight-speed of the V1, before it could be released. The start-up of the V1 produced an exhaust flame visible for miles at night. When this new tactic became known later in the month, patrolling defence fighters kept a good look-out for these tell-tale flames. It is possible that the failure rate of air-borne launches may have reached about 40%.

CONFUSION UNRESOLVED

Intelligence reports reaching the British at this time still confused the two types of long-range weapon being developed, a matter not resolved until the end of November 1943. Then RAF reconnaissance photographs taken over the Peenemünde complex clearly revealed the existence both of the Fzg 76, the flying bomb, and an upright rocket, the A4. Uncertainty as to the rocket's size, performance, and range remained. Also open to speculation was the critical matter of the size of the explosive warhead to be carried. This lack of positive, decisive, information persisted for many months, and was not resolved until June 1944.

On the day the first V1s landed in England, an A4 rocket was test-fired from Peenemünde. The day, 13 June, also brought to England, by accident and by an unintended route, the very first of the A4 rockets. Following the precedent set by the *Vergeltungswaffe 1* – the 'revenge' title suggested by Goebbel's propaganda machine – the new rocket weapon was soon known simply as the V2.

On 13 June, the Germans test-fired a V2 to experiment with another form of guidance control. For some time they had been trying out a procedure for guiding bombs to their target by radio. The Peenemünde scientists wished to establish the feasibility of guiding a rocket by the same procedure. A bomb-aiming expert, used to controlling the radio-directed glider-bombs, was to have charge of the rocket's guidance-system. Winston Churchill's account of what followed is precise:

> The Peenemünde experimenters were well accustomed to seeing a rocket rise, and it had not occurred to them that the glider-bomb expert would be surprised by the spectacle. But surprised he was, so much so that he forgot his own part in the procedure. In his astonishment he pushed the control lever well off to the left and held it there. The rocket obediently kept turning to the left, and by the time the operator had pulled himself together it was out of control range and heading for Sweden. There it fell.

The rocket fell on a farm in Backebo. The Swedish authorities allowed two British officers to examine the rocket in Stockholm, and their report went some way towards resolving the details of the weapon. Then, by a covert arrangement, the Swedish authorities allowed the remains of the rocket to be flown back to England, where they duly arrived at the end of July. They were sent to the Royal Aircraft Establishment at Farnborough, where they were re-assembled and accurate analyses of the rocket's workings prepared.

A flying bomb coming to earth beyond the Law Courts in the Strand, and the explosion a few seconds later, off Drury Lane

Already it was evident from earlier appraisals made by the British analysts that the threat posed by this rocket was much more menacing than that of the V1 flying bomb, which was at least vulnerable to both ground and air attack. Given their estimate (in fact, an underestimate) that the rocket would take only three or four minutes to reach London from launch-sites in northern Europe, and given its manner of delivery – an inverted U-trajectory to the stratosphere and a vertical descent – there could be no defence against the weapon.

It was therefore imperative for the allied troops to press on as quickly as possible through the Low Countries into Germany, having already over-run the bomb-proof launch pads in northern France from which it had been the German intention to mount the V2 assault against England. The only way of dealing with the V2 would be its capture.

On the last day of August Hitler issued his command for V2s to be used against both London and Paris, though his orders were not implemented for some days. They came after the day on which British defences had virtually eliminated every V1 flying over its coasts.

THE NEW MENACE

On 7 September the British Government announced that the danger from the V1 flying bombs was largely over, all launch-sites having been officially reported as cleared the day previously. There still remained the possibility of air-launched V1s, but that was considered a lesser threat. What was not known, however, was that on the day before this press briefing a German Army battery tried to put into effect the orders from Hitler to attack Paris with V2s. On the 6 September they prepared two V2 rockets, near Vielsalm in Belgium, to be fired against the French capital. Neither, however, could be successfully fired. Another coincidence which could not have been known at the time, was that at the moment when Duncan Sandys was addressing the members of the press a V2 launch battery arrived in The Hague, whence it was to direct its first missiles against London.

Following the British Government's press conference the next day's newspapers were celebrating the end of the missile assault and the lifting of blackout regulations which had been in force since the start of the war. Unknown to the British public, the V2 launch crew that morning successfully got away two missiles which had failed two days before. The first disappeared without trace, but the second hit a Paris suburb where it killed six people. Then at 6.43 that evening a V2, launched from The Hague batteries, struck Stavely Road, Chiswick, creating a large, deep crater, and a large area of destruction and blast damage. The explosion claimed the lives of three persons: a woman, an Army private, and a 3-year-old girl. A second V2 fell upon farmland at Epping just 16 seconds after the first exploded.

After these initial incidents no other V2s followed for two days. When the missiles did return their targeting was erratic. One rocket landed near Southend on the evening of 10 September, and during the week after that, between one and five V2s were recorded over a wide area. Places close to Eastbourne and Southend (again) received hits, as did locations in Kent, Surrey, and Essex. Within the London area Kew Gardens, Woolwich, Southgate, Wembley, East Ham, and Lambeth were all struck.

The attempt to maintain official secrecy about the V2 – which had been code-named 'Big Ben' – was continued, the authorities ascribing V2 incidents to 'exploding gas mains'. The pretence was hardly successful. There was, first, the nature of the explosion itself, a deafening thunderclap accompanied by an intense blue flash of light, followed by the roar of the rocket catching up with its own supersonic descent and a secondary boom of the broken sound barrier. The sound of the impacting explosion reached the ears before the sound of the rocket's approach. There was the fact too that news of these incidents travelled quickly by word of mouth, and soon members of the public were referring to 'flying gas mains' – a jibe at the style of official announcements referring to V2 incidents.

On September 17 the Allies began Operation Market Garden – the attempt to recapture the Rhine bridges in Holland, and also to deny the Germans the use of Holland as a V2 launching area. The V2 batteries withdrew to safer places in eastern Holland. Within days, as the British paratroops at Arnhem were overwhelmed by the German counter-attack, a V2 battery made its way to a new location in a wooded region close to the hamlet of Rijs in south-west Friesland on the edge of the Zuider Zee. From there the only English targets with sizeable populations within the V2's maximum range of 200 miles were Norwich and Ipswich. The first V2 missile directed against the east coast of England was fired in the early evening of 25 September. It landed on farmland in Hoxne in Suffolk. Two days later the Germans began their bombardment of Norwich, sending four rockets on their way. Of these three arrived close to the target zone, the second, in fact, arriving alongside the City Sewage Works. From then until 12 October the Rijs battery, with occasional interludes of a day or rather more, kept up a steady release of missiles aimed on Norwich. In this short period the Rijs battery sent nearly 50 rockets on their way, most aimed at Norwich with a few directed towards Ipswich. At least 15 of the missiles, however, failed to make English landfall, ten of them falling into the North Sea, and three of them exploding in mid-air before impacting. At least two of the rockets actually fell back into the launch-zone itself, in the wooded area of Friesland.

While the Rijs battery was conducting its operation against East Anglia, other V2 batteries, with orders to resume the attack upon London, were moving back to locations at The Hague, as the Allies' advance from the south was now checked. The first of the V2 missiles in this renewed campaign landed alongside Wanstead Flats. Eight people were killed in the explosion at Blake Hall Crescent. The renewed campaign against London put its eastern approaches under a special threat, at a time when V1 activity continued with the *Luftwaffe's* air-borne drops of flying bombs.

Despite the Allies' continuing advance on the Continent in October, the Luftwaffe persisted in their night-time air-borne launches of V1s from Heinkel 111s. But now fewer flying bombs were successfully launched and the impact points of those which did penetrate the defences were more widely scattered than hitherto. A few got through to London, but others fell over a much wider area, including parts of Hertfordshire, Bedfordshire, Suffolk, Norfolk and Kent. They fell mainly on lightly populated areas and consequently the damage was limited. Exceptions to this were almost all in the London region (for example, Harrow, Edmonton, Hackney, West Ham), while towards the end of the month the majority of flying bombs fell in East Anglia. In October, too, the Germans began to direct both V1s and V2s against Antwerp in an attempt to deny the port to the advancing Allied armies, and the scale of this attack increased dramatically towards the end of the month. In a savage and sustained bombardment, both before and during the Allies' occupation, Antwerp received many more V1s and V2s than fell on the London region – indeed, almost twice as many V1s and three times the number of V2s. When the destructive power of the V1 and the even more devastating power of the V2 are recalled, this makes a sobering comparison.

A V2 rocket being fuelled, and final adjustments made before launch – a long and complicated procedure

Airborne launches of V1s continued throughout November and early December, but by then they were relatively infrequent, certainly not crossing the coastline in anything like the numbers of the earlier land-based launches. Of those which were aimed at the capital, many were destroyed, and others fell in the Home Counties wide of their intended mark. Other flying bombs penetrated to Suffolk and Leicestershire. Most reported incidents were relatively minor in character.

Then, in the early hours of Christmas Eve, the Luftwaffe tactics suddenly changed yet again. So far all V1s had been directed to the southern part of England, but on the 24 December, 45 Heinkels, from 40 miles off the east coast, aimed their flying bombs towards the Manchester area. The landing-zones covered several counties: impact-points were reported in Yorkshire, Lancashire, Cheshire, Derybshire, Nottinghamshire, Shropshire, Northamptonshire, and Lincolnshire. A 'cluster' (but a very loose cluster) of fifteen bombs struck on a line from south-east of Manchester to the north-west, from Buxton to just east of Preston.

The Christmas Eve airborne launch of V1s aimed at Manchester proved to be one of the last attacks the Luftwaffe was able to mount, for by now the RAF's bombing campaign was becoming increasingly successful in reducing German oil and petroleum supplies.

Such airborne launches of flying bombs against southern England as had continued throughout December and into the New Year, ceased altogether after mid January. The last air-launched V1 attack on London took place in the early hours of Sunday 14 January 1945, a fact which was naturally not appreciated at the time. Not until some weeks had gone by, free of V1s, did it begin to appear likely that the worst of the threat was now at an end. V2s were still falling at regular intervals, but during February 1945 no V1s were launched against England.

However, British intelligence reports had indicated that a new long-range version of the weapon was being developed. From ground launch-ramps at sites around The Hague, which the Germans still occupied, numbers of these new flying bombs were released against England, starting on 3 March. On that same night, when the Luftwaffe made scattered bombing sorties over southern and eastern counties, air-launched flying bombs were also aimed at London. Of the 21 V1s released, only seven reached the London area.

The threat posed by the final, and intermittent, employment of the V1 weapon from The Hague sites remained, in the event, at a comparatively minor level. Few of the bombs launched against England got through: most of those approaching the coast were accounted for by AA gunners.

In the entire V1 campaign nearly 10,000 flying bombs, ground and air-launched, were directed at Britain, though more than 4,000 were destroyed by anti-aircraft fire, fighters, or barrage balloons. Of the 5,552 which crossed the English coast, 2,420 got as far as the London area. V1s killed 5,187 civilians, all but 462 of them in the London area. Flying bombs also killed 302 Service men and women. The grim equation of one person killed per flying bomb, which Churchill had forecast in the House of Commons on 6 July 1944, contined to hold good to the very end of the campaign.

On the first day of the last year of the war the Germans tried to break out of the grip to which the Allies were subjecting them in their drive across the Continent.

While the German army was being put on the defensive on the ground, its rocket batteries allowed southern England no respite from their missiles. From the first day of 1945 until the 29 January, with the exception only of the 18th, V2 incidents were recorded every day in southern England. On some days there were unusually large numbers recorded, the heaviest single day of the month being 20 January (16 recorded), whilst on seven other days of the month ten or more rockets fell. Throughout the month there totalled 13 separate V2 incidents, in each of which 12 or more persons were killed. The greatest number of casualties in a single incident was in Lambeth, where a V2 fell at about 8.30pm and 41 fatalities were recorded. In the month as a whole 585 deaths were directly attributed to V2 rocket explosions.

Despite this loss of life and the destruction caused by the rockets, the accuracy of the V2 landfalls was not in

Total numbers of flying-bomb and long-range rocket incidents reported

By Counties

Counties	Flying-Bombs	Long-Range Rockets
London (Region)[1]	2,420	517
Kent	1,444	64
Sussex	886	4
Essex	412	378
Surrey	295	8
Suffolk	93	13
Hertfordshire	82	34
Hampshire	80	–
Buckinghamshire	27	2
Norfolk	13	29
Berkshire	12	1
Bedfordshire	10	3
Lancashire	8	–
Yorkshire	7	–
Cheshire	6	–
Cambridgeshire	5	1
Northamptonshire	4	–
Oxfordshire	4	–
Isle of Ely	3	–
Derbyshire	3	–
Huntingdonshire	2	–
Lincolnshire	2	–
Durham	1	–
Nottinghamshire	1	–
Leicestershire	1	–
Rutland	1	–
Shropshire	1	–
Total	5,823[2]	1,054[2]

[1] London Region received 41 per cent of flying-bombs, and 49 per cent of long-range rockets.
[2] 271 of these flying-bombs and 4 of the long-range rockets fell in the sea. Source: HMSO

fact increasing, as might have been expected. One reason for this was undoubtedly that the machines themselves were still uncertain, and refinements were continuing even as the rockets were being employed. But the second reason, as with the V1 flying bombs, may be attributed again to deceptions practised by military Intelligence. The Germans could calculate very accurately the estimated arrival-time of a V2 rocket. Therefore, Intelligence attached to actual incidents the times of V2s which had in fact over-shot the intended target-point in London by some miles. As with V1s the German agents who were under the control of MI5 fed this information back to Berlin. The evidence suggests that as a result of this information the Germans did indeed steadily decrease the mean distance of travel of their rockets launched from the east so that the impact-point of rockets tended therefore similarly to creep further eastwards from London. Hence, as January gave way to February, more and more rockets tended to fall eastward, outside the London region.

Towards the end of March the Allies crossed the Rhine, and within days they advanced to The Hague where they cut off the remaining German forces and their V-weapon launch-sites, thus ending the V-weapon campaign. The last of the V1s to land in England came down at 9.35am on the 29th of the month at Datchworth in Hertfordshire. There were no casualties. It was not, however, the last to cross the British coast. That V1 was destroyed by AA fire over Iwade in Kent just an hour later. And the very last V1 to approach the British coast was shot down off the Suffolk coast, at Orford, at 12.43pm on the same day. This was the last hostile air activity of any kind over Britain of the Second World War.

In this month, of the rockets launched by the German Army, 229 incidents were officially recorded, including several in which the missile fell into the sea just off the English coast. Two incidents, however, took an especially heavy toll of life. On the morning of 8 March a V2 fell on Smithfield Market. From the twelfth century pigs, sheep and cattle had been traded in 'a smoth field where every Friday there is a celebrated rendezvous of fine horses to be sold, and in another quarter are placed vendibles of the peasant, swine with their deep flanks, and cows and oxen of immense bulk' (William FitzStephen, clerk, 1173). The rocket which crashed upon the 'smoth' or 'smooth-field' of the market fell directly on the building housing the meat, fish, and poultry sections of the market and cut its way to the railway beneath before exploding. 110 persons were killed.

Excluding V2s which fell into the sea close to British shores, 1,054 rockets exploded on (and a few over) English soil. Of that number, 517 landed in the London region. In close to seven months the V2s landing in England killed 2,855 persons, a figure which may be compared with the 4,483 dead recorded in Belgium.

The German battery at The Hague, even as its last rockets were being fired, was beginning to make preparations to withdraw. Within two days its personnel moved to the east, transporting with them several dozen unfired missiles. The war in Europe was just weeks away from its conclusion – yet its ending would signal another beginning. On 29 September 1945 sixteen 'Reich technicians', including Dr Wernher von Braun, disembarked from a troopship at Boston Harbour. Twenty-four years later the Americans landed men on the moon.

Estimated tonnages of bombs, flying-bombs and long-range rockets reported falling on the British Isles

	Bombs Excluding I.B.s & A.P.s	Flying-Bombs (War-head)	Long-Range Rockets (War-head)	Total (Metric Tons)
3 Sept 1939–6 Sept 1940 7 Sept 1940–31 Dec 1940	34,970	–	–	34,970
1941	22,176	–	–	22,176
1942	3,039	–	–	3,039
1943	2,232	–	–	2,232
1944	1,960	5,731	390	8,081
1 Jan 1945–8 May 1945	16	92	664	772
Total	64,393[1]	5,823[2]	1,054[2]	71,270

[1] Though the tonnages or numbers of incendiary bombs dropped in particular raids have sometimes been given in the text these were often in practice incalculable. No reliable total can therefore be given for these or for armour-piercing bombs.
[2] Since the war-heads of both flying-bombs and rockets were about one ton these figures are equivalent to the numbers reported to have fallen. Source: HMSO

Postlude

In the perspective of history, it is possible to distinguish a number of phases in the German campaign to bomb Britain into submission. In the first phase, following the fall of France, the Luftwaffe made attacks on British coastal targets and shipping, while the German army assembled fleets of barges and landing craft for Hitler's planned invasion of England.

During this phase Göring stationed his fleets of bombers and fighters in occupied France, the Low Countries, Denmark and Norway. From air bases just across the Channel he mounted a campaign to smash the RAF Fighter Command's front-line Groups by means of intense attacks on its airfields – attacks which were soon carried forward to fighter stations further inland. If Göring and Hitler had persisted, this strategy might have succeeded, but the balance of the evidence, viewed in simple mathematical terms, suggests that at the point of destroying the RAF, the Luftwaffe might have also destroyed itself. There remains no doubt, however, that this phase of the battle was Britain's hour of greatest danger, possibly in the entire war.

If an 'accident' can change the course of a war, it was the Luftwaffe's accidental bombing of London on 23 August – described on an earlier page of this book – which changed the course of the Battle for Britain. For in retaliation for that attack the RAF mounted an ineffective raid on Berlin on the night of 25/26 August, aimed at the armament factories to the north of the city. Three nights later, in a repeat RAF raid, German civilians were killed, and on 6 September there was a further raid on Berlin. Hitler's fury over these raids provoked a switch of policy: he ordered the Luftwaffe's attacks to be concentrated on London, diverting them from RAF's fighter bases and control centres. Thus began the London Blitz, starting with daylight raids on the city which continued until the end of the month.

THE COST

The cost of this policy in aircraft and crews proved unacceptably high to the Luftwaffe, forcing another change of strategy: a night-bombing campaign which was extended from London to other British cities and industrial centres. In the early spring of 1941 the Luftwaffe began a new phase in their campaign, and between 19 February and 12 May it launched some 61 attacks, mostly aimed at ports, including London.

As these raids were reaching their climax, the whole strategic balance of the war was being shifted to eastern Europe, and the Luftwaffe *Gruppen* were being withdrawn from their bases in France and the Low Countries and moved towards the Soviet frontier, where another *Blitzkrieg* was about to be opened. From the raid on London on 7 September 1940 until the end of May 1941, the Luftwaffe had dropped some 46,000 tons of high-explosive bombs and well over 10,000 incendiaries on target-areas in Britain. In the same period more than 40,000 British civilians had been killed in the raids.

This massive effort, however, achieved little in military terms, and the campaign was a failure. Britain's industrial production was not significantly affected, despite local disruptions which put individual factories out of action for days, or even weeks. In most cases production at damaged plants was merely reduced, not stopped. The most effective precaution against destructive raids proved to be dispersing centres of production and assembly instead of concentrating them in individual sites. Similarly, the nation's vital supply lines remained open, and despite constant heavy attacks the ton-

Major night attacks on United Kingdom cities and towns from 7 September 1940 to 16 May 1941

	Major Attacks[1]	*H.E. Tonnage*		*Major Attacks*[1]	*H.E. Tonnage*
London	71	18,291	Southampton	4	647
Liverpool-Birkenhead	8	1,957	Hull	3	593
Birmingham	8	1,852	Manchester	3	578
Glasgow-Clydeside	5	1,329	Belfast	2	440
Plymouth-Devonport	8	1,228	Sheffield	1	355
Bristol-Avonmouth	6	919	Newcastle-Tyneside	1	152
Coventry	2	818	Nottingham	1	137
Portsmouth	3	687	Cardiff	1	115

[1] The Luftwaffe definition of a 'major attack', i.e. one in which 100 tons or more of high-explosive bombs were successfully aimed at the target, has been adopted for this table. Source: HMSO

Civilians killed and injured in Great Britain by enemy action 1939-1945
(Compiled by Ministry of Home Security from police and medical reports)

	Killed			Admitted to Hospital (in most cases seriously injured)			Slightly Injured			Treated at First Aid Posts and Mobile First Aid Units (estimated one-fifth sent on to hospital)[1]
	London	Elsewhere	Totals	London	Elsewhere	Totals	London	Elsewhere	Totals	
3 Sept 1939-6 Sept 1940	257	1,441	1,698	441	1,848	2,289				
7 Sept 1940-31 Dec 1940	13,339	8,730	22,069	17,937	10,303	28,240				
3 Sept 1939-31 Dec 1940 (bracketed)							33,756	20,264	54,020	54,700
1941	6,487	13,431	19,918	7,641	13,524	21,165	13,236	20,880	34,116	43,775
1942	27	3,209	3,236	52	4,096	4,148	63	7,097	7,160	8,719
1943	542	1,830	2,372	989	2,461	3,450	1,015	4,412	5,427	6,598
1944	7,533	942	8,475	19,611	2,378	21,989	33,212	6,343	39,555	41,116
1 Jan 1945-9 May 1945	1,705	155	1,860	3,836	387	4,223	7,560	1,202	8,762	10,835
Northern Ireland	–	967	967	–	678	678	–	1,793	1,793	–
	29,890	30,705	60,595	50,507	35,675	86,182	88,842	61,991	150,833	165,743

[1] Source: *Report of the Chief Medical Officer of the Ministry of Health 1939 1945*.

nage moving through the ports was not seriously disrupted. Communication-links were frequently severed but were always repaired – often with surprising swiftness.

The morale of the British people generally held up well in most of the stricken cities and towns – even though the 'We can take it' response of contemporary newsreels and other propaganda does not tell the whole story. People did not always endure with cheerful confidence: there was real fear, and on occasion the government was concerned that morale was about to break in some of the most devastated areas. It has also to be said that if the public had been aware that the official expectation of casualties from Luftwaffe raids was far higher than in the event they were, its morale might well have been lower.

With its strength mainly concentrated on the eastern front, the Luftwaffe failed to renew its bombardment of Britain in the winter of 1941/42. When better weather conditions returned in the spring of 1942, however, it began to mount heavy raids once more. But once again, the Germans were diverted from pressing home their attacks – this time by the RAF's bombing of Lübeck and Rostock, which provoked the retaliatory 'Baedeker' raids. Occasional severe raids occurred throughout the period from July 1942 until January 1944, but most of what remained of the Luftwaffe's effort was spent on raids of the 'tip and run' variety – high-speed, low-altitude attacks on coastal targets by a few (or just one) aircraft, which rarely ventured far inland.

THE 'LITTLE BLITZ'

There was one final concentrated effort by the Luftwaffe, and that was between January and March 1944 – usually referred to as the 'Little Blitz' or the 'Baby Blitz'. The typical raiders of this period released heavy loads of incendiaries, and the duration their attacks tended to be shorter than the massed night raids of 1940/41. Most of these raiders aimed at London.

The final attacks launched against Britain by the Luftwaffe and the German Army – the V.1 and V.2 missiles – represented their last throws. In some ways the sheer unpredictability and unexpectedness of these weapons produced greater fear in the areas they hit than earlier bombing, but as a military weapon their effectiveness was limited.

The Blitz over Britain, in all its forms as described in this book, caused massive destruction and loss of life in the country's cities and towns. In the most intense period of the Blitz – September 1940 to May 1941 – some two million houses were demolished. The most serious threat to Britain's survival, however, was not posed by aerial bombardment but by the U-boat. In the early years of the war the U-boat campaign might have cut off the nation's food and other supplies, condemning the population to slow starvation. The ultimate cost of the Blitz was, of course, in human lives: the killed and the injured, and those whose lives were blasted by the death or injury of loved ones. The official figures for those who died in air attacks on the British Isles are recorded in the table above.

REAPING THE WHIRLWIND

It is clear that the casualty figures were highest during the 1940/41 period. The dramatic fall in civilian deaths caused by the Luftwaffe during 1942 and 1943 can best be highlighted by comparison with road death figures. In each of those two years more people were killed in car accidents (despite restrictions in the use of private cars, but under black-out conditions) than by enemy action. Indeed, during the entire war deaths due to motor accidents amounted to almost two-thirds of the number attributed to enemy bombardment.

There was another consequence of the Luftwaffe's bombardment of Britain. Germany had sown a wind, but she reaped a whirlwind in the form of RAF Bomber Command's massive raids and later of the Allied Combined Bomber offensives. The British learned from the Luftwaffe the lesson of combining fire-bombs with high-explosives, and they then taught the German people what it could mean.

In the first Operation Gomorrah raid on Hamburg on the night of 24 July 1943, more than 1,500 civilians were killed, and during the next few days the city was bombed to destruction. On the 28th over 2,300 tons of bombs, a large proportion of them incendiaries, set the whole city ablaze. An inferno developed, and at the centre of the firestorm a wind was generated, driving the flames further, until eight square miles of the city had been burned out.

In the last year of the war, it was Dresden which was destroyed in firestorm conditions. On the night of 13 February 1945 Bomber Command struck the city twice. The next day American bombers attacked the city, where eleven square miles were already on fire, and on the morning of the 15th another force of American bombers hit the city.

The fire of Dresden burned for seven nights and seven days. The final death-count can never be established with any degree of accuracy, although the official toll records 39,773 dead. At least another 20,000 were not recorded: these were residents buried beneath the ruins, or bodies burned beyond recognition.

Residents in the worst bombed areas of Britain were most likely to be among those who did not wish the same treatment to be given to German towns and cities, while others in more secure regions might call loudly for retaliation. In the event, the destruction of German cities was awesome, and the casualties exceeded several times those of British centres. German civilians killed as a direct result of air raids during the course of the war amounted to some 410,000. When foreigners, prisoners-of-war, and civilian personnel attached to the armed forces and the police are added to this figure, the air-raid death toll in Germany exceeded 590,000.

Such figures tend to put the British losses in some perspective, but such comparisons do not in any way reduce the sense of personal tragedy and loss involved in each death, wherever it occurred. Decades after the end of this, the most destructive war in history, in which 57 nations were involved, we may recall as an epitaph the words of John Donne:

> No man is an island, entire of itself; every man is a piece of the continent, a part of the realm; if a clod be washed away by the sea, as well as if a promontory were, as well as if a manor of thy friend's or of thine own were; any man's death diminishes me, because I am involved in mankind; and therefore never send to know for whom the bell tolls; it tolls for thee.
>
> From John Donne: Devotions

●

Attacks on London compared with those on other Cities and Towns

Throughout the war London had 101 daylight attacks and 253 night attacks, a total of 354, by piloted aircraft. It was attacked at some time during the day or night, with the exception of only two twenty-four periods, for the whole of September, October and November 1940. London received 41 per cent of the attacks by flying-bombs, and 49 per cent of those by rockets.

	Number of Attacks (Cross-Channel shelling included)		
	Day	*Night*	*Total*
1. Dover	76	49	125
2. Yarmouth	25	72	97
3. Folkestone	56	27	83
4. Hull	6	70	76
5. Hastings	54	21	75
6. Lowestoft	27	47	74
7. Romford	4	68	72
8. Portsmouth	15	57	72
9. Plymouth	13	58	71
10. Margate	30	40	70
11. Liverpool	—	68	68
12. Southampton	18	49	67
13. Southend	10	57	67
14. Portland	28	38	66
15. Eastbourne	39	27	66
16. Ramsgate	37	26	63
17. Gillingham	22	38	60
18. Bristol	5	51	56
19. Birkenhead	—	52	52
20. Birmingham	—	51	51

London suffered over 80,000 of the estimated total for the country of 146,777 fatal and serious casualties. Outside London, only Birmingham and Liverpool suffered more than 5,000 such casualties.

Source: HMSO

Newspapers

(various issues and dates)

Bath Evening Post
Bath and Wiltshire Chronicle and Herald
Belfast Telegraph
Birmingham Evening Despatch
Birmingham Evening Mail
Birmingham Gazette
Birmingham Post
Bristol Evening Post
Bristol Evening World
Coventry Chronicle
Coventry Evening Telegraph
Daily Dispatch and Manchester Evening Chronicle
Daily Record and Mail (Scotland)
Derby Evening Telegraph
East Anglian Daily Times
Exeter Express and Echo
Folkestone Herald
Glasgow Evening Citizen
Glasgow Herald
Great Yarmouth Mercury
Hampshire Telegraph
Hull Daily Mail
Kent & Sussex Courier
Lancashire Life
Leicester Mercury
Liverpool Post & Echo
Manchester Evening Chronicle
Manchester Evening News
Manchester Guardian
Midland Daily Telegraph
Newark Advertiser
Newcastle Evening Chronicle
Newcastle Journal
Northern Whig
Nottingham Evening News
Nottingham Evening Post
Nottingham Journal
Nottingham News
Portsmouth Evening News
Sheffield Morning Telegraph
Sheffield Star
Southern Daily and Evening Echo
South Wales Echo
South Wales Evening Post
Sunderland Echo
The Times
West Bridgford and Clifton Standard
Western Daily Press and Bristol Mirror
Western Evening Herald
Western Morning News
Yarmouth Mercury

Select Bibliography

BAILEY, Val (ed.), *Woodseats at War*, Yorkshires Arts Circus, Castleford, 1988

BIALER, Uri, *The Shadow of the Bomber*, Royal Historical Society, London, 1980

BICKERS, R. T. Townshend, *The Battle of Britain*, Salamander Books, London, 1990

BILLS, L. W. *A Medal for Life: biography of Lieut. W. L. Robinson VC*, Spellmount Ltd., Tunbridge Wells, 1990

BOYLE, Gerard, *The Clydebank Blitz*, Strathclyde Regional Council, Dumbarton, 1980

BOWYER, Michael, *Air Raid! The enemy offensive against East Anglia 1939-45*, Patrick Stephens, Wellingborough, 1986

BROWN, Anthony Cave, *Bodyguard of Lies*, W. H. Allen, London, 1976

BROWN, D., SHORES C., & MACKSEY K., *The Guinness History of Air Warfare*, Guinness/Purnell, Abingdon, 1976

CALDER, Angus, *The People's War*, Jonathan Cape, London, 1969

CASTLE, H. G., *Fire over England: German Air Raids in World War I*, Secker & Warburg, London, 1982

CHIGNELL, Philip, *From our Home Correspondent*, Highgate Publications, Beverley, 1989

CHURCHILL, Winston, *The Second World War, Vols 1, 2, 5, & 6*, Cassell, London, 1949

CITY OF COVENTRY, *Information Officers' Guide*, After Raid Information Service, Coventry, 1943

CLYDEBANK DISTRICT LIBRARIES/MUSEUM SERVICE, *The Clydebank Blitz in Pictures*, Clydebank, 1980

CLAYTON, Anthony, *The British Empire as a Superpower, 1919-39*, Macmillan, London, 1986

COLLIER, Basil, *A History of Air Power*, Weidenfeld and Nicolson, London, 1974

COLLIER, Basil, *The Defence of the United Kingdom*, HMSO, London, 1957

CRAMPTON, Paul, *The Blitz of Canterbury*, Meresborough Books, Rainham, 1989

DALLAT, C. and GIBSON, F., *Rooms of Time: Memories of Ulster People*, Greystone Books, Antrim, 1988

DIKE, John, *Bristol Blitz Diary*, Redcliffe, Bristol, 1982

DOHERTY, J. E. and HICKEY, D. J., *A Chronology of Irish History since 1500*, Gill and Macmillan, Dublin, 1989

DONALDSON, P., *Yes, Matron: A History of Nurses and Nursing at the Royal Victoria Hospital, Belfast*, The White Row Press, 1989

FORTY, George and DUNCAN, John, *The Fall of France*, The Nutshell Publishing Co. Ltd., Tunbridge Wells, 1990

FRANKS, Norman, *Battle of Britain*, Bison, London, 1981

FREDETTE, R. H., *The First Battle of Britain*, Cassell, London, 1976

FULLER, J. F. C., *The Conduct of War, 1789-1961*, Eyre & Spottiswoode, London, 1961

GERAGHTY, T., *North-East Coast Town: Ordeal and Triumph (1951)*, Mr Pye Books, Howden, 1989

GILBERT, Martin, *The Second World War*, Weidenfeld and Nicholson, London, 1989

GILBERT, Martin, *Finest Hour: Winston S. Churchill 1939-41*, Heinemann, London, 1983

GUNSTON, Bill, *Encyclopaedia of the World's Combat Aircraft*, Salamander Books, London, 1976

HAINING, Peter, *Spitfire Summer*, W. H. Allen, London, 1990

HARDY, Clive and HARRIS, Paul, *Tyneside at War: a Pictorial Account*, Archive Publications, Manchester, 1988

HARRISSON, Tom, *Living through the Blitz*, Collins, London, 1976

HARROD, Roy, *The Prof.: A Personal Memoir of Lord Cherwell*, Macmillan, London, 1959

HILL, Ted, *Tell Your Mother There's a War On: the Wartime Memories of a Bedminster Boy*, Malago Publications, Bristol, 1986

H.M.S.O., *Fire over London: the Story of the London Fire Service 1940 41*, London, 1942

H.M.S.O., *Front Line 1940/41*, London, 1942

HOYT, Edwin P., *Hitler's War*, McGraw-Hill, New York, 1988

HUMPHRIES, Roy and others, *Kent Airfields in the Battle of Britain*, Meresborough Books, Rainham, 1981

JOHNSON, Brian and COZENS, H.I., *Bombers: The Weapon of Total War*, Thames Methuen, London, 1984

JONES, R. V., *Most Secret War*, Hamish Hamilton, London, 1978

KEEGAN, John, *The Second World War*, Hutchinson, London, 1989

KEEGAN, John (ed.) *The Times Atlas of the Second World War*, Times Books Ltd., London, 1989

LEWIN, Ronald, *ULTRA goes to War: the Secret Story*, Hutchinson, London, 1978

LEWIS, Peter, *A People's War*, Methuen, London, 1986

LONDON COUNTY COUNCIL, *Fire over London*, Hutchinson, London, 1941

LONGMATE, Norman, *How We Lived Then*, Arrow Books, London, 1973

LONGMATE, Norman, *Air Raid*, Hutchinson, London, 1976

LONGMATE, Norman, *The Doodlebugs*, Hutchinson, London, 1981

LONGMATE, Norman, *Hitler's Rockets*, Hutchinson, London, 1981

MACK, Joanna & HUMPHRIES, Steve, *London at War*, Sidgwick & Jackson, London, 1985

MacPHAIL, I. M. M., *The Clydebank Blitz*, Clydebank Town Council, 1974

MARWICK, Arthur, *The Home Front*, Thames and Hudson, London, 1976

MESSENGER, Charles, *World War Two: Chronological Atlas*, Bloomsbury, London, 1989

MOORE, Brian, *The Emperor of Ice Cream*, Mayflower, London, 1967

NEWBOLD, E. B., *Portrait of Coventry*, Hale, London, 1975

O'BRIEN, T. H., *Civil Defence*, H.M.S.O., London, 1955

PEAKE, Nigel ed., *The People's War, 1939-1940*, Portsmouth Publishing and Printing Ltd., Portsmouth, 1989

PILE, Sir Frederick, *Ack-Ack*, Harrap, London, 1949

PRESTON, Anthony (ed.)., *Decisive Battles of Hitler's War*, New Burlington Books, London, 1988

PRICE, Alfred, *The Battle of Britain: the Hardest Day*, Macdonald and Jane's, London, 1979

ROTHNIE, Niall, *The Bombing of Bath*, Ashgrove Press, Bath, 1983
SAUNDBY, R., *Air Bombardment: the Story of its Development*, Chatto & Windus, London, 1961
SAUNDERS, H., St. George, *Per Ardua: The Rise of British Air Power, 1911-1939*, Oxford, 1944
SCRIVENER, Keith, *Plymouth at War. A Pictorial Account 1939-45*, Archive Publications, Runcorn, 1989
SIMS, Charles, *The RAF: The First Fifty Years*, Chatto & Windus, London, 1968
SMITH, Mark, *Britain's Front Line Town – Dover*, Buckland Publications Ltd. & Dover D.C., Dover, 1990
STONES, Donald, *Operation Bograt*, Spellmount Ltd., Tunbridge Wells, 1990
TALFAN-DAVIES, Aneurin ap., *Dyddiau'r Ceiliog Rhedyn (The Locust Years)*, Gwasg Gymraeg Foyle
TAYLOR, A. J. P., *The Origins of the Second World War*, Hamish Hamilton, London, 1961
THOMAS, Hugh, *The Spanish Civil War*, Eyre & Spottiswoode, London, 1961
TWYFORD, H. P., *It Came To Our Door: an Account Of Plymouth at War*, Underhill, Plymouth, corrected ed. 1949
ULYATT, Michael E., *Hull at War: a Photographic Recollection 1939-1945* Dalesman Books, Lancaster, 1989
WALLINGTON, Neil, *Firemen at War*, David & Charles, London, 1981
WALTON, Mary and LAMB, J. P., *Raiders over Sheffield*, Sheffield City Libraries, Sheffield, 1980
WARD, Arthur, *A Nation Alone: the Battle of Britian 1940* Osprey, London, 1989
WESTALL, Robert, *Children of the Blitz*, Viking, London, 1985
WIMHURST, C., *The Bombardment of Bath*, Mendip Press, Bath, 1942
WINSTONE, Reece, *Bristol Blitzed*, Reece Winstone, Bristol, 1973
WINTERBOTHAM, F. W., *The Ultra Secret*, Weidenfeld and Nicholson, London, 1974
WRIGHT, Michael, ed., *The World at Arms*, Readers Digest Association, London, 1989

1-7-92 Hamilton 10.95 48015